D1274397

DEVELOPMENTS IN FOOD SCIENCE 2

PROCEEDINGS OF THE FIFTH INTERNATIONAL CONGRESS OF

FOOD SCIENCE AND TECHNOLOGY

DEVELOPMENTS IN FOOD SCIENCE

Volume 1   J. G. Heathcote and J. R. Hibbert
            Aflatoxins : chemical and biological aspects

DEVELOPMENTS IN FOOD SCIENCE 2

PROCEEDINGS OF THE FIFTH INTERNATIONAL CONGRESS OF

FOOD SCIENCE AND TECHNOLOGY

Edited by

Hideo Chiba
Department of Food Science and Technology, Faculty of Agriculture,
Kyoto University, Kyoto

Masao Fujimaki
Department of Food Science and Nutrition, Ochanomizu University,
Tokyo

Kazuo Iwai
Department of Food Science and Technology, Faculty of Agriculture,
Kyoto University, Kyoto

Hisateru Mitsuda
Laboratory of Food Science and Technology, Research Institute for
Production Development, Kyoto

Yuhei Morita
The Research Institute for Food Science, Kyoto University, Kyoto

KODANSHA LTD.

Tokyo

ELSEVIER SCIENTIFIC
PUBLISHING COMPANY
Amsterdam-Oxford-New York

1979

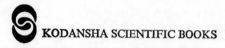

KODANSHA SCIENTIFIC BOOKS

Library of Congress Cataloging in Publication Data

```
International Congress of Food Science and
     Technology, 5th, Kyoto, 1978.
     Proceedings of the Fifth International
Congress of Food Science and Technology.

     (Developments in food science ; 2)
     Includes bibliographical references and indexes.
     1.  Food--Congresses.  2.  Food supply--
Congresses.  3.  Food industry and trade--Congresses.
I.  Chiba, Hideo, 1925-      II.  Title.
III.  Series.
TX345.I562  1978          641.3          79-20898
ISBN 0-444-99770-9
```

ISBN (Vol. 2) 0-444-99770-9
ISBN (Series) 0-444-41688-9

Copublished by

KODANSHA LTD.
12-21 Otowa 2-chome, Bunkyo-ku, Tokyo 112

and

ELSEVIER SCIENTIFIC PUBLISHING COMPANY
335 Jan van Galenstraat, P.O. Box 211, 1000 AE Amsterdam

ELSEVIER NORTH-HOLLAND, INC.
52 Vanderbilt Avenue New York, N.Y. 10017

PRINTED IN JAPAN

Preface

The Fifth International Congress of Food Science and Technology took place at the Kyoto International Conference Hall in Kyoto, Japan from September 17–22, 1978. The Congress was sponsored by the International Union of Food Science and Technology (IUFoST) with preceding Congresses having taken place in London (1962), Warsaw (1966), Washington, D. C. (1970) and Madrid (1974). The Congresses were designed with the purpose of: 1) promoting the international exchange of ideas in scientific disciplines relating to the production, processing, distribution, conservation and utilization of food, 2) assimilating and calling attention to major progress made in the field of food science and technology since the previous Congress and 3) obtaining stimulation for and increasing world-wide collaboration on topics of great importance.

The host organization for the 1978 Congress was the Union of International Food Science and Technology of Japan, a member of the IUFoST and representative of the following national organizations: the Institute of Food Technologists—Japan Section, the Japanese Society of Food Science and Technology, the Agricultural Chemical Society of Japan, the Japanese Society of Food and Nutrition, and the Food Hygienic Society of Japan. The Ministry of Education, Science and Culture of Japan, the Science Council of Japan and the Japan Association for the Promotion of Science also supported the Congress in conjunction with the IUFoST.

The theme of the 1978 Congress was "Food Availability and Quality through Technology and Science—FAQTS—". The program consisted of plenary sessions, subplenary sessions, contributed paper sessions, and round table meetings.

Plenary Sessions

The opening and closing sessions were dedicated to a comprehensive assessment of the present and future roles of food science and technology in solving world food problems. Two internationally recognized authorities addressed the plenary sessions with respect to this most urgent matter. The opening plenary lecture was given by Professor Emil M. Mrak, Chancellor Emeritus of the University of California, Davis (U.S.A.), with the title of "The World Food Problem and Meeting the Challenge". Professor John Hawthorn of the University of Strathclyde (UK), immediate past president of the IUFoST, gave the closing plenary lecture entitled "Every man and Food Science".

v

Subplenary Sessions

Four subplenary sessions were held in the mornings from Monday, September 18th through Thursday, September 21st. These sessions were designed to focus in on the topical areas outlined below. More than fifty papers were presented by invited speakers selected by the Scientific Program Committee of Japan.

Main Topic I.	Resources of Food
1.	Exploitation of Food Protein Resources
2.	Efficient Utilization of Conventional Food Resources
3.	Utilization of Rice
Main Topic II.	Safety and Nutritional Aspects of Food
1.	Food Safety
2.	Nutritional Aspects of Food Processing
Main Topic III.	Preservation and Processing of Food
1.	Food Preservation
2.	Enzymes in Food Processing
3.	Fermentation
Main Topic IV.	Physical, Chemical and Sensory Properties of Food
1.	Physical Properties of Food
2.	Chemical Aspects of Food Quality
3.	Taste and Chemical Structure

Contributed Paper Sessions

The contributed paper sessions were open to original research papers on any aspect of food science and technology. The contributed papers were selected by the Scientific Program Committee of Japan which accepted about 350 papers and classified them into the eleven sections listed below with regard to relevance to the program and variety of subject matter. All papers were allotted time for oral presentation during the regular sessions from Monday, September 18th through Thursday, September 21st.

Section	1.	Exploitation of Food Resources
Section	2.	Food Safety
Section	3.	Food Engineering and Technology
Section	4.	Organoleptic Properties
Section	5.	Basic Problems on Food Constituents
Section	6.	Biochemical Techniques in Food Science
Section	7.	Food Analysis and Standard

Round Table Meetings

The round table meetings were designed to permit the exchange of thoughts and ideas on any subject of food science and technology that was not covered in the Subplenary Sessions. Seven round table meetings were held.

These Proceedings include the full texts of the plenary lectures and abridged versions of the papers submitted for the subplenary sessions. It is regrettable that, due to financial limitation, the presentations of the contributed paper sessions and round table meetings are not included. Readers are kindly requested to refer to the "Abstracts of the Congress" for these papers. The credit for the quality and the success of the Congress must go to the participants. We owe much to them.

April, 1979
The Editors

Contents

Preface
Editorial Board

Main Topic II: Safety and Nutritional Aspects of
Food

Main Topic III: Preservation and Processing of
Food

Plenary Sessions

Plenary Sessions

The World Food Problem and Meeting the Challenge

Emil M. Mrak*

We hear so much about feeding the world and how simple it should be to do so. Some say that all we need to do is to produce more food—but we are producing more food. The facts of the case are that population increase in the world is outstripping the increase in food production. In brief, it certainly looks as though we are losing the battle.

In the past few years there have been many symposia, books, pamphlets, articles, reports, discussions, political considerations, studies, and conferences on the world food situation. The large amount of oratorical material has, without doubt, caused the subject to be obscured by rhetorical overkill.

While there seems to be a unanimity of opinion on the seriousness of the situation, there doesn't seem to be a consensus on the ability of the world to cope with the problem or what to do about it.

Many reasons have been given for our failure to solve the problem, but most seem to concentrate on population increase and the lack of resources with which to purchase food.

As a result of my travels around the world, I have come to the conclusion that a considerable part of our problem relates to culture, food habits, education, the lack of training and information transfer and, above all, yes indeed above all, political and governmental interferences and constraints.

The seriousness of the situation was manifested at a conference held by the New York Academy of Sciences about a year ago on the world food gap. Several experts spoke, all of whom seemed to have a grim outlook, except one, and that was Dr. Jean Mayer, now president of Tufts University. Mayer opened the session by declaring that since the famines of 1974 and the World Food Conference held in Rome, there may have been a turning point. Mayer, however, did not state the basis for his optimism.

At the same meeting, Dr. Sol Chafkin, who oversees social development programs in developing countries for the Ford Foundation, indicated he

*Chanceller Emeritus, University of California, Davis

3

saw little cause for optimism. He pointed out, for example, that one Latin American country increased the production of soybeans during the past few years, but unfortunately these are mostly exported, and the land now used for soybeans was previously used to produce food for home consumption.

At the same meeting, Dr. Peter Timmer, a food economist from Cornell University, indicated that the world now produces enough food to feed the entire human race, a nutritionally adequate diet of 65 grams of protein and 3,000 calories daily. He went on to say, however, that hunger and malnutrition afflict one-half billion people because the mechanisms for determining access to this food are inadequate. In other words, distribution, not production, is the problem. I am certain, from my firsthand observations in the hinterlands of Latin America and Africa, that changes in distribution to help these people will be slow in coming.

Other speakers, at the same conference, dealt with politics and generally pointed out that most national leaders in underdeveloped countries derive little power from rural populations that need food and, therefore, do little to improve the lot of these people.

I have mentioned this conference because it is an indication of the rhetoric that has been pouring forth without realities of accomplishment.

Many reasons have been given for the failure of crop production or adequacy of foods in various sections of the world and some of these are indeed obvious.

The matter of climate, according to Reid Bryson of the University of Wisconsin, for example, is not reassuring for the future. He indicates that climate is changing and we may be confronted with some very serious situations. The years since 1900 have had unusual warmth and reliable rains around the world in contrast with the cooler, drier and more erratic weather patterns of the previous millenium.

According to Bryson, it is only in the present unusual period of favorable weather that agriculture has blossomed into its present abundance and the human population began growing rapidly. New climate monitoring techniques indicate that the present unusual situation might be coming to an end with a return to a colder and drier climate. I can only hope that Bryson is wrong.

A most extreme point of view has been taken by Dr. Hardin of the University of California at Santa Barbara. He has raised the question as to whether or not Americans and perhaps Europeans and other advanced countries can continue to be well fed in a starving world.

He even wonders about triage or "the lifeboat ethic." He has indicated that as global food shortages become more intense, the advanced countries may not be able to give aid to others and, therefore, the world may experience more famines.

A fantastic number of suggestions have been made on how to solve the problem, and some of these I find interesting, amusing, and even unbelievable. Some very distinguished people, including one of our former senators, have suggested that we curtail our food consumption to help the rest of the world. The amount of food saved in this manner, however, would be far from doing much to solve the problem.

It has been suggested by some that we reduce the consumption of beef and even eliminate it from our diet in order to save grain, without realizing that much of the animal production is on range land that is not suitable for other agricultural uses.

Furthermore, marginally productive and often untillable land can be best utilized for human benefit by supporting livestock. In fact, the only way in which millions of acres of range land can be used for human benefit is by grazing livestock on it. I am afraid that those who have suggested giving up livestock are not familiar with the total and true situation.

A recent statement was made by a distinguished person to the effect that "isn't it wrong to feed grain to animals when many people are starving in the world today?" It is true that certain feeding practices involve the use of grains, but this is small when compared to the other advantages of raising livestock. I doubt if our culture or our food habits would permit such a drastic change, but more important is the fact that beef and sheep are ruminants, and can extract energy from forages that would otherwise be wasted. Their unique digestive systems enable them to transform huge quantities of waste and fibrous materials into high quality protein.

These animals, in fact, have utilized as much as 9.3 million metric tons of waste from milling, brewing and sugar industries in the United States in a single year. This is what we might call constructive recycling. Some have also suggested that we give up growing tobacco and use the land for the production of food materials. Likewise, I doubt if this is realistic.

About two years ago a very interesting suggestion for improving the world situation came out of Great Britain. There, the question was raised as to whether or not it is justifiable for that country to feed 700 million dollars worth of foodstuffs to cats and dogs each year when the richer countries distribute only a little over a billion dollars worth of foodstuffs to the hungry people of the world during the same period.

Excluding dogs from our friendship is something that is hardly realistic in any country. It must be realized that the dog was one of the first domesticated animals and has lived with man for perhaps 20 thousand years.

It will be difficult to induce a divorce of an association of such long standing, in spite of all the arguments against such a friendship, no matter what country it might be.

A more recent realistic suggestion has been that every effort be made to reduce food waste throughout the world. This is constructive and an area that deserves much attention and research. For one reason or another, it has not been given enough consideration.

It has been estimated that in some parts of the world as much as 50% of the food supply is lost between harvest and consumption. In humid tropical climates, the problem is acute since food deteriorates rapidly and methods of preservation are lacking, or insufficient and costly. We need to know more about the magnitude and nature of these losses and how to control them. Technology must be simple, relatively low in cost, and easily applicable in rural areas if it is to be effective.

Professor Mitsuda and colleagues have recently done some very interesting and original work on the storage of rice. They certainly recognize the problem and have come up with an imaginary approach to solving the problem.

Losses not only occur in less developed nations, but also to developed nations. In the United States, the losses between harvest and consumption are substantial.

According to Barrons, in his recent book, authorities on the scene have estimated that 15% of all the rice and other cereal crops raised in the Orient are destroyed by rats either in the field or in storage. Fifteen per cent of Asia's cereal crops must be equated with nearly 50 million acres of land, and area equal to the size of the entire state of Kansas. Barrons has also stressed the importance of storage insect pests.

Canby and Stanfield state that rats will destroy approximately a fifth of all the food crops planted, and that in India degradations by rats will deprive a hungry people of enough grain to fill a freight train stretching more than 3,000 miles.

I have often wondered why we have overlooked this very destructive animal. I have wondered on many occasions if we could find a way to control these pests sufficiently to minimize their destructiveness.

As already indicated, Professor Mitsuda and his colleagues have developed a new procedure to eliminate these destructive processes-not only from rodents but, also, by insects, mold, and chemical deterioration.

Now, I would like to go on to another suggestion and that is fish culture. It has been suggested that this offers great possibilities and perhaps they are substantial. A great deal of effort has been devoted to growing fish in fresh waters under controlled conditions. It has indeed been successful in Japan, where eel production is a successful industry and is promising for those who have water and will eat eels.

Other experiments and trials in fish production are promising, and this is something that may eventually prove worthwhile.

I am certain you have all heard about the Green Revolution. It has certainly offered hopes and appears to be promising, but there are difficulties. In discussing these, I would like to quote from an interesting article by Dr. Clifton Wharton entitled, "The Green Revolution—Cornucopia or Pandora's Box?"

On the positive side, the U.S.D.A. reveals that in Asia alone, the estimated acreage planted with the new high-yield variety of wheat rose from 200 in 1964 to 20 million in 1968. In view of this, food-importing nations, such as the Philippines and Pakistan, may become self-sufficient and conceivably could become net food exporters. Apparently, this was the case in Mexico, until the population increase not only caught up with food production, but went ahead of it.

Increase in production as a result of the Green Revolution, however, automatically produces a whole new set of second-generation problems which must be faced, if development is to be sustained and accelerated.

There are other factors that in one way or another may impair increased production and the most important in this connection are the cultural constraints. Every nation is different: the people, the culture, the education and the economics, as well as the weather and geographic location. These differences can be serious constraints and very often are.

Distribution, of course, is a serious problem in the underdeveloped nations. In a recent issue of THE LIPTON MAGAZINE, it was pointed out that much has been made of the fact that starvation in countries such as Bangladesh and Ethiopia is much more attributable to the failure to distribute available food supplies than to the food shortage as such. The article gave as examples official corruption, bureaucratic incompetence, hoarding and black marketing to such an extent that some of the people often feel that aid is not worth the effort.

Now, I would like to change the subject and consider the food conference held in Rome a few years ago. Some very distinguished people attended, and among these were Secretary of State Kissinger and Senator Humphrey from the United States. Upon their return home, there was action and new legislation. Secretary Kissinger wrote a letter for the President's signature to the National Academy of Sciences asking for advice on what the United States might do to help improve the world food and nutrition situation.

A steering committee with fourteen subcommittees was established by the Academy and funding was obtained in order to make a study.

It was indeed an intensive and extensive study. The various committees were asked to consider fourteen areas which were: pest control, crop and animal production, animal health, fish, soils and plant nutrition, weather and climate, crop production, agricultural systems, information systems, highly imaginative ideas, new approaches to alleviate hunger, research organizations in the U.S. and, of course, food science and nutrition.

The study resulted in the publication of 6 volumes containing many suggestions and ideas. I can only cover a few of these.

To me, the most important areas were production, processing, storage and distribution. I have already stressed the importance of storage and the need for technological investigations in connection with storage.

From the standpoint of long-time research, two important areas stressed were biological nitrogen fixation by plants other than legumes, and improvement of the photosynthetic process. A study of the effects of stress factors on the growth and production of plants was also emphasized. Other suggested studies were food losses and the need for fact gathering about losses throughout the world, the role of small animals such as the guinea pig as a source of food, forage improvement, fish culture, treatment of organic wastes as a part of the farm system, soil erosion and development of an improved non-biological process for drawing nitrogen from the air to produce ammonia. Much was also said about nutrition in various countries.

I would like now to cover the area of greatest interest to us, and this relates to food processing and food technology. Before doing this, however, I must quote Aykroyd, who said, "It would be foolish to claim that advancing food technology—by no means confined to the affluent countries—can itself solve the world's great food problems." On the other hand, he also stated that it would be equally foolish to minimize what modern food technology has already achieved, and still more its potential achievements. He went on to say it is a new factor in the world food situation, likely to have remarkable consequences.

The study for the President pointed out that food processing and preservation are extremely important and these certainly include minimizing crop losses and waste and especially during storage.

Food processing and preservation vary widely among countries and with products. Methods that have evolved over the centuries are influenced by culture, wealth, climate, food preferences, health standards, and a host of other factors.

Food production alone cannot solve the world food problems. Present supplies of food need to be better used; new food services must be developed; and food trade must be expanded—all of which require improved food processing and preservation.

The general consensus of the committees making the study for the President was that the need for processing and preservation of food increases as nations advance. Urbanization and development bring about specialization in food which then require the processing, preservation, and improved distribution and marketing, all of which are related.

A number of areas were stressed with respect to food research. These involve the utilization and/or the upgrading of food materials. Developing new methods of processing and preservation were given a high priority for countries where energy may be scarce and the climatic conditions are such that simple methods of preservation are unfeasible.

There was great stress on the efficiency of water removal, or in other words, drying and, especially, dehydration. This is especially important for rice and wheat produced in humid areas where they cannot rely on natural drying to prevent mold and microbial deterioration. Professor Mitsuda's work on rice indicates that even though the product may be dry, storage losses may be great and, accordingly, we need to develop new methods of storage.

It has been suggested that a study be made of food formulations in order to improve the nutritional quality of many foods throughout the world. For example, where casaba, which is low in protein, is eaten extensively, the quality could be improved by the addition of protein-containing substances.

With respect to utilizing and upgrading food materials, it was pointed out that there are possibilities to extract important food components from very dilute solutions, such as protein from whey.

It was also pointed out that where monoculture is the practice, such as the production of bananas in some countries, significant quantities of culls are either discarded or underutilized as animal food. This practice needs to be examined within the context of utilizing such materials for human consumption.

Another area that is considered important is a study of the removal of natural toxicants and other undesirable constituents from products that might be used as foods. Potentially, large quantities of high quality protein are excluded from the world food supply because of the presence of certain natural toxicants that make products unacceptable for human consumption. Many of these toxicants have been identified and techniques for removing them, or reducing them to acceptable levels, have been developed to various degrees. Examples include gossypol in cottonseed meal, tannins in sorghum grains and glucosides in rapeseed.

Nonfunctional protein resources also need intensive study. Many protein-rich coproducts or byproducts exist essentially as inert powders, lacking any functional properties such as water-binding or the capability of being texturized. Their only use has been as inert additives to simple protein systems. Generally, protein-fortified foods based on such materials as single-cell protein, algal protein, leaf protein and fish protein concentrate have not become realities. As a general rule, these foods are organoleptically unacceptable. A study should be made of ways of preserving the native protein or of incorporating it functionally into the processed protein.

Potentially nutritious food materials need to be studied and a good example of this is oil palm kernel meal, an extraction by-product of which is a potentially utilizable protein source. World production of palm kernel meal was over 550,000 tons in 1975. This product represents an exploitable source of about 100,000 tons of good quality protein, most of which is currently either burned or fed to animals. A still greater quantity of by-product protein is available from coconut oil extraction operations. There are other examples in this general category.

There is need to make a study of the possibility of upgrading the nutritive value of carbohydrate foods. Certain microorganisms can be grown on carbohydrate-rich media that contain, or to which may be added, simple materials such as ammonia, phosphates, minerals, etc. These microorganisms can be harvested and utilized as food materials containing nutrients, including protein.

Research devoted to analyzing properties of foods would result in the development of methodology for standardizing the measurement and characterization of physical, chemical and functional properties of foods so the effects of processing storage and transportation can be identified and quantified.

For all significant foods, their properties need to be defined as to the effects of storage, processing, and transportation. Standard testing procedures should be adopted or developed to measure the physical and chemical properties of foods in their intact state, as well as the processed states. These properties would then be valuable to technologists and engineers for use in developing procedures and equipment.

There is a great need for quantifying and locating losses. One study team pointed out the most important immediate research task is to study more accurately the kind and extent of losses by commodity, by countries, and by different locations in the marketing chain. This is important and would certainly help meet the challenge.

It is needless to mention the importance of preventing losses caused by pests and, as I already indicated, especially rodents. These are other significant losses due to animals such as birds, chemical deterioration, especially the so-called browning reaction and, of course, enzymatic changes.

Increased research is needed to reduce these tremendous losses and the deterioration in the quality of foods occurring during handling, shipment, storage and merchandizing. The improvement of storage, packaging and transportation is indeed a must and would do much to help meet the challenge. Both food quantity and quality are lost because of improper methods of processing, packaging, transportation and storage. As an example, I have already indicated a number of times the importance of considering storage from the standpoint of rice. This is receiving serious consideration in Japan.

Research must be directed toward developing and applying technology that will permit the design of acceptable methods, especially for developing nations. The unique demands placed on their food systems, such as marketing requirements, product life, product properties, and distribution requirements need to be identified.

Research on the physiological and biological interactions in foods has a number of important purposes: (1) to attain a stable state for foods before losses can occur; (2) to aid in regulating the biological factors of food during preharvest and postharvest so losses during the storage, packaging, processing, and transporting are reduced; (3) to learn more about preharvest and postharvest changes affecting losses during storage, packaging, and transporting; and (4) to learn more about antemortem and postmortem physiology and mechanisms causing chemical and physiological changes in the components of land and marine animals used for food.

The importance of the use of microorganisms was stressed so I cannot refrain from spending a little time on this subject, since I was brought up as a microbiologist with a great interest in molds and yeasts.

Algae seems to hold great promise if anyone can prepare economically a product that can be eaten. I know that workers in Japan have conducted studies on chlorella and have been leaders in the world. I also know that a great deal of work is underway in Thailand. Professor Bhumirtana, in association with German scientists, has been working on *Scenedesmus acutus* as a potential source of protein.

Much has been written about the use of yeast for human and animal food. While the opportunities here are great, and especially for some of the developing nations, for some reason or another, this has not gotten very far. Professor Harry Snyder wrote a review on microbial sources of protein in which he covers yeast very well, and also algae and fungi.

While on the subject of yeast, I might point out that in a book entitled "The Science of Life", microbes are considered as an unseen resource. While it stresses the great variety of uses for microorganisms, specific ones relate to improved nutrition, food and vitamin production. It also stresses protein from microorganisms as a new vista and that yeast produced on an industrial scale, using petroleum or related hydrocarbon substrates, is an active and worldwide enterprise. Some experts have estimated that a billion tons of crude oil are used by mankind each year and that converting 10 per cent of this into single-cell material consisting of about one-half protein would provide 50 million tons annually of high quality food supplement. The organism used for this is *Candida lipolytica*. It is estimated that the protein deficit between now and the year 2,000 could be entirely overcome by this process.

Dr. Peppler, in his book, "The Yeasts", also points out the great possibilities for the use of yeast for protein and for animal food.

A new and exciting development insofar as the use of microorganisms for food is concerned, relates to the work done at the Natick Laboratories of the U.S. Department of Defense. At this laboratory they have developed a procedure for the use of *Trichoderma viride* to convert cellulose into glucose. Cellulose-containing materials such as waste pulp from a paper mill, ground-up cobs, trash from cotton gins, or old cardboard containers, and so on, are exposed to *Trichoderma* to be converted to glucose, which can be fermented to alcohol, if so desired. Recently, I was told that by using this process, alcohol can be produced for seventy cents a gallon.

A curious use for microorganisms may be in the development of flavors for certain foods.

Now that I have presented the positive side of microorganisms, I must remind you that there is a negative side. There are, of course, aflatoxins, and it is important to give them serious consideration, particularly with respect to cereal grains, peanuts and, at times, even milk.

I have covered a wide range of subjects and have discussed many ideas. I am not sure that I have been constructive, although some of the research mentioned could help over a period of years.

There is, without doubt, a strong feeling that each nation must develop its own food production procedures and must be interested in obtaining information concerning not only production, but processing, distribution and storage of foods. It is apparent that there are as many constraints ranging from cultural, geographic, and economic to political.

Political constraints to food production, in many instances, are most important. These must be overcome if developing nations are to increase food production for home use. In the meantime, the other points I mentioned should gradually come into play. No matter what we do, we must consider the politicians, their political activities, and how these influence food availability.

In developing this paper, I have reviewed a great deal of the recent literature. I should like to quote from a few of these as an indication of the diversity and extremeness of views, and especially by nonscientists.

Gale Johnson in 1975 stated, "The possibility of improving food consumption of the poorer people of the world clearly exists. The world does not lack resources required, nor are there biological or technical factors that would prevent us from realizing this desirable objective."

Lester Brown, on the other hand, in his recent book, "The 29th Day", is far from optimistic. Brown believes the world stands on the threshold of a basic social transformation and that the choice will be between voluntary simplicity or enforced austerity. He feels that the call is for a new international economic order that has both ecological and political dimensions.

Tudge, in his new book, "The Famine Business", indicates that famine is not the result of overpopulation or exhausted natural resources, but is the logical consequence of the way food is grown—for profit—and the way it is marketed.

It is apparent that there are many ideas, some realistic and some unrealistic. It is apparent, too, that those who seem to know—the scientists, do not speak, and those who do not know—the economists and politicians, do speak.

In conclusion, I cannot refrain from mentioning Jonathan Swift who lived in the years 1667–1745. He stated, "Whoever could make two ears of corn or two blades of grass grow where only one grew before, would deserve better of mankind and do more essential service to his country than the whole race of politicians put together". How wise he was, for the situation that existed 200 years ago is still with us. I have high hopes that the technologists will do their part, but the politicians and others must work along with them.

SELECTED REFERENCES

1. Altschul, Aaron, M. 1976. "New Protein Foods, Vol. 2, Technology, Part B," Academic Press, New York, N.Y.
2. Aykroyd, W. R. 1974. "The Conquest of Famine." Ghatto and Windos, London, England.
3. Barrons, Keith C. 1975. "The Food in the Future—Steps to Abundance." Van Nostrand-Reinhold Co., New York.
4. Ben-Cera, Hamar and Kramer, Amihud. 1969. The Utilization of Food Industries Wastes. *Advances in Food Research* 17, 77–152.
5. Brown, Lester R. 1970. "Seeds of Change—The Green Revolution and Development in the 1970's." Praeger Publishers, Inc., New York.
6. Brown, Lester R. 1971. "The Social Impact of the Green Revolution," No. 581, Carnegie Endowment Fund for International Peace.
7. Brown, Lester R. 1978. "The 29th Day." Worldwatch Institute, Washington, D.C.
8. Camby, Thomas Y. and Stanfield, James L. 1977. The Incredible Rat. *National Geographic* 152(1), 60–87.
9. Chen, S. L. and Peppler, Henry J. 1978. Single-Cell Proteins 19, 79–949.
10. Fisher, K. D. and Nixon, A. U. 1977. "The Science of Life—Contributions of Biology to Human Welfare." Plenum Publishing Co. Rosetta paperback.
11. Garst, Jonathon. 1963. "No Need for Hunger." Random House, New York.
12. Goldblatt, Leo A. 1969. "Aflatoxin—Scientific Background Control, and Implications." Academic Press., New York.
13. Harrison, Kelly; Henley, Donald; Riley, Harold and Shaffer, James. 1974. Improving Food Marketing Systems in Developing Countries: Experiences From Latin America." Research Report No.6, Latin American Studies Center, Michigan State University, East Lansing, Michigan.
14. Johnson, Gale, 1975. "World Food Problems and Prospects." Foreign Affairs Studies, American Enterprise Institute for Public Policy Research, Washington, D.C.
15. Kahn, Herman; Brown, William and Martel, Leon. 1976. "The Next Two Hundred Years." William Morrow and Co., Inc. New York.
16. Kasetsart University. 1974–1975. "Algae Project." Office of the Prime Minister, Institute of Food Research and Product Development. Bangkok, Thailand.
17. Mitsuda, Hisateru; Kawai, Fumio and Yamamoto, Aijiro. 1971. Hermetic Storage of Cereals and Legumes Under the Water and Ground. *Memoirs of the College of Agriculture*, Kyoto University, Food Science and Technology Sereis No. 1 (100) 49–69.
18. Mitsuda, Hisateru; Kawai, Fumio and Yamamoto, Aijiro. 1972. Underwater and Underground Storage of Cereal Grains. *Food Technology* 26(3) 50–56.
19. Mitsuda, Hisateru and Nakajima, Kenji. 1977. Storage of Cooked Rice. *Journal of Food Science* 42(6) 1439–1443.
20. National Research Council. 1970. Vertebrate Pests: Problems in Control. *Principles of Plant and Animal Pest Control*, Vol. 5. National Academy of

Sciences, Washington, D.C.
21. National Research Council. 1972. "Genetic Vulnerability of Major Crops." National Academy of Sciences, Washington, D.C.
22. National Research Council. 1974. "Food Science in Developing Countries— A Selection of Unsolved Problems." National Academy of Sciences, Washington, D.C.
23. National Research Council. Report of the Board on Agricultural and Renewable Resources. 1975. "World Food and Nutrition Study—Enhancement of Food Production for the United States." National Academy of Sciences, Washington, D.C.
24. National Research Council. 1975. "Understanding Climatic Change." National Academy of Sciences, Washington, D.C.
25. National Research Council. 1976. "Genetic Improvement of Seed Proteins." National Academy of Sciences, Washington, D.C.
26. National Research Council. 1977. "World Food & Nutrition Study—The Potential Contributions of Research." National Academy of Sciences, Washington, D.C.
27. National Research Council. 1977. "Supporting Papers: World Food and Nutrition Study." Vol. I: Study Team 1, Crop Productivity; Study Team 2, Animal Productivity; Study Team 3, Aquatic Food Sources. Vol. II: Study Team 4, Resources for Agriculture; Study Team 5, Weather and Climate. Vol. III: Study Team 6, Food Availability to Consumers; Study Team 7, Rural Institutions, Policies, and Social Science Research; Study Team 8, Information Systems; Study Team 10, Interdependencies. Vol. IV: Study Team 9, Nutrition; Study Team 12, New Approaches to the Alleviation of Hunger. Vol. V: Study Team 14, Agricultural Research Organization. National Academy of Sciences, Washington, D.C.
28. Peppler, Henry J. 1967. "Microbial Technology." Reinhold Publishing Corporation, New York.
29. Protein Advisory Group of the United Nations System. 1972. "Nutritional Improvement of Food Legumes By Breeding." United Nations, New York.
30. Report of an Ad Hoc Panel of the Advisory Committee on Technology Innovation. 1975. "Underexploited Tropical Plants with Promising Economic Value." Board on Science and Technology for International Development, National Academy of Sciences, Washington, D.C.
31. Snider, Harry. 1970. Microbial Sources of Protein. *Advances in Food Research* 18, 85–140. Academic Press, New York.
32. Teranishi, Roy. 1978. "Agricultural and Food Chemistry: Past, Present, Future." Avi Publishing Company, Inc., Westport, Connecticut.
33. Tudge, Colin. 1978. "The Famine Business". St. Martin's Press, London, England.
34. Wharton, Jr., Clifton R. 1969. The Green Revolution: Cornucopia or Pandora's Box? *Foreign Affairs* 47(3) 464–476.
35. Wittwer, Sylvan H. 1975. Critical Issues Relating to Land Use for the Production of Food and Other Renewable Resources. Summary of remarks on land use issues presented at the CNR mini-symposium, Michigan State University, East Lansing, Michigan.

Everyman and Food Science

John Hawthorn*

The implications of my theme "Everyman and Food Science" are obvious. Except for a few tribes in the remoter parts of the earth's surface, no man escapes the influence of our subject, since all must eat. Were I to pick a random half dozen of this professional audience and ask "What is the most important single influence that Food Science and Technology has had on the society within which you live?" I would receive answers such as "health standards improved by clean food", "nutritional well-being raised by the increased range of foodstuffs available", "reduction of waste and of seasonal dependence by effective preservation processes", "improvements in food safety through progressive legislation", "transformation of kitchen drudgery to pleasure by convenience packs", and so on.

These are all valid statements yet none goes far enough. Over the past hundred years, unobtrusively to the point of being almost unnoticed, food science and technology have altered the structures of our societies, and the process is continuing. The most obvious example is that, whereas a century ago three quarters to nine tenths of our citizens lived by agriculture and on the land, in the developed countries at least, the work of one farmer feeds forty to fifty others. This is not merely due to agricultural science but equally to the back-up of our food processing industries. This escape from the bondage of unremitting labour on the land is the unique feature of modern life which has released a degree of creativity in the other fields of science, engineering, medicine and the arts unparalleled by any other event in human history.

As I have emphasised elsewhere and on other occasions, the reorganisation of human food supply has produced not merely the material changes I have described but also more subtle changes in outlook which find public expression in ways which we scientists sometimes find difficult to understand. In a sense, the partaking of food as satisfying the primary human need, has always had mystical, almost sacred overtones recognised symbolically in the religious rituals of feast and fast of all the major and most of the minor religions of the world. At a lesser level, family meals help to

* President of International Union of Food Science & Technology

bind the family together, and the sharing of food equally acts as a cement to wider social structures. Food as proteins, fats, carbohydrates, vitamins and minerals as seen by the scientist is very different to a well-prepared meal as eaten by the same scientist in the company of his family and friends.

If then some of our modern techniques appear to challenge the simple traditional attitudes to food which have their long-forgotten roots in man's evolutionary history, we must not be surprised to find them challenged by the kind of social movement which has come to be known as consumerism. Food science and technology are for everyman. If our science is modern our objectives are classical and humanitarian. When our activities meet with what appears to us as irrational reasoning, we must guard against an equally irrational response and try to understand the real as opposed to the expressed reasons of our critics.

Twenty-seven years ago, when I had just entered academic life after eight years in industry, I came across a book called "Four Thousand Million Mouths" (1). Edited by Le Gros Clark and Pirie, it contained chapters by eleven other well-known British scientists of the time all engaged in a range of food-related subjects. I would like to read you the opening paragraph of that book. Remember please, that these words were written in 1950.

"Within the lifetime of some of our children the world's population may be expected to reach 4,000 millions. It stands at present at about 2,300 millions; and it is said to be increasing at the rate of about 1 per cent per year. This rate of increase will almost certainly be exceeded before long. It was considerably exceeded in many western countries when they were passing through their early stages of industrialisation and sanitary reform; and the fact that these changes are only now beginning to influence the countries of the Orient is often overlooked.
How shall we work the miracle of feeding the 4,000 millions?"

If you take out your pocket calculator you will find that on the basis of a starting population of 2,300 millions increasing at the rate of 1 per cent per annum from 1950, the figure of 4,000 millions would have been reached by the year 2006. In the event the figure was reached in 1976 (2). Between 1950 and the present the mean rate of population increase has been 2.1%.

To the authors of 1950, nothing short of a miracle could prevent world starvation by the year 2006. How much greater is the miracle of providing for these numbers by 1976? But if we look below the surface the miracle is compounded, because despite the huge increase in demand, the food supply *per head* has increased substantially over this period.

Let me contrast the year 1962, the year of our first Congress, with 1974, the most recent year for which figures are available on a world-wide basis. During this period the world food supply on a *per capita* basis has increased by 5% in terms of calories, by 4.7% in terms of protein and 7.8% in terms of fat. Having read so many prophesies of doom over the past two decades, this to me is an amazing achievement, and had I used the 1950 figures as a starting point the increases would have been greater. The figures can be broken down between the developing and the developed countries. Over the same period the developing countries have improved their situation by 3.1%, 1.1% and 4.2% in terms of calories, protein and fat. The corresponding figures for the developed countries are 6.0%, 5.9% and 14.1%. The developed countries, it seems, are still ahead of the game. But the developing countries started on this race far behind the developed ones, and because their progress has been slower, the gap between the two is widening rather than narrowing.

To put it another way, the average citizen of a developing country has only 66% of the energy intake 57% of the protein intake and 27% of the fat intake of his counterpart in the developed countries (3). In considering these figures, it is helpful to remember that the populations of the developed countries represent about one sixth of the world's population, although this figure depends somewhat on the definitions used.

The lesson of these figures is clear and has been stated in this and in other ways by many speakers during this Congress. Our scientific and economic strengths lie mainly in the developed countries. The major task of our Union before it meets again in five years' time is to contribute to redressing this imbalance in food supply in the developing world. Over such a short time we shall not achieve miracles, but let us make whatever contributions are open to us.

If food supply and distribution were simply a matter of science and technology our task would be easy because it is not difficult to demonstrate that the biological resource of our planet can support a human population greater than our present four thousand million by a factor of at least three and probably by much more (4). Unfortunately, economic and cultural factors often dominate and sometimes swamp the sweet reason of our scientific disciplines. On such factors our influence can only be indirect. But we can influence the scientific situation in five ways within our structure and constitution and I suggest these as a framework for our Union's activities during the period of tenure of the Executive Committee which took office yesterday.

Our first and most obvious mechanism is through our Committee on the Needs of the Developing Countries, which has made excellent progress during the past four years under the leadership of our new President, Mr. Joseph H. Hulse. This committee has met the problem of having the whole world as its parish by establishing regional committees to care for areas of similar climates and cultures. These committees have met with varying fortunes but the successes of the most active give encouragement for this approach. Local problems require local solutions.

In these regional activities it sometimes becomes clear that situations of unusual promise exist. It is at this point that the Scientific Activities Committee of our Union can step in and give help to the organising of a meeting involving a regional committee of CNDC, and I expect that such meetings will assume importance over the next five years. Not only will they allow high-level analysis of regional problems, but they can have a morale-building effect, providing encouragement in situations in which individuals may be working in relative isolation. In addition to such regional meetings our Scientific Activities Committee is aware of the occasional need for a really large-scale joint international venture. To this end it can call in the assistance of our International Liaison Committee, one of whose functions is to retain friendly and largely informal links with other International Unions and this mechanism forms the third point of attack.

For example, a joint meeting of the Applied Chemistry Division of the International Union of Pure and Applied Chemistry and our own Union was held in Hamburg in 1973 on the topic of the "Contribution of Chemistry to Food Supply". It was a resounding success which exceeded the expectations of its parent bodies. A further joint venture to follow up this meeting is at present at the early planning stage, and is exciting interest not only amongst the scientists and technologists involved, but also in certain quarters which I am not at the moment free to mention but which operate at the highest levels of international aid. I hope that our Union will be in a position to make a formal announcement of this large and important undertaking before the end of this year.

A fourth line of attack is through our Education Committee. As the events of this week have shown, the educational problems of the developing world are inextricably mixed with its food problems. Education is not merely a matter of training agriculturalists, food scientists, food technologists and nutritionists, but also one of communications, of water supply, of transport, of marketing, of investment and above all, of management. These skills cannot flourish without educated leaders in each field working within a situation of reasonable continuity and political stability. Our Education Committee has plenty of scope!

The CNDC is therefore supported by the back-up of three other Committees of the IUFoST Executive. But that is not all.

Reflect for a moment, please, on the scope and functions of IUFoST. We are poor in treasure, we give no grants, we do not support research or development projects in the developing countries, we pack no financial punch. In contrast, we are rich in intellectual resource. I claim that in the short sixteen years of our history we have become the richest intellectual body of our kind in the world.

During the past four years as your President, I have been conscious of the rapid growth in prestige which this Union enjoys, a respect which is unchallenged by any other international body of its kind. I am both humble and proud: humble at the increased responsibility which this status brings yet proud at the capacity of our Union to sustain it.

This intellectual wealth is not based on the formal structures of the Union, but on the world-wide distribution of the individuals who make up its members at grass-roots level. Our strength is in our working professionals–the everyman, the everywoman of food science and technology. The skills and knowledge of the thousands of individual scientists who contribute to our membership is our most valued resource.

So to the great task ahead of attempting to redress the balance between the developed and undeveloped countries, our fifth line of attack is to find means of tapping into this resource. I know that it is a topic high in the priority list of our new President. He has raised it with me many times over the past two years and I am confident that he will not be content until he has found means of mobilising this great reserve of knowledge, skill and experience.

I am now almost finished and I thank you for the patience with which you have listened to this address. But I have a final thought of leave with you. Our Union has grown to maturity in the sixteen years since our first Congress. Sixteen years from now our leadership will be in the hands of our present generation of young scientists some of whom may well have offered their first papers at this very gathering. I believe that we should give them part of the action now. After all, our own Professor Erik von Sydow first became involved in Union affairs as a member of its first Executive Committee when still a young man in his thirties and few have rendered more signal service to our affairs than he has done. It is a further task for our new Executive to identify and encourage those like him who will be our future leaders.

These are the future tasks of the Union as I see them: we approach them in as healthy a state as I could have wished. Since we last met our membership has increased by 25% and is still rising. Our executive and committee structures are strong and well-established and our inter-congress activities have a thrust and penetration which is the envy of other Unions. We are equal and more than equal to the tasks which face us.

To close this lecture without paying tribute to our Japanese colleagues and friends who have made this Congress possible would be ungrateful and ungracious. But to name them all and to pay tribute to each would be impossible in the time at my disposal. The organisation of the Congress has set a standard in efficiency and courtesy which will be difficult to sustain in the future. The facilities provided by the Kyoto Congress Centre were superb, and the patience with which the hundreds of little problems which arise at large meetings of this sort were dealt with set an atmosphere of friendliness and co-operation from the first day of our meeting. Those who were responsible deserve my thanks on behalf of all the participants.

REFERENCES

1. Le Gros Clark, F. and Pirie, N. W., "Four Thousand Million Mouths", page 1, 1951 (Oxford University Press, London)
2. Population and Vital Statistics Report, Statistical Papers, Series A, Vol. XXX (1), January, 1978. (United Nations, New York)
3. The figures quoted are calculated from Production Year Book, Volume 30, 1976, Tables 97, 98, and 99. FAO Rome, 1977. They exclude the Centrally Organized Economies (Russia and China) which have in their separate ways obtained large increases in *per capita* food supply during the corresponding period.
4. Hawthorn, J., "The Future of Food Science and Technology", Proc. Second International Congress of Food Science and Technology, (Ed. Tilgner, D.J. and Borys, A.), Warsaw, 1966.

Subplenary Sessions

Main Topic I: Resources of Food

1. Exploitation of Food Protein Resources
2. Efficient Utilization of Conventional Food Resources
3. Utilization of Rice

1. Exploitation of Food Protein Resources

1.1 An Overview on Protein Sources: Past, Present and Future

Ricardo Bressani*

Vegetables in the form of leaves, roots, grain or fruits have always been components of the diet of human populations. However, their significance as sources of nutrients, particularly of protein, was brought into focus some 30–35 years ago, when the world became aware that large groups of people suffered from protein-calorie malnutrition. Such populations, particularly those requiring higher intakes of better quality protein like small children and women, were protein deficient due to a lack of consumption of good quality protein such as that found in animal products. It was recognized that these proteins were too costly for such people.

The concept of utilizing properly combined vegetable protein sources was thus developed. Economic reasons behind the need to supply high quality protein provided the initial momentum to study plant proteins in greater detail, and this has resulted in significant technological advances for the benefit of mankind.

The present paper aims to present an overall assessment of the factors of importance in the production and utilization of protein resources, with emphasis on vegetable sources.

1.1.1 COMMON FACTORS IN THE PRODUCTION AND UTILIZATION OF VEGETABLE PROTEINS

Within the context of the production and utilization of vegetable proteins in human nutrition, there are a few common factors. These will be discussed first.

Division of Agricultural and Food Sciences, Institute of Nutrition of Central America and Panama (INCAP), P. O. Box 1188, Guatemala, Guatemala, C.A.

A. Nutritional value of protein

It is well known that protein represents one of the 5 major groups of nutrients necessary for animals, including man. To be efficiently utilized, protein as a nutrient requires the presence of energy, vitamins, minerals and water. Furthermore, the protein must also provide the essential amino acids in the correct amounts and proportions plus some additional non-specific nitrogen. The significance of providing all necessary nutrients is demonstrated in Table 1 based on studies carried out with young swine. Greater performance resulted only when the basic diet was supplemented with energy, vitamins, minerals and the amino acids that limit the protein from corn and beans, as compared to the performance of other partially supplemented groups[1].

TABLE 1.   Weight gain of young pigs fed on corn/bean diets with various supplements alone and combined

Supplement	Corn/bean diet 87/13	Corn/bean diet 70/30
None	2.35 kg	10.88 kg
+ Vitamins	8.50	15.88
+ Minerals	14.63	17.88
+ Calories	6.00	8.63
+ Lys + Try + Met	14.75	13.63
All nutrients	35.00	37.00
Control	54.88	54.88

Animal protein sources display a higher content and more efficient balance of essential amino acids. These and other factors such as a higher digestibility and absence of undesirable nutritional factors endow animal protein sources with a higher nutritional quality. Table 2 summarizes certain results obtained with human subjects[2-9]. The values shown represent the amount of ingested protein necessary for maintenance purposes. Clearly, animal protein sources are superior to vegetable sources, although some of the latter do approach the values of animal sources.

Determination of the efficiency of utilization of protein in man is at present limited by two important questions. One is related to the human requirements for protein or essential amino acids, and the second concerns the evaluation of the quality of protein in foods.

B. Evaluation of protein quality

In recent years, numerous conferences have maintained a continuous discussion of this problem[10]. The primary objective of present methods

TABLE 2. Protein intake from various foods required for maintenance
purposes in human subjects

Protein source	Protein intake (g/kg) for N equilibrium	Ref.
Children		
Whole milk	0.52	Viteri & Bressani
Whole egg	0.57	Viteri & Bressani
Cottonseed/corn	0.62	Viteri & Bressani
Soy/corn	0.57	Viteri & Bressani
Sesame	1.13	De Maeyer & Vanderborght
Peanut	1.16	De Maeyer & Vanderborght
Cottonseed	0.91	De Maeyer & Vanderborght
Adult		
Whole milk	0.63	Young & Scrimshaw
Whole milk	0.57	Bressani, *et al.*
Egg	0.42	Inoue, Fujita, Nuyama
Rice	0.51	Inoue, Fujita, Nuyama
Beef	0.64	Young & Scrimshaw
Bean	0.71	Bressani, *et al.*
Soy isolate	0.68–0.71	Young & Scrimshaw
Whole wheat	0.83	Young, Rand, Scrimshaw

TABLE 3. Comparative results of the protein quality of various
proteins using a short-term assay and the conventional method

Protein	Protein intake for zero N retention (g/kg.day)	
	Conventional[1] assay	Short term[2] assay
Soy protein isolate	0.67	0.54
50/50 Beef/soy isolate	0.59	0.57
Beef	0.64	0.53
Milk	0.63	0.62

[1] MIT.
[2] INCAP.

such as PER, NPR, NPU, BV, etc., has been to predict the value of a protein sufficient to supply the essential amino acids and nitrogen, thus predicting the amounts required for maintenance and normal growth. Animal bioassay methodology for the measurement of protein quality must be verified in human subjects. Present methods generally require a relatively long time and are of high cost. Recently a short, 9–day bioassay in human subjects has been proposed[5,6]. Comparative results for this short modification and the conventional method are listed in Table 3. They indicate a very good agreement between the two methods as performed in the two different laboratories[5,9].

The main point is that protein utilization needs improved methods for protein quality evaluation. These must be accurate, rapid and inexpensive to be of practical use to plant breeders, the food industry and regulating agencies.

C. Economics of vegetable proteins

From the viewpoint of efficiency of utilization of available resources, including energy, vegetable proteins are produced more efficiently than animal proteins. Based on the amount produced per unit of land, vegetable crops yield from 2 to 9 times as much protein as animals. Besides the production of protein/ha, economic productivity must also incorporate such factors as (1) the number of additional products obtained from a particular source, (2) the potential or actual uses of these additional products, (3) the technological inputs in the production of a product which meets specific functional and organoleptic characteristics, (4) the nutritional aspects of the product, and (5) the process of incorporation of vegetable proteins into food systems. All these factors serve to reduce the economic difference which is apparent between vegetable and animal proteins. Economic nutritional efficiency indices should be made available to guide both manufacturers and consumers. Such assessments should be based on nutrient composition, the protein value of the food including its digestibility and biological value, and cost.

D. Toxic factors in plant proteins

Vegetable protein sources may contain toxic compounds. These can be present in the original material or acquired during storage or processing.

Natural toxic compounds which have received attention include the well-known trypsin inhibitors and hemagglutinin compounds found in food legumes. These groups of foods also contain other toxic compounds, which may be even more active than those just mentioned. Such antiphysiological substances can be eliminated by thermal treatments, as shown in Figure 1 for *Phaseolus vulgaris*, which resulting in an increased animal performance and utilization of the protein.[11] Other natural toxic compounds which have limited the use of vegetable proteins include gossypol in cottonseed, and cyanogens in certain food legumes, nuts, and roots such as cassava and sorghum. Saponins are widely distributed, as are goitrogens.

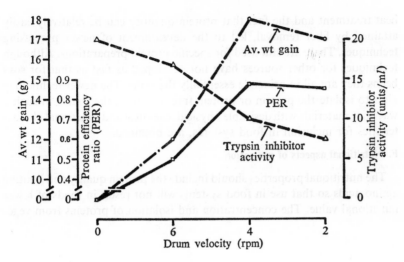

FIG. 1. Effect of heat in the inactivation of trypsin inhibitor activity in *Phaseolus vulgaris* (black coat) (after Bressani *et al.*, 1977).

The naturally occurring toxic substances also include nucleic acids, which tend to limit the potential use of foods in which they are found.

Toxic substances in vegetable protein sources may be acquired after harvesting due to poor storage conditions. Examples include compounds derived from fungal growths. Similarly, insect infestation in addition to the obvious product losses it causes, leads to contamination of food with uric acid, and possibly other undesirable substances. Of similar importance is deterioration of the fat fraction of foods, particularly of those composed of highly unsaturated fatty acids.

Toxic compounds may also develop during processing. One example is the formation of lysinoalanine as a result of the alkaline process used to produce protein isolates. Fat overheating and oxidation may result in the formation of deleterious compounds as well as protein degradation products of protein-carbohydrate complexes, which apart from reducing the quality of the protein, may cause harmful effects on the health of animals. On the basis of the above considerations and if such proteins form an increasing part of the human diet, attention must clearly be given to safety controls. Regulatory agencies must then show concern.

E. Technology for the production and utilization of plant proteins

In the case of oilseeds, processing has previously consisted essentially of removing the oil content to give a product with a higher protein concentration. However, recognition of the loss of protein quality due to extreme heat treatment and the fact that protein quantity can be relatively easily attained by fiber removal, led to the development of newer processing techniques. These are still used for specific protein preparations. Although techniques for other sources have not developed as fast as that for soybeans they are all in principle essentially the same. The newer technology aims to isolate the protein or protein fractions from the source in such a way that materials with desirable physical, chemical and functional characteristics for inclusion in food systems, are obtained.

F. Nutritional aspects of utilization

The nutritional properties should include the protein quality and limiting amino acids so that use in food systems will not result in foods of lower nutritional value. The concentration and isolation of proteins from vege-

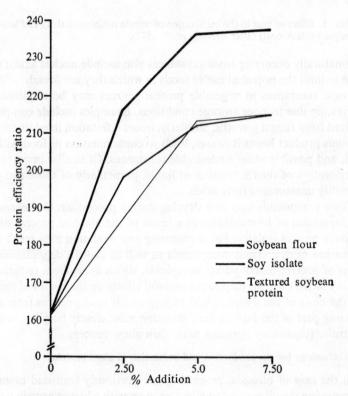

FIG. 2. Effect of protein level in 3 soybean products and corn mixtures on the protein efficiency ratio of rats.

table sources in many instances results in products of lower protein quality than the starting material. This may be due to removal of protein fractions with a better amino acid pattern[12]. A second possibility is that antiphysiological factors may be concentrated in the isolated protein[13]. A third possibility concerns the effects of processing conditions *per se* which may decrease amino acid availability. An example is given in Figure 2. In this case, 3 products from soybeans, a flour, a TVP and an isolated protein, were used as supplement to corn. The results indicate that they were not equally effective in improving the protein quality of the final product[14-17].

1.1.2 SOURCES

Animal protein sources are fewer in number than plant proteins, although insufficient attention has yet been given to small species whose flesh could well be employed in the manufacture of specific types of foods with vegetable proteins. It is important (1) to increase the number of studies on sources and products, (2) to expand the number of applications, and (3) to develop the sources in integrated systems of utilization for the feeding of man and animals.

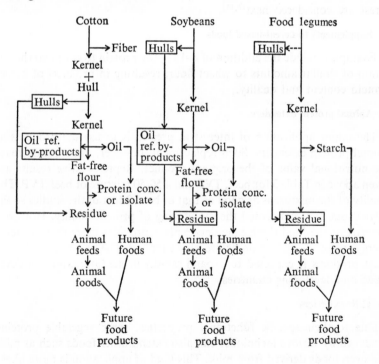

FIG. 3. General uses and products of processing various plant sources.

Many conferences have been held and reviews written on the various plant protein sources. It would appear that in order to increase the number of sources, selection should be based on the basis of protein per ha, as well as on the number of products to be obtained from the source. Various examples are shown in Figure 3.

From this viewpoint, cotton offers more than soybeans, and could, therefore be utilized more efficiently than soybeans in certain areas in terms of an integrated system. Similarly, the selection of legume grains must be based on the value of the starch as compared to the value of the oil from an oilseed. Individually derived systems may of course be combined with others, leading to even more efficient utilization of world resources.

Clearly other factors must also be taken into account, such as the cost of obtaining a product with the desirable characteristics for utilization in various food systems.

1.1.3. Applications

The sources of vegetable proteins will depend in part on how diversified its uses are in food systems. Some applications of current and future interest are considered next[16,17].

A. Supplements to cereal-based foods

Examples include the addition of 8–15% soy protein to corn and the addition of similar amounts to wheat flour, resulting in products of higher protein content and quality.

B. Animal protein extenders

The major application of interest at present is to use the products as animal protein extenders. Such replacement, however, must not decrease the nutritional value of the original product. Representative results are given above in Table 3 for beef, TVP and a 50/50 mixture of beef/TVP. The quality of the mixture is as good as that of beef. Most of the studies so far carried out have concerned the monitoring of protein quality. However, the part of the food these extenders replace provides more than protein: energy, minerals and vitamins are also supplied. The use of extenders in meat products is expected to expand rapidly in the future, both in developed and developing countries.

C. Milk extenders

Due to their specific functional properties, some vegetable proteins produced by various techniques can also extend other foods such as milk and even foods derived from milk. This kind of application is more likely to be developed in areas of the world where milk production is not keeping pace with demand. However, due to the high quality of milk proteins, the danger of decreasing quality by extending them with protein isolates is high.

D. Meat analogues

An additional application which is likely to expand in the future is the production of meat analogues. Since vegetable proteins are lower in quality than animal proteins, meat analogues may also be of inferior quality. However, two other factors may be of importance in this respect. One is that various proteins may be selected for spinning without differences in final texture. Secondly, if various proteins can be used, these may be combined so as to compensate for deficiencies in protein quality which arise from the use of only a single source. These factors must be emphasized since success in the utilization of such products will depend to a great extent on their nutritive value.

In conclusion, it can be said that the problem in all the above applications is the dependence on one source such as soybeans. Efforts must therefore be made to develop other sources. Indeed, such work is now being carried out with rapeseed, green leaves, legume grains and single cell proteins. It is believed that as direct or indirect economic pressures increase, they will stimulate increased research, and significant advances in the development of products from vegetable sources will follow. By-products of these developments will be increasingly used as feeds for animals, the products of which, when properly combined with those derived from the vegetable kingdom, will feed man in the future.

REFERENCES

1. Contreras, G., Elias, L. G., and Bressani, R., Limitación de dietas a base de maíz y frijol como fuente de calorías y proteína, *Informe Anual*, INCAP (1974).
2. Viteri, F. E. and Bressani, R., The quality of new sources of protein and their suitability for weanling and young children, *Bull. World Health Organ.*, **46**, 827 (1972).
3. De Maeyer, E. M. and Vanderborght, H., A study of the nutritive value of proteins from different sources in the feeding of African children, *J. Nutr.*, **65**, 335 (1958).
4. Young, V. R. and Scrimshaw, N. S., Soy protein in adult human nutrition: An update with original data, *Proc. Intern. Soya Protein Food Conference*,

p. 18, Rep. of Singapore, January 25–27, 1978. American Soybean Association, Hudson, Iowa.

5. Bressani, R., Navarrete, D. A., Elías L. G., and Braham, J. E., A critical summary of a short term nitrogen balance index to measure protein quality in adult human subjects, Keyston Conf. Soy Protein and Human Nutrition, Ralston Purina Co., St. Louis, May 22–28, 1978.

6. Navarrete, D. A., Loueiro de Daqui, V. A., Elías, L. G., Lachance P. A., and Bressani, R., The nutritive value of egg protein as determined by the nitrogen balance index (NBI), *Nutr. Repts. Intern.*, **16**, 695 (1977).

7. Inoue, G. Fujita, Y., and Nuyama, Y., Studies on protein requirements of young men fed egg protein and rice protein with excess and maintenance energy intake, *J. Nutr.*, **103**, 1673 (1973).

8. Young, V. R., Rand W. M., and Scrimshaw, N. S., Measuring protein quality in humans: A review and proposed method, *Cereal Chem.*, **54**, 929 (1977).

9. Scrimshaw, N. S. and Young, V. R., Soy protein in adult human nutrition: A review with new data, Keystone Conf. Ralston Purina Co., St. Louis (1978).

10. Institute of Food Technologists, Overview: Protein Efficiency, Outstanding Symposia in Food Sci. Technol., Proc. Midlands Conf. New Concepts for the Rapid Determination of Protein Quality, Univ. of Nebraska, Feb. 20–22, 1977.

11. Bressani, R., Elías, L. G., Huezo, M. T., and Braham, J. E., Estudios sobre la producción de harinas precocidas de frijol y caupí, solos y combinados mediante cocción-deshidratación, *Arch. Latinoamer. Nutr.*, **27**, 247 (1977).

12. Elías, L. G., Sánchez Loarca, S., and Bressani, R., Estudio comparativo de diferentes métodos para evaluación del valor proteínico de harinas de semilla de algodón, *Arch. Latinoamer. Nutr.*, **19**, 279 (1969).

13. Bressani, R., Viteri, F. E., Elías, L. G., de Zaghi, S., Alvarado J., and Odell, A. D., Protein quality of soybean protein textured food in experimental animals and children, *J. Nutr.*, **93**, 349 (1967).

14. Bressani, R., Nutritional contribution of soy protein to food systems, *J. Am. Oil Chem. Soc.*, **52**, 254A (1975).

15. Bressani, R., Calidad proteínica de la soya y su efectividad suplementaria, Meorias Primera Conf. Latinoamericana sobre la Proteína de Soya, México, Nov. 9–12, 1975, Asociación Americana de Soya p. 118 (1975).

16. American Soybean Association, Proc. Int. Soya Protein Food Conf., Republic of Singapore, Jan. 25–27, 1978.

17. American Soybean Association, Proc. World Soy Protein Conf., Münich, Nov. 11–14, 1973.

1.2 Food Protein from Unconventional Cereals and Cereal-like Grains

Olusegum. L. Oke*

There is probably no group of plants which has been more important to man than cereals. In fact, it has been predicted that if other groups of plants became unavailable, man could still survive and remain reasonably healthy, but failure of cereals would lead to starvation and malnutrition in most parts of the world.

In view of the present world shortage of protein and the desire to seek plants with greater drought resistance, unconventional cereals and the problem of finding ways to improve the quality and quantity of their protein, are relevant factors in both the short- and long-term goals of bridging the protein-energy gap. This review therefore attempts to focus attention on these unconventional cereals and cereal-like grains as sources of protein.

1.2.1 THE RANGE OF UNCONVENTIONAL CEREALS AND CEREAL-LIKE GRAINS

In general, these unconventional cereals considered here grow wild, are drought resistant, have less than half the water requirement of the major cereals, do not possess any serious toxic problems, and produce reasonable yields even on poor soils. Some are more nutritious than conventional cereals.

Quinoa (*Chinopodium quinoa*). This is one of the most resistant crops to a combination of frost, salty soil and pests, and requires very little care in its cultivation. No organic or mineral fertilisers, irrigation or other treatment is necessary except for occasional weeding. Fortunately, it is not seriously attacked by plant diseases. It matures in about 4–5 months producing abundant white or pink seeds in large sorghum-like clusters, with a yield of 350–800 kg/ha which can be increased to as much as 4000 kg/ha on experimental plots[2]. Quinoa is very rich in protein (12–19%), which is higher than wheat (12%), barley (9.7%) or maize (9.4%). It contains a balanced amino acid pattern, with a lysine content of 6.6 g/16 g N which is higher than that of any of the conventional cereals and equivalent to that of milk.

*Chemistry Department, University of Ife, Ile-Ife, Nigeria

35

Other chinopods occur but are used mainly as poultry feed. These include Russian thistle (*Salsolakali* var. *tennifolia*), garden atriplex (*Atriplex hortensis*), *Kochia scoparia*, etc. Such chinopods are drought resistant and can yield up to 1680 kg/ha. In all cases feeding trials with mice at protein levels of 7% and 14% gave weight gains of 11.5–13.6 g in 14 days which was the same as casein controls.

Job's tear (*Coix lacrymajobi*). This is usually grown in areas that are suitable for hill rice but are now replaced entirely by rice and maize. Its advantage over rice and maize are that it is more wholesome, contains more protein (13.6%) and is less subject to locust attacks[4]. It is the best substitute for rice in Ceylon.

Eel grass (*Zostera marina*). This plant is one of the few groups of fully submerged flowering plants. Since it grows in shallow sea water, it has the advantage of not requiring manure, mineral fertilizer, fresh water or pesticides. These properties give it a positive environmental value and so its usage should be encouraged. It is richer in protein (13%) than the major cereals.

Amaranth (*Amaranthus* spp.) This produces grains in large sorghum-like seed heads which are delicious and used extensively in the tropical highlands of the Americas as the major cereal grain. Experiments with rats have shown that the PER is comparable to that of casein[5]. Even in a neglected genetic state, unimproved amaranth grains are still better nutritionally than most of the major cereals with respect to protein, and they contain more methionine.

Teff (*Eragostris tef*). This is grown only in Ethopia as a cereal plant, and is used as a staple food grain. The seeds contain about 9.1% protein and the amino acid pattern compares favorably with that of egg except for the low lysine content (273 mg/100 g). Compared to the FAO pattern, the absolute amount of individual amino acids is greater and also exceeds the normal requirements of rats for growth.

Finger grass (*Digitaria* spp.) There are over 100 species of this plant scattered through the drier parts of the tropics. It is valued mainly as a fodder crop but a few species are known to yield edible grains. A good example is Acha or Hungry Rice (*D. exilis*). This is an annual grass growing up to 1.5 ft, and produces numerous small seeds.

The above is not an exhaustive list of all the unconventional cereals, but it does give an insight of what possibilities exist in this area. It could be said the list gives the recognizable unconventional cereals. Apart from this, poorer peoples eat a host of other unconventional cereals in times of scarcity, such as *Brachiaria deflexa, Cenchrus biflorus, C. prieurii, Echinochloa staguina, Dactyloctenium aegypticum, Hygroryza aristata, Ischaemum*

rugosum, Oryza rufipogon, Saciolepis interrupta, Setaria pallide-fusca and
S. glauca.

1.2.2 USES AS FOOD

In general, the cereals are usually sun-dried, threshed with wooden clubs
and the fruit loosened by rolling the seed heads between the palms of the
hands or trampling with the feet. Winnowing is usually accompanied by
tossing the fruit into the air and allowing the debris to blow away before
grinding to flour. In some cases like quinoa which contains some saponin,
the fruit has to be soaked first to remove the bitter taste. The flour can
then be mixed with water in a container as in the case of teff when making
injera, and fermented.

Alternatively, as in case of amaranth, the grains can be parched, milled
and the dough formed into pancakes or else toasted first in earthenware
jars, milled on a saddle stone and used as such or else mixed with wheat to
give a composite flour as in the case of quinoa. A composite flour with 30%
Job's tear makes excellent biscuits[4].

The seeds can also be cooked for gruel, popped and made into confections or powdered and made into drinks[1].

1.2.3 PROBLEMS ASSOCIATED WITH UNCONVENTIONAL CEREALS

The question that is often asked is why these nutritious unconventional
cereals have been supplanted by less nutritious ones like barley or even
maize in which about 50% of the protein in the kernel is not digestible by
monogastric animals such as man. One main difficulty is that the seeds
are very small. For example, the size of teff seed is only about half the size
of a pinhead. They are also very loosely attached to the stock and so are
very difficult to handle or harvest mechanically. In many cases the seeds
are attacked by birds and they also scatter when mature so that they have
to be harvested before maturity in order to minimize losses. It is thus not
surprising that they have been displaced by larger cereals such as maize
with convenient packaging.

1.2.4. AREAS FOR FURTHER DEVELOPMENT

In general, lysine is a limiting component of cereals, resulting in a low
biological value. In some of the above unconventional cereals, especially
amaranth, because of the small size, most of the seed volume is occupied
by the embryo: this is possibly related to their unusually high lysine content[3]. This factor may assist plant breeders to develop varieties of higher
nutritional quality. At present, there are few plant breeding experiments
although there are many varieties with different yields, protein contents,

height, etc. The yields are especially uneven due to lack of proper selection, some being about 4–5 times others. This should aid plant breeders to undertake a proper selection for different altitudes and rainfall regions.

In 1921, Wester[6] concluded, "It would appear then, that with lower production cost and larger yield of a better grain/unit area adlay (i.e. Job's tear) is destined to supplant rice as the leading staple grain not only in the Philippines but probably throughout a very large part of the tropics". This prediction is fast becoming a reality. Through systematic research in Brazil a variety called the "dwarf variety" has been developed which possesses superior features such as a high yield which is even greater than that of maize or rice (2500–3000 kg/ha, or up to 4000 kg/ha in experimental plots).

1.2.5. Conclusion

The research effort on improving the production of cereals which has been made in the past decade, has led to the breakthrough now referred to as the Green Revolution. At about the same time, plant breeders have also been searching for genes which could improve both the quality and quantity of the major cereal proteins and thereby improve their biological value. The present author would like to advocate that an extension of this systematic approach now be made to unconventional cereals also.

References

1. Downton, W. J. S., *Can. J. Bot.*, **48** 1975 (1973).
2. FAO, *Agriculture in Altiplano of Bolivia*, Development Paper No. 4 (1950).
3. Nelson, O. E., *Advan. Agron.*, **21**, 171 (1969).
4. Schauffhausen, R., *Econ. Bot.*, **6**, 216 (1962).
5. Subramanian, N and A. Srinivasan, *Bul. Cent. Fd. Tech. Res. Inst.*, **3** 183 (1952).
6. Wester, P. J., *Philip. Agr. Rev.*, **15**, 159 (1921).

1.3 Oil Seeds as Protein Sources

Mario R. Molina* and
Ricardo Bressani*

Oil seeds have long been recognized as not only an oil source but also a possible protein source for diets. When the oil is removed a high protein by-product (flour or meal) is obtained. The protein content of several defatted oil seed meals and/or flours is in the range of 25–50%. For this reason, such by-products have generally been regarded as protein sources for either food or feed formulations. Besides the high protein content, their relatively low cost represents another important factor which has ensured constant interest in increasing their utilization as protein sources.

The significance of defatted oil seed meals and/or defatted oil seed flours as a protein source is thus not new, and studies related to their possible utilization appeared in the literature 40–50 years ago[1]. The limitations and/ or problems in their utilization both as food or feed were also noticed a few decades ago. Although technology has now been developed to overcome the major problems in some cases, we are still a long away from saying that maximum possible utilization of oil seed by-products as protein sources has been reached. The main factors which still restrict the optimum utilization of oil seed by-products as protein sources are summarized in Table 1.

The present paper attempts to review the main technological achievements which have served to obviate these limitations, and to indicate those studies which are still required to maximize and realize an optimum utilization of oil seed by-products as protein sources.

1.3.1. LIMITATIONS IN THE UTILIZATION OF DEFATTED OIL SEED FLOURS AS A PROTEIN SOURCE

A. Amino Acid Imbalance

The protein quality of oil seed proteins is, with very few exceptions, low. This is due mainly to an inherent amino acid deficiency in the constituent protein. Oil seed proteins do not exhibit similar amino acid patterns. For example, soybeans are deficient in methionine but are a good source

*Division of Agricultural and Food Sciences, Institute of Nutrition of Central America and Panama (INCAP), P. O. Box 1188, Guatemala, Guatemala, C.A.

39

Table 1.   Main factors restricting the maximum utilization of oil seed by-products
as protein sources

---

1. Amino acid imbalance
2. Protein damage through processing
3. Presence of anti-nutritional factors
   3.1.   Inherent factors
        3.1.a.   Toxic factors
        3.1.b.   Anti-nutritional components such as phytic acid, fiber, polyphenols,
                 etc.
   3.2.   External factors
        3.2.a.   Microbial contamination and toxins
        3.2.b.   Insecticide and pesticide residues

---

of lysine; sesame is deficient in lysine but a good source of sulfur-containing amino acids; cottonseed and peanut are deficient in both these amino acids[3].

To overcome these deficiencies, technologies for fortification and complementation have been developed. The protein complementation principle has permitted the development of engineered foods consisting mainly of mixtures of cereals, legumes and oil seed flours, in which the protein of each component complements the amino acid deficiency of the others yielding as a whole a high protein quality food item. An example of this type of food is INCAPARINA, a food item developed by INCAP. Several other formulations and products have been developed in different countries utilizing the same principle[3].

In general, the amino acid deficiency problem of oil seed proteins no longer represents a major limitation to their utilization as a protein source in food items, due to the advances which have been made in both protein complementation and protein fortification technology. The latter is also actively supported by the great developments which have been made in synthetic amino acid production through fermentative processes.

B. Thermal Damage to the Protein Fraction of Oil Seeds

In general, the processing damage shown by oil seed proteins has been characterized as thermal damage occurring during oil extraction. Such damage has been shown to magnify the amino acid deficiency of the oil seeds, as well as to interfere with other nutritional characteristics such as the digestibility and availability of the protein fraction. The thermal processing damage to the protein fraction also affects the functional characteristics of the final oil seed flour to be included in food items[3].

To overcome the above limitations, oil extraction technology has adopted several alternative approaches. The pre-press solvent extraction and direct solvent oil extraction techniques so far represent the most popular technologies offering oil seed defatted flours with minimum thermal damage, resulting in flour products with a high nitrogen solubility index as well as several other functional properties desirable for their inclusion in different food systems[21]. The above-mentioned techniques have permitted the inclusion of defatted oil seed flours in bread making, pasta products and different food systems, since they offer a defatted flour with improved water absorption and functional characteristics[16,23].

C. Anti-nutritional Factors Limiting the Utilization of Oil Seeds as a Protein Source

Inherent anti-nutritional limitations. Several oil seeds contain anti-nutritional toxic factors. The latter include gossypol (cottonseed), trypsin inhibitors and hemagglutinins (soybeans and peanuts), goitrogenic compounds (rapeseed), and ricin, ricinine and other unidentified factors (castor oil seeds)[1]. Techniques have been developed to overcome this limitation especially in cases where the toxic substances are thermolabile. Also, in the case of cottonseed, techniques have been developed to bind the free gossypol to ions such as iron through treatment of the defatted cottonseed flour with iron and calcium hydroxide, where the latter gives an alkaline pH[11]. The agricultural development of glandless (gossypol-free) cottonseed varieties has offered another alternative[4,13]. This case illustrates a multilateral approach with agriculture, biochemistry and food science and technology working together in order to optimize the utilization of cottonseed by-products as a protein source. Although several problems still remain to be solved in this type of approach, such as the agricultural yield and insect susceptibility of the glandless cottonseed varieties, we believe that the approach is valid and has every possibility of success.

In the case of rapeseed and other oil seed flours (i.e. tung, aceituno and castor bean), several techniques, mainly based on solvent extraction, have been proposed to detoxify them. Efforts are currently being made to simplify the technology of detoxification of several of these materials such as rapeseed[14]. However, the challenge still remains to supply a low-cost material free from any toxic factor. A multilateral approach to the toxicological problems of oil seed by-products would seem advisable as in the case of cottonseed.

Another factor which could be classified as an anti-nutritional factor characteristic of some oil seed meals or defatted oil seed flours, is a relatively high fiber content, which apart from affecting the nutritional characteristics also affects the functionality of the by-product[12,15]. The fiber content varies from material to material. In coconut, rapeseeds or peanut flours it oscillates between 10–15%, but it can go as high as 20–30% in palm kernel or cohune nut flours. Various approaches have been adopted to obviate this limitation or eliminate the problem, ranging from wet oil extraction processes starting from the full fat material, to protein extraction from the defatted flour. The wet oil extraction technology has recently been studied in detail but economic limitations still affect its use on an industrial scale.[9,10,20] Nevertheless, this process can be applied relatively easily as an intermediate technology for the preparation of "cream" or "milk" from different oil seeds such as soybeans, coconut, peanuts, etc.[18,22] Work along these lines has been carried out in various countries and several products have been developed. Among the possibilities is the utilization of the oil seed "cream" or oil seed "milk" for the preparation of a wheat flour dough prior to the production of cookies or bread, involving a bakery product formulation with a high protein and high energy content. This has the advantage of lowering the cost primarily of the high caloric compound, viz. the oil. However, we consider that every effort should also be made to develop uses for the wet oil extraction technology on an industrial scale in the near future.

The protein extraction method starting from a defatted material has been developed considerably. Several extraction techniques have been devised utilizing different principles. At present these can be classified as chemical, enzymatic and chemical-enzymatic procedures. The protein concentrates or protein isolates obtained by the chemical extraction method have found a wide range of possible applications in the food industries, mainly as meat or milk extenders, milk substitutes, high protein beverages, etc.[4,21] However, nutritional evaluations have shown that these products as well as the protein concentrates or isolates obtained by the wet oil extraction process, are of lower protein quality than the original flour or whole oil seed from which they were derived. A possible explanation of this is a change in amino acid pattern away from that of the flour or raw material on which the protein extraction was started. In addition, it has been shown that protein extraction carried out at an alkaline pH and relatively high temperature, leads to complex formation between the amino acids, lysine and alanine. This complex has also been blamed for the lower protein quality of the final products and has been shown to affect kidney function in animals fed on a relatively high concentration of this compound.[7,26] Clearly, further studies are required to assure a higher nutritive quality of the final protein product.

The enzymatic and chemical-enzymatic protein extraction methods have been shown in the laboratory to be very efficient and to provide a protein product of higher nutritive quality than the original and with favorable functional characteristics for the preparation of nutritional bever-ages.[6,12,15] However, these techniques appear unlikely to be developed for practical use on an industrial scale in the near future, due mainly to the relatively high cost involved in the present technology. There is thus a need for research into the possibility of attaining a detoxification of the oil seed protein through an enzymatic or chemical-enzymatic technology, since this should enhance the possible industrial or large-scale application of these methods.

Anti-nutritional factors deriving from external contamination. This type of limitation is exemplified by the aflatoxin production by *Aspergillus flavus* seen particularly in the case of groundnut or peanut meal,[2] and by the residual insecticide or pesticide contamination observed in our labora-tories in defatted oil seed flours derived from cottonseed, etc. In the case of aflatoxin contamination of peanut meal, several technologies had been developed to obviate this limitation. These consist mainly of using chemi-cals such as sodium hypochloride (or hypochloric acid) to inactivate the toxic factor.[19] Agronomic efforts are also of some significance since several peanut strains or varieties resistant to *Aspergillus flavus* contamina-tion have been developed in this way.[2] Here again, a multilateral approach to the problem seems valid. Moreover, in the case of the residual con-tamination of cottonseed flour,[25] a multilateral approach is needed to obviate this limitation and the possible inefficient utilization of oil-seed flours which are so needed in the developing countries as another source of protein for the diet.

1.3.2. POSSIBLE UTILIZATION OF FULL FAT OIL SEEDS

Several routes for the utilization of whole full fat oil seeds as a protein and calorie source in different food systems have recently been developed. Among the main achievements is the introduction of whole full fat soy-beans in bakery product formulations.[24] This technology offers the pos-sibility of preparing a bread-type product with a high protein quality and protein content as well as a high caloric density.

Another technology which has been developed recently and offers the opportunity of utilizing full fat oil seeds such as soybeans, cottonseed, sesame, etc. for the manufacture of high protein and high caloric food items, is extrusion cooking. This type of technology is daily becoming more valuable with the development of relatively low-cost extrusion cook-ers which are adequate for the processing of full fat oil seeds.[17]

The above examples of the processing and utilization of whole full fat oil seeds are considered to be of value especially in countries where particular oil seeds or new oil seeds are not being utilized primarily due to the prevalence of another oil seed of lower cost and higher oil content.

1.3.3. New Oil Seeds as Possible Protein Sources

Due to the increasing world demand for oil and protein sources, new oil seeds which could be utilized as sources of both these nutrients are being investigated. Included in this category are the seed from the fruit called "morro" or "jicaro" (*Crescentia alata*) which grows widely in the tropical humid areas of Central America, and the winged bean which is a high oil-containing legume seed. In these and other cases, a multilateral approach is recommended involving the agricultural production technologies as well as the food science and technology aspects.[5,8]

1.3.4. Conclusions

From the above discussion, it can be said that recent technological achievements have permitted the improved utilization of oil seeds as protein sources, both as flour and as the whole oil seed. However, it is considered that we are still a long way from attaining an optimal utilization of oil seeds or oil seed by-products as protein sources for human or animal diets. More research is clearly needed to eliminate or inactivate the toxic factors of oil seeds, both those inherent to the seeds and those deriving from the external environment. This research may often be done best through a multidisciplinary approach. Also, more research is clearly needed to develop lower cost technologies for improving the functional quality of oil seed proteins so that they can be included in multiple food systems.

References

1. Altschul, A. M., (ed.) *Processed Plant Protein Foodstuffs*, Academic Press, New York (1958).
2. Amaya, J., Young, C. T., Mixon A. C. and Norden, A. J. Soluble amino and carbohydrate compounds in the testae of six experimental peanut lines with various degrees of *Aspergillus flavus* resistance, *J. Agr. Food Chem.*, **25**, 661 (1977).
3. Bressani, R. and Elías, L. G. Processed vegetable protein mixtures for human consumption in developing countries, *Advan. Food Res.*, **16**, 1 (1968).
4. Carter, C. M., Mattil, K. F., Meinke, W. W., Taranto, M. V., Lawhon J. T. and Alford, B. B. Cottonseed protein food products, *J. Am. Oil Chem. Soc.*, **54**, 90A(1977).
5. Cerny, K. Comparative nutritional and clinical aspects of the winged bean, Workshop/Seminar of the Potential of the Winged Bean, Los Baños, Philippines, Jan. 1978, 53 pp. (1978).

6. Childs, E. A. and Forte J., F. Enzymatic and ultrasonic techniques for solubilization of protein from heat-treated cottonseed products, *J. Food Sci.*, **41**, 652 (1976).

7. De Groot, A. P. and Slump, P. Effects of severe alkali treatment of proteins on amino acid composition and nutritive value, *J. Nutr.*, **98**, 45 (1969).

8. Gómez-Brenes, R. A. and Bressani, R. Evaluación nutricional del aceite y de la torta de la semilla de jícaro o morro (*Crescentia alata*). *Arch. Latinoamer. Nutr.*, **23**, 225 (1973).

9. Hagenmaier, R. D., Carter C. M. and Mattil, K. F. Critical unit operations of the aqueous processing of fresh coconuts, *J. Am. Oil Chem. Soc.*, **49**, 178 (1972).

10. Hagenmaier, R. D., Carter C. M. and Mattil, K. F. Aqueous processing of coconuts: economic analysis, *J. Am. Oil Chem. Soc.*, **52**, 5 (1975).

11. Jarquín, R., Bressani, R. Elías, L. G. Tejada, C. González M. and Braham, J. E. Effect of cooking and calcium and iron supplementation on gossypol toxicity in swine, *J. Agr. Food Chem.*, **14**, 275 (1966).

12. Lachance, P. A. and Molina, M. R. Nutritive value of a fiber-free coconut protein extract obtained by an enzymatic-chemical method, *J. Food Sci.*, **39**, 581 (1974).

13. Lawhon, J. T., Carter C. M. and Mattil, K. F. Evaluation of the food use potential of sixteen varieties of cottonseed, *J. Am. Oil Chem. Soc.*, **54**, 75 (1977).

14. Macfarlane, N., Shah E. and McFarlane, M. Aqueous fractionation of rapeseed, *Tropical Sci.*, **18**, 211 (1976).

15. Molina, M. R. and Lachance, P. A. Studies on the utilization of coconut meal. A new enzymatic-chemical method for fiber-free protein extraction of defatted coconut flour, *J. Food Sci.*, **38**, 607 (1973).

16. Molina, M. R., Mayorga, I., Lachance P. A. and Bressani, R. Production of high-protein quality pasta products using a semolina-corn-soy flour mixture. I. Influence of thermal processing of corn flour on pasta quality, *Cereal Chem.*, **52**, 240 (1975).

17. Molina, M. R., Bressani, R. Cuevas, R., Gudiel H. and Chauvin, V. Effects of processing variables on some physicochemical characteristics and nutritive quality of high protein foods, *Am. Inst. Chem. Eng. (AIChE) Symp. Series*, **74** (172), 153 (1978).

18. Nadkarni, B. Y., La noix de coco, source de protéines. Une méthode d'extraction artisanale, oléagineux, **21**, 519 (1966).

19. Natarajan, K. R., Rhee, K. C., Cater C. M. and Mattil, K. F. Destruction of aflatoxins in peanut protein isolates by sodium hypochlorite, *J. Am. Oil Chem. Soc.*, **52**, 160 (1975).

20. Orr, E. and Adair, D. *The Production of Protein Foods and Concentrates from Oilseeds*, Tropical Products Institute Rept. G31, Tropical Products Institute, London, June 1967.

21. Smith, A. K. and Circle, S. J. *Soybeans: Chemistry and Technology, Vol. 1, Proteins*, The AVI Publ. Co., Inc., Westport, Conn. (1972).

22. Steinkraus, K. H., David, L. T., Ramos L. J. and Banzon, J. Development of flavored soy milks and soy/coconut milks for the Philippine market, *Philip. Agriculturist*, **52**, 268 (1968).
23. Tsen, C. C. and Hoover, W. J. The shortening sparing effect of sodium stearoyl-2 lactylate and calcium stearoyl-2 lactylate in bread baking, *Baker's Dig.*, **45** (3), 38 (1971).
24. Tsen, C. C. and Hoover, W. J. High-protein bread from wheat flour fortified with full-fat soy flour, *Cereal Chem.*, **50**, 7 (1973).
25. Whitaker, T. B. and Whitten, M. E. Evaluation of cottonseed aflatoxin testing programs, *J. Am. Oil Chem. Soc.*, **54**, 436 (1977).
26. Woodard, J. C. and Short, D. D. Toxicity of alkali-treated soyprotein in rats, *J. Nutr.*, **103**, 569 (1973).

1.4 SCP for Animal Feeding

Pieter. van der Wal*

1.4.1 INTRODUCTION

During the opening session of this congress a number of crucial statements were made.

The shortage of food in the world is well known. The director general of FAO[1], emphasized recently again the special need in densily populated rural areas of the developing countries.

We need new sources and we should not just play around with the existing ones to meet this demand[2].

In our attempts to develop these potentials we should avoid, however, the often occurring theoretical overkills[3].

In this paper we will try to take these points into account while studying the question as to whether or not new sources could be tapped to a significant extent and we could produce from these sources, in rural communities, food which is affordable and sufficiently acceptable gastronomically, nutritionally and toxicologically.

In view of the latter point we would like to emphasize that especially in rural areas the most critical consumers are to be found. This is by no means specific for those countries that are at present developing. In the Netherlands too we were teaching the children that what "a farmer does not know he does not eat either".

1.4.2 THE SOURCES OF NUTRIENTS AVAILABLE

An inventory of these sources is rather illuminating. There are approximately 9 billion hectares of land in the world. Close to 50% of that consist of wood, shrubs and forests. Another 35% is pasture and grassland, 15% finally is arable land. Of the products from arable land by far the major part is discarded as a residue. That means that approximately 95% of the products mentioned in Table 1 can be considered to be an untapped source of nutrients in the sense of not being utilized directly for human consumption.

*ILOB, Institute for Animal Nutrition Research, Haarweg 8, 6709 PJ, Wageningen, The Netherlands.

47

Table 1.   Land production of potenial nutrients

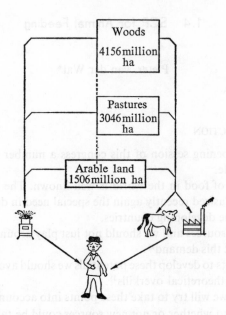

Food Science and Technology is at present concentrating predominantly on the 5% of the annual production of potential nutrients that can be used after relatively simple forms of processing like cooking or baking. The other 95% needs very considerable processing be it physical, chemical or *via* some form of bioconversion.

In this paper we will concentrate on the products that we refer to as organic residues. They are the residues of agricultural production, sometimes left behind on the land (straw), on the farm (manure) or in agro-industries. They are relatively easily available for conversion into food.

In Table 2 some of the most important agricultural crops are represented. There is a line along which we can divide these products. On the left hand side we find the percentage considered as the main product of the crops. They can be used without severe processing by the human consumer (grain, oil, starch, vegetable protein). On the right hand side we find the residues forming approximately 2/3 of the total production.

For the conversion of the residues two routes are available, as indicated in Table 2: *via* animals or *via* some industrial process. Because these residues form the major part of agricultural production, their conversion into food *via* efficient and safe systems seems to deserve far more attention than we have given them so far.

Tremendous efforts are required to make such new systems operational.

TABLE 2.   Agricultural crops

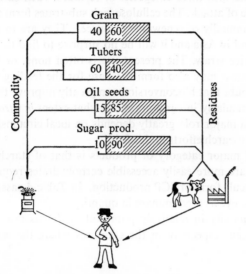

So if we want to achieve something we should concentrate on a limited number of the most promising systems and attack them by a multidisciplinary action.

Those of us who were involved in developing new conversion systems will agree that the creation of acceptable food from novel sources usually requires animal conversion as a last step. Microbial conversion alone produces in most cases biomass, e.g. Single Cell Protein that is not accepted as a food by most consumers.

1.4.3. THE MOST RELEVANT MATERIALS FOR BIOCONVERSION

To identify the most relevant areas in which bioconversion of residues

TABLE 3.   Straw production 1974 (million tons)

Crop	World	Africa	South America	Asia
Paddy rice	323	8	10	294
Wheat	360	8	10	90
Maize	586	54	58	100
Other straws	441	41	18	123
Total straws	1710	111	96	607
Sugar cane	116	9	28	46
Total	1826	120	124	653

may be of importance and are therefore particularly worth our while, we divided the field into three categories of residues, each category having a common angle of attack. The cellulose-rich substrates form a total of 1800 million tons annually of renewable resources. They are to a great extent (Table 3) found in Asia and it will be no surprise to find that they consist primarily of rice straw. The present use is often none, or for fuel. To a great extent straw may also form the base for the feeding of ruminants. There is no doubt that bioconversion can greatly improve the use of these materials, particularly in rural areas. To what extent *in vitro* SCP production can play a major role greatly depends on local circumstances and on the results of research efforts in this field.

The second major category of products is that of starchy and sugary wastes. They are more easily accessible carbohydrates requiring a somewhat less difficult form of SCP production. In Table 4 cassava and sugar beets catch the eye as predominant in quantity.

High productivity in relatively poor soil made cassava popular. This happens to occur especially in the countries where the largest need for food is.

TABLE 4. Starchy, sugary and other residues (million tons)

Crop	World	Africa	Latin America	Asia
Cassava	106	42	33	30
Sugarbeets	482	4	5	39
Bananas	8	1	4	2
Citrus fruits	12	1	3	3
Coffee	5	2	3	—
Total	613	50	48	74

TABLE 5. Chemical composition (% dry matter)

	grain[1] (straw)	leaf[1] (grass)	citrus[2] (pulp)	manure (poultry)
Organic matter	95	91	93	77
Ash	5	9	7	23
Crude protein	3	17	7	32
Crude fiber	48	27	14	—
Nitrogen–free extract	43	44	69	27

[1]O. Kellner, M. Becker, 1959, Grundzüge der Futterungslehre
[2]Nutrient Requirements CVB, Netherlands

A third category of residues is manure, being the residue of all animal production systems. It is calculated that approximately 1900 million tons of manure per year is produced.

1.4.4 CHARACTERISTICS OF RESIDUES

When questioning why these residues are not used as a food, we may identify the basic shortcomings that have to be overcome by bioconversion.

In Table 5 it is shown that the chemical composition of most residues is not attractive. In straw 48% crude fiber and 3% crude protein is found. It is hardly a good product for human consumption. Grass is better for both parameters, but if it were to be used for monogastric consumers, like humans, we would still meet severe problems because of the relatively high crude fiber content.

Poor digestibility is another reason why materials may become rejected residues. In Table 6 the digestibility for ruminants is presented. The organic matter of straw is even then only 38% digestible. For monogastric organisms as humans, poultry and pigs, the coefficients are even lower. Grass is better but less suitable for monogastrics.

TABLE 6.   Digestibility coefficients in ruminants

	grain[1] (straw)	leaf[1] (grass)	citrus[2] (pulp)	manure (poultry)
Organic matter	38	72	—	72
Crude protein	12	75	42	78
Crude fiber	40	65	80	—
Nitrogen–free extract	38	77	95	69

[1]O. Kellner, M. Becker, 1959, Grundzüge der Futterungslehre
[2]Nutrient Requirements CVB, Netherlands

For citrus and animal wastes, the digestibility is reasonable, but not particularly good.

A number of other reasons may make a product be considered as a residue.

Logistic aspects and low dry matter content may be expensive to overcome. Seasonal variability makes it often difficult to cope with the material by advanced technology. Chemical and microbial contamination, and also organoleptic and psychological aspects may offer problems.

In the above mentioned characteristics we have listed the problems to be overcome if we want to convert a residue into food.

1.4.5. BIOCONVERSION SYSTEMS

In Table 7 the bioconversion of residues into food is shown along different routes.

TABLE 7.   Bioconversion

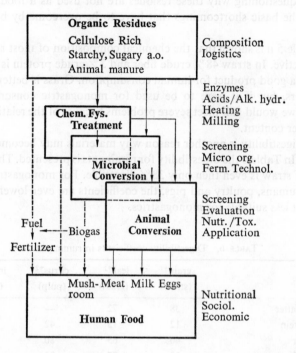

In the upper box the cellulose-rich, starchy, and sugary residues and animal manure are represented. In the lower box the goal of bioconversion systems is given: human food. In most cases this will be in the form of meat, milk and eggs.

It is often said that there seems to be a certain competition for food between animals and humans. One easily overlooks at present that this is an exception rather than a rule. The animals are kept for producing food in by far the most cases. They are mainly converters (biological ones) of products inedible by men. As such they do not run into significant competition in the ability to make products for the same price, from the same raw materials and equally acceptable. The options we have in making food from the wastes are many. The ones bypassing the animals are represented by dotted lines. The direct use is non-existent, otherwise the product would not be a waste. Chemical and physical treatments seldom lead to food.

Microbial conversion, directly or after pre-treatment, leads to mushrooms and to fermented oilcakes. Unfortunately these do not yet form a major contribution for the conversion of millions of tons of residues either.

The drawn lines on the right hand side of the table represent the bioconversion systems making use of animals. Grass, straw and some poor quality roughage follow the direct route to food. We may also reach the animal box *via* chemical or physical treatment and/or *via* microbial conversion. The potentials and efficiency of the bioconversion may thus greatly be improved.

In general it can be assumed that on this side of our scheme the realistic potentials for bioconversion of the bulk of the residues are presented.

1.4.6 PHYSICAL AND CHEMICAL PRE-TREATMENTS

The alkali treatment of cellulose-rich materials like straw (1800 million tons in rural areas) asks for special attention. Digestibility for ruminants improves from 45% up to 68%. What does that imply?

TABLE 8.   Effect of treatment on straw digestion in sheep

Treatment	Organic matter	Digestibility (%)
Alkali	Untreated	45
	Treated	68
Ammonia	Untreated	38 (56)
	Treated	52 (69)

In major rural areas of India untreated rice straw provides hardly enough nutrients to maintain the live weight of cattle, in other words to cover the maintenance requirements. Let us assume that 90% of the feed is used for maintenance, then 10% is available for production of live weight, offspring and milk. When digestibility is increased by 50%, it provides in our example a five–fold increase of the nutrients available for production (Table 8).

1.4.7. MICROBIAL CONVERSION

In fact in our above–mentioned example we gave the pretreated straw to small fermentation plants located in the rumen of a cow, buffalo or goat. The microorganisms in these "SCP plants" are able to convert the treated residue into protein. The process has been fairly stable through the ages.

Microbial conversion can also be carried out outside the animal. By applying appropriate technology we will then be able to produce protein products that can be converted into food by monogastric animals like poultry and pigs.

If the microorganisms used remain combined with the remnants of the organic residue that was used as a substrate, we call the product Biomass Product (BMP). If the microorganisms are harvested and separated from the substrate, we refer to the product as Single Cell Protein (SCP).

SCP compare in their composition favourably with the substrates on which they are grown, as shown in Table 9.

The crude protein content and the amino acid composition (Tables 9 and 10) put bacteria, yeasts, fungi and algae in the category of high quality protein sources like soybean oilmeal. The crude fiber content is low with the exception of the algae.

The digestibility (Table 11) compares again well with conventional high quality protein sources like soya. Only for algae the digestibility is lower and the data inconclusive. Further evaluation is required. It is often as-

TABLE 9.   Chemical composition (%)

	Yeast	Bacteria	Fungi	Algae	Soybean Oilmeal
Dry matter	96	90	86	94	88
Ash	6	8	2	7	6
Organic matter	90	81	84	87	82
Crude protein (N × 6.25)	60	74	32	52	45
True protein (amino acid-N × 6.25)	47	55	22	46	38
Crude fat	9	8	5	15	1
Crude fiber	—	—	28	11	6
Nitrogen–free extract	20	—	20	12	30

TABLE 10.   Amino acid composition (g/16 g N)

	Yeast	Bacteria	Fungi	Algae	Soybean oilmeal
Lysine	7.0	5.5	4.8	4.6	6.2
Methionine + Cystine	2.9	3.1	2.5	3.2	2.9
Arginine	4.8	4.7	5.2	—	7.2
Histidine	2.0	1.9	2.0	—	2.5
Isoleucine	4.5	3.9	4.1	3.1	4.9
Leucine	7.0	6.3	6.4	7.0	7.6
Phenylalanine + Tyrosine	7.9	6.2	8.1	6.0	8.4
Threonine	4.9	4.2	4.4	4.9	4.2
Tryptophane	1.4	0.8	1.4	1.7	1.3
Valine	5.4	4.8	5.6	4.7	5.0

TABLE 11. Digestibility coefficients in pigs

	Yeast	Bacteria	Fungi	Algae	Soybean oilmeal
Organic matter	92	90	79	—	83
Crude protein	90	93	71	54	91
Crude fat	95	87	34	—	34
Crude fiber	—	—	99	—	—
Nitrogen–free extract	94	—	—	—	94
Metabolisable energy (kcal/kg)	3860	3720	2940	—	3190

sumed that small scale SCP production can be made operational relatively easy. This can be considered as a serious under-estimation of the problems involved. Low key technology that can be made operational on the scale of a farm cooperative or a village, and that is nevertheless effective, and stable, asks for elaborate research and development efforts. Positive results are more likely to be achieved if experienced industrial fermentation research groups participate.

1.4.8 THE ANIMAL CONVERSION PHASE

In order to apply successfully the SCP products, a thorough nutritional and toxicological evaluation is necessary. Such an evaluation has to be carried out with the animals for which the material will be used.

The digestion of an animal is specific and so is the absorption of the nutrients after digestion. The metabolism of the nutrients and potential toxic substances is specific as well, and again this is the case with the susceptibility to toxic substances and the requirements for nutrients.

The consequence of this specificity is that experimental data obtained in animal testing are not necessarily transferable to other animal species. The nutritional and toxicological evaluation has to incorporate animals for which the product is destined, the target species. In guidelines for testing the nutritional and safety aspects of novel sources of protein, as formulated by the Protein Calory Advisory Group of the United Nations System (PAG)[4,5], this is taken into account.

In Table 12 digestibility coefficients for the same product in two different monogastric species, poultry and pigs, are given.

The digestibility of the organic matter whilst being close to 80 for the pigs, is hardly 24 for the chickens. Protein digestibility differs somewhat less dramatically. The Table seems to suggest that the difference is probably due to the difference in digestibility of the crude fiber. In the final analysis the metabolisable energy for the chickens is only 1/3 of that for the pigs.

TABLE 12.   Digestibility coefficients of a fungal product

	Pigs	Chickens
Organic matter	79	24
Crude protein	71	59
Crude fat	34	18
Crude fiber	99	6
Metabolisable energy (kcal/kg)	2940	1000

The difference between species is usually less marked, but the figures illustrate that specific reactions of animals must be taken into account in the
evaluation of SCP.

When the basic nutritional and toxicological evaluation has been completed with satisfactory results, the product can be submitted for approval
by the governmental authorities.

TABLE 13.   Number of animals (millions)

	World	Africa	Latin America	South Asia	S.E. Asia	Near East
Cattle	1214	160	266	199	23	46
Buffalo	132	2	—	73	14	4
Sheep	1038	159	120	77	3	137
Goats	413	127	41	87	9	62
Pigs	645	8	72	7	25	—
Chickens	6116	488	721	192	307	236

When producing the product commercially, biological testing has to
make sure that the product complies with the specifications of the product
for which approval was obtained. For modifications of the product the experimental data are not always applicable.

With respect to testing, the final stage concerns the optimum application
of the product in the rations and with the animals used in the countries
where the product will be applied. Here too specific factors may play a
major role.

The animals available and the acceptability of their products differ greatly
among regions.

REFERENCES

1. E. Saouma, Director General of the Food and Agriculture Organization (FAO).

Statement at the opening session of the *Fifth International Congress of Food Science and Technology, Kyoto, Japan,* 17–22 September, 1978.

2. F. Aylward, Food safety: Novel foods. *Proceedings of the Fifth International Congress of Food Science and Technology, Kyoto, Japan,* 17–22 September, 1978 (see 140 page).

3. E. M. Mrak, The world food problem and meeting the challenge. *Proceedings of the Fifth International Congress of Food Science and Technology, Kyoto, Japan,* 17–22 September, 1978 (see 3 page).

4. Protein Advisory Group (1970). *PAG Guideline No. 6.* Guideline for pre-clinical testing of Novel Sources of Protein. Protein Advisory Group, United Nations, New York 10017, USA.

5. Protein Advisory Group (1974). *PAG Guideline No. 15.* Guideline on Nutritional and Safety Aspects of Novel Protein Sources for Animal Feeding. Protein-Calory-Advisory Group, United Nations, New York 10017, USA.

6. P. van der Wal. The Future of Single Cell Proteins: The nutritional and safety aspects. Paper presented at the *Fifth International Conference on Global Impacts of Applied Microbiology, Bangkok,* 21–26 November, 1977.

1.5   Fish Protein from Underutilized Species

Poul Hansen*

World fish catches include a very large number of species of which only a few are traditional food fish. Among the other species, many are utilized for reduction to fish meal, while others are discarded at sea because they are of low commercial value or of a size which is unsuitable for the handling system on board. The storage life of small wet fish is often short and insufficient for delivery to food fish markets. High contents of blood, bone or oil limit the value of many fish on the traditional food fish markets. Moreover, in the present world fisheries, squid, krill and other intervertebrates are underutilized. However, these organisms are not included in the present account which concentrates on the food use of fish.

The majority of the shoaling or pelagic species are oily and range in size from small to medium. They are mostly taken near the surface by purse seine or other fishing gear which gives rather uniform catches comprising only one or a few species. The demersal or bottom-dwelling species range in size from small to large. Many demersal species are "white" fish, i.e. they have almost white, non-oily flesh. Reserve fats are stored mainly in the liver. The greater part of the demersal fish catches are taken by trawl. Each haul contains a variety of species and sizes, which complicates the catch handling and causes considerable losses of fish resources.

Various hake, whiting and poutassou species are very abundant and form one of the most important groups of underutilized species in the present world fisheries. Another important group of underutilized species is the by-catches taken by shrimp trawlers. Recent estimates indicate that at least 3–4 million tons of fish per year are discarded at sea from shrimp trawlers, mainly those operating in tropical waters, where the by-catches of fish are many times larger than the shrimp catches.

1.5.1. TRADITIONAL FISH PROTEIN CONCENTRATION AND PRESERVATION

Food fish have been concentrated and preserved by salting, marinating,

---

* Director, Technological Laboratory, Ministry of Fisheries, Technical University, Building 221, DK 2800, LYNGBY, DENMARK

smoking and drying since ancient times. In 1976, about 15% of the world fish landings was cured. While fish curing methods have changed or been replaced by other processing methods in the industrialized countries, they prevail as the main means of preserving fish protein in the developing countries. Many Asians, Africans and Latin Americans are therefore used to the strong fishy odors and flavors of hard cured fish. "Pink" halophile microorganisms are common in fish salting premises and may in severe cases cause considerable losses, particularly in humid climates, where salt is gradually leached out and the fish spoil and liquefy. Other substantial losses occur through insect attacks on dried unsalted fish.

Traditional fish curing requires considerable manual labor and time, and is therefore becoming increasingly expensive. At the same time, increasing quantities of fish are being reduced to fish meal. These developments have given rise to new initiatives aimed at the concentration and preservation of fish protein for human consumption.

1.5.2. PRESENT-DAY FISH PROTEIN CONCENTRATION AND PRESERVATION

Fish species may be divided into 3 main groups according to size and established handling techniques in high sea fisheries. These are (1) large fish which are normally eviscerated soon after being caught, (2) medium-size fish, and (3) fish which are too small to be eviscerated before processing.

A. Large Fish

Large fish are probably utilized almost fully in many developing countries, where the heads and frames from filleting may be sold to low-income consumers for use in soups or other composite meals. When the fish are eviscerated at sea, the entrails are normally discarded there, even though they contain almost as much protein as fillets and could provide valuable protein feed for livestock if recovered and preserved on board. Entrails are highly perishable but could be converted into a stable fish silage by mixing with formic and sulfuric or propionic acid. Entrails can also be preserved on board in dilute ammonia. Acid or alkaline silage of entrails autolyzes rapidly at temperatures between 20°C and 40°C, and may be divided into oil, slurry and an aqueous solution of protein, peptides and amino acids. Spray-dried, oil-free hydrolyzate from fish viscera forms a light-yellow powder with a fishy odor and bitter taste.

Low-oil fish. The filleting industries produce large quantities of protein-rich offal which is not recovered for human consumption. Heads constitute about 1/6 and other filleting offal about 1/3 of the weight of round fish. White fish meal produced from such offal does not meet the PAG

(Protein Advisory Group of the UN) guidelines for fish protein concentrates for human consumption: it has too little protein and too high a content of total ash. If bones were removed before drying, however, the resultant fish meal could meet the PAG guidelines for FPC, type B.

Modern bone separators may divide the fillet offal of gutted white fish into about 40% bones and skin and 60% mince, each fraction having about 14% crude protein[1]. Some of the protein in the bone fraction may be extracted by alkali or enzyme treatment to be returned to the mince. The main constituent of such mince is small particles of white meat, but the mince is strongly discolored by blood and other parts which are undesirable in food. It also has small amounts of oils, which readily oxidize and become rancid, and of trimethylamine oxide (TMAO) which may break down to give formaldehyde during processing and subsequent storage. Any formaldehyde formed in mince is believed to lower the water holding capacity and the content of salt-extractable proteins[2]. Drying of unpurified mince of fillet offal from gutted gadoid fish gives discolored meals with an off-taste and poor texture, even if low-temperature drying methods are employed. The cheaper methods of drying at high temperatures for a short time may be advantageous, since they may reduce formaldehyde formation in the dried product[3].

Experience with frozen white fish mince points to blood and tissues with a high blood content, such as kidney and dark muscle, as the main agents causing oxidation[2] and formaldehyde formation. Blood pigments are clearly responsible for the reddish-brown discoloration that occurs in white fish offal minces, and they must be removed or reduced if mince products of light color are desired. Simple water washing of the mince does much to reduce blood pigments, but at the same time large quantities of protein tend to be lost[4]. Another way to obtain mince and mince products of light color and good storage stability is to avoid those parts of the fillet offal which contain high blood tissues. This measure, however, greatly reduces the quantities of fillet offal available for processing.

B. Medium-size Fish

Some wet fish of medium size keep better or as well in the round than when eviscerated. In other cases, evisceration at sea is desirable but impracticable due to the very large number of fish per catch. Catches of medium-size food fish are therefore often chilled and stowed in the round at sea. Their storage life at 0°C varies from a few days when the fish are feeding to about 10 days when their stomachs are empty.

Machines are now available or being developed to fillet the round fish. In this case, the fillet offal comprises heads, entrails and backbones. Other machines remove the heads and entrails or the entrails only. Heads and entrails are normally reduced to fish meal. The heads could be recovered separately for deboning. The resulting mince would be very discolored by blood, but may be suitable for FPC, type B products.

Medium-size white fish. The principal hake, whiting and poutassou raw materials for food processing are fillets or headed and gutted (HG) fish, dependent on the state of development of the butchering machinery. Fillets of the more valuable species end up as frozen products, while those of less valuable species such as poutassou may be dried, retaining the shape of the fillets. They are thin and do not take as long to dry as the larger gadoids, traditionally split for drying.

An interesting new dried white fish product has been developed in the Faroe Islands. Fillets with skin are treated briefly in salt brine and then air-dried and beaten on the meat side to loosen the muscle fibers from the skin. The dry fibers may be picked by hand for consumption without further treatment.

Headed and gutted hake, whiting and poutassou have been deboned to produce minces for freezing or drying. In both cases, the natural content of TMAO may break down to DMA and formaldehyde as described above. Kidneys discolor the mince and accelerate fat oxidation and formaldehyde formation. They should therefore be removed before mincing. Even so, the mince of HG gadoid fish will contain more blood than minces prepared from fillets.

Some modern methods of concentrating and preserving white fish minces include dewatering, which removes some blood pigments and TMAO. According to a Canadian procedure, white fish mince is mixed with fine salt and held briefly at a slightly elevated temperature. The free brine is separated and the salted mince shaped and dried, all within one day, if desired. A salted and dried mince of HG cod contained about 20% water, 40% salt and 40% fish solids (mainly protein)[5]. Salt-cured and dried minces are not attacked by microbes, insects, rodents or birds.

While at least 15% salt is required to cause a substantial reduction in the water binding capacity of raw mince in a normal, i.e. almost neutral, reaction, much less is required if the pH is lowered to about 4. Recent Danish studies have indicated that cod or blue whiting mince acidified to pH 4, after the addition of about 2% salt, can be compressed by a simple hand press to less than half its weight, which means removal of more than half of the original content of water and TMAO[3]. Subsequent mechanical break-up, neutralization with NaOH solution and air drying produced a light greyish granulate with only a very slight salty taste.

Substantial removal of water and TMAO from white fish mince before drying can also be effected by processes similar to the traditional reduction to fish meal, i.e. cooking and pressing. The meal obtained by drying the presscake, however, is gritty and without the functional properties desirable in a food ingredient.

According to a recent report from Taiwan[6], "fish bits" or fried shredded fish may be produced by steaming, compression, seasoning and drying. These "fish bits" are well accepted in China, Japan and Indochina, which indicates that considerable room still remains for improvement of the fish meal process.

Medium-size oily fish.   Some oily fish such as herring and mackerel are in such great demand for food that they are being overfished in many waters. They are traditionally prepared in numerous ways, fresh or frozen, canned or cured. They are normally fully utilized except where the market is temporarily glutted. The South-East Pacific jurel (jack or horse mackerel) and sardina (Spanish sardine, pilchard) represent examples of similar species which are now mainly used for reduction to fish meal. The methods developed for the handling and processing of herring and mackerel will no doubt go a long way to improve the utilization of such species for food. Direct drying is less feasible as it would introduce oxidation and rancidity problems.

C. Small Fish

Although small fish species contain protein which is of comparable quality to that of the larger species, only a few small species are considered as food fish. The main reason for small fish being discarded or reduced to fish meal may simply be that they cannot be eviscerated economically on a large scale by present technology. As fish entrails are rarely considered edible, neither are small whole fish. The main consumer objection to the fish entrails may be the content of feed being digested. This problem has been overcome by Norwegian sprat processors by keeping the live sprat trapped until they have emptied their stomachs. For various reasons, similar measures have failed in the case of Peruvian anchovetas, and cannot be regarded as a general solution to the fish entrails problem[7].

Small whole fish may be fermented or autolyzed to produce sauces or aqueous solutions of protein, peptides and amino acids. The processes may be controlled using acid, alkali or salt. While the acid and alkali controlled processes have not yet been used on a large scale for food purposes, various salty fish sauces are traditionally produced as condiments in South-East Asia. The high salt content, however, limits consumption.

Low-oil species.   The by-catches of demersal fish taken by shrimp trawlers are large in tropical waters. In the Gulf of California, shrimp trawlers take on an average 8 times more fish than shrimp. Most of the fish by-catches are discarded at sea. Recent studies show that the vast majority of the fish are small, 87% measuring between 7 and 17 cm in length[8].

A product-developing group working on the by-catches of shrimp trawlers in the Gulf of California has elaborated on the saltfish cake production mentioned above. Using a meat and bone separator, they obtained an almost 70% flesh yield from mixed by-catches of small whole fish. Some minces were prepared from whole fish, others from headed and eviscerated fish. The mince samples were mixed with salt, left to stand for 30 min, pressed into cakes and dried. Addition of 20% salt to the mince appeared to represent the best concentration for cake formation. At this concentration the salt could easily be removed by soaking and most of the samples were fairly bland in flavor. Hedonic scaling of the cakes produced no significant difference between cakes made from whole fish and those prepared from eviscerated fish[8].

High-oil species. Of the more than 20 million tons of fish annually reduced to fish meal and oil, most are small and fatty. The main species are anchoveta, sardines, capelin, sprat, and sand-eel. Bacterial spoilage, autolysis and fat oxidation of these fish are fast and the storage life as wet fish is consequently short. Salt curing and holding under strong brine may improve the storage life considerably, but the resultant strongly flavored fish have a very limited market at present.

Current efforts in Denmark to concentrate and preserve sand-eel for food are based on mechanical deboning and mixing the resultant mince with low-oil materials prior to drying. Starchy materials such as corn, millet, wheat, barley and rice, and proteinaceous vegetables such as lentils and chick peas are being tested together with skim-milk powder to lower the oil content of the material to dry. Addition of tomato, onion and certain spices is also being tested.

While pure fish mince containing more than 2% oil cannot be properly drum dried, it is possible to drum dry mixtures of fish mince and certain starchy materials with oil contents of up to 7%. The drum dried products in general have a much better appearance than products dried by other methods[9].

Oily fish minces which are dried tend to oxidize and become rancid. The Danish group working on the drying of sand-eel products has attempted to overcome the rancidity problem by avoiding delays in processing and by adding antioxidants or spices. Among the latter, rosemary appears to have a good antioxidant effect.

1.5.3. Future Developments

While most people in the industrialized countries eat animal protein in excess of their needs, there is a growing shortage of animal protein in some developing countries. The greatest needs for fish protein are foreseen in certain South-East Asian countries with large populations of traditional fish consumers. Since the resources of marine fish are often far from the consuming centers, and many sea fisheries are highly seasonal, a large part of the marine catches must be concentrated and preserved.

Concentrated fish proteins for developing countries. The traditional cured products of low-oil fish need better protection than at present against insect and other animal attacks during storage and distribution in tropical climates. Such protection may be obtained by improved packaging and by adjusting the composition so that the product becomes unattractive to insects. Comminuted low-cost products of white fish may be produced by mechanical deboning, dewatering by compression and drying. Very oily fish are probably best concentrated by the traditional curing and canning methods, which preserve not only the fish proteins but also the valuable fish oils providing much needed calories to underfed populations.

Concentrated fish proteins for industrial countries.   The FPC, type A products are now being replaced by functional fish proteins (FFP) with high solubility and emulsifying properties. The new processes can be expected to take advantage of pH adjustments during processing to control the water binding capacity and facilitate the removal of undesirable components. Protein fibers simulating the muscle fibers of intact fillets may soon appear[10].

REFERENCES

1. Legendre, R. and Hotton, C., Separation of Flesh and Bones from Fish, New Series Circular No. 50, Environment Canada, Fisheries and Marine Service (1975).
2. Proc. Conf. on Production and Utilization of Mechanically Recovered Fish Flesh (Minced Fish), 7/8 April 1976. Torry Research Station, Aberdeen (1976).
3. Annual Report 1977, Technological Laboratory, Ministry of Fisheries, Technical University, Lyngby, Denmark.
4. Spinelli, J., Koury, B., Groninger Jr., H. and Miller, R., Expanded uses for fish protein from underutilized species, Food Technol., **31** (5), 184, (1977).
5. Bligh, E. G., A note on salt minced fish, Proc. Conf. on Handling, Processing and Marketing of Tropical Fish, 5–9 July 1976, Tropical Products Institute, London (1977).
6. Pan, B. S., Low-moisture fishery products, Fishery Products of Taiwan (Chung, J. L., Pan, B. S. and Chen, G. C., eds. p. 43), JCRR Fisheries Series 25 B, Taipei (1977).
7. Loayza, E., Aprovechamiento de la anchoveta para consumo humano en el Perú, Fishery Products (Kreuzer, R., ed.), p. 215, Fishing News (Books) Ltd., West Byfleet (1974).
8. Young, R. H., Studies on shrimp by-catch utilization in Mexico, Proc. 3rd Ann. Tropical and Subtropical Fisheries Technological Conf. of the Americas, New Orleans., April 23–26, 1978.

9. Nielsen, J., Personal communication.
10. Mackie, I., Protein fibres from fish, Spectrum, No. 152, 9 (1977).

2. Efficient Utilization of Conventional Food Resources

2.1 Developments in the Processing of Traditional Soybean Foods in Japan

Tokuji Watanabe*

The importance of soybeans as a food material in Japan is evident from the fact that nearly 1 million metric tons of soybeans including those used after oil extraction are consumed annually to make *tofu, kori-tofu, natto, miso*, soy sauce and other foods. The development of automated equipment for continuous processing has made mass production of these foods possible, ensuring evenness of quality and lowness of price, to the benefit of consumers. Popularization of these foods in supermarkets has been promoted by their mass production, as well as by developments in distribution technology such as cold chain, packaging and sterilization systems. This ensures long survival of these foods in food markets, combined with a compatibility for cooked rice which is the most important staple food in Japan. However, it must be remembered that mass production can also cause problems such as in product safety, decreased local character of the products, and pollution by wastes.

The present paper attempts to explain recent developments in the processing of the main traditional soybean foods such as *tofu, kori-tofu, natto, miso* and soy sauce, to point out some of the problems encountered, and also to suggest possible countermeasures for solving these problems.

2.1.1. TOFU

Tofu is a kind of curd made from soybean milk. It is highly digestible and nutritious, since the insoluble components of soybeans are completely removed giving a product which is rich in protein and oil. To prepare *tofu*, soybeans are soaked overnight in water and ground. The mash is then cooked with added water and filtered to obtain the soybean milk.

* *Kyoritsu Women's University, 2-2-1, Hitotsubashi, Chiyoda-ku, Tokyo 101, Japan*

66

To this milk (5–6% solid), calcium sulfate is added at a level equivalent to 2–3% of the soybeans at about 70°C to coagulate the protein and oil. The resultant curd is transferred to a wooden or aluminum box equipped with holes and pressed to mould as *tofu*[1]. The process is summarized in the upper part of Fig. 1. Treatment of the whey and residue represents a serious problem for the *tofu* industry, since these substances often cause environmental deterioration. The whey is at present all abandoned in the sewage, while the residue is partially utilized as feed for cattle. Some trials have been made to apply reverse osmosis technology to concentrate the

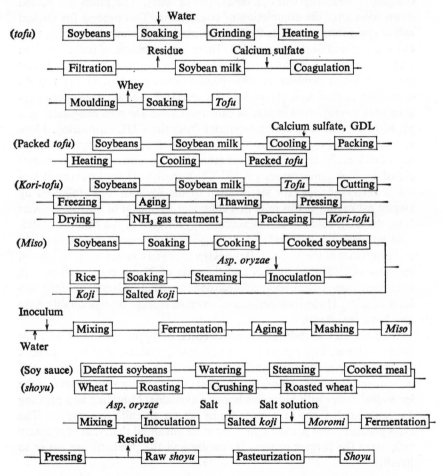

Fig.1. Flow sheet for the production of traditional soybean foods: *tofu*, packed *tofu*, *kori-tofu*, *miso* and soy sauce

whey, and to find new uses. Residue which contains 20% protein on a dry basis can be used as feed material if an economical method of drying is available.

The scale of *tofu* production remains fairly small. However, it is undergoing expansion due to extension of the shelf-life.

With a view to maintaining improved sanitary conditions, "packed *tofu*" has been developed. Soybean milk with 9–10% solid is, after being rapidly cooled, placed in small polystyrene or polypropylene boxes together with calcium sulfate. Each box contains some 200–300 g of the milk. After sealing, the boxes are heated in a water bath (90°C) for 40–60 min. The milk coagulates gradually without separation of whey. The boxes are cooled down soon after the completion of coagulation. This process for packed *tofu* is also shown in Fig. 1. Packed *tofu* made in this way is sanitary, easy to transport and fairly preservable. There is no problem of pollution from whey, since the whole whey is included in the product. Several factories exist which can produce 50,000–100,000 boxes per day. In the process of making packed *tofu*, glucano-δ-lactone, (GDL, a newly developed coagulant) can be employed instead of calcium sulfate. The milk coagulates to a gel with gluconic acid which separates from the GDL on heating. More recently, packed *tofu* which can be distributed at ambient temperature has been developed[2]. It can be kept for more than 3 months at 25°C. It is completed by high temperature (> 130°C)-short time (1 sec) treatment (so-called HTST heating) for sterilization of the soybean milk, followed by aseptic packaging of this milk in a container. Removal of microorganisms from the GDL solution can be successfully effected with a Millipore filter.

In *tofu* making, the quality of the soybeans themselves affects the yield and properties of the product. Besides the nitrogen content of the soybeans, the ratio of total P to total N and the ratio of 7S protein to 11S protein have been found to be closely related to the coagulation behavior of the soybean milk[3,4]. Undesirable effects of soybean storage on *tofu* quality have also been reported[5].

With the aim of reducing product costs, mass production of *tofu* has been developed. Equipment for the automatic production of soybean milk is now fairly popular through the introduction of continuous cookers and centrifuges. Recently, semi-continuous moulding equipment instead of the individual boxes with holes has become available. Moulding and pressing are both carried out in a large frame set on an endless conveyor. The mass production of packed *tofu* is far more advanced than that of ordinary *tofu*, since the former process is simpler and the products are easier to handle.

2.1.2. KORI-TOFU

Kori-tofu is dried *tofu*. It is prepared in a special way by drying *tofu* into porous products without case hardening. It is a yellow, porous and therefore light cake of square form. It swells to a large size when cooked in hot water and becomes like a sponge.

The *tofu* used for making *kori-tofu* is much harder, more sandy and more homogeneous than ordinary *tofu*. After cutting, the *tofu* is frozen at −10°C and then stored at −1 to −3°C for 2–3 weeks. On thawing, the texture of the stored (aged) *tofu* becomes like sponge and it can easily be squeezed out with a press or centrifuge. It is then dried in forced hot air. The process is summarized in Fig. 1. About 45–50 kg of product is obtained from 100 kg of soybeans.

Kori-tofu differs from fresh *tofu* in its production scale, perhaps because of the differences in shelf-life and ease of handling. Several factories consume over 10 tons of soybeans per day. Continuous equipment has been introduced into the process to a greater extent after coagulation than before it. The innovations are generally the same as those in fresh *tofu* processing. One recent trend in the *tofu* preparation in this industry has been enlargement of the *tofu* size itself. For freezing, thawing, dehydration and drying, new types of continuous and labor-saving equipment are popular in larger plants.

It has been found that protein denaturation plays an important role in the aging process, which lasts 2–3 weeks[6]. New technology to promote protein denaturation will thus shorten the aging time. Methods of active sludge treatment of waste water consisting mainly of whey on *kori-tofu* manufacture are now available.

2.1.3. MISO

Miso is a fermented food prepared from soybeans, rice and salt. It is a pastelike, tasty and flavoring food and is mainly used in *miso*-soup. *Koji* is a very important starting material in *miso* manufacture, since it represents a source of enzymes during the fermentation of the *miso*. *Koji* is made from steamed rice by inoculating *Asp. oryzae* onto its surface and incubating for 2 days. It is mixed with cooked soybeans, salt and water to give a final water content of about 50%. This mixture is then fermented in wooden or concrete tanks for 3–6 months[7]. The process is summarized in Fig. 1. Usually the rice is steamed for about 40 min at atmospheric pressure and the soybeans are cooked for 20–40 min at 0.7–0.8 kg/cm², both after overnight soaking in water.

There are many varieties of *miso*, according to the materials used with the soybeans, the ratio of rice (or barley) to soybeans and the salt content. The variations are usually related to locality, and involve the flavor and/or color of the products.

There are several types of continuous rice cookers which can be used. Soaked rice is fed continuously on a moving belt conveyor made of stainless steel netting. It is steamed under atmospheric pressure during conveyance at a certain speed. For cooking soybeans, high-temperature short-time cookers have recently been developed. It is desirable to prevent overcooking of the soybeans since this may be accompanied by an unwanted browning of the product and destruction of basic amino acids. Continuous two-step cookers using rotary valves, at 1.5 kg/cm² for 6 min and 1.3 kg/cm² for 10 min, are available.

In *koji* making from rice, small wooden trays were formerly used. However, these have now been almost completed replaced by *koji* rooms which can be strictly air-conditioned. Steamed rice, after being inoculated, is spread out on the floor of the room and kept warm and humid for the growth of *Asp. oryzae*. Large rotating trommels are also available for *koji* preparation.

The aging of the *miso* usually starts under ambient temperature, although sometimes it is carried out in a warm room to shorten the fermentation period. Control of the microorganisms during the fermentation appears to be critical yet difficult, since the fermentation proceeds under a so-called open system liable to contamination by undesirable microorganisms. *Saccharomyces rouxii*, *Torulopsis* sp., *Pediococcus halophylus* and *Streptococcus* sp. have been identified as useful microorganisms in *miso* manufacture, and pure cultures of these microorganisms are now available as starters just like the lactic starter of cheese manufacture.

In the *miso* available on the market, fermentation still continues unless the product is pasteurized or otherwise treated. Swelling of packed *miso* thus prevented its popularization. However, the problem has been solved by the introduction of new heating equipment for pasteurization, and the use of food additives such as sorbic acid and ethyl alcohol. Packed *miso* in 500 g and 1 kg bags is now very common in supermarkets.

With expansion of the production scale of *miso*, cooking drains in soybean steaming were found to need treatment by the active sludge method. However, although this is perhaps the only way to solve this problem at present, from the viewpoint of resource economy ways must be found to use the discarded material as food, or at least as feed. Recent research has shown that the drain effluent can be employed as a culture medium for *Asp. oryzae*, resulting in a decrease in COD to as low as 20% of original[8]. Mycelia so obtained contain about 40% protein and, when added to *miso*, exert a desirable effect on the progress of the fermentation.

2.1.4. SOY SAUCE *(Shoyu)*

Shoyu represents one of the most important seasonings in Japan, and is widely used in restaurants and other catering facilities as well as at home. It is now an international seasoning as shown by the introduction of a new plant in the USA. *Shoyu* is a salty, transparent liquid, usually reddish-brown in color, and has a characteristic flavor.

Shoyu manufacture begins from *shoyu-koji* preparation. Defatted soybean meal is hydrated and steamed at a pressure of 0.9 kg/cm² for 50–60 min. This is mixed with roasted crushed wheat and then with an inoculum of *Asp. oryzae*. The mixture is incubated until it is virtually covered by the mold with spores that are yellowish-green in color. This so-called *shoyu-koji* is mixed with brine and fermented for 8–12 months at ambient temperature. The resultant mixture is the so-called *moromi*. After completion of the fermentation, the *moromi* is separated from solids with a filter press. The separated liquid, known as raw *shoyu*, is pasteurized at 65–80°C. After removing the precipitates formed, the final transparent liquid is bottled in glass jars, small plastic containers for home use or wooden casks. The process of *shoyu* production is summarized in Fig. 1. Use of preservatives such as butyl ester of *p*-hydroxybenzoic acid and sodium benzoate is permitted to prevent the growth of mold-like yeasts (*Zygosaccharomyces*) during storage.

The mass production of *shoyu* is more advanced than that of other soybean foods, perhaps because of its long shelf-life and ease of handling. Continuous cookers are now employed in several large factories. These are set inclined and have an internal screw conveyor. The moistened soybean meal which is fed into the cooker is completely cooked as it moves on the conveyor by steam injected from the top of the cooker. The cooked meal must be rapidly cooled to prevent overheating which may lower the nitrogen utility. NK type cookers are also designed to cool the steamed meal as early as possible. Recently, a new type of continuous cooker for HTST heating has been used[9], as mentioned in the case of *miso*. It is effective for avoiding overheating. Moreover, air-conditioned rooms are now popular for making the *koji* in large plants. This is not only laborsaving but also effective in preventing contamination by undesirable microorganisms. When ripened in a fermenter, the *moromi* is passed to the filter press by a plunger pump. Since usually it takes 4–6 days for pressing, several attempts have been made to save time and labor in this process. For pasteurization, continuous pipe or plate heaters have become more popular in large plants. Aseptic bottling with no requirement of preservatives is now employed in *shoyu* plants.

When making *shoyu*, the nitrogen utility ratio is very important. This ratio indicates how much of the nitrogen in the materials becomes soluble in the *shoyu*. It varies according to many factors, such as the steaming conditions of the soybean meal, the quality of the inoculum, and the fermentation conditions. It has been found that overheating of the soybean meal lowers the ratio, perhaps due to the difficulty in carrying out enzymatic degradation of over-denatured protein in the meal. The newly developed HTST cooker mentioned above was found to raise the nitrogen utility ratio to 90%, i.e. about 5% higher than that for the NK type cooker which has been used widely for maintaining a high nitrogen utility ratio.

2.1.5. NATTO

Natto is a soybean food prepared by cooking soybeans, inoculating them with pure-cultured *Bacillus natto*, and then fermenting for approximately 16 hr. If the fermentation is allowed to progress too far, ammonia gas is produced and lower quality product is obtained. With expansion of the production scale, the products are stored in warehouses at low temperature to retard the fermentation. Frozen natto is also available on the market.

2.1.6. CONCLUSION

In the traditional soybean food industry, many kinds of modern equipment have now been developed for mass production, so ensuring evenness of product quality and lowness of price. This trend is expected to continue in the future, although problems have been encountered with these new innovations. Fresh technology is required to solve such problems, as exemplified successfully by the introduction of HTST heating.

REFERENCES

1. Watanabe, T., Fukamachi, C., *et al.*, Research on tofu making, *Rept. Food Res. Inst.*, No. 14B, 1 (1960).
2. Okada, K., Ogasawara, K., Kuwabara, K., *et al.*, Research on aseptic tofu (I), Annual Mtg. Japan Agr. Chem. Soc. (1978).
3. Saio, K., Watanabe, T., *et al.*, Protein-calcium-phytic acid relationship in soybean, I, II, III, *Agr. Biol. Chem.*, **31** (10), 1195 (1967); **32** (1), 447 (1968); **33** (1) 36 (1969).
4. Saio, K., Watanabe, T., *et al.*, Food processing characteristics of soybean 11S and 7S protein, I, II, *Agr. Biol. Chem.*, **32** (9), 1301 (1969); **35**(6), 890 (1971).

5. Saio, K., Nakagawa, I., and Hashizume, K., Determination of soybean quality in storage, concerning the preparation of non-fermented foods as *tofu* and *aburage*, Annual Mtg. Japan. Soc. Food Sci. Technol. (1978).

6. Hashizume, K., Watanabe, T., *et al.*, Denaturation of soybean protein by freezing, *Agr. Biol. Chem.*, **35** (1), 449 (1971).

7. Watanabe, T., Industrial production of traditional soybean foods in Japan, Soybean Expert Mtg. by UNIDO (1969).

8. Nikkuni, S., Ito, H., Ebine H., *et al.*, Return back utilization of cooking drain of soybean in miso making, Proc. Symp. Ferm. Foods, Brewing Society of Japan, (1978).

9. Suzuki, T., Comparison of cooking method between NK steam apparatus and continuous steam apparatus for soysauce brewing, *J. Japan Soy Sauce Res. Inst.*, **1**(2), 90 (1975).

2.2 Progress in the Technology of Soymilk Production

Julian A. Banzon* and Elias E. Escueta*

There is continuing interest in the technology of soybean milk production as attested to by the number of recent patents and publications on the subject. For reference, nutrient recoveries and compositions of soymilks are listed in Tables 1 and 2.

2.2.1 PROGRESS IN PROCESSING

The greatest activity is in technology aimed at (1) inactivation of trypsin inhibitor (T.I.), (2) removal of beany flavor, and (3) increasing the yield of soymilk. The presence of T.I. lowers the nutritional value. A time-temperature dependent heat treatment readily destroys the T.I. but also tends to insolubilize the proteins, so lowering the yield (and quality) of soymilk. The bigger problem is how to avoid the beany flavor which is produced by the traditional cold grinding of water-soaked soybeans. This undesirable flavor is formed when lipoxidase liberated during the grinding acts on polyunsaturates thereby releasing the offending compounds. Methods developed to solve this problem include (1) elimination of these compounds by steaming (prolonged boiling), (2) use of defatted soy flakes, (3) destruction of the lipoxidase as it is formed by grinding (with water) at 80°C, and (4) inactivation of the lipoxidase before the grinding operation by heat treatment.

Processes employing preheat treatment to destroy the lipoxidase have been described as follows. (1) Soybeans are heated for 45 min at 100°C, dried, dehulled, ground, and the powder slurried with warm water. The slurry is then homogenized and spray dried resulting in a product which disperses easily in water, forming soymilk[6], (2) Dehulled soybean flakes properly conditioned with moisture are fed into an extruder. The product formed comes out cooked, puffed and dried and can be fine-ground and slurried in water to form soymilk[7]. (3) Autoclaved soybean flakes (whose protein is heat denatured) are redispersed in water by ultrasonics[11].

Water soaking prior to grinding is found to be advantageous. It softens

* Department of Food Science and Technology, University of the Philippines at Los Banos College, Laguna, The Philippines

TABLE 1. Nutrient recoveries

Protein (%)	Solids (%)	Fat (%)	Variety	Source
83	65	—	Clark	Hand *et al.* (1964)
80	65	—	Bragg	Wu and Bates (1972)
72.7	—	—	—	de Man (1975)
78.5	48	54	30 cultivars	Bourne *et al.* (1976)
71.8	42.2	—	Hsi-Hsi	Escueta (1973)
91.5	80	—	Clark	Hand *et al.* (1964)
95	89	—	—	Nelson *et al.* (1976)

TABLE 2. Composition of soymilks

	A	B	C	D	E	F	G
Water	92.5	81.4	85.1	86.1	87.8	88.6	95.0
Protein	3.4	4.2	2.1	1.6	3.0	2.7	3.1
Fat	1.5	2.1	3.1	1.8	3.2	1.0	1.0
Ash	.5	.7	.4	.3	.5	—	—
Carbohydrate	2.1	11.6	9.1	10.3	5.5	(7.6)	.9

A – Cheng and Chung (1973).
B – Kasetsoy (Amara, 1978).
C – Local Bangkok sample (Amara, 1978).
D – Local Bangkok sample (Amara, 1978).
E – Soyalac
F – Av. of 30 cultivars (Bourne *et al.*, 1970).
G – Escueta (1973).

the beans, removes undesirable substances, increases protein and fat extraction, and decreases the extraction of raffinose and stachyose. Use of NaOH, Na_2CO_3 or $NaHCO_3$ in the soak water is known to be beneficial for improving flavor and for facilitating thermal destruction of T.I. Bourne[2,3] concludes that the flavor effect is due to sodium ion.

2.2.2 Progress in Increasing Acceptability

Fifty percent of a Filipino taste panel preferred a "hot grind" milk, and only 33% preferred the cold grind. Between a plain water presoak and an alkali presoak, the latter was voted as better in flavor. An unsweetened soymilk was definitely unacceptable. Being accustomed to soft drinks, the taste panel preferred a sweet beverage (about 7% sucrose). Chocolate flavor increased acceptability but this is expensive to introduce. Addition of coconut milk tended to decrease the sugar requirement for the same acceptability score.[10] However, Bhumiratana and Nondasuta[1] have reported a lower acceptability with added coconut milk. Water buffalo milk added to a 25 % level was not well received by the taste panel[9]. Addition of coconut oil imparted whiteness.

2.2.3 Nutritional Improvement

Soymilk has a composition similar to cow's milk although it is rather low in fat (see Table 2) and calcium; it is high in iron and niacin[4]. Bhumiratana and Nondasuta attempted to fortify their soymilk with 0.02 % methionine, 15,000 I. U./1 vitamin A, 100 I.U./1 vitamin D, and 1 % Ca (OH)$_2$ solution (10 % w/v). Miller's Soyalac manufactured in Manila had 3000 units vitamin A, 400 units vitamin D, 2 mg thiamine, 12 mg niacin and 2 mg riboflavin per quart. The fat content of soymilk is low (about 1 %) and needs to be increased to combat protein-calorie malnutrition. Addition of vegetable oils corrects this deficiency but coconut milk blends easily without the need for a homogenizer.

2.2.4 Soybean Varieties

Of 30 Philippine cultivars, Bourne et al.[2] found 6 as giving soapy flavor; one gave a chocolate brown milk while 8 had low protein extractability. Similar studies have been made of cultivars in Canada and Brazil by de Man et al. (1975) and Da Costa (1974) as cited by Bourne.[2]

2.2.5. Customer Presentation

In urban areas, anything called milk is expected to taste like cow's milk, so that it is not advisable to call soymilk a milk. Names actually used include Vitasoy, Soyalac, Kasetsoy, and Philsoy. Soymilk served ice-cold had a higher acceptability score than warm soymilk. The soymilk "ice candy" of Steinkraus et al. was extremely popular with school children. In Hong Kong, Vitasoy is served piping hot during frosty mornings and Winston Lo uses a beverage heater.

2.2.6 Philippine Experience in Soymilk Production

In recent years, the economics and improved flavor of the hot grind process have suggested promising commercial exploitation. CDCP, a construction group involved in a variety of ventures, entered into a contract with the Food Science/Technology Department of U.P. Los Banos, to produce PHILSOY, using the latter's 600 bottle/day pilot plant. PHILSOY was well received and production reached 3500 bottles/day. The retail price was kept below a competing skim milk chocolate-flavored beverage, and at about the same price as the better soft drinks. After about 3 years of operation, the venture stopped due to breakdown of the processing equipment which had been made to run at 3500 bottles/day even though it was designed for only 600 bottles/day. Acquisition of additional equipment was imperative but the contracting parties failed to make a decision. The CDCP experience proved that soymilk production can be profitable in the Philippines. The need for a nutritious beverage is in the hinterlands where transporting a bottled product from a distant processor is expensive. The buying power is low[10], so that the unit price must also be low. The most expensive step is in-bottle sterilization. A cheaper system lies in serving soymilk "on draught", and prepared locally as a "home brew", a system not uncommon in the villages. Unsold soymilk can be converted to *tofu*, and the soy press-cake can be used as an ingredient of the locally made rice cakes (puto).

2.2.7 SIMPLIFIED SOYMILK PRODUCTION

The hot grind method results in a very acceptable soymilk but requires an expensive grinder. The Illinois method also needs an expensive homogenizer. Escueta[5] has worked out a simple, satisfactory process whereby soaked beans (Hsi-Hsi variety) are given a 2 to 3 min immersion blanch which adequately destroys the T.I. without severely reducing protein extractability. The treated beans are then cold ground with water in a stone grinder, diluted, cloth-filtered and then boiled for 10 min or more. The slight "beany" flavor is not objectionable when formulated with 7% sugar and served cold like a soft drink. The addition of pasteurized coconut milk (1:25 v/v) improves the flavor and increases the calorific value.

2.2.8 CALCULATION METHODS

For theoretical yields, consider soybeans containing 38% protein, where 80% of the protein is recovered in the milk. Assume solid recovery to be 60%. It is desirable to prepare 1000 g soymilk with a 3.0% protein content, so that the total protein needed is 30.0 g. The weight of soybeans furnishing 30 g protein is $30/(0.8 \times 0.38) = 98.68$ g. The solids in the milk calculate as $0.60 \times 98.68 = 59.21$g. The weight of dry press cake is thus 39.47 g. Since the actual press cake (wet) is 75% water, the weight of this cake is 157.9 g.

$$\text{Beans} + \text{Water} = \text{Milk} + \text{Cake solids}$$

or

$$98.68 + W = 1000 + 39.47, \qquad W = 940.8 \text{ g.}$$

$$\text{Milk} + \text{Cake solids} = \text{Recovered milk} + \text{Wet cake}$$

or

$$1000 + 39.47 = M + 157.9, \qquad M = 881.6 \text{ g.}$$

Hence, useful ratios are:

$$\text{Beans: Water} = 98.7:941 = 1:9.5$$

$$\text{Beans: Recovered milk} = 98.7:881.6 = 1:8.9$$

$$\text{Beans: Bean slurry} = 98.7:1039 = 1:10.5$$

$$\text{Beans: Press cake} = 98.7:157.9 = 1:1.6$$

To increase the fat content of soymilk from the usual 1.0% to 2.5% by the addition of coconut milk (40% fat, 4.8% protein), the calculation is as follows. When 1000 g of fat-enriched soymilk is desired:

$$0.40C + 0.01S = 0.025 \times 1000, \quad C + S = 1000$$

Hence, the weight of coconut milk, C, is 38.46 g.
The weight of soymilk, S, is 961.5 g. (1000–38.5) Since the original soymilk contained 3.0% protein and 1% fat, the weight relations are:

Milk	Weights	Protein	Fat
Coconut	38.5	1.85	15.38
Soybean	961.5	28.84	9.61
Total	1000.0	30.69	25.00

References

1. Bhumiratana, A. and A. Nondasuta, *Rept. Inst. Food Res. Ind. Dev. Kasets art U. Bangkok* (1978).
2. Bourne, M. C. *et al.*, *J. Food Sci.*, **41**, 62 (1976).
3. Bourne, M. C. *et al.*, *J. Food Sci.*, **41**, 1204 (1976).
4. Chen, P. S. and Chung, H. D., *Soybeans*, Keats Publ. Inc., Canaan, Conn. (1973).
5. Escueta, E. E., *Master's Thesis*, Univ. of the Philippines, (1973).
6. Hand, D. B. *et al.*, *Food Technol.*, **18**, 139 (1964).
7. Mustakas, G. C. *et al.*, *Food Eng.*, **36** (10), 52 (1964).
8. Nelson, A. I., Steinberg, M. A., and Wei, L. S., *J. Food Sci.*, **41**, 57 (1976).
9. Puertollano, C. L. *et al.*, *Philip. Agric.*, **24**, 227 (1970).
10. Steinkraus, K. H. *et al.*, *Philip. Agric.*, **52**, 268 (1968).
11. Wang, L. C., *J. Food Sci.*, **40**, 549 (1975).
12. Wu, L. C. and Bates, R. P., *J. Food Sci.*, **37**: 40 (1972).

2.3 Utilization of Soy Protein Isolates in Meat and Fish Applications

C. D. Decker* and C. W. Kolar*

2.3.1 INTRODUCTION

The use of vegetable proteins to extend and replace more expensive animal proteins is essential if future protein demands are to be met. The soybean is one of the most successful sources of vegetable protein. While whole soybeans have been used for food in the Orient for centuries, processed soybean protein products, which as food ingredients can replace and extend meat and fish proteins, have only gained prominence within the last 10 years. Flours, concentrates, and isolates are the major forms of processed soy protein, and all forms are important to the world's food supply. These processed soybean products have evolved on the basis of their protein content. Soy protein isolates are the most recent forms of soy protein and contain over 90% protein on a moisture free basis. The purpose of this paper is to discuss principles for the optimum utilization of soy protein isolates in combination with meat or fish.

The intact muscle such as roasts, steaks, hams and fillets, and comminuted products such as sausages, fishballs and Japanese style fish paste products, are examples of the two principle forms in which meat and fish are consumed. Comminuted products were one of the first meat and fish applications for soy protein isolates. Technology based on techniques for cured meat preparation has recently made it possible to augment whole cuts of meat and fish. A slurry of soy protein isolate, water, and salts can be injected into the muscle using a stitch pump, or the slurry can be massaged into the muscle using other forms of cured meat technology. Because soy protein isolates are the most recent form of soy protein, there has been little information published concerning ways in which soy protein isolates can be used so as to optimize their functionality in meat and fish systems. This subject will be addressed by first reviewing economic considerations, since they are largely responsible for the expanded use of soy protein and determine the way in which meat and fish products must be formulated to contain soy protein isolates. Next, important hydration prin-

* *Ralston Purina Company, Checkerboard Square, St. Louis, Missouri 63188, USA*

ciples will be reviewed, since many isolates must be properly associated with water before optimum functional properties are expressed in many foods. Finally, these principles will be reviewed in more complex meat and fish applications which illustrate the latest concepts of soy protein isolate utilization.

2.3.2 Economics and the Basic Philosophy of Using isolated Soy Proteins

The successful commercial utilization of soy protein isolates occurs when they are used in combination with meat and fish such that the unit cost of a traditional product has been lowered. A portion of the expensive animal proteins can be replaced or extended with less expensive soy protein. In addition to extending the supply of meat or fish proteins, the unit cost of the food will be lower so that the processor can increase his profits or offer lower cost foods to the consumer. Changes in food consumption patterns, which are strongly embedded in the culture of all societies, require considerable time, education, and are often unsuccessful. As opposed to a complete replacement, partially replaced foods more successfully compare to the traditional counterparts and minimize changes in these basic consumption patterns.

2.3.3 Important Hydration Principles

Generally, soy protein isolates must be properly hydrated before certain desirable properties are expressed in many foods. Moreover, the addition of salt to a soy protein isolate before it has been properly associated with water can have a detrimental effect upon some functional properties. Both kinetic and thermodynamic factors are important since mechanical energy, heat energy, and time affect protein hydration. Operationally, these interactions can be controlled so as to optimize soy protein isolate functionality in meat and fish systems.

Ideally, most isolates should be added with the water of hydration, or as a pre-hydrated slurry to the food product prior to salt addition, and at a point where isolate mixing time will be maximized. The exact means by which these hydration principles can be translated into a commercial fish or meat application depends upon the equipment, layout of the process, personnel, properties of the isolate, and properties of other functional constituents in the product. No two operations are exactly the same.

2.3.4 Comminuted Applications

The importance of following basic hydration principles in a comminuted system can depend upon the product and mechanical energy associated with the process. This point can be illustrated using bologna, a popular sausage in the U.S., and *kamaboko*, a popular Japanese fish paste product. Bologna is made using a process which is higher in mechanical energy than that used to make *kamaboko*. The order of ingredient addition is similar for both products in that meat or fish is chopped with salt to extract the myofibrillar proteins before other ingredients are added.

For the purpose of illustration, both products were prepared with approximately 5% isolated soy protein. Representative formulas were used in which meat and fish were replaced with 1 part isolate and 4 parts water. The bologna was prepared using a high energy input silent cutter and emulsifier according to procedures consistent with industrial practice. *Kamaboko* was prepared with a low energy input silent cutter using conditions which simulate many commercial processes. Various combinations of addition sites (before salt or after salt) and addition methods (isolate added as a prehydrated slurry; isolate added as a powder with the simultaneous addition of hydration water; isolate added as a powder without hydration water which was added near the end of the process) were investigated. The finished products were evaluated using an Okada Gelometer. Similar textural values (Figure 1) were obtained for all samples of bologna. *Kamaboko* texture was weakened by adding the isolate as a powder without the simultaneous addition of hydration water.

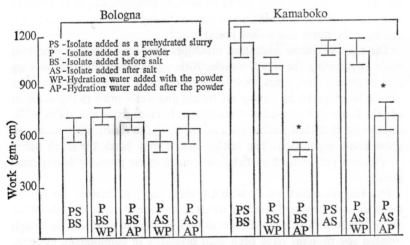

FIG.1. Effects of isolate addition method upon Okada Gelometer textural properties of bologna and *kamaboko*. Values represent the mean ± standard deviation of 4 replicates conducted on single batches of product. The term work is defined by Toda *et al.*, 1970, *J. Texture Studies*, **2**, 207. Measurement Parameters included: 700 ml/min flow rate, 5mm diameter spherical probe, 110 mm/min chart speed, 25°C sample temperature, and a cylindrical sample shape 35 mm in diameter and 30 mm in height. Organoleptically, all bologna was judged equivalent.
*These were noticeably softer than the other samples of *kamaboko*.

Isolated soy proteins are easy to use in comminuted products. Isolate can be added in a variety of ways with good results in processes with high mechanical energy. The low mechanical energy processes, such as those employed in *kamaboko* manufacture, tend to be a little less flexible although isolate can usually be added before or after salt addition provided that the water of hydration is added along with the isolate. However, problems in any application such as poor final texture, or an emulsion breakdown, are reasons to re-evaluate soy protein isolate addition in terms of basic hydration principles.

2.3.5 Muscle Augmentation

One of the most recent developments in the utilization of soy protein isolates is the augmentation of whole cuts of meat or fish. Most of the work has been conducted with ham. Slurries for injection into ham have been prepared with 8–10% isolated soy protein, 6–12% salt, phosphate, sucrose, sodium erythorbate, and sodium nitrite. Many variations in composition are possible. The optimum method of preparing a slurry is to gradually add the isolate to cold water (4° C) under conditions of agitation. After the isolate has been mixed with the water, salts and other dry ingredients can be added. A stitch pump can then be used to pump the slurry into the green ham. After pumping, the hams must be either massaged or tumbled to extract the meat proteins and disperse the soy proteins. Standard processing procedures can follow massaging.

The need to follow hydration principles appears especially important when augmenting the intact muscle. Although augmentation technology is in its infancy, it appears essential that slurries for incorporation into the muscle be prepared by mixing the isolate and water prior to the addition of salt. Properly hydrated slurries remain homogeneous and stable while improperly hydrated slurries (salt added to the water before isolate) can show phase separation. The settled isolate may block the stitch pump needles and precipitated particles may not disperse properly during massaging.

Injecting the intact muscle with a protein slurry to increase the yield is a new development and research needs to be done to define conditions for the optimum utilization of isolate in various muscle products. Although isolated soy proteins have been used primarily in comminuted systems, advances in muscle augmentation should make isolated soy proteins available to nearly all meat and fish applications. The soybean is an attractive source of protein as the world demand for protein expands while traditional sources of protein become more expensive. By using some very simple principles, soy protein isolates can be easily used in meat and fish applications to provide a cost advantage while maintaining product quality.

2.4 Starch Utilization: Present Status and Its Potential in the Future

Roy L. Whistler*

Carbohydrates supply 80% of the total calories consumed by the human population of the world. Starch supplies two thirds of these calories. With development of new sweeteners from starch, the total amount of starch consumed directly or indirectly will increase.

The abundance and low price of starches assures them of a continuing strong position as ingredients in human diets. A good example is the enormous amount of corn available for starch production. Production of corn in the United States continues to rise with 165,000 metric tons produced in 1977 (Table 1). About 5–7% of this grain is processed by the wet milling industry to starch, protein, oil and other components. The amount of wet milled corn is increasing each year (Table 2). Of prime importance to business is the continuously low price of corn (Table 3). This indicates its continuous use in food products and its use as starting material for the development of new products such as food additives and modifiers or for producing new structures or replacements for hydrocolloids that are becoming scarce or are high priced.

Because the existing uses for starch have been so well outlined, I will discuss here several new and increasing uses for starch in foods and I will present several areas where food starches may be used if investigators are able to bring about appropriate and low cost modifications.

2.4.1 SWEETENERS FROM STARCH

The corn wet milling industry brought enzyme engineering into its first enormous use.

The initial application was to replace acid hydrolysis by hydrolysis with glucoamylase immobilized on columns. Starch paste could be hydrolyzed to glucose in high yields with the production of very few by-products in the form of sugars, oligosaccharides or dehydration products, such as hydroxymethylfurfural and organic acids which cause off-flavors and colors. The second significant development was the use of immobilized isomerase to produce a mixture of glucose and fructose with the same sweetening

* Department of Biochemistry, Purdue University, W. Lafayette, IN 47907

83

Table 1.   U.S. corn production

Year	Metric tons $\times 10^6$
1972	144.39
1973	146.28
1974	120.81
1975	153.30
1976	162.35
1977	164.70
1978	175.12

Table 2.   Wet milled corn

Year	Bushels $\times 10^6$	Pounds $\times 10^9$
1972	265	14.8
1976	350	19.6
1977	375	21.0
1978	400	22.4 (projected)
1979	425	23.8 (projected)
1980	500	28.0 (projected)

Table 3.   Corn price

Year	Dollars/Pound
1972	0.021
1973	0.037
1974	0.053
1975	0.048
1976	0.045
1977	0.037
1978	0.042

Table 4.   1978 Consumption of sugars (Dry basis)
(Billions of pounds)

Crystalline glucose	1
Glucose syrup	4
Glucose-fructose syrup	2.6

power as obtained from invert sugar. This brought about the opening of an entirely new market for starch in the sweetener field (Tables 4 and 5). While glucose-fructose syrups find applications in soft drinks, jams and jellies, baking, table syrups and salad dressings, the market was still further expanded by further increases in the fructose content of the syrup. Fructose was found to be removable from the glucose-fructose syrup by separation on cation exchange resins in the calcium form. Whereas, pure fructose can be made in this way, a syrup of 90% fructose content is most readily produced and can be used to enrich the normal glucose-fructose syrup to 55% fructose which also finds wide acceptance (Table 6). The prime use of the 55% fructose syrup is in the soft drinks, salad dressings, frozen desserts, jams, jellies and cereals. The 90% fructose syrup is suited for products where reduction in calorie level is desired as indicated in Table 7.

TABLE 5.   U.S. population sweetener consumption (pounds/capita)

Year	Glucose syrup	Glucose-Fructose syrup	Sucrose
1960	9.4	0	97.4
1965	12.3	0	96.8
1975	16.2	6.8	91.5
1978	17.6	13.9	91.5 (projected)
1980	18.2	15.5	91.3 (projected)

TABLE 6.   Typical glucose-fructose syrup composition

	Normal syrup	55% fructose	90% fructose
Glucose	52	40	7
Fructose	42	55	90
Higher saccharides	6	5	3

TABLE 7.   Some food uses of 90% fructose syrup and calorie reduction

Soft drinks	Up to 50% calorie reduction
Table syrups	Up to 70% calorie reduction
Jams and Jellies	Up to 70% calorie reduction
Salad dressings	At least 30% calorie reduction
Wines	"Light types"

2.4.2 MALTOSE

Hydrolysis of starch with a debranching enzyme and β-amylase leads to syrups of high maltose content. Expanded use of this type of syrup is occurring because it can be used at high concentrations to produce body without increasing sweetness.

Perhaps its greatest potential is in its use as a mild sweetener with low cariogenicity compared to sucrose. Sucrose is acted upon by the transglu-cosidases produced by normal bacteria of the mouth, as for example *Streptococcus mutans,* to produce glucans that adhere bacteria together and adhere to the enamel of the teeth, thus retaining metabolic products such as acids that can attack the tooth enamel. Maltose is not so easily amenable to transglycosilation and tends to prevent insoluble glucans from forming thereby reducing plaque formation and, consequently, carie production.

2.4.3 Maltodextrins

Maltodextrins are a class of saccharides (corn syrup solids, Table 9) of D.E. less than 20 obtained by partial acid or enzyme hydrolysis of starch. The composition approximates that shown in Table 8. Almost all mal-todextrins are sold as spray-dried powders readily soluble but relatively non-hydroscopic. They are essentially tasteless, but in foods give a de-sirable mouth feel due to viscosity characteristics. They are excellent bulk-ing agents, carrying agents, maintain free-flow properties of mixes and can absorb moisture vapor but still remain free-flowing. It may be expected that these useful, digestible carbohydrates will undergo increased use in the food industry.

Table 8.   Maltodextrins

Component	Percent
Monosaccharide	1–3
Disaccharide	2–5
Trisaccharide	5–9
Tetrasaccharide	4–7
Pentasaccharide	4–9
Higher saccharides	65–80

Table 9.   U.S. sales of starch and starch products (1977)

Product	Pounds × 10⁶ dry basis
Starch, unmodified	2,000
Starch, modified	1,500
Syrup, conventional glucose	4,000
Syrup, high fructose	2,500
Crystalline glucose	1,000
Corn syrup solids	150
Total	11,150

2.4.4 Gels

An important growth area for starch is likely to be in the development of new and improved gelling agents. Many gelling agents are becoming expensive and new requirements for gels are fast developing. Old established gelling agents or aids to gelling agents are either not increasing or are decreasing in supply. This is especially true of agar and tragacanth. This comes at a time when the food industry has need for improved gelling agents. Gels are required that are firm but low in brittleness, do not synerese and do not change strength or develop brittleness with age. Gels are needed that have melting characteristics like agar or that set permanently with characteristics somewhat like curdlan. Such gels prepared by modification of starch are a possibility and work toward their production is proceeding.

2.4.5 Starch in Fluid Flow

Need for agents to reduce the friction fluid flow is increasing, especially in non-food areas, such as pipeline transport of coal. However, such agents could be useful in many food handling systems. Okra gum is excellent in friction control and polysaccharides like guar are potentially useful. It is likely that modified starches could also be designed for this application.

2.5 Progress in the Utilization of Whey Protein in Human Nutrition

Leif Hambraeus*

Whey is a highly nutritious by-product of cheese manufacture. It remains when casein has been precipitated from milk enzymatically by the addition of rennin ("rennet whey" or "sweet whey") or isoelectrically by the addition of acid ("acid whey"). Although the properties of whey vary with the type of cheese manufacture, it contains all the lactose of the milk, which constitutes about 5 % of the liquid whey, but as much as 74 % of the dry whey, as well as minor amounts of minerals and water-soluble vitamins which together constitute another 0.7 % of the liquid whey. The protein content is low, being only about 0.6 % or about one quarter of that of skim milk. It is comprised of whey proteins as well as fragments of casein, mainly κ-casein, which remain after curd formation. Whey powder on the other hand has a protein content of about 12 % which is of the same order of magnitude as that of most cereals.

The amount of whey production is rather impressive. According to the FAO[2], world whey output was estimated at more than 74 million tons in 1973 and there had been a 25 % increase since 1966. The production of whey during cheese manufacture is still a great problem for the dairy industry although the dilemma over whey utilization has been studied for several decades.

Whey has traditionally been considered as an undesirable element of very little use. The most common way to dispose of it has been to dump it into the sewage system. Disposal of liquid whey, which becomes a powerful pollutant through the sewage system, has, however, been prohibited in many countries. As a result, the dairy industry has been forced to develop a whey processing industry under pressure from ecological and legal forces. Economic interest in whey products *per se* has, however, remained lacking.

A less wasteful use of liquid whey is to employ it in the feeding of animals such as pigs and cows. With the development and expansion of the cheese industry, however, such measures are still inadequate to cope with the problem of whey disposal and the problem has grown in magnitude during the last years. It has still not been possible to stimulate sufficient

* *Institute of Nutrition, University of Uppsala, P.O.Box 551, S-751 22 Uppsala, Sweden*

new areas for whey products to solve the surplus problem of the dairy industry. Despite intensive research efforts resulting in many new potential uses,[10-12,17-19] whey still represents one of the most important reservoirs of high value food proteins which is not used for human consumption.

The use of whey powder in human food is more due to its unusual functional properties which have enhanced its potential application in foods[15], and there is almost no mention whatsoever about the nutritional properties of the product. It is also symptomatic that much work has been devoted to the deproteinization of whey in order to use it in various types of beverages, although from the nutritional viewpoint the whey proteins would seem to represent the most valuable constituents.

Although whey has been considered mostly as an undesirable surplus product in the dairy industry, there are some traditional whey products to be found in the human diet. These include whey beverages, both alcoholic and non-alcoholic, and whey cheese. Nevertheless, such traditional uses of whey involve only a minor and marginal portion of the total whey available. Whey beverages have been employed previously for therapeutic purposes in folk medicine. Most of the beverages, however, are based on deproteinized whey.

Holsinger *et al.*[7] recently published a review of whey beverages. They classified them in 4 major groups: (1) beverages from whole whey, (2) non-alcoholic beverages from deproteinized whey, (3) alcoholic beverages, some containing protein, and (4) protein beverages in the form of milk-like beverages and beverages resembling soft drinks. The use of whole whey in beverages usually takes advantage of the fact that the flavor of acid whey is well compatible with citrus flavors. Consequently, a number of citrus-flavored beverages of high nutritive value have been developed in the US.

From the nutritional viewpoint, the protein-containing beverages based on whey are of course of greatest interest. A number of imitation milk products or extended milks have been developed mainly in the US. Some of these are based on a combination of whey and soy, where the low contents of lysine and sulfur-containing amino acids in soy are balanced by the whey protein, which is rich in lysine and also contains appreciable amounts of sulfur-containing amino acids.

The development of new techniques for the production of whey protein concentrates has also resulted in trials to produce protein-fortified soft drinks. The problem of producing and marketing whey beverages thus does not seem to be a technological one, nor a question of acceptability. The main problems are still economic.

Whey cheese in the form of the Scandinavian type "mesost", which is produced by prolonged boiling, or in the form of the Italian type of "Ricotta cheese", which is manufactured by heat coagulation of the whey proteins, takes advantage of the protein components of the whey.

From the human nutritional viewpoint, the whey proteins are the components of the various whey products which have by far the greatest interest as they comprise a series of nutritionally well-balanced high value proteins, some of them with interesting physiological functions.

The major protein component of bovine whey is β-lactoglobulin, which constitutes about 50% of the bovine whey proteins. Although this is a milk-specific protein which is synthesized in the mammary glands, its physiological role remains unknown. α-Lactalbumin represents another milk-specific protein. It is a component of the enzyme lactose synthetase and its concentration seems to be related to the lactose content when milk specimens from various mammals are compared[8]. Interestingly, α-lactalbumin appears to have the most optimal amino acid composition and consequently the highest nutritional value according to biological evaluations.[3] The immunoglobulins, which mainly comprise IgG and IgM in bovine milk, as well as serum albumin are not milk-specific but derived from the serum. However, in human milk the dominant immunoglobulin, IgA, appears to be milk-specific and to play an essential role in the defense against gastrointestinal infections. The concentration of IgA in bovine milk is however very low. There are also several other proteins present in small quantities in the whey, which may possibly play a significant physiological role. These include lactoferrin, lactollin, transferrin, glucoprotein and various enzymes.

The role of whey proteins in the field of human nutrition is two-fold. First, substitution of whey powder for part of the skim milk powder used in animal feed increases the supply of the latter for human consumption. Whey powder has also been replacing fishmeal and oilcake protein in cattle, poultry and pig feeding. A combination of whey powder and petroleum based single cell proteins has also been developed as a calf feed ingredient which is physiologically and economically capable of replacing skim milk powder to a considerable extent[2]. It should be stressed, however, that the substitution of whey protein for casein or skim milk powder does not essentially solve any problem for the dairy industry since it leads merely to a surplus problem of the products which are replaced.

Direct use of whey products in human food is therefore of greater interest. This can be divided generally into three categories: (1) use of whey protein as a major protein source for its nutritional, physiological and pharmacological characteristics, (2) use of whey protein as a supplement to protein of less nutritional value, and (3) use of specific whey protein fractions for specific (e.g. pharmaceutical) purposes.

The use of whey protein for infant feeding in products such as adapted milk formulas might represent the first real approach taking advantage of its nutritional characteristics. In the adapted formulas, whey protein concentrate is added to skim milk powder in order to give a casein/whey protein ratio of 40/60 which was earlier assumed to be the actual ratio in human milk. However, there are still great differences both from quantitative and qualitative viewpoints[5]. Recent studies by Lönnerdal at our laboratory have shown that the casein percentage in human milk might be as low as 20%. Furthermore, there is a great difference in composition of whey proteins between human milk and cow's milk[5]. The nutritional significance of these differences is still not known.

The use of whey protein concentrate as a major protein source in clinical dietetics has also been reported[9]. This application is based on the fact that the amino acid pattern of the whey proteins is apparently highly optimal for human beings and the whey proteins are easily digested. Interestingly, the content of the aromatic amino acids, tyrosine and phenylalanine, is rather low, indicating the possiblity of using whey proteins in the dietary treatment of hyperphenylalaninemia and phenylketonuria[6].

One of the essential roles of whey proteins in milk is probably to supplement the casein, since they contain a considerable amount of the essential amino acids and have a higher nutritive value than casein. This indicates that they could also be of value as supplements to other proteins of less nutritional quality.

The effect of replacing skim milk by whey protein concentrate in protein-rich weaning foods has been studied by Forsum[3]. These foods are usually based on cheap and readily available vegetable protein sources which are enriched with animal proteins which should comprise at least 5%[15]. Skim milk powder is generally used. Forsum was able to show that whey protein concentrate was superior to dried skim milk as the animal protein source in a number of protein-rich weaning food mixtures. Interestingly, the USDA and USAID have tested a whey-soy mix for use as a supplementary food for children in developing countries when they were faced with shortage of skim milk powder. This mixture comprised 41.5% sweet whey and 36.5% full fat soy flour as protein components, 12.2% soybean oil, 9% corn syrup solids and 1% of a vitamin-mineral premix. It contained approximately 20% protein and 2,100 calories per pound.

Ahmed and Ismail[1] recently reported the use of whey protein for the enrichment of Zabadi. Whey protein concentrates have also been used as a milk extender[13]. During processing, whey is often subjected to heat treatment which might decrease the supplementary effects. However, Forsum and Hambraeus[4] have been able to show that the protein nutritional quality of denatured whey products was sufficient even after considerable heat treatment.

It is quite obvious and has already been stated that whey contains a considerable amount of proteins which appear to have specific effects of physiological importance. One example is provided by the lactoperoxidase system which has been so extensively studied and discussed by Reiter and his collaborators[16]. Lactoferrin is another example of a protein with a specific physiological function which is worthy of further study. It might have a two-fold effect, as an iron-binder in the defense against gastrointestinal infections, and also for the transport of iron from mother to infant, and for the absorption of iron from the human milk in the infant's gastrointestinal tract. It might also be of interest to undertake further studies of other compounds in milk, i.e. enzymes such as lysozyme.

It is not impossible that whey could be of further use in the pharmaceutical industry as a source of specific proteins. However, any project dealing with the utilization of whey products must always take into account the need to provide a complete solution for the use of all the components of the whey. The interesting composition of whey with all its minerals, vitamins and trace elements in addition to its high value protein, indicates that this might not represent an insoluble problem. However, more research is clearly needed to determine the proper role of whey products in human nutrition and to reduce the high costs involved in concentrating demineralized and delactosed whey since these still represent the real limiting factor against the wider utilization of whey proteins in human food. Herein lies the principal challenge to dairy industry innovators.

REFERENCES

1. Ahmed, N. S. and Ismail, A. Enrichment of Zabadi by whey proteins, *Milchwissenschaft*, **33**, 228 (1978).
2. FAO Commodity Note, Whey—an important potential protein source, *Monthly Bull. Agr. Econ. Stat*, **23**, 12 (1974).
3. Forsum, E., The use of whey protein concentrate as animal protein source in protein-rich weaning foods, *J. Trop. Ped. Envir. Child Health*, **19**, 333 (1973).
4. Forsum, E. and Hambraeus, L. Nutritional and biochemical studies of whey products, *J. Dairy Sci.*, **60**, 370 (1977).
5. Hambraeus, L., Proprietary milk versus human breast milk in infant feeding. A critical appraisal from the nutritional point of view, *Ped. Clin. North Amer.*, **24**, 17 (1977).
6. Hambraeus, L., Hardell, L. I., Forsum, E. and Lorentsson, R. Use of a formula based on a whey protein concentrate in the feeding of an infant with hyperphenylalaninemia, *Nutr. Metabol.*, **17**, 84 (1974).

7. Holsinger, V. H., Posati, L. P. and De Vilbiss, E. D. Whey beverages: a review, *J. Dairy Sci.*, **57**, 849 (1974).

8. Jenness, R., The composition of milk, *Lactation, a comprehensive treatise* (ed. B. L. Larsson, and U. R. Smith), vol. III, p. 3, Academic Press (1974).

9. Law, D. H., Kaplan, Z. M., Sandstead, H. H. and Roberts, W. L. Whey protein formula for clinical use, Proc. Xth Int. Congr. Nutr. Kyoto, Japan, p. 684, Aug. 3–9, 1975.

10. Mann, E. J., Whey beverages, *Dairy Ind.*, **37**, 153 (1972).

11. Mann, E. J., Whey processing and utilization, *Dairy Ind.*, **36**, 44 (1971).

12. Mann, E. J., Some aspects of whey utilization, *Dairy Ind.*, **38**, 77 (1973).

13. McDonough, F. E., Alford, J. A. and Womach, M. Whey protein concentrate as a milk extender, *J. Dairy Sci.*, **59**, 34 (1976).

14. McDonough, F. E., Hargrove, R. E., Mattingly, W. A., Posati, L. P. and Alford, J. A. Composition and properties of whey protein concentrates from ultrafiltration, *J. Dairy Sci.*, **57**, 1438 (1974).

15. Protein Energy Advisory Group of the UN system, Guidelines on protein-rich mixtures for use as weaning foods, U. N., New York (1971).

16. Reiter, B., Pickering, A. and Oran, J. D. An inhibitory system—lactoperoxidase thiocyanate peroxide—in raw milk, 4th Int. Symp. Food Microbiol. (ed. N. Molin), p. 297, Almqvist & Wiksell, Stockholm (1964).

17. Webb, B. H., Whey Utilization Conf. Proc. Agr. Res. Serv. US Dept. Agr. Philadelphia (1970–71).

18. *ibid.* (1972).

19. *ibid.* (1974).

3. Utilization of Rice

3.1 Biochemical Aspects of Rice Utilization

Yuhei Morita*

Rice is one of the leading crops in the world. More than 250 million tons of rice are produced every year, and over 95% of the world production is used for human consumption. In Japan, rice is the most important food and 12–13 million tons are produced annually. The Japanese people, on average, take 1000 calories and 23 g of protein from rice per capita per day, the latter quantity representing about one third of the required amount of protein. This paper gives a review of recent biochemical research on the rice kernel, primarily based on Japanese studies, with respect to the utilization of rice (*Oryza sativa* L. var. *japonica*).

The chemical composition of rice has been analyzed by many workers[1]. The nutrient components are not distributed evenly in the kernel: starch is limited only to the inner endosperm cells, while protein, lipids and minerals are rich in the outer endosperm and embryo. In addition to these analyses, scanning electron microscopy has revealed the fine structure and localization of the cell constituents of the rice caryopsis[2]. The caryopsis consists of the pericarp, tegmen, aleurone layers, embryo and starchy endosperm. Most of the ventral portion contains a single layer of aleurone cells, while the dorsal portion contains two to several layers. Small spherical particles called aleurone particles, which consist of proteins and minerals, fill these cells. Between the aleurone particles are small spheroplasts which consist of lipids. The scutellum cells in the embryo have the same structure and constituents as the aleurone cells. The constituents of these cells will be described in detail later.

On the other hand, the inner endosperm cells contain mainly starch granules and proteins. The starch granules of the peripheral cells of the in-

* The Research Institute for Food Science, Kyoto University, Gokasho, Uji, Kyoto 611, Japan

ner endosperm are few and small but those in the central portion are larger and occur in closely packed compound groups. Up to 95% of the protein of the inner endosperm exists in the form of protein bodies, which were identified by Juliano and Mitsuda *et al.* in 1967. Furthermore, Mitsuda *et al*[3]. observed the fine structure of protein bodies which were composed of concentric layers of very small unit particles. The size of the unit particles was about 150 μ in diameter, which corresponds to the molecular weight of glutelin, 2×10^6 daltons, as described later. About 80% of the endosperm protein consists of glutelin. Sawai and Morita[4] established a simple method for the purification of rice glutelin. The large molecule of glutelin is constructed from small subunits. The critical isolation of 3 different kinds of subunits, I, II and III, was achieved by cation-exchange chromatography of cyanoethylated glutelin in the presence of urea. The molecular weights of the subunits were determined as 32,000, 54,000, and 20,000, respectively. The *N*-terminal amino acids of the minor, basic subunits II and III were both found to be glycine, while that of the major, neutral subunit I could not be established by the FDNB- and PTC- methods. The weight ratio of the 3 subunits was found to be 8:1:1 for the variety "Manryo". The amino acid compositions of the neutral and basic subunits were considerably different[5], especially as regards the essential amino acid, lysine. From the nutritional viewpoint, the relationship between the total protein and lysine contents of rice has been extensively investigated and some workers have reported a negative interrelation between them. However, our recent work has shown that such a relationship did not exist in the same variety ("Nihonbare") cultivated under different conditions of nitrogen fertilizer. In this case, the compositions of the protein components of brown rice with different protein contents exhibited similar patterns (see Table 1). Moreover, as shown in Fig. 1, the chromatographic profiles of the subunits were almost the same for the 3 glutelin preparations from "Nihonbare" with different protein contents. The ratios of the subunits were all found to be 12: 1 :6, however, which differed from the

TABLE 1. Relative amounts of protein in rice ("Nihonbare")

	Protein (g/100 g)		
	A	B	C
Total	5.60 (100.0)	6.13 (100.0)	7.28 (100.0)
Albumin	1.24 (22.1)	1.30 (21.2)	1.34 (18.4)
Globulin			
Prolamin	0.19 (3.4)	0.23 (3.8)	0.35 (4.8)
Glutelin	4.17 (74.5)	4.60 (75.0)	5.59 (76.8)

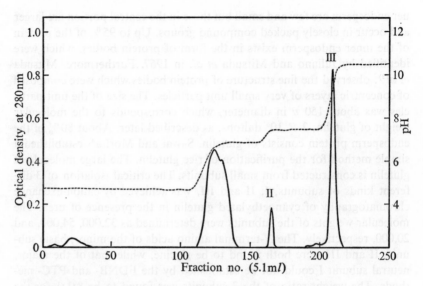

FIG.1. Chromatography of S-cyanoethyl glutelin on a CM-Sephadex C-50 column (2.5 × 40 cm). Solid line, optical density at 280 nm; broken line, pH.

results for "Manryo". A similar composition was found in another variety, "Koshihikari", with a total protein content of more than 10%, based on SDS gel electrophoretic patterns of the isolated glutelins as compared with those of "Nihonbare". Further analyses will be necessary to demonstrate the full variety-specificity of the composition of glutelin subunits. In any case the nutritional value of glutelin will be determined by the content of basic subunits with high lysine contents. Recently, many trials for the enrichment of the protein in rice have been carried out by breeding or γ-ray irradiation. From the nutritional viewpoint, rice breeding should be concentrated in this direction. Concerning other nutritional and biochemical aspects of glutelin, Kasai et al. have recently shown that 2 different types of protein bodies are present in the rice endosperm. One is that found by Mitsuda et al., in which an ultrafine structure of concentric layers was observed; the other exhibits no such fine structure but is evenly dense in texture. As regards physical strength, the first type of protein bodies shows high rigidity but the second type does not. Reports also exist on the indigestive protein bodies of rice, so that the digestibility and utilization of these different types of protein bodies in the human intestine should be examined.

One of the most important problems in rice utilization is the effective use of bran constituents. Usually, about 10% of brown rice on a weight basis, is removed as bran fractions in the milling process. These fractions contain

TABLE 2.   Molecular characteristics of γ_1-and γ_3-globulins of rice embryos

	γ_1	γ_3
Molecular weight (daltons)	200,000	120,000
Intrinsic viscosity (dl/g)	0.0424	0.0404
Partial specific volume (ml/g)	0.721	0.725
Frictional ratio	1.74	1.1
Axial ratio	14	1
No. of subunits	10	4
N-Terminal	Arg 4	Arg 3
	Glu 2	Gly 1
	Phe 2	
	Lys 1	
	Gly 1	
Molecular weight of subunits	36,000	35,000
	24,000	13,000
	21,000	
	15,000	
	13,000	
Extinction coefficient at 280 nm, E_{1cm}^1	6.25	8.55
Secondary structure	α-helix 3%	
	β-structure 38%	β-structure

pericarp, tegmen, aleurone cells, embryo and peripheral portions of the inner endosperm. The complex composition of such rice bran gives rise to considerable difficulties in utilization. As described above, aleurone cells as well as scutellum cells contain aleurone particles and spheroplasts, which consist mainly of protein and oil, respectively. The major protein components of the aleurone particles are albumin and globulin. The albumin is quite heterogeneous and consists of histone-like basic proteins, many enzymes and other active proteins. On the other hand, up to 80% of the globulin consists of 7S globulins, or γ-globulin. This γ-globulin can be easily isolated on the basis of its solubility and by gel-filtration chromatography. However, it is not a homogeneous protein, but is fractionated into 3 components (γ_1-, γ_2-, and γ_3-globulins) by cation-exchange chromatography. Table 2 summarizes some of the molecular characteristics of the γ_1-and γ_3-glublins for comparison[6]. γ_2-Gluobulin can be distinguished by electrophoresis and ion-exchange chromatography, but the molecule is very similar to the γ_3-component except for a small difference in electric charge. In any case, these globulins are synthesized as reserve proteins or possible proenzymes in part, and the physicochemical characteristics resemble the 7S or 11S globulins of soybean seeds. Although γ-globulins aggregate on heating of a solution, especially in the presence of calcium or magnesium salts, the solubility and other properties of the head-denatured globulin as well as albumin differ from those of the glutelin in the endosperm. Therefore, a critical separation of the aleurone layers from the inner endosperm on milling rice is necessary for the effective utilization of the bran proteins. This is also true of the other nutrients, starch and oil, as will be described below. In connection with the utilization of bran proteins, it should also be noted that phytin is concentrated in the aleurone particles[7]. Since phytin is known to disturb the absorption of minerals (especially alkaline earth elements) from animal intestine, removal of the phytin will form a necessary part of the utilization of bran proteins.

One of the most important problems in bran utilization is the stabilization and extraction of bran oil. Bran oil of high quality is known to be useful as a good edible oil. An example of the fatty acid composition of rice bran triglyceride is given in Table 3. The recent work of Fujino et al[8]. has

TABLE 3.   Lipid content and fatty acid composition (wt%) of rice bran

		Total lipid	Triglycerides
Lipid content			
weight basis		18.7	14.5 (77.7)
glyceral basis			14.7 (78.7)
Fatty acid			
myristic	14:0	0.1	0.3
palmitic	16:0	17.6	17.9
palmitoleic	16:1	0.2	0.5
stearic	18:0	2.0	2.1
oleic	18:1	38.9	38.8
linoleic	18:2	39.2	38.4
linolenic	18:3	0.4	0.4
arachidonic	20:0	1.3	1.3
lignoceric	24:0	0.3	0.3

determined the major molecular species of triglyceride as 16:0– 18:2 – 18:1 16:0 – 18:2 – 18:2, and 18:1 – 18:1 – 18:1. The triglycerides are localized in the spheroplasts of aleurone and scutellum cells, so that critical separation of these tissues from the inner endosperm containing mainly starch is necessary for the effective extraction and utilization of bran oil. Moreover, it should be noted that the embryo and aleurone layers are the most biologically active portions of the rice grain and many active enzymes are concentrated in these portions. Mechanical isolation of these tissues from the inner endosperm by milling thus tends to disturb the biological equilibrium of the cellular metabolism and promote marked change in the cellular constituents. The greatest changes occur by hydrolysis and oxidation. Among them, the hydrolysis of lipids and oxidative breakdown of unsaturated fatty acids are the most serious as regards the utilization of bran. Triglycerides and other lipid materials are easily hydrolyzed by the catalysis of lipase to form free fatty acids, so leading to a rapid increase in the acid value of the bran.

The lipase of rice bran has been studied by Aizono *et al.*[8], who isolated and characterized 3 kinds of lipase. Among these, the major component (lipase I) has been the most extensively investigated. It has a molecular weight of 38,700 daltons, and is constructed from 324 amino acid residues. It has one serine and one histidine residue at the active center and these are modified by DFP or photosensitized oxidation and diazonium-1-H tetrazol, respectively, to cause inactivation of the lipase. This enzyme is known to bind calcium ion as a stabilizer and the enzyme activity is lost by treatment with chelating reagents. The catalytic mechanism is one of hydrolyzing triglyceride at the 1 or 3 position, and fatty acid at the 2 position is transferred to the 1 or 3 position by the same enzyme. Lipase I exhibits a wide specificity of substrate from C_2 to C_{18}, but increasing the carbon chain decreases the activity. The optimal pH is 7.5. Lipase II has similar enzymatic properties but shows a somewhat lower stability on heating. In practical use, stabilization of rice bran is achieved by freezing or heating the bran immediately after milling, but consideration of such enzymatic properties will be useful in the future.

Another form of deterioration of bran oil is caused by the oxidation of unsaturated fatty acids by molecular oxygen automatically or by the catalysis of lipoxygenase, as shown in Fig. 2. Many carbonyl compounds will be formed by the breakdown of peroxide compounds of the unsaturated fatty acids. The storage of rice grain under partially anaerobic conditions increases the accumulation of ethyl alcohol as a metabolic product and also causes a reduction of the carbonyl compounds from unsaturated fatty acids to give the corresponding alcohols. However, when the grain is again placed under aerobic conditions, especially on milling, the alcohols are reoxidized to produce aldehydes, which not only give rise to an off-flavor but also bind to amino groups of lysine residues to decrease the nutritive value of the bran proteins.

Finally, it is pointed out that the major constituent of rice, i.e. starch, is the most important factor determining the quality of rice. In milled rice, up to 77% on a weight basis is starch. Rice starch is present as specific granules in many amyloplasts in the endosperm cells. These granules are

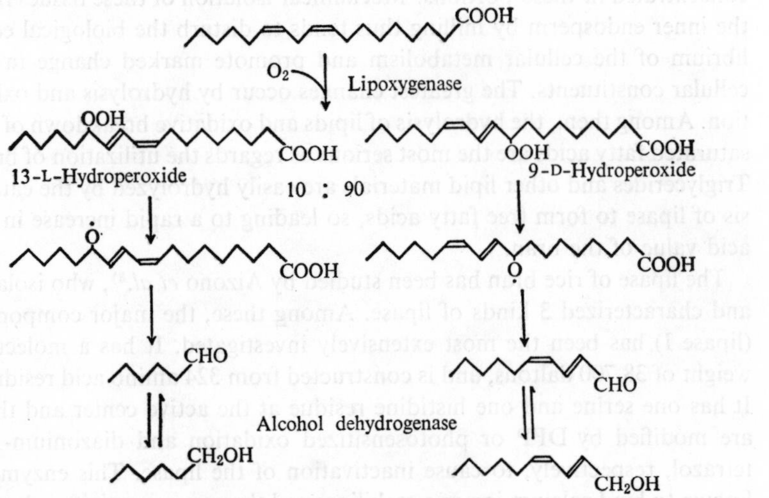

Fig.2. Oxidative breakdown of unsaturated fatty acids.

constructed from further, small polyhedral particles of starch. The composition of rice starch varies widely, and it seems to be characteristic according to variety of rice. Waxy strains contain 0–1.8 % amylose, while non-waxy rice contains 7–33 % amylose. The mechanism of starch synthesis during rice development has been extensively studied by Akazawa and his co-workers[10]. However, this mechanism is valid for the synthesis of amylose; that of amylopectin remains unknown. Resurreccion et al.[11] have reported that the day temperature during the ripening stage affected the amylose contents of rice. Further studies on external factors controlling amylose content are thus worth while.

References

1. Juliano, B. O., *Rice, Chemistry and Technology* (ed. D. F. Houston), p. 16, American Association of Cereal Chemists, (1972).
2. Tanaka, K., Yoshida, T., Asada, K., and Kasai, Z., *Arch. Biochem. Biophys.*, **155**, 136 (1973).
3. Mitsuda, H., Murakami, K., Kusano, T., and Yasumoto, K., *Arch. Biochem. Biophys.*, **103**, 678 (1969).
4. Sawai H. and Morita, Y., *Agr. Biol. Chem.* **32**, 76, 496 (1968).
5. Sawai, H., Nikaido, H., and Morita, Y., *Agr. Biol. Chem.*, **34**, 1039 (1970).
6. Morita Y. and Horikoshi, M., *Agr. Biol. Chem.*, **36**, 651 (1972).
7. Tanaka, K., Yoshida, T., and Kasai, Z., *Plant Cell Physiol.*, **15**, 147 (1974).

8. Miyazawa, T., Tazawa, H., and Fujino, Y., *Cereal Chem.*, **55**, 138 (1978).
9. Aizono, Y., Funatsu, M., Sugano, M., Hayashi, K., and Fujiki, Y., *Agr. Biol. Chem.*, **37**, 2031 (1973).
10. Akazawa, T., *Rice, Chemistry and Technology* (ed. D. F. Houston), p. 75, American Association of Cereal Chemists (1972).
11. Resurreccion, A. P., Hara, T., Juliano, B. O., and Yoshida, S., *Soil Sci. Plant Nutr.*, **23**, 109 (1977).

8. Minawaa, T., Tsuruta, H., and Fujino, Y., Cer. of Chem., 55, 118 (1978).
9. Aizono, Y., Funatsu, M., Sugano, M., Hayashi, K., and Fujiki, Y., Agr. Biol. Chem., 37, 2031 (1973).
10. American Association of Cereal Chemists (1972).
11. Resurrección, A. P., Hara, T., Juliano, B. O., and Yoshida, S., Soil Sci. Plant Nutr., 23, 109 (1977).

3.2   Progress in Methods for Evaluating the Quality of Rice

Katsuharu Yasumatsu*

It is widely recognized that rice constitutes one of the most important food sources of mankind. Moreover, in different countries rice is consumed in various different ways. In Japan, the consumption of rice has shown a steady decline in recent years, presenting various problems. Even so, 34% of the calorie intake and 19% of the protein intake of the Japanese are still dependent on rice. This means that, in Japan, rice remains as the staple food. On the other hand, according to the cookery books of western countries, rice is regarded as one of many vegetables, which means that it forms an ingredient of dishes and is far from being thought of as a staple food. With this difference in the role of rice in the daily diet, it is little wonder that the manner of cooking rice and the form in which it is served vary.

According to a 1975–76 menu survey in Japan, more than a half of the carbohydrate food taken at home was rice and more than 70% of this was consumed as plain, white rice. The Japanese usually eat unseasoned, cooked rice with chop-sticks, not with a spoon. This is why in Japan a particular kind of rice which provides a white, glossy and sticky product on cooking is preferred. On the other hand, in western countries as well as in some other oriental countries, rice is often fried, seasoned, or used as an ingredient of soup. A rice which is cookable into a less sticky product with a stable textural integrity during cooking is therefore preferred in these countries. This means that the qualities expected of rice will vary with different countries and that the methods used to evaluate these qualities will also vary between them.

In discussing the quality of rice, several viewpoints can be taken. For example, quality from the nutritional viewpoint is important; also, storage stability and high yield during milling are indispensable factors in the evaluation of rice as a commodity. In this paper, however, only the eating quality of rice will be reviewed.

* Food Research Labs., Takeda Chemical Industries, Ltd., Juso-honmachi, Yodogawa-ku, Osaka 532, Japan

3.2.1 KEY FACTORS IN THE EVALUATION

As in the case of most foods, cooked rice is evaluated according to 4 different organoleptic attributes, viz. appearance, odor, taste and texture. The 4 kinds of scores so obtained are integrated to give an overall score. How these terms are weighted varies from country to country.

According to data compiled in our sensory tests on groups of polished rice stored under different conditions, overall flavor showed a high correlation with flavor, taste and hardness. This means that the quality of cooked rice depends largely on its flavor and hardness. On the other hand, due to the recent advance of gas chromatography as an analytical tool for investigating flavor, many studies have been made on the flavor of cooked rice by gas chromatography. Concerning texture, the texturometer, an instrument capable of measuring texture in a form quite similar to the human sense, has recently enjoyed widespread use. The present report will thus focus essentially on the flavor and texture of cooked rice.

3.2.2 FLAVOR

A. Chemical Components of Rice Flavor

The first report on the flavor of cooked rice was made by Obata *et al.* in 1965. They found that when cysteine or cystine was subjected to photolysis in the presence of riboflavine, a flavor similar to cooked rice was produced. They also noted that when hydrogen sulfide, acetaldehyde and ammonia are admixed, the flavor of cooked rice is produced. It is apparent therefore that sulfur compounds and carbonyl compounds play an important role in the flavor of cooked rice, as they do in the flavor of various other cooked food products.

B. Carbonyl Compounds

Many carbonyl compounds were found to be involved in the cooking flavor of rice. We also clarified that 5 kinds of carbonyl compounds existed in the volatiles from cooked rice, viz. acetaldehyde, propion-aldehyde or acetone, methylethylketone, *n*-valeralidehyde and *n*-capro-aldehyde. Following our report (1966), Mitsuda *et al.* (1971), Suzuki *et al.* (1971), Endo *et al.* (1977) and Aisaka *et al.* (1977) also investigated the volatile carbonyl compounds of cooked rice and found other related compounds such as *n*-butylaldehyde, *iso*-butylaldehyde and *iso*-valeraldehyde in the volatiles of cooked rice.

C. Sulfur Compounds

In the case of volatile sulfur compounds, Sato *et al.* (1976) found hydrogen sulfide, methyl mercaptan, dimethyl sulfide, dimethyl disulfide and sulfur dioxide in distillates during the steaming of milled rice, using a gas chromatograph fitted with a flame photometric detector. Since the threshold values of these compounds are very low, it is reasonable to assume that they are associated with the odor of cooked rice.

D. Flavor of Carbonyl Compounds

The next problem is how carbonyl compounds are related to the flavor quality of cooked rice. Stored rice and newly harvested rice are clearly different as regards their cooked flavor. The Japanese prefer the flavor of newly harvested rice and regard the flavor of stored rice as stale. Table 1 shows results for the quantitative analysis of carbonyl compounds contained in the volatile fractions of fresh and stored rice. Clearly, cooked rice with a stale flavor is rich in carbonyl compounds: the concentrations of n-valeraldehyde and n-carpoaldehyde, both of which have a relatively high boiling point, increase. If these aldehydes are added to fresh rice and the rice is cooked, stale flavor is perceived. On the basis of these data, it is considered that these aldehydes are important factors in the stale flavor of rice. The carbonyl compounds, especially n-caproaldehyde (hexanal), have been considered as the major materials of the off-flavor of various oil-containing food products such as potato chips, potato granules, green peas and fried meat.

TABLE 1.   Composition of volatile carbonyl compounds in distillate of cooked rice[†]

Storage temperature of rice		5°C	40°C
Carbonyl	Acetaldehyde	50.8%	25.1%
	Propionaldehyde or acetone	31.0	42.1
compounds	Methylethylketone	11.0	8.9
	n-Valeraldehyde	trace	4.9
	n-Caproaldehyde	7.2	19.0
Total volatile carbonyl comp. (μmol)		1.7	3.7

[†] Calculated from the peak height on gas chromatograms.

It is supposed therefore that, during the storage of rice, lipids are oxidized and decomposed to yield carbonyl compounds, and that these carbonyl compounds give rise to the unpleasant flavor formed when stored rice is cooked. Measurements by us of changes in the amounts of fatty acids during rice storage also support this conclusion. Further confirmation has been provided by several other studies. Endo *et al.* (1977) published gas-chromatograms for the head space vapor of cooked rice prepared from 16 classes of milled rice from different harvest years. To clarify the relation between the pattern of the gas-chromatograms and the quality of rice, they calculated the degree of pattern similarity and prepared a pattern distribution diagram on the basis of the radian distance. They reported that, while rice samples of the same harvest year showed very similar patterns to each other, a clear difference occurred between the patterns of fresh rice and stored rice. Among the different groups of stored rice, sub-grouping could be made into 1-yr-stored rice and 2-yr-stored rice. Fresh rice could be identified from stored rice by comparing the patterns of gas-chromatograms of the vapors of the cooked rice.

E. Flavor of Sulfur Compounds

The flavor quality of the sulfur compounds in the volatiles of cooked rice will next be discussed briefly. Table 2 shows that milled rice stored at 5° C, which has a good flavor, contains a relatively large amount of hydrogen sulfide. On the other hand, in the milled rice stored at 40° C, which has a stale flavor, carbonyl compounds are abundant and there is only a minor amount of hydrogen sulfide. The volatile fraction of rice which is of good quality for the Japanese, is thus rich in sulfur compounds and relatively poor in carbonyl compounds. In other words, the flavor quality of cooked rice is largely dependent on the balance between the contents of both these chemical compounds.

TABLE 2. Contents of hydrogen sulfide and carbonyl compounds in distillate of cooked rice

	Hydrogen sulfide (μmol)	Carbonyl compounds (μmol)
Rice stored at 5°C	1.51	1.6
Rice stored at 40°C	0.41	3.8

3.2.3 TEXTURE

The preferred texture of cooked rice varies widely with different nations. In certain countries, a less-sticky, rather fluffy, dry and well-separated cooked rice is preferred. In Japan, however, sticky cooked rice is more acceptable. Data on textural preferences in cooked rice are thus not applicable universally. When evaluations of the texture of cooked rice are to be discussed internationally, the analysis must be based on objective criteria such as hardness or cohesiveness, and not on subjective data such as preferences.

It should be remembered that rice is largely consumed in the state of granules as they are. Generally speaking, determination of the texture of granular foods involves various problems. In the case of rice, therefore, many studies have first investigated the physicochemical properties of rice powder with an amylograph or photopastegraph, and then attempted correlations between the data obtained and the texture of the granular cooked rice. Many excellent reports such as those of Juliano *et al.* have been published, so that the significance of these studies has been well established. Recently, with the development of texturometers, it has become possible to determine the texture of granular cooked rice as it is, and a standard method for such determinations has been established. The parameters of hardness, adhesiveness and cohesiveness are obtained from the texturograms.

We have found that correlations between the hardness or cohesiveness obtained with a texturometer, and data of corresponding sensory evaluation scores are not statistically significant. However, a significant correlation was observed between the adhesiveness or hardness/adhesiveness ratio (H/A) and the hardness or cohesiveness obtained from sensory evaluations. Moreover, the fact that the correlation coefficient between the hardness perceived in sensory evaluations and the H/A obtained with a texturometer was higher than that for the texturometer hardness suggests that the hardness actually perceived by a person involves not only physical hardness but also a component of adhesiveness.

Endo *et al.* (1976) have also studied the correlations between cooking qualities, amylogram parameters, texturometer parameters and sensory scores. It was concluded that, among the texturometer parameters, hardness/adhesiveness had the highest correlation with the taste of cooked rice.

3.2.4 Future Prospects in Japan

Finally, a brief discussion will be given of the recent changes in pattern of food consumption by the Japanese people in relation to changes in their rice intake. As mentioned above, the amount of rice intake has been steadily decreasing over the last 13 years. On the other hand, the intake of vegetables, milk, milk products and meat has increased. Moreover, the intake of processed foods from wheat has not decreased. It must be asked therefore whether the Japanese people have come to prefer wheat food products to rice.

Questionnaire surveys on food acceptance have been conducted in our laboratories over the last 10 years. The results indicate a consistently higher score for cooked rice over bread or related products; no significant change was observed over the 10-years period. In other words, while a higher degree of preference for cooked rice over bread has been maintained, the actual consumption of rice has decreased steadily. Even though the foods consumed by the Japanese people may have become more abundant in variety, the

amount of food eaten has not itself increased. In other words, although
the preference of the Japanese people for cooked rice has not declined, the
amount of rice consumption has apparently decreased in accordance with
the increasing consumption of other kinds of foods.

When the changed pattern of food consumption of the Japanese people
is widely recognized, it is believed that a need to diversify the forms of
rice consumption in Japan further may arise. It will then be necessary for
the quality of rice to be discussed not only in the context of the quality for
cooked rice, but also the quality for processed rice foods. A change in methods for quality evaluation can then be expected.

amount of food eaten has not itself increased. In other words, although the preferences of the Japanese people for cooked rice has not declined, the increasing consumption of other kinds of foods.

When the changed pattern of food consumption of the Japanese people is widely recognized. It is necessary to diversify the forms of rice consumption in Japan further processing. It will also be necessary for the quality of rice to be discussed not only in the context of the quality for cooked rice, but also the quality for processed rice foods. A change in rice quality evaluation can then be expected.

3.3 Post-Harvest Rice Requirements for Southeast Asia

Dante B. de Padua*

The breakthroughs in rice production through increased yields and double cropping are now of significant extent and magnitude that requires the complementary investments in a post-production delivery system capability. Losses are incurred because of the lack of capability to handle, store, and process the increased volumes. The provision of this capability is the real issue today. It appears deceptively as a straightforward and well established industrial operation and it is, except for the incompatability of the technologies available to the situation in Southeast Asia, where 80 % of its approximately 300 million people depend on the rice industry for their livelihood.

The development of the post-harvest capability for Southeast Asia must recognize the following unalterable conditions.

(1) Cultivated farms are small, ranging from 1/2 to 3 ha per family. This has many implications. Harvesting and threshing will remain labor intensive, either manual or with small machinery unless farm operations are consolidated under a single management where larger combines can be used. With small independent farmers, a larger number of varieties are planted, and with planting unsynchronized, the harvest comes in small batches of different grades. If high milling quality and yields are desired, these different batches should not be mixed.

(2) The increase in rice production is not only due to the use of higher yielding varieties, but also because of its nonphotoperiodicity. The rice plant can be planted anytime of the year where irrigation and water management is available. A second crop is possible and is harvested during the rainy months of September to November. This has created an entirely new harvesting and handling situation. The rice straw is wet and has a tendency to clog harvesting machines. The grain moisture is in the 24–28 % range and is extremely unstable. If drying cannot be initiated within 24 hr the grain quality suffers from heat damage, discoloration due to fermentation, molding and even rotting at the extreme case, as well as germination (sprouting of roots). An option therefore is to provide small capacity dryers

* SEARCA, College, Laguna, The Philippines

on the farm which can be owned or leased and operated by the farmers, and provide the necessary price incentive for the farmers to dry the grain. If such a capability is provided, the biological deterioration of the grain can be arrested, and the grain can be held, stored, or transported without the time pressures.

A second option is to develop an efficient system of assembling the harvested wet grain from the farmers and delivering it to drying stations or directly to millers. The requirements for such a system are the provision of a network of farm roads for mechanized transport, a method of receiving, grading, and handling the many different grades of wet paddy, and a flexible continuous flow and auto-mixing type of industrial dryer. The existing large capacity single receiving pit type dryers are not suitable. The management of such a system requires highly trained technicians.

A third option, which may be considered innovative and definitely merits consideration, is the development of an entirely new technology of handling wet grain. Some of the merits of parboiled rice are the sterilization of the grain and the cementing of fissures during the gelatinization of the starchy endosperm resulting in high head grain recoveries. The primary objection to the parboiled rice using the traditional process are the aroma and discoloration, which can be overcome. Research should be carried out to explore the feasibility of wet threshing and cleaning, and partial cooking of the grain in its own moisture to sterilize the grain and to gelatinize and eliminate fissures, and combined with flash drying—the rapid removal of the surface moisture, either by conduction heating, or in a fluidized bed arrangement. If the surface moisture can be removed to an extent that the grain moisture is reduced to 18%, the raw rice will remain stable with no appreciable deterioration for about 21 days. Such a process may be a batch type process for on-farm application or a more sophisticated process for on-plant application.

(3) The high yielding varieties (HYV) have made the green revolution possible, to fill the rice bowls of Asia, but those responsible have concentrated on breeding the new varieties and developing the associated cultural practices of growing them. This has resulted in increased tons of paddy in the standing crop but not necessarily at the consumer's table. The HYV's shatter easily, do not ripen uniformly, have a high percentage of immature kernels, and have much poorer milling and eating qualities compared to the traditional varieties. These deficiencies in the grain characteristics until they are corrected by the agronomists, must be accommodated in the processing system. Paddy graders, cleaners, sifters, and scavengers must be designed and incorporated into the system.

(4) Since much of the damage to grain quality, as well as physical loss, occurs before the paddy reaches the rice mill, the milling systems in South-

east Asia have not been able to take advantage of new technology. About 50% of production is still milled in one-pass iron hullers of the "Engelberg" type. These mills are notorious for grinding the grain, resulting in head grain yields of only 35%, and total milling yields as low as 55%, and very rarely making 62%, where a potential milling yield of 68% is possible. These mills are cheap, rugged, and grind the husk that mixes with the bran. The latter is used for backyard animal feed. These features account for the popularity and contained utilization of these type of mills. The most significant development in the milling industry has been the development of the rubber roll huskers for removing the rice hull to produce brown rice. The two rubber rolls operating at different speeds are resilient and accept ungraded paddy. The traditional husker consists of two circular disks, coated with emery stone, the upper disk stationary and the lower rotating. The clearance between the two disks is adjusted to husk about 80% of the paddy. Too tight a clearance to hull the small grains crushes the bigger kernels. Intensive tests in an IDRC supported study at the University of the Philippines at Los Baños have indicated that rubber roll huskers have a hulling efficiency of 83.24% compared to only 58.23% for stone disk huskers. (The husking efficiency is a product of the husking coefficient, a measure of the percentage of paddy husked, and the coefficient of wholeness, a measure of the brown head rice produced.) The significance of this finding is that the rubber roll husker produces about 3% more brown rice than the stone disk husker. This 3% is lost with the husk and chips in a stone disk husker. With the same whitening and polishing efficiencies, the after-husking operations, the 3% more brown rice is passed on and means 4.5% more milled rice from the same paddy stock. The drawback in using rubber roll huskers is that due to the abrasive nature of the paddy hull, the rubber rolls wear out fast.

The above discussion suggests that the requirements in the Southeast Asian region are unique, and complex in a way that makes the introduction of innovations, and of the necessary hardware a much more difficult undertaking than is generally recognized. It has been declared repeatedly by many that post-harvest expertise and post-harvest technology are available. This is true in the context of the requirements of developed countries but these expertise and technology require considerable adaptive changes for application in the Asian region. These changes are necessary to make them compatible with the physical, environmental, economic, and social conditions, as well as the levels of education prevailing in the region. The hardware must make use of indigenous resources as much as possible.

REFERENCES

1. Houston, D. F. (ed.), *Rice Chemistry and Technology*, American Association Cereal Chemists, Inc., St. Paul, Minnesota (1972).
2. National Grains Authority, Philippines, Comparative Study and Test Evaluation of Village Type Rice Threshers, Presented at the Southeast Asia Post-Harvest Workshop, Bangkok, Thailand, January 1978.
3. National Grains Authority, Philippines, Comparative Study and Test Evaluation of Village Type Single Pass Rice Mills, Presented at the Southeast Asia Post-Harvest Workshop, Bangkok, Thailand, January 1978.
4. Maitrie Thongswang, *et al.*, Design and Development of Farm Dryer. Paper from the Division of Agricultural Engineering, Dept. of Agriculture, Thailand (1978).
5. Manalabe, R. E., *et al.*, Milling Parameters for Maximum Milling Yield and Quality of Milled Rice. U. P. at Los Baños, Agricultural Engineering Institute. A progress report to IDRC, 1978.
6. Maitrie Naewbanij, *et al.*, Small Scale Rice Milling Unit, Thailand. Presented at the Southeast Asia Post-Harvest Workshop, Bangkok, Thailand, January 1978.
7. Rapusas, R. S., *et al.*, Pre-drying, Handling of Fresh Paddy, U. P. at Los Baños, Agricultural Engineering Institute. A Progress report to IDRC, 1978.
8. Chung, C. J., Determination of Optimum Timing of Paddy Harvesting Based on Grain Loss and Milling Quality, Dept. of Agricultural Engineering, Seoul National University, Suweon, Korea, June 1977.

3.4 Rice Bran as a Potential Source of Food

Salvador Barber*

3.4.1 INTRODUCTION

The world rice bran production can give annually around four million tons of proteins, five million tons of edible oil, 75,000 billion calories, plus vitamins and minerals. Out of this immense potential, the oil, and only a minimum part of it, goes to direct human consumption. Although bran is produced in regions where the full utilization of all food resources is a must, paradoxically it is underutilized and frequently wasted. This is a dramatic situation. The potential food value of bran has been known for a long time and food grade bran products are available but investors do not show interest in new alternatives. Therefore, an analysis of present status is advisable to ascertain possible causes impeding progress. It is attempted below under three major headings: 1) rice milling technologies and rice bran production, 2) microscopic structure, chemical composition and physical properties, and 3) rice bran products and factors affecting their potential food uses.

3.4.2 RICE BRAN TECHNOLOGIES AND RICE BRAN PRODUCTION

Quality and quantity of the bran produced at the mill are key factors in the utilization of the byproduct. Mills throughout the world differ greatly in this respect. Milling methods vary from simple handpounding, with a mortar and pestle, to large scale processing in highly mechanized mill plants. Handpounding, although declining in use, still accounts for a major percentage in many areas, reducing dramatically the quantity of bran actually available for utilization.

The Engelberg huller type of mill, which removes husk and bran in a single operation, is also widely used in spite of its inefficiency. In Egypt, 50 percent of the rice crop is processed by this method, in the Philippines 55 percent. These mills are scattered throughout rural areas lacking roads and transportation means, raising hard procurement prob-

---

* Cereals and Proteaginouses Laboratory, Instituto de Agroquímica y Tecnología de Alimentos, Jaime Roig, 11, Valencia-10, Spain

lems. Mills generally are of 1/2 ton paddy per hour capacity or less. The bran produced is of a very poor quality: too low in oil (around 6 percent) and too high in fiber and ash (around 20 percent each). In summary, huller bran can only be used as livestock feed. Because of its importance in rural areas, efforts to improve its feeding value by simple, lowcost procedures would be worthwhile. A different alternative might be the improvement and partial modernization of the huller mills, since complete replacement of them will be very difficult and slow. Such an approach has proved promising.[16]

Multistage rice mills are the only mills which produce the kind of bran with potential for food utilization. Unfortunately, not all of them are of appropriate capacity. Many of these mills process 1/2–1 ton/hr, what in many countries means only 20–40 kg bran/hr. And most of them are scattered throughout rural areas making bran procurement difficult. Quality of bran is frequently low. Inadequate milling unit components and/or inefficient operation are the major causes for it. The under-runner disk huller and the rubber rolls huller still are in competition, confronting maintenance vs. performance. Even when the adjustment of the former is optimum (which very often is not), damage of the pericarp and germ can not be avoided. In addition to cargo rice of low keeping quality, up to 2.5 percent (on a paddy basis) of very poor quality bran (with 6–8 percent oil) is produced. Bran from whitening will also be lower in fat.

Separation of grain fractions at the discharge of the sheller is important. Mills differ greatly both in facilities and efficiency. Unless the paddy separator and the return sheller work efficiently, the husk incorporated into the bran in subsequent whitening will be significant—whitening 95 percent purity brown rice at 4 percent degree of milling will give bran with about 20 percent husk.

Abrasive type machines and friction type machines are used for removing bran from brown rice. It has been suggested that the former type cuts off bran like an orange skin, little by little, in small pieces, with a sharp razor blade, whereas the second system loosens and pulls off the bran layer in rather big flakes[9]. Abrasion machines scratch the grain reaching into the starchy endosperm. Friction milling produces bran richer in oil.

Lack of uniformity in bran layers removal during the first stage of whitening is usual. It demands deeper milling and produces admixture of particles of different layer composition, which results in lowered total milling outturn and poor quality bran. Today, the uniformity of bran layers removal can be assessed[1] and both rice milling machinery manufacturers and rice millers should take advantage of it to check scientifically the performance of machines. Also, researchers have with this method a helpful tool to search possibilities for serial removal of successive anatomic bran layers from the caryopsis. Bran fractions with sharp differences in composition could be produced, justifying their individual segregation as distinct commercial products, attractive for specific markets.

In producing good quality bran, removal of the small brokens and the husk particles passing along with bran is essential. Unfortunately the importance of this step is frequently disregarded.

In summary, there is a need to improve the quality of bran and this should be achieved by identifying and correcting inadequate milling machinery and/or improving their performance. Changes in sector structure involving increased milling capacity and geographic concentration of mills, as well as complete modernization of machinery, are very desirable but slow in coming. Better quality bran will contribute to increase market demand, specially from oil extractors, and the miller will have the necessary incentive to become interested in his bran.

3.4.3 MICROSCOPIC STRUCTURE, CHEMICAL COMPOSITION AND PHYSICAL PROPERTIES

The majority of works done on histology and histochemistry refer to bran as it is in the rice caryopsis, not as individual discrete particles. The mechanism of the formation of bran particles during milling has hardly been investigated even in its most fundamental aspects. It is very surprising since this information is essential not only for improved bran production but for improved rice milling.

In a recent study[4] 15 different kinds of discrete particles were identified in commercial bran (Table 1). Eight of them were simple in composition, the remaining seven were compound. The particles were characterized morphologically, histologically and histochemically. The information has been included in a book on rice production and utilization now in press[10]. The germ, entire or in fragments, was one major component of commercial bran amounting up to 20–40 percent. Fragments of pericarp and of pericarp plus seed coat were abundant. They contribute notably to cellulose, hemicellulose and lignin contents of bran. Particles made up only of starchy endosperm were also abundant, denouncing unnecessary deep milling and/or high grain breakage. Although aleurone cells are a part of endosperm, they come out of the rice caryopsis preferably stuck to the seed coat (particles j and k) rather than with the starchy endosperm (particles m). Compound particles of types k, 1 and o, containing fiber- and lignin-rich layer tissues along with protein- and fat-rich ones, are undesirable. They minimize quality differences between successive bran fractions from multistage whitening and make difficult any further improvement of them. k particles were abundant in bran from abrasion cone mills. In addition to fragments of florescent glumes and sterile glumes, conic, transparent, incoloured, empty trichomes, entire or in frag-

TABLE 1. Types of discrete particles identified in Spanish commercial rice bran[†]

Simple particles		Compound particles	
Type	Composition	Type	Composition
a	Fragments of florescent glumes	i	Fragments of pericarp and seed coat
b	Fragments of sterile glumes	j	Fragments of seed coat and aleurone layer
c	Fragments of trichomes	k	Fragments of pericarp, seed coat and aleurone layer
d	Fragments of pedicel	l	Fragments of pericarp, seed coat, aleurone layer and starchy endosperm
e	Fragments of pericarp	m	Fragments of starchy endosperm and aleurone layer
f	Fragments of starchy endosperm	n	Fragments of germ, flattened cells layer and starchy endosperm
g	Germ, whole or fragments	o	Fragments of germ, aleurone layer, seed coat and pericarp
h	Fragments of fibers		

[†] From Barber *et al.* (1978)

ments, of 100–360 μ of length and 30 μ of maximum diameter were found in numbers exceeding 3 millions/kg bran in some samples. Carbohydrates (presumably cellulose) and lignin were identified in them, but histochemical tests failed to detect proteins.

Much research remains to be done on the morphology, histology and histochemistry of bran from existing milling systems (friction milling, especially). Such knowledge will contribute to improving rice milling technology and consequently to the production of a better quality bran.

There is an immense amount of data available on the proximate analysis of bran and very thin bran layers, and on the individual components of each major group of chemical constituents[2]. However, the latter has received little attention in recent years. A few exceptions such as proteins and lipids should be noted. A recent contribution has been the isolation and characterization by electron microscopy and chemical analysis of aleurone grains[15,17] which, along with the protein bodies found in the endosperm[14], constitute an important further step in our knowledge of the major bran proteins.

The chemical composition of rice bran depends of a variety of factors associated with the rice grain itself and the milling process, namely, average chemical composition, distribution of chemical constituents, thickness of anatomical layers, size and shape of grains, resistence of grain to breakage and abrasion, processing diagram, machines used and milling conditions as they affect degree and uniformity of milling. Because continuous evolution of both paddy and milling conditions, data on commercial bran from specified regions should be systematically revised as existing information is insufficient or too antiquated to be used in industrial projects.

Adequate handling, processing and storage of bran demands extensive knowledge of its physical properties. However, published information in this field is meager. Variability in size and shape, histological and chemical composition, and processing history make the few data available of limited value and engineering designs and calculations difficult. Much research should be done on this subject of fundamental importance in developing appropriate technologies for food utilization of rice bran. Since the stabilized bran will be the regular product, this should be more extensively studied.

3.4.4 RICE BRAN PRODUCTS AND FACTORS AFFECTING THEIR FOOD USES

Several rice bran products are known, namely, stabilized bran, defatted bran, dephytinized bran, defibered bran, protein concentrates and isolates. They can be prepared either as full-fat or as defatted products. Purified rice germ could be added to the list. At present only the first mentioned stabilized rice bran has significant use in foods—and this is solely as a source of oil. The other bran products exist almost exclusively on the bench of R & D laboratories. Accordingly, the two groups are dealt with here separately.

Concerning stabilized rice bran, the expected increase of world demand for vegetable oil has originated a spiraling interest of oil extractors in this byproduct. In the developing countries of South East Asia and the Far East the per capita consumption of oils and fats is on an average 4.4 kg, as against 20 kg in developed countries, 8 kg in Latin America, 7.4 kg in Western Asia and 5.1 kg in Africa. Oils and fats consumption in developed countries has reached a peak level. However, it will increase significantly in developing countries where almost all of the expansion of this industry in the next 20 years is expected to take place[18]. To play its role as a source of edible oil, high oil content and good keeping quality are two essential requisites for rice bran.

Although it is claimed that 10–12 % oil content is sufficient to make bran oil extraction economically feasible, this is a low limit. Raw bran is expected to contain as an average 15 to 20 % oil and parboiled rice bran 25 to 30 %. Lower levels demand major causes of low oil content—listed before—to be revised.

Bran of good keeping quality is a must. It can now be produced commercially. Heat resistance of enzymes responsible for bran deterioration was evaluated as a function of temperature and time of treatment and moisture content of bran. Conditions were thus optimally combined to achieve irreversible inactivation of enzymes, necessary for good storage ability. Microorganisms, very often accounting for several millions per gram, and insects, present as adults, larvae or eggs, other major causes of bran deterioration, are also destroyed or their activity arrested under conditions selected to inactivate enzymes. The machine in Fig. 1 is a commercial stabilizing unit which processes bran continuousiy by steaming, flash drying and cooling. Properties of bran stabilized in it were extensively studied and reported elsewhere[2]. The quality of stored stabilized bran was entirely satisfactory for oil extraction and refining. Moisture content of bran and fat acidity were kept below 12.5 and 6.0 percent respectively. The latter level brings refining losses to a minimum. With unstabilized rice bran losses range from 1.5 to 6 times the FFA content, the higher the FFA the higher the loss. Plants process bran up to 15–18 FFA percent. With the low FFA bran refining plants of lower investment and cheaper processing costs are also required. The pelletizing properties and the colour of the oil of the cited stabilized bran were also satisfactory. Even though heat treated rice bran is reported to be difficult to pelletize, entirely acceptable pellets were obtained by using a conventional roller type pelletizer,

Fig.1. IATA fluidized bed stabilizer.

with 4 mm ϕ die. No additive or binding agent was used. Although crude oil from the cited stabilized pelletized rice bran was more coloured than that from raw bran, colours of the neutralized and bleached oils were similar, free of green and blue tinges and conformed to standard specification requirements for edible refined rice bran oil.

Efficient technology is therefore available for production of food grade high quality rice bran for extraction and refining edible oil. However, as there are several stabilization systems and designs[2] there is an urgent need for reliable data on techno-economic feasibility of existing stabilizing alternatives, considering prevailing local conditions, to guide decision makers in the most appropriate selection.

No commercial process is operating for the industrial production of protein from rice bran although promising laboratory and pilot plant scale processes have been developed. Approaches consist in: a) isolation of proteins and/or protein rich particles, and b) removal of fiber-richer particles. Both dry and wet methods have been used. They have been reviewed recently[2]. Protein concentrates with different chemical composition (up to 90 % protein and less than 1 % fiber) have been prepared from either raw bran or defatted bran by different alkaline-extraction procedures and conditions, involving heat or acid precipitation of protein from the solubilized material[7,11]. In a Japanese process bran is ground in water, solids are separated by centrifugation and a protein-oil mixture is separated from the colloidal solution by chemical coagulation[12]. A Spanish process characterized by selective grinding and particle size classification all in water medium, extracts a relatively high-protein (around 15–20 percent) flour with a fiber content of about 3 percent, in yields of about 50–60 percent[5]. Another Japanese process, intended to be attached in the conventional rice bran oil production system, involves grinding of bran and fractional sedimentation in n-hexane. A concentrate of about 22 percent protein and 4 percent fiber is obtained[13].

Major constraints for development and expansion of food-grade protein flours, concentrates and isolates from rice bran are the additional energy requirements in the processes, especially drying costs, the large proportion of secondary fractions of feed grade value and the consumer acceptability which will be dealt with later. Meanwhile substantial improvements come, prospects are limited. Dry fractionation processes yield fractions with slightly increased protein content, high in fiber, and low yields. Solution is to be found in the serial removal of very thin bran fractions with significantly different anatomo-histological composition through improved milling machinery and techniques.

Bran has a light tan colour and a characteristic bland flavor that easily turns rancid, bitter and sour if not stabilized. Compounds responsible for the characteristic odor and taste are not known. Relevant contributions have been made recently[8]. Among 270 compounds detected, of which 170 were identified, 4-vinylguaiacol and 4-vinylphenol were reported to be main components in the characteristic flavor of cooked bran. Recently developed bran products like full-fat and defatted defibered brans and protein concentrates, are blander in flavor and lighter in colour than raw bran. They have a reasonable good keeping quality. However after 5 minutes cooking in water they become browner and both bran and bran products are similar in color. Heating also enhances flavor. Flavor and colour deserve much research. They are still major constraints in consumer acceptance, limiting to low levels the proportion of bran and bran products in formulated foods.

Nutrients in bran have been extensively investigated. This is not the case with bran products although some essential information (amino acid composition, PER, enzyme inhibitors) is available[2]. In general, there is a lack of data concerning availability of nutrients and nutritional value based on animal tests.

Extensive data on functional properties including protein extractability and solubility, water and fat absorption, emulsifying and foaming capacities and rheological characteristics of water pastes of bran and bran flours, protein concentrates and isolates have been accumulated in recent years[3,6]. Results of model tests have not been evaluated in predicting performance in real food systems—bread is an exception. In general, functional properties did not show remarkable values. Some bran fractions, however, combine interesting properties. A defatted bran high-fiber fraction showed water absorption capacity similar to that of commercially available soya bean 70% protein concentrate (which is around 270) along with low protein solubility (NSI = 5) and fat absorption capacity around 2.5 times that of the soya bean concentrate (which is around 105). The fraction seems promising for meat products. Stabilized bran and defibered bran were successfully incorporated at various replacement levels in wheat flour breads. French type bread with bran compared favourably with breads formulated with rye-wheat flour mixes of consolidated market in Europe.

In summary, many problems remain to be solved before an extensive use of the full potential of bran and bran fractions in formulated foods is achieved. But prospects are good. Research and industry, in a parallel effort, should place emphasis on improving bran quality for edible oil production as this is a key step in the food processing chain of bran. Simultaneously, new or improved processes for preparation of bran fractions of low cost and high consumer acceptability should be sought.

REFERENCES

1. Barber, S. and Benedito de Barber, C., 1976. An approach to the objective measurement of the degree of milling, *RPEC Reporter*. Vol. 2, no. 2. 1–8.
2. Barber, S. and Benedito de Barber, C. Rice bran: Chemistry and technology. In: Rice: Production and utilization, B. S. Luh (ed.), Chapter 24. Avi Publishing Co., Inc., Westport, Conn., USA (in press).
3. Barber, S., Benedito de Barber, C. and Martinez, J., 1978. Potential value of rice bran fractions as protein foods ingredients. Presented at: 5th International Congress of Food Science and Technology. Kyoto, Japan, 17–22 September.
4. Barber, S., Pineda, J. A. and Benedito de Barner, C. Histochemistry of commercial rice bran. Presented at the Congress of the Royal Spanish Society of Physics and Chemistry, 75 Anniversary, 2–7 October, 1978, Madrid, Spain.
5. Barber, S., Flors, A., Tortosa, E., Camacho, J. M. and Cerni, R. 1977. High protein flours from rice bran by wet fractionation process. In: Proceedings Rice By-products Utilization, International Conference, Valencia, 1974. Vol. IV. Rice Bran Utilization: Food and Feed. S. Barber and E. Tortosa (eds.), Inst. Agr. Tecnol. Alimentos. Valencia, Spain.
6. Barber, S. and Maquieira, A. 1977. Rice bran proteins. I. Extractability of protein of raw and heat-stabilized bran. Rev. Agr. Tecnol. Alimentos, 17/2, 209–222 (in Spanish, English summary).
7. Connor, M. A., Saunders, R. M. and Kohler, G. O. 1977. Preparation and properties of protein concentrates obtained by wet alkaline processing of rice bran. In: Proceedings Rice By-products Utilization, International Conference, Valencia, 1974. Vol. IV. Rice Bran Utilization: Food and Feed. S. Barber and E. Tortosa (Editors). Inst. Agr. Tecnol. Alimentos. Valencia, Spain.
8. Kato, H., Tsugita, T., Kurata, T. and Fujimaki, M., 1978. Volatile components of rice and rice bran. Presented at: 5th International Congress of Food Science and Technology, Kyoto, Japan, 17–22 September.
9. Koga, Y., 1969. Rice milling. In: Drying, husking and milling in Japan, 25–40, Japan Agr. Machinery Man. Ass.
10. Luh, B. S. (ed.) Rice: Production and utilization. Avi Publishing Co., Inc., Westport, Conn., USA (in press).
11. Lynn, L., 1969. Edible rice bran foods. In: Protein-enriched cereal foods for world needs, 154–172. M. Milner, (ed.). Am. Ass. Cereal Chem., Inc., St. Paul. Minn. USA.
12. Mihara, S., 1970. Nakataki water process separating rice bran components. Chem. Ec. Eng. Rev., 36–38, 42.
13. Mitsuda, H., Kawai, F., Suzuki, A. and Honjo, J., 1977. Studies on the production of a protein-rich fraction from rice bran by means of fractional sedimentation in *n*-hexane. In: Rice Report 1976. S. Barber, H. Mitsuda, H. S. R. Desikachar and E. Tortosa (Editors). IUFoST Working Party on Rice Utilization. Inst. Agr. Tecnol. Alimentos, Valencia, Spain.

14. Mitsuda, H., Yasumoto, K., Murakami, K., Kusano, T. and Kishida, H. 1967. Studies on the proteinaceous subcellular particles in rice endosperm: electron microscopy and isolation. Agr. Biol. Chem. (Tokyo), 31/3, 293–300.

15. Ogawa, M., Tanaka, K. and Kasai, Z. 1975. Isolation of high phytin containing particles from rice grains using an aqueous polymer two phase system. Agr. Biol. Chem., 39/3, 695–700.

16. Pillaiyar, P., Chandrasekaran, R., Narayanasamy, R. V., Kutharathulla, K. Md. and Ramachandran, K. Low cost modernisation of huller rice mills for the production of High quality bran and its stabilisation. Proceedings of the Seminar on Edible Rice Bran Oil, 9–15, Bombay, India, 25 November 1977.

17. Tanaka, K., Yoshida, T., Asada, K. and Kasai, Z. 1973. Subcellular particles isolated from aleurone layer of rice seeds. Arch. Biochem. and Biophys., 155, 136–143.

18. Unido. 1977. Seminar on Oils and Fats Insdustry. Madrid. December.

3.5 Small Capacity Rice Bran Oil Extraction Plants

Horst R. Koenig*

3.5.1 THE RAW MATERIAL "RICE BRAN"

Nearly all of the oil contained in the rice kernel is concentrated in the germ, pericarp and polish, commonly forming the "rice bran". The composition of rice bran thus depends on the intial paddy composition and to a high degree on the particular rice milling technology used.

With an average oil content of 15%, rice bran is, in principle, a valuable raw material for vegetable oil production. Naturally occurring enzymes liberated at the moment of separation of the bran layers from the kernels, however, cause rapid hydroysis of the rice bran oil resulting in a rapid increase in its FFA value.

3.5.2 RICE BRAN OIL AND MEAL

Crude rice bran oil is dark brown to greenish-yellow in color and contains pigments such as carotenes and chlorophyll. Oxidation, particularly in the presence of iron, can render the color resistant to normal bleaching methods.

The relatively low linolenic acid content (0.5–1.0%) gives rice bran oil a distinct advantage over cottonseed or soya oil. From this viewpoint, rice bran oil compares favorably with other "soft oils" if it is carefully produced and refined.

The high content of wax (up to 9%) in crude rice bran oil and the normally high FFA value make the oil refining process difficult and may lead to high refining losses. The wax, therefore, needs to be removed during the first stage (dewaxing) of the refining process. Although purified rice bran wax can be used as a carnauba wax replacer, it has not yet become a competitive trade commodity.

Deoiled rice bran meal (12–14% protein) is a most suitable animal feed component despite its fibrous structure. Its lower energy content compared to crude bran is compensated for by its stability and easy handling.

* Industrial Operations Division, United Nations Industrial Development Organization, P.O.Box 837, A 1011, Vienna, Austria

3.5.3 THE RICE BRAN SITUATION

Rice milling operations in most paddy producing countries are predominantly post-harvesting activities and can hardly be considered to constitute an industry. Milled rice is normally produced as the only main product and little attention is paid to the concurrent production of quality rice bran. As a result of this situation, numerous small capacity, technically inefficient rice milling units have been set up that produce white rice and leave a mixture of bran, husk and impurities which is completely unsuitable as a raw material for the production of rice bran oil and quality protein meal. A precondition for optimum utilization of rice bran is thus the improvement of the rice milling industry's structure combined with techno-economic up-dating.

3.5.4 THE RICE BRAN PROCESSING PROBLEM

When discussing small capacity rice bran oil extraction plants, two basic factors require consideration. These are the suitability of such plants in view of the existing rice bran raw material situation, and the principle techno-economic requirements of rice bran processing operations. Little doubt exists that efficient rice bran processing operations for the production of rice bran oil require solvent extraction. Solvent extraction plants, however, follow the principle of economy of scale. This techno-economic fact conflicts with the limited quantities of quality rice bran raw material that can generally be made available. The particular situation which results, combined with the usually very high FFA content of the rice bran, may represent the main reason for the global underutilization of rice bran for the production of edible oil. The capacity of rice bran solvent extraction plants or their location is thus not the root problem. Rather, development of the rice bran oil industry is hampered by the nature of the rice bran itself: it has first to be converted into an acceptable vegetable oil raw material with regard to both quality and quantity.

3.5.5 RICE BRAN STABILIZATION

The application of suitable rice bran stabilization techniques appears to be a very promising method in this respect. Stabilization, i.e. inactivation of the enzymes that cause hydrolysis, needs to take place at the rice mill and should form an integrated part of its operation. Suitable stabilization equipment must be developed and adjusted to individual rice milling conditions, the principle criteria being small capacity, husk fuelling, continuous operation with minimal of labour attendance, and simple design with limited maintenance and repair requirements. The success of a rice bran stabilization operation stands and falls on its economic feasibility. Low FFA rice bran is required that can be sold more favorably by the rice miller and yet to remain competitive for the solvent extractor.

3.5.6 Solvent Extraction Technology

While no preparatory cell rupturing operations are needed, rice bran requires pelletization prior to extraction in continuous countercurrent extraction plants. Hexane (inflammable!) is the most effective solvent. Although modern solvent extraction plants have a high degree of technical processing security, certain safety measures must be carefully observed and implemented by trained operation personnel.

The hexane dissolves the oil from the bran, thereby forming "miscella" (20–25% oil). In special continuous vacuum distillation units, the solvent is separated from the oil in several stages and recycled to the extractor. The crude rice bran oil should immediately be cleaned and dewaxed. Only filtered and dewaxed oil should be forwarded to the refinery. Long intermediate oil storage in mild steel tanks should be avoided.

The extracted rice bran pellets which remain rather stable during the hexane treatment are de-solventized until they are completely free of solvent. The recovered hexane is recycled to the extractor. The pellets are dried, cooled and (if required) milled. They are light-brown in color, have a pleasant "nutty" smell, and are easily stored and transported.

3.5.7 Continuous Percolation Type Extractors

The solvent or miscella, respectively, is spread on a stationary bed of rice bran pellets through which it percolates. The pellet bed acts as a filter by retaining unavoidable fines. No additional miscella filtration equipment is normally required. The miscella when leaving the extractor is, however, not completely free of fines and the condensers and coolers of the oil and meal desolventizing units should be equipped with removable pipe packages to facilitate cleaning. Modern percolation type extractors are suitable for rice bran oil extraction.

3.5.8 Continuous Immersion Type Extractors

The rice bran pellets need to be moved counter-current to the solvent and miscella flow through the extractor. A certain "washing" effect takes place and the unavoidable friction partially damages the pellets. A considerable amount of fines is necessarily produced and no self-filtration by a stationary pellet bed is possible. The miscella must therefore pass an additional filtration unit prior to distillation. Miscella filtration units are usually difficult to handle (solvent!) and cause higher solvent losses. The filtered miscella is, however, almost free of fines and virtually no problems normally arise with the coolers and condensers.

3.5.9 BATCH EXTRACTORS

Batch extraction plants are now technically and economically outdated installations. However, some plants are still in operation in developing countries, predominantly processing rice bran. For quite some time batch extraction plants were—rightly—considered the only type of plant that could process rice bran with its characteristic fine particle structure and could also be operated on a small scale. This situation has, however, been changed by new technical developments and economic considerations which one can no longer ignore.

3.5.10 THE RICE BRAN PELLETIZING PROCESS

The production of crude bran pellets prior to extraction must be carefully executed by conditioning, pelletization and pellet drying. The most effective size for the pellets is 3 mm in diameter. Larger pellets permit a capacity increase but exert an unfavorable influence on the extraction. While "white" bran can easily be pelletized, difficulties are met with parboiled bran. Stable pellets also cannot be easily produced from stabilized (heated) bran. Additional applied research is thus still required on the pelletizing properties of the various rice bran varieties.

3.5.11 MECHANICAL PRESSING OF RICE BRAN

The common design of mechanical screw presses is not suitable for rice bran processing because the fine particle structure of the bran makes it difficult to build up the required pressure sufficiently quickly. Even if a new technically suitable press design can be developed, intensive conditioning (cooking) of the bran will be necessary with all its unfavorable effects on production costs and product quality. The residual oil content of the press cakes can hardly be expected to be lower than 5–7%, indicating a production yield of only about 50%. The considerable wear and tear problems and high electric energy consumption of screw presses also hardly make mechanical pressing of rice bran a desirable processing method.

3.5.12 CONCLUSION

Appropriate utilization of the large global amounts of rice bran for the production of edible oil constitutes a very complex problem. It must begin with techno-economic improvement of the rice milling sector and end with efficient production of edible oil and protein feed meal not to mention food. The setting-up of viable smaller capacity single purpose rice bran oil extraction plants may be called for under very special circumstances. The more promising rice bran utilization method, however, appears to involve stabilization at the rice mill and processing of the stabilized rice bran in modern multi-purpose solvent extraction plants combined with oil refining operations. The crucial point is undoubtedly the initial conversion of the by-product rice bran into a quality product obtainable from rice mills as an acceptable raw material for the vegetable oil industry.

Subplenary Sessions

Main Topic II: Safety and Nutritional Aspects of Food

1. Food Safety
2. Nutritional Aspects of Food Processing

1. Food Safety

1.1 Problems Associated with Evaluating Food Safety

A. C. Kolbye, Jr.* and R. M. Schaffner*

I will attempt to provide an overview of some of the food safety problems we in FDA have faced in the past and will continue to face in the future.

Toxicology, as you know, has its roots in forensics. Earlier, the question was whether or not a substance could cause death and at what levels. Acute toxicity was the major index of measurement. The earlier laws incorporated the poisonous *per se* doctrine, but it became clear to toxicologists that this doctrine would lead to inappropriate restrictions on many beneficial substances such as pesticides which were intrinsically toxic and yet were required and useful compounds. Studies were designed in which varying doses were employed and duration of exposures increased. Longer term feeding studies were undertaken and throughout the 1950's, various feeding studies were conducted using relatively small numbers of animals at that time when our abilities to measure chemicals in substances ranged in the parts per thousands. The major aim of such studies was to identify and quantify toxic effects in terms of ascertaining dose levels below which no adverse or toxic effects occurred. Carcinogenicity was considered as one of the parameters to be investigated rather than as a goal unto itself. As we entered the turbulent 60's, various legislation was enacted creating profound effects on the field of toxicology. FIFRA[1] and the laws concerning food and color additives[2] clearly placed the burden of proof of safety on the manufacturer. Substances found to induce cancer were prohibited from intentional addition to the food supply if those substances fell under the legal classification of food and color additives.

The DES clause[3,4] enacted by Congress in 1962 created an exception to

* Bureau of Foods, Food and Drug Administration, 200C St., S.W., Washington, D.C. 20204, USA

the Delaney Amendment[4,5] and established the principle that carcinogenic drugs could be used legally in food-producing animals provided they did not harm the treated animal and provided that no residue was detectable by an analytical method approved by the Secretary.

In the 60's, long–term feeding studies became a more pronounced requirement to support the safety of direct food and color additives and exploratory investigations were undertaken in the field of mutagenesis and teratology. Multigeneration reproduction studies had been done selectively since the 1950's, but following the PSAC[6] recommendation that they be done for all pesticides having a tolerance limit on foods, these studies were required by the FDA in the early 1970's. At the same time, greater emphasis was given to the safety of metabolites of drugs used in food-producing animals.

In the 70's, associations were established between the potential properties of a chemical to induce mutagenic and carcinogenic effects. At the same time, efforts in preventive medicine to achieve greater control of cardiovascular and pulmonary diseases had the effect of decreasing mortality in middle-aged people, thus contributing to a longer life span. Greater numbers of people lived to older age. As the denominator of the population in the older age range increased, more people then fell victim to the onslaught from cancer, although the cancer rates, with the exception of lung cancer, have generally remained remarkably stable[7]. However, greater evidence became available that occupational exposures to certain chemicals were associated with an increased risk of cancer. The National Cancer Institute embarked upon a major program of testing chemicals and a number of these "cancer bioassays" came out positive. Politicians, the press, and consumer advocates became increasingly concerned about cancer. Some epidemiologists stated the proposition that 80 or 90 percent of cancer is related to environmental factors, including personal habits. Some advocates make the allegation that most cancer is related to chemicals in the environment and it has become fashionable to say that food and color additives are primary culprits in this regard. The cases of vaginal adenocarcinoma in some daughters of women who had received substantial therapeutic doses of DES during pregnancy drew further attention to chemical carcinogenesis, as did the controversies concerning cyclamates and saccharin.

The expected response of government has been to increase its requirements for proving safety with respect to potential carcinogenic effects. The recent passage of the Toxic Substances Act in the wake of PCB and PBB[8] has intensified pressures on manufacturers to perform safety testing prior to marketing chemicals.

Concern with the beta error of statistics (that of failing to detect a true positive because of limitations on sample size) in relation to animal feeding studies, combined with the concern of experts about radiation–induced cancer, have led to the hypothesis of the "one–hit" phenomenon: that relatively low exposure levels to chemicals will still be associated with the induction of cancer in humans, and thus, a "no threshold" policy continues in force today.

Some scientists now claim that positive mutagenesis tests are sufficient to identify a chemical as a carcinogen. Both regulatory agencies and manufacturers are actively exploring usage of short-term tests to identify potential carcinogens because limitations on testing resources will not permit long-term animal feeding studies for all substances of interest. Pressures on regulatory agencies to adopt mutagenic testing for decision-making purposes to restrict potential carcinogens are mounting day-by-day.

With that overview, I would recommend that we re-explore some rather fundamental considerations that pertain to semantics and law. The word "safety" is an everyday word that appears also in various statutory language. We all use the word, but frequently the word is misused and abused. We really are talking about a concept embodied in a word which means different things to different people and, in turn, the word is used with the force of law not only by a variety of regulatory agencies in different ways but also in the courts. The word essentially represents a value judgment when used as an adjective: something is safe or it is not. The value judgement represents some process of weighing risks and when something is safe, the risk for harm is considered acceptable. Most people do not use conscious criteria but appear to make comparisons with their viewpoints on other factors they have experienced in life, such as their chances of injury from riding in automobiles as compared to riding in an airplane. Whenever the term "risk" is used, it creates an emotional impact which includes fear. While all would like to live a risk-free life, most of us recognize that to live life is to live with the risks that are involved with the reality of everyday life. We accept certain risks essentially because we have to and not because we want to. If we are mature, we are willing to recognize conceptually that there is no such thing as absolute safety (i.e., absolutely zero risk), if there is any statistical chance of exposure to a potential source of harm. We all have to eat and few of us have ever experienced any recognized toxicity from foods unless we include gastrointestinal upsets from bacterial or viral causation and allergic or intolerance reactions to food ingredients. And thus, the desire of all of us is to have safe and nutritious food to eat. A worthy desire, but what does the term "food safety" embody? Again the answer depends on the value judgments of each person, and the subconscious desire is to be risk-free as much as possible. Most people have no meaningful scale of reference to compare issues dealing with food safety, and thus, when they learn that experimental animals become ill or die from certain exposures to test substances, their reaction is one of concern and fear. Toxicologists know that "the dose makes the poison" and that all substances in food are potentially toxic if exposure levels are high enough. Hence all foods, be they composed entirely of natural ingredients or contain added substances (whether the additives are natural or man-made), are also potentially toxic.

In most instances, if normal eating habits are practiced, overt toxicity never occurs because the exposure to the particular food component is below the range of the susceptibility of particular individuals to untoward reactions to the potential toxicities involved. Some people have greater susceptibility than others and if the exposure is increased, there is an increasing probability of an untoward reaction occurring in some of the more sensitive people.

And so, we have three fundamental parameters involved in food safety: *potential toxicity, exposure,* and *susceptibility.* Absolutely precise information is never available for any of the three parameters involved because each parameter involves a quantum of information generated or estimated under the influence of probability theory, and thus, considerations dealing with statistical extremes enter into the picture. Extreme-case "what if" questions are raised. What if a sensitive person received a substantial exposure to a particular food component? Will his or her range of susceptibility be invaded by that exposure? These questions can only be answered in terms of a value judgement predicated on other value judgments concerning potential toxicity, exposure, and susceptibility which, in turn, involve interpretation of complex toxicological data, if available. Insight into exposure and susceptibility is gained by studying the dose-response relationships involved in experimental or epidemiological data. I use the term "if available" because there is very little or no toxicological data available for most natural foods and their natural components which include many potentially toxic natural chemicals never characterized nor evaluated for safety. Largely by trial and error throughout prehistory and history, we humans have learned about the safety of food and its nutritional value. The public-at-large has never given conscious recognition to this fact, but instead has been captivated by "natural food fads" and motivated to fear and concern over the safety of our food by the "instant toxicologists" and "instant nutritionists" in the information media, including the press. As a result, many secondary markets have been created that capitalize and thrive financially on misinformation or information-out-of-context.

Any value judgment is easy to attack, hence, any judgment concerning food safety can be attacked by questioning the reliability, relevance, and completeness of the data concerning toxicity, exposure, and susceptibility. Thus, we come to the "*safe/not safe*" confrontation which is frequently presented to the public-at-large as an "either/or" semantical proposition:

either something is safe or it is not safe. In actuality, there is frequently a huge expanse of middle ground between the two extremes. What is poorly understood is the distinction created by the food additives legistlation of 1958 and subsequent laws which essentially shifted the burden of proof to industry instead of FDA: industry was now required to provide data demonstrating safety under proposed conditions of use to FDA's satisfaction before approval for use could be granted. As expected, especially in the context of the revolutionary biomedical and scientific issues rapidly emerging in the last two decades, regulatory agencies asked more and more questions which required satisfactory answers before the government institution issued a particular pronouncement of food safety. Consequently, the steeplechase that faced the food industry became more and more difficult. If the water-jumps and hedges proved too difficult to surmount in good style, institutionalized approval was withheld. A proposed usage can be deemed "not demonstrated to be safe" and accordingly, become subjectable to attack by other parties as being "unsafe". Therein is described a major problem. The point of it all is this: just because the full burden of demonstrating safety was not satisfied before approval for use can be granted does not *ipso facto* mean that such exposure is necessarily dangerous to human health. The safe/not safe spectrum of considerations when compressed into an either/or framework contributes substantially to public confusion and hysteria.

All value judgments about "so-called" safe exposures should encompass a margin of safety to compensate for the unusual sensitivity of certain humans, and for some errors of translating animal data into safety judgments for humans. A relevant question then becomes: what should the margin of safety be before granting approval for use in the food supply? How should we categorize potential hazards to public health, and which criteria should be applied to a particular potential hazard? Some advocates demand the equivalent of a "zero tolerance" for all substances demonstrated to induce cancer or mutagenic changes without considering the full implications involved that could affect many activities of mankind.

As far as intentional additives to food are concerned, there is major disagreement concerning some of the critical aspects of safety testing and the interpretation of results. Should the maximum tolerated dose approach be used for all cancer bioassays or should modifications be made when anticipated human exposure is very low? Are all substances that can be demonstrated to contribute to increases in the incidence of cancer observed in test animals as compared to controls necessarily carcinogens *per se*? What about modifiers and promoters of carcinogenesis that may not be carcinogenic *per se*?[7] The Delaney philosophy currently embodied in various sections of the Food, Drug, and Cosmetic Act essentially has been interpreted to require the banning of all intentional additives except drugs in food-producing animals if such additives have been demonstrated to induce cancer: the exception for animal drugs requires that no residue be detectable in foods. What about residues of carcinogenic animal drugs that appear to be firmly bound to macromolecules in the tissue of recipient animals? Currently, we are approaching that problem on a total residue basis, but additional data are needed to clarify whether or not potential hazards can be expected when such molecular binding is involved. The various extrapolation models that have been constructed to estimate human risk from dose-response data generated in animal feeding experiments rely more on mathematical statistics than biological science but they appear to be the "only game in town". A modified Mantel-Bryan[9] model is now being employed by FDA to determine what detection capabilities should be required of an analytical method for a carcinogenic drug used in food animals to satisfy the no-detectable-residue requirements of the Act. A linear extrapolation model may be adopted shortly to supplant the Mantel-Bryan model. Such models generally assume that the same mechanisms involved with cancer induction in animals exposed to biologically substantial doses also operate at much lower dose levels. This philosophy has been generated in keeping with the precept that there is no such thing as a "safe" exposure to a carcinogen which, in turn, was largely generated by scientists concerned with radiation-induced cancer. The models differ mathematically and thus a linear extrapolation model may predict a higher cancer incidence for a given exposure than would, for example, a probit model. A major problem is that none of these hypothetical models is testable by animal experiments although efforts are underway at the National Center for Toxicological Research to explore low dose effects. Such information would be very helpful as would more information concerning potential interactive effects. Concern has been expressed that low-level exposures to a variety of substances in the environment may, in the aggregate, have a pronounced influence on the incidence of human cancer. Just as we know that some interactions can be synergistic as far as toxicity is concerned, we know that protective interactions also take place. Further exploration is needed in this area.

The last two decades brought dramatic improvements in the ability of analytical chemists to detect smaller and smaller amounts of a particular substance in a food matrix. Detection levels went from parts per thousand to parts per trillion in the "blink of an eye" when considered in perspective of human history. A whole new world suddenly became visible. We can now detect substances that migrate from packaging or that occur naturally or as environmental contaminants in food with increasing accuracy for every-decreasing amounts. And so, more and more "chemicals" are found in foods. The public becomes further confused by the legal distinction between substances purposefully added to foods (intentional additives) and those not intentionally present in foods. The latter include indirect or incidental additives and environmental or natural contaminants.

The substances that can transfer to food during processing and packaging are called indirect or incidental additives and usually occur in very small quantities in only those foods processed or packaged in a particular way. FDA requires safety data concerning such substances prior to approval for use but if anticipated human exposure is very low, less safety data are likely to be required unless there is reason to suspect unusual toxicity or carcinogenicity.

Trichloroethylene, vinyl chloride monomer, and acrylonitrile are examples of recent problems in this category. Concern has been expressed over whether our society can afford to always treat unintentional additives present in low levels in certain food products in the same way as intentional additives if the former additives are potentially carcinogenic when tested at substantial dosage levels in animals. Some uses of chemicals are deemed technologically very important by the food processing and food packaging industries—such as particular solvents and polymers. There is a finite number of chemicals in particular categories to choose from, and sudden prohibitions on using some chemicals could have far-reaching technological consequences and adverse impacts on the consumption of energy. Similar concerns have been raised with regard to the availability of drugs for use in food-producing animals. FDA is not permitted to evaluate the societal benefits when making a determination of safety for a food additive whether the additive is direct or indirect. Until better experiments in animals are performed to elucidate the biological mechanisms of chemical carcinogenesis, FDA would still have difficulty in evaluating risks for cancer and the so-called risk-benefit equations for additives would be difficult to resolve.

When environmental contaminants such as PCBs and PBBs get into the food supply, major problems arise because there is no magic wand to wave to eliminate the problem. You cannot prohibit addition to food because it is already present. The only immediate recourse is for FDA to ban certain foods from interstate commerce and to provide public health advice and estimates of risk to State authorities with jurisdiction over intrastate food commerce and non-commercial sources of foods such as sport fishing. FDA bears a heavy legal and scientific burden in this regard. We have to *prove potential danger to health* and are required to consider adverse impacts on the availability of food in view of the pre-existent contamination. Our limited resources to rapidly mount comprehensive scientific investigations into the chemistry and toxicity of such contaminants are stressed in view of the many competing priorities for our energies. The lack of certain data when preliminary decisions have to be made to protect public health is frequently used against FDA by those who disagree on where the line should be drawn as far as action levels are concerned. Many questions arise concerning toxicity and potential carcinogenicity as well as exposure and human susceptibility. The public frequently infers risk from lack of hard data especially when "experts" have opinions at variance with one or another. Since FDA cannot require safety data from the food industry, FDA has to evaluate all available data on the chemistry and toxicity, make epidemiological judgments as to the degree of risk presented by potential exposures, and perform additional investigations where required. Disagreements over the interpretation and emphasis placed on particular data are compounded by semantical confusion as to the distinctions concerning "safe", "not-shown-to-be-safe", "not safe", "unsafe", "degree of risk or hazard", "threat to health", "hazardous", and "dangerous".

Aflatoxins are potent carcinogens produced by molds growing in grain used for human food or to feed food-producing animals. Such molds thrive under certain conditions of temperature and humidity and prevention of mold growth can be difficult or impossible to attain under such conditions in fields or in stores. If a "no detectable residue" philosophy against carcinogens in food were to be required for foods containing PCBs or a-flatoxins, a very significant disruption of the American food supply would result because much grain, milk, meat, eggs, and fish would have to be condemned. Fortunately, most human exposure to such contaminants in this country is not at systematically high levels. Enforcement of FDA action levels "trims off" the more substantial exposures and the expected frequency of ingesting food-servings actually containing residues is in most instances very low as long as the diet is reasonably well-balanced. Clearly we prefer that no such residues be present in food, but reality dictates some toleration of risk although such risk is not precisely quantifiable. Will such exposures "cause" or "induce" cancer in humans exposed to such residues?

We now come to another term that creates many semantical problems: the word "*cause*". Again this word is frequently used in a variety of imprecise ways. If one observation is made in conjunction with another parameter, the true descriptor of that relationship is "association", not cause *per se*. Causation in terms of biomedical science has been described by Koch's postulates and more recently in the 1964 Surgeon General's Report on Smoking[11]. If one delves into the depths of knowledge and ignorance concerning the etiology of chronic diseases in humans, one appreciates that many diseases involve multiple "risk factors". These risk factors may act independently or dependently, i.e., obesity and hypertension are two recognized risk factors for atherosclerotic cerebro-cardio-vascular disease but obesity may to some degree influence hypertension, although not always. It is likely that a variety of risk factors contribute to the etiology of cancer in humans. When one looks at dose-response curves for the incidence of cancer in test animals, some distinction should be made between responses at biologically substantial doses as compared to much smaller doses. Why? Because each dose-response curve is saying something about biological susceptibility of animals to cancer induction. Animals with increased susceptibility, i.e., responsive to relatively low doses of the test substance in question, are more likely to have other factors operating in the total causation pattern of cancer. The increased biological susceptibility should be explored on the basis of genetics, constitutional development, comparative metabolism, or concurrent disease processes (based on infection, toxic co-factors or nutritional abnormalities). This is *not* to say that all carcinogens operate or are influenced by the same mechanisms; thus low-level exposures should not be dismissed lightly. But the converse does not appear to be necessarily true either: not all low-level exposures to carcinogens appear to be equally dangerous to human health. In this context, we currently label as carcinogens most substances that when fed to animals are associated with increases in observed tumors. We tend to say that they "caused" cancer when in fact such may not always necessarily be true, although in fact they may have "modified" the incidence of observed tumors. We do know that substantial human exposures to certain chemicals administered as human drugs or present in occupational environments have been strongly associated with human cancer. The same can be said for substantial exposures to inhaled cigarette smoke and ingested alcohol as well as for over-nutrition in the form of obesity.

The point here is that greater perspective must be attained with regard to estimating the factorial (or vectorial) strength of all exposures likely to affect the etiology of cancer. You will recall much of the testimony before Congress supporting the proposition that there is no such thing as a "safe" exposure to a carcinogen. The implication is made that because a precise determination of safety has not been made, therefore any exposure to any "carcinogen" is dangerous to human health. Such may or may not be the case depending upon the particular substances and whether or not carcinogenically active molecules are proximate to susceptible biological targets. Good answers are lacking at the present time and thus we are in status quo. This is a real problem upon us now and likely to contribute greatly to prolonged scientific and public confusion because needed research is not being done to the extent desirable.

We need better answers to the questions that follow. Should we label

as carcinogenic risks to health all extraneous factors that can modify up-
wards the incidence of cancer in test animals as compared to controls? Or
are there risk factors that can modify the expression of cancer (and non-
cancer diseases) that should not necessarily be deemed carcinogens? How
does one evaluate susceptibility to cancer and factors that may increase
susceptibility but that are not carcinogenic *per se*? Can some of these
factors create greater risks for cancer induction as compared to certain exposures to substances labeled as carcinogens?

Are the toxicological characteristics (of a substance deemed carcinogenic) of importance when assessing cancer risk? What about fat soluble
compounds with long biological half-lives in the mammalian body? What
about compounds that induce enzymatic changes? What about substances
that can easily penetrate body barriers without deactivation as compared
to compounds that respond to some of the biological defense mechanisms?
What about substances that pass through the placenta or enter breast
milk? What about substances that induce increases in cancer in test animals that are also mutagenic as compared to those substances that are negative for mutagenesis? Or are all substances equally carcinogenic in the
sense of presenting equal risks for cancer induction in humans?

Are all exposure routes for a given carcinogen equally dangerous? If no
"safe level" can be found, does this mean that any exposure to any carcinogen presents the same degree of danger or anticipated hazard to human
health? Or are certain exposure patterns of greater risk than others?

Are carcinogenic substances that, when tested in animals, have steep
slopes of the dose-response curve in the observed experimental range,
tantamount to being more powerful carcinogens and hence of greater risk
to human health? Or do the so-called weak carcinogens or those of flat
slope present the same degree of risk as the so-called strong carcinogens?

How do dose-response observations from experimental data have
relevance to predicting hazards to human health? Which mathematical
extrapolation models have relevance to which situations and when? What
assumptions underlie each model? Should mathematical extrapolations be
modeled only on radiation and radiomimetic substances? How does our
knowledge of biology and toxicology influence our choices? Do extrapola-
tive mathematical projections within a species provide informational judgments that can be trans erred to humans whose exposure pattern may differ
substantially from the experimental dosing regimen in animals? What
about repair phenomena between intermittent exposures? Extrapolation
models have implications that involve allocating national resources for
public health. Does everyfexposure to every "carcinogen" have to be
minimized to infinitesimal levels in order to minimize cancer risk to an
acceptable level?

If safety is construed as being of acceptable risk, or the absence of a certain level of expected hazard to health, then how much safety evidence is needed to prove acceptable risk? How much evidence is needed to make risk judgments as to the severity of the hazard if it can occur and the probability that it will occur as a result of a given pattern of exposure to the substance in question?

Risk assessment operates in the public arena—and is influenced by social values. Honesty about the strengths and limitations of our current scientific capabilities or lack thereof must prevail. Misperceptions of risk can occur both by scientists and by the public at large due to misinformation or the lack of accurate information concerning overall perspective. We all face inherent and competing risks in life. Our ability to ask relevant questions about safety must be placed in the context of our ability to provide relevant answers in timely fashion.

REFERENCES

1. Federal Environmental Pesticide Control Act of 1972 (86 Stat. 973, 40 U. S. Code).
2. Federal Food, Drug, and Cosmetic Act As Amended, Sections 409, 706 (21 U. S. Code, 348, 376).
3. FD&C Act, Section 512(d) (1) (H), (21 U. S. Code, 360 (b)).
4. FD&C Act, Section 409 (c) (3) (A), (21 U. S. Code 348).
5. FD&C Act, Section 706 (b) (5) (B), (21 U. S. Code 376).
6. President's Science Advisory Committee, 1963, *Use of Pesticides*, Government Printing Office, Washington, D. C.
7. Kolbye, A., Cancer in Humans: Exposures and Responses in a Real World, *Oncology*, **33**: 90–100 (1976).
8. Final Report of the Subcommittee on the Health Effects of Polychlorinated Biphenyls and Polybrominated Biphenyls, July 1976, Department of Health, Education, and Welfare, Washington, D. C., *Environmental Health Perspectives*, **24**, (June 1978).
9. Mantel, N., and Bryan, W. R., "Safety Testing of Carcinogenic Agents," National Cancer Institute, 27 (2): 455–470 (1961). Mantel, N., et al., "Improved Mantel.-Bryan Procedure for 'Safety' Testing of Carcinogens," *Cancer Res*, **35**: 865–872 (1975).
10. Guess, H., Crump, K., and Peto, R., "Uncertainty Estimates for Low-Dose-Rate Extrapolations of Animal Carcinogenicity Data," *Cancer Res.* **37**: 3475–3483 (October 1977).
11. *Smoking and Health, Report of the Advisory Committee to the Surgeon General of the Public Health Service*, U. S. Department of Health, Education, and Welfare, Public Health Service, Public Health Service Publication No. 1103.

1.2 Food Safety—Novel Foods

Francis Aylward*

1.2.1 INTRODUCTION

Many of the traditional foods of different regions of the world have never been subjected to modern methods of biological testing. It is known, however, that a number of *natural* or *accepted* food preparations from both plant and animal sources contain toxic materials or anti-nutrients, which may or may not be removed or destroyed in traditional or newer methods of post-harvest treatment. In assessing food safety, we have to use information from biological experimentation and the more refined methods of analysis now available, and also from human experience. This experience is gradually being codified in epidemiological data on the potential relationships of food and other environmental factors to disease in different geographical regions.

Current interest in the safety of novel foods arises because of the wide variety of new food preparations and processes recently introduced in many countries. Because of the speed of introduction—in contrast to a relatively slow diffusion in earlier centuries—there is often little information from human experience, and the food scientist has responsibilities for securing reliable information so that he can (i) advise the food industries and (ii) demonstrate to the consumer that adequate precautions are being taken. International bodies, such as the Committees of the Codex Alimentarious of FAO/WHO and the Commission of the European Economic Community, and many national organisations, are now concerned with the safety of both traditional and novel foods.

Problems relating to new *protein* foods are often stressed, but fats and other products must also be considered.

Attention has to be given not only to *foods* for *direct* human use, but also to *animal feed*, which can modify the flesh or other animal materials (such as milk or eggs) subsequently used as human food.

In this paper we omit from consideration the importance of water supplies and microbiological aspects of food safety, while recognising that

* Queen Elizabeth House, 21, St. Giles, Oxford OX1 3LA, England

140

these require attention at all points in the food chain—during storage, processing and preparation procedures, whether in the factory, restaurant or home.

1.2.2 CLASSIFICATION OF NOVEL FOODS

Throughout recorded history crops and animals have been transferred from one geographical area to another. A crop—or a foodstuff derived therefrom—may be well-established and *normal* in one part of the world, *novel* in another. Thus the *soya bean,* long known in Eastern Asia, has only in the past half-century been extensively cultivated in North America and elsewhere (e.g. in Brazil).

Food *sources* may be classified under three broad divisions: plants, animals and micro-organisms and, in respect to novel foods may be summarised:

- (A) *Plant Materials:* (1) oil seeds;
  - (2) legumes other than oil-seeds;
  - (3) leaves and other chlorophyll containing materials;
  - (4) other land crops;
  - (5) algae and related marine crops.
- (B) *Animal Materials:* (1) meat and products;
  - (2) milk, eggs and products;
  - (3) fish and products.
- (C) *Micro-organisms:* (1) yeasts;
  - (2) fungi;
  - (3) bacteria.

In considering novelty we have to take into account, both the *sources* of foods, and also the *processing and preparation* methods used; there are obvious differences between the traditional methods—often based on fermentation techniques—for the food use of soya in Asia, and the large-scale operations of the modern soya industry. There are even wider contrasts between local methods to produce bakers' or brewers' yeast and the biochemical engineering operations used to obtain microbial protein. The processing techniques may be all-important in determining the composition and structure, the nutritional value and health safety of the food *as eaten*, in contrast to the composition and other properties of *freshly harvested material.*

The different processes used may be summarised under six headings as follows:-

- A. *Extraction* and *refining* including fractionation by physical and chemical techniques.
- B. *Modification* by *chemical* methods—including enzymes.
- C. *Modification* by *physical* and mechanical methods—extrusion and other techniques.

D. *Compounding*—before or after *B.* or *C.*

E. *Preservation* and *processing* by heat treatment, dehydration fermentation and other methods.

F. Kitchen *preparation* (including mixed dishes) and *cooking* procedures.

1.2.3 Foods of Plant Origin

The novelty may consist (i) in introducing a crop for direct human use into a region where it was formerly unknown or (ii) in making or introducing a new product from the crop by relatively simple procedures or (iii) in using a crop—well-established or novel—as the raw material for factory processing operations. With (i) and (ii) human experience may provide a guide to safety; with (iii) there is the need for experimental work on each *source* and each on the *process* used, and for well-defined criteria of quality.

In many countries efforts are being made to introduce new types of food crops which can contribute to the total food resources, provide a more varied diet and supply greater quantities of proteins and/or other nutrients. Even in such relatively simple programmes, attention has to be paid to safety. This can be illustrated from cassava (manioc), many cultivars of which contain a cyano-phoric glycoside. Traditional methods of grating the root, followed by exposure to air, liberates hydrogen cyanide and yields a safe product; deaths have been reported when these precautions are not taken. A programme for cassava should involve therefore (a) the use of cultivars low in the glycoside (b) advice on the treatment of the root on a kitchen or factory scale (c) quality appraisal for manufactured materials.

In industrial preparations from different crops it must be recognised (i) that a processing operation may lead to a concentration of a toxic component in the final product and (ii) that an individual who, for genetic or other reasons (e.g. allergies), avoids a 'fresh' foodstuff may be unable to identify an extracted product. Refined and accurate routine methods of quality appraisal are therefore all-important.

Much research and development work has been carried out on oil seeds; it is known that toxic materials can occur in raw materials (e.g. pesticide residues), during storage (e.g. aflotoxins from mould growth) and during processing (e.g. reactions between chlorinated solvents and some amino-acids). For soya and several other oil seeds (e.g. groundnut) safe procedures are well-established; clearance has been given by different agencies (e.g. the Food and Drug Administration in the U.S.A.), and increasing quantities of protein concentrates in textured or other forms are being used as foods in their own right or as 'extenders' for meat or other dishes. Active research is being conducted on other oil seeds, e.g. cotton seed (to remove gossypol) and rape-seed (to remove sulphur components). Parallel work is taking place on non-fatty legumes and other crops.

Current research on edible fats includes the safety levels of long-chain fatty acids (such as erucic), of highly unsaturated acids and of branched chain acids.

1.2.4 FOODS OF ANIMAL ORIGIN

Time does not permit any detailed discussion of animal products but several areas may be noted: (i) the utilisation of offal, blood and other abattoir products and of whey and related materials; (ii) work on fish protein concentrates; (iii) increased interest in fermented products such as yoghurt, well-known in south-eastern Europe, now introduced commercially in many countries; (iv) new fish products, successfully launched by the frozen food industries, with investigations, especially in Europe, on the use of lesser known species of fish (to remedy the acute shortage of some traditional species.)

Safety aspects of animal products often centre around microbial spoilage, but active work is in progress on processing problems (e.g. on the (effects of smoking, and of nitrates and nitrites).

1.2.5 FOODS FROM MICRO-ORGANISMS; BIO-SYNTHESES

Old examples of 'single-cells' used as food include yeast, widely used in breadmaking and sometimes as a food component, and edible fungi (*single*-celled, but necessary *micro*-organisms).
Recent work has for its major objective the cultivation of the cell, to obtain a protein-rich bio-mass to be used as animal feed or as a component of human food. Such products can be classified in terms of (a) micro-organisms (b) the source of carbon and (c) the process. In addition to the carbon substrate, (a carbohydrate, or hydrocarbon or some simpler compound), nutrients must be provided—and in particular ammonium salts or some other nitrogen source.

Toxicological problems relating to bio-syntheses have to be considered in terms of (i) the composition of the basic raw materials and (ii) the products of fermentation. It is impossible here to survey the many scientific and other reports which have been published over the past twenty years; a few points only can be selected for comment.

Most enterprises have been concerned *primarily* with the production of *animal feed* protein. Many authorities believe that the direct *human* use of products of bio-syntheses must await some years of experience in animal use but there are perhaps two exceptions, namely the use of (i) traditional yeasts and (ii) some micro-fungi with a mushroom-like character, grown on simple carbohydrates (or material such as low-protein wheat flours.)

Problems in the direct human use of biosynthetic materials arise from the levels of non-protein materials (in particular nucleic acids) produced parallel to the protein; there are upper limits to the desirable levels of nucleic acids in the diet. Reliable methods are now available to remove non-protein materials from the bio-mass.

Major debates have centred round the use of single-cell protein for animal feed. It is accepted that the animal can, with certain types of components (potentially toxic to man), serve as a 'filter'; on the other hand some lipid and other components in the feed may accumulate in the animal tissues. Special attention has been given therefore to (i) polynuclear (and potentially toxic) hydrocarbons in basic raw materials (especially those derived from petroleum sources) and (ii) branched-chain or odd-numbered fatty acids or other 'un-natural' lipids formed during biosynthesis. Experimental work has been carried out on the composition of animal flesh (meat, organs and fat deposits) and on milk and eggs, of laboratory and farm animals which have been fed on the protein products.

Much of the experimental work shows that under suitable production, extraction and purification conditions, protein feeds can be manufactured which pass safety tests. On the other hand it has been emphasised that ordinary crops and animals have relatively stable compositions determined largely by genetic considerations—and only to a limited extent modified by environmental (i.e. cultivation) conditions. By contrast, micro-organisms because of the rapidity of growth and the rapid 'turnover in generation' are potentially more liable to give variations in composition, especially in respect to minor components. In all the large-scale fermentation processes it will be necessary to maintain systematic and detailed monitoring of the composition.

Toxicologists (and public health authorities) are still debating the quality appraisal standards and the nature of monitoring which they consider necessary. It is probably true to say that fermentations based on relatively simple chemicals (such as methanol) have certain advantages. On the other hand we cannot under-estimate the importance of the basic developments, namely the demonstrations that micro-organisms can be cultivated on a wide variety of hydrocarbon (as well as carbohydrate and other) substrates, so that the new processes are likely in future decades to make an important contribution to national and international supplies of animal feed protein, and directly or indirectly to foods for man.

1.3 Food Additives: Current Trends and Problems

Richard L. Hall*

Governments employ a wide range of measures in the regulation of food additives. Larger, more economically developed countries characteristically have the most complex and far-reaching regulatory systems. The most extreme example is the cyclical review of a total positive list now planned in the United States, but Japan and many of the countries of Western Europe are not far different. The general pattern for the regulation of food additives in these countries is one of positive lists of permitted materials often grouped by food categories. A number of countries greatly simplify this task by not regarding flavoring ingredients as food additives. Some nations then regulate flavors only by short lists of permitted artificial and prohibited natural flavors, permitting all others without listing. This is often called the "mixed system". Some countries also exclude nutrients from the definition of food additives, thus eliminating the second largest group of intentionally added ingredients. Unfortunately, this commendable economy of effort has not been universally accepted.

At the other extreme are a number of developing nations which adopt the regulatory framework of an economically more advanced country with which they have had a long association. Perhaps the simplest approach of all is that which simply stipulates that imported foods must observe the laws of the country of origin. Spain has one of the most flexible arrangements, regulating synthetic flavors and colors, but otherwise, through advisory regulations, leaving the authorities free to decide, case by case, as they deem best.

Two major inter-governmental efforts are those of the Codex Alimentarius and the Council of Europe. The Codex establishes food standards, partly to assist those countries which cannot afford to develop their own, and partly to encourage trade. The Codex commodity groups set standards for food product categories and agree on the admissibility of particular additives. The FAO/WHO Joint Expert Committee on Food Additives

* *McCormick & Company, Inc., 11350 McCormick Road, Hunt Valley, Maryland 21031, U.S.A.*

145

then reviews these for safety, along with other additives which it considers on its own initiative.

Among its other activities, the Council of Europe attempts to harmonize national food additive regulations. This is no easy task, since the use of additives is inseparable from broader aspects of food processing and reflects differing economic, cultural, and historical interests.

All of these activities terminate in approval or disapproval of substances for use in food. The judgments are based on accumulated biological and toxicological information, and to a varying extent, past experience with the substance as an intentional ingredient or natural constituent. Although several efforts have been made to outline criteria for safety, few, if any, have been detailed, formal, explicit, official, and wise. Indeed, these probably are mutually conflicting characteristics.

During the past three years, the Food Safety Council, unofficial, but with broad international industrial, academic, governmental, and consumer participation, has addressed this difficult task. It was established not to review specific substances, but to devise a means to bring more rationality and consistency to decisions on the safety of food ingredients. Over the years, several million dollars each has been spent on the safety evaluation of saccharin, Red. No. 2, cyclamates, aspartame, and monosodium glutamate; yet there is not a unanimous opinion on their safety. To extend this effort to every additive would be ridiculous. We must have a structure for evaluation which devotes to each problem no more effort than is necessary in terms of risk or justified in terms of benefit. We cannot run every conceivable test in order to be able to say, in retrospect, where we might more wisely have stopped. To arrive at a consensus on a rational system requires two concessions. First, we must in virtually every case permit some socially acceptable residual risk in order that we need not test everything by every possible means. Likewise, we must adopt certain minimum testing standards, and forego the development of some potentially practical or useful agents if early indications of risk are sufficiently serious to suggest that effort should be more wisely allocated to other substances.

The Scientific Committee of the Council has prepared a report which arrays testing steps in the form of a "decision tree". At several points in the tree is a decision to accept a substance, to reject it, or to proceed with further testing. The objective of the Social and Economic Committee is to study the nature and size of residual risks on accepted substances and to develop means for determining the social acceptability of such risks.

If the Council succeeds, as there are hopeful signs it will, it will be only because of the strenuous inputs of talented people, including, very significantly, a number of individuals from the consumer movement.

Improved analytical tools have continually made us aware of ever smaller traces of substances. Improved toxicological tools have made us newly aware of many risks, a few large, many remote, mostly indeterminate. All require a decision on how far they are to be pursued, and by what means. This leads to three categories of current problems.

1. The problem of extrapolation of high-dose effects;
2. The problem of low-level exposures; and
3. The problem of appropriate measures of protection.

It has long been conventional wisdom in toxicology to subject experimental animals to highly elevated levels of exposure to a test substance, with the highest level intentionally designed to produce some adverse effects. Obvious adverse effects at the highest level(s) provide clues to more subtle effects at lower levels. Typically, response depends on dose illustrated by a sigmoid curve with a fairly straight middle portion. Thus, one may hope to observe an adverse effect with fewer animals at higher feeding levels as a substitute for the more expensive alternative of feeding larger numbers at lower levels. But, conventionally, one hopes to find a lower feeding level at which there is no observed adverse effect. In common practice, one then reduces this no-observed-adverse effect level by a suitable safety factor in order to obtain the total amount of which humans may be exposed. Even those who are skeptical of no-effect levels or who reject the concept of a threshold, would usually concede that there is some low dose at which the risk is so small as to be practically negligible— the "virtually safe dose".

The investigation of carcinogenic potential has developed this concept of elevated doses into that of the "maximum tolerated dose" (MTD). The MTD is estimated after a review of the subchronic data. It is defined as "the highest dose of the test agent. . . . that can be predicted not to alter the animal's normal longevity from effects other than carcinogenicity. . . . (and) . . . that causes no more than a 10% weight decrement . . ." This definition depends on the realization that tumor induction requires a major part of the life span of the animal. Feeding at doses so high that, in short-term tests, they elicit early and serious toxicity does not not permit the animals to survive long enough for tumors to develop. Moreover, if the dose results in seriously reduced food intake or weight restriction, this may protect against tumor formation. Thus comes the provision against no more than a 10 percent weight decrement.

All of this seems pragmatic and useful, but it leads to further difficulty. Rarely does an organism handle the same substance in an identical manner at very high and at low levels of intake. Characteristically, metabolic pathways shift as progressively higher doses overwhelm the organism's capacity to cope. This means that different sets of reactions may take place, or to different extents, at different points on the response curve. Thus, the dose-response relationship alters and with it, the estimate of risk obtained by extrapolation of the levels fed animals to the much lower levels to which humans are exposed.

This is a difficult problem because the range of human exposure is usually several log cycles below that of the experimental dose levels. Thus our evidence is on one part of the curve, and our concern on another.

In addition to the traditional approach of using large safety factors, we have available mathematical models for making this dose/response extrapolation. These vary in conservatism; each has a rationale. The linear model, and the slightly less conservative Mantel-Bryan Method generally permit a dose at a socially acceptable risk, say one adverse event in 100 million, so low that the dose is of no practical value, and the substance may not be used. Both use *assumed* slopes, and thus can be used even with only one dose/response data point. The Food Safety Council has proposed another mathematical model which uses experimentally derived slopes and, at least in some cases, would permit higher, more useful, safe levels. The choice between these probably cannot now be settled in some cases on available data, since it rests on assumptions about the nature of the toxic and, particularly, the carcinogenic process. In fact, the difference between the approaches is a matter of where one puts one's faith—in experimentally derived data points, with all of their uncertainties, or in theoretical descriptions of the possible nature of the carcinogenic process.

Another approach is to find out what is happening to the test substance in the test animal and man. This is the science of comparative metabolism and pharmokinetics. Presumably, if we can know enough about the metabolic fate of the test substance, we can make judgments on safety based on the knowledge of the human body's ability to dispose safely of the substance and all its subsequent metabolites.

Low level exposures raise another problem. Since the total number of small threats is very large, we cannot possibly investigate all of them simultaneously. There are still many categories of substances: natural toxicants, food contaminants, indirect additives, and flavors which either have not been addressed at all in terms of thorough safety evaluation, or which need periodic review. There is also the matter of newly discovered constituents, contaminants, or proposed intentional additives. The Food Safety Council's report outlines a rational scheme for the experimental examination and evaluation of a substance, but does not address the issue of the order in which the substances still before us shall be attacked.

Some priority-setting devices consist of "*in vitro*" or "short-term" tests, most of them involving microbial or cell cultures. They promise, if successful, prediction at least of carcinogenic potential, though probably not of most other forms of toxicity. We desperately need valid short-term tests. But their current limitations are severe. They produce some "false negatives" because no single test system can provide all of the activating enzymes and target molecules of a higher organism such as man. They also produce "false positives" because they do not have the protective mechanisms a higher organism may interpose. It seems probable that the short-term tests will take their place as a useful but not definitive tool when used *as a battery of tests*, after successful validation of the tests themselves by collaborative study in several laboratories. This is underway but has not yet happened.

Several methods have recently been proposed for establishing priorities. Two published procedures treat environmental contaminants (A. D. Little, Inc., 1977) and food additives, contaminants, and natural toxicants (Cramer *et al.*, 1978). The latter consists of a decision tree, which largely deals with chemical structure and which leads to the classification of every ingested, structurally defined, organic or metalloorganic substance into one of three classes of presumptive toxicity. It further combines this classification by presumptive toxicity with data or trustworthy estimates of consumption in order to obtain a "protection index" which is a measure of relative risk. This tree has been tried so far on more than 2,000 substances without apparent serious misclassification. Certainly some such devices for allocating scarce experimental effort must be developed and employed.

We come finally to the most troublesome problem of measures of protection. These are difficult because they transcend science, and must be resolved by society at large. How much risk is acceptable is not easy to quantify, predict, or rationalize. As Chauncey Starr has pointed out, our behavior indicates that we are about one thousand times more willing to accept a risk we perceive as voluntary than an involuntary one (1969). As others have discussed, acceptance depends upon the benefits which are believed to accompany the risks or upon the alternative risks which are to be avoided (Lowrance, 1976). It is reasonable to suggest, as Hutt has done, that risks can be divided somewhat simply for purposes of regulation into those major risks that are to be reduced or eliminated by a limitation or ban, those small but intermediate risks which can be controlled by labeling and education, and those very small risks which can safely be ignored (Hutt, 1978). Dr. Richard Wilson has further suggested that risks smaller than 10^{-5} are so small and numerous that it is not possible or practical to focus regulatory attention on them. Those risks greater than 10^{-2} are sufficiently large, so that they deserve severe limitation or banning (1977). In between are those we label. We need to consider whether there are sufficient alternatives in the marketplace so that the risk can truly be voluntary. And we can, in many instances, transform an involuntary risk into a voluntary one by sufficiently prominent and informative labeling.

Such a scheme is well worth pursuit. We cannot fritter away scarce regulatory effort anymore than we can fritter away scarce toxicological effort. But there are limitations. We cannot ban many substances without serious consequences for the cost and quality of the food supply. We cannot apply warning labels to many, or we lose their effectiveness by overload, and we cannot ignore or fail to label truly significant risks. Here is where the Food Safety Council and other efforts may perform a really useful service in promoting a consensus on the management of these different risks. Finally, one should be able to consider not only risks, but benefits, although the frequently mentioned concept of risk-benefit analysis is in fact almost never rigorously possible in the area of foods. The risks are almost invariably remote and uncertain or we would have known about them before and refused to tolerate them. Furthermore, they have seldom, if ever, been demonstrated in humans, but are usually only implied from animal studies at vastly higher levels. Finally, they are, to the extent they exist at all, vital risks not easily measurable in dollars. The benefits, on the other hand, are different but by no means easier to quantify and compare. The benefits, typically, are in an improved product. It may be more economical or convenient, or last longer, or taste better. These and other product properties have economic consequences measurable directly or indirectly in dollars. Consumer acceptance is measured in dollars for share of market, but how much is due to a particular additive and how much to other factors of packaging, product characteristics, promotion, or to the availability of competing and alternative products remains uncertain. We may *evaluate* risks and benefits, but not in the same units, and without rigorous comparison. Balanced judgments are our best hope.

But perhaps the greatest hope for those of us involved in this area is that practical limitations will force prioritization of effort in such a way that we will not endlessly allocate equal concern and effort to the trivial as well as to the urgent. Unfortunately, it may be a long time before that lesson is learned.

REFERENCES

Arthur D. Little, Inc. (1977). Pre-screening for Environmental Hazards—A System for Selecting and Prioritizing Chemicals. Prepared for Environmental Protection Agency, Office of Toxic Substances, Washington, D. C. PB 267 093. U. S. Dept. of Commerce, National Technical Information Service, Springfield, VA.

Cramer, G. M., R. A. Ford, and R. L. Hall (1978). Estimation of toxic hazard—a decision tree approach. Fd Cosmet. Toxicol. **16**, July.

Hutt, Peter Barton (1976). Public policy issues in regulating carcinogens in food. Presented at the Conference on the Scientific Basis for Interpretation of the Delaney Clause, sponsored by the International Academy of Environmental Safety, Washington, D. C.

Lowrance, William W. (1976). Of Acceptable Risk. Science and the Determination of Safety. William Kaufmann, Inc., Los Altos, California.

Starr, Chauncey (1969). Social benefit versus technological risk. *Science* **165**, 1232.

Wilson, Richard (1977). OSHA Docket 8–090 before the U. S. Department of Labor, Assistant Secretary of Labor for Occupational Safety and Health Admin., Washington, D. C.

1.4 Present Status of Studies on the Safety of Irradiated Foods

Masuo Tobe*

Studies on food irradiation have a history of about 20 years in Japan. Initially, research was concerned only with efficacy of food irradiation and was carried out in certain universities and other institutions. In 1965, a Special Committee on Food Irradiation was established under the auspices of the Japan Atomic Energy Conference. In 1976, studies on the efficacy of food irradiation, irradiation techniques and wholesomeness of irradiated food were begun on potatoes and 6 other food items by a project team consisting of scientists from various broad academic fields under the sponsorship of the Science and Technology Agency. The present author was a member of this project team, and as such has been engaged in studies on safety aspects, which constitute a major factor in the wholesomeness of irradiated foods. The present paper gives a brief outline of the results of our experimental studies so far, with the emphasis on irradiated potatoes. It also gives an account of overseas studies and discusses the safety evaluation of irradiated foods in general.

Table 1, quoted from the Food Irradiation Information of the International Project in the Field of Food Irradiation (IFIP), lists the countries which have so far authorized various items of irradiated food for human consumption. Clearly, 12 countries have authorized irradiation of one or more food items, covering a total of 8 different items in all. Irradiation of potatoes has been most widely authorized, followed by onions and wheat. Irradiation of garlic, dried fruits, mushrooms, dry food concentrate, and strawberries has been authorized by single countries only. The USSR shows the greatest number of food items authorized for irradiation, followed by Canada, the Netherlands and Italy. The first authorization of food irradiation was that of potatoes in the USSR in 1958, and the most recent was that of potatoes in South Africa in 1977. In Japan, irradiation of potatoes was authorized in 1972.

It is extremely difficult to decide the scope of experimental research which is necessary for giving a proper evaluation of the safety of irradiated

* Department of Toxicology, Biological Safety Research Center, National Institute of Hygienic Sciences, 1-18-1 Kamiyoga, Setagaya-ku, Tokyo 158, Japan

TABLE 1. Irradiated foods permitted in various countries for human consumption

Country	Potatoes	Onions	Garlic	Dried fruits	Mushrooms	Wheat	Dry food concentrate	Strawberries
Canada	+ 1960	+ 1965				+ 1969		
Denmark	+ 1970							
Israel	+ 1967	+ 1968						
Italy	+ 1973	+ 1973	+ 1973					
Japan	+ 1972							
Netherlands	+ 1970	+ 1975			+ 1969			+ 1975
South Africa	+ 1977							
Spain	+ 1969	+ 1975						
Thailand		+ 1973						
Uruguay	+ 1970							
USA	+ 1964					+ 1963		
USSR	+ 1958	+ 1973		+ 1966		+ 1959	+ 1966	

+ Unconditional clearance for unlimited human consumption.

foods in man. However, consideration of the experimental studies so far carried out on irradiated potatoes, which have the longest and widest history, may provide useful pointers.

In 1961, the FAO/IAEA/WHO Joint Committee formally recognized the importance of the wholesomeness of irradiated foods, and in 1969 the Joint Committee evaluated the wholesomeness of irradiated potatoes, wheat and onions. Table 2 summarizes the details of animal experiments then available on the safety of irradiated potatoes. The short-term experiments covered 9 studies, including 4 in the pig, 3 in the rat, and 2 in the dog. The rat study by Jaarma and Henricson (1964) was characterized by the use of a very high irradiation dose. Two groups of 14 rats including both sexes just after weaning were given diets containing 53% raw potato, irradiated or not irradiated with 200 krad, for 40 days. No difference in growth between the groups was observed. The 4 males and 10 females were taken from the 2 groups and mated. No difference in litter size between the groups was observed. After feeding on a high protein diet during the lactation period, both groups were fed a diet containing potatoes and again mated. Again, no difference in litter size between the groups was observed.

Recently, it has been suggested that amount of radiolytic products may be dose-dependent in the range up to Mrad. Although the significance of 200 krad irradiation is not clear from the viewpoint of radiolytic products, the fact that no adverse effects were noted in rats fed on potatoes irradiated at such a dose may be considered important.

In the study of Lang and Bässler (1966), a very high concentration of potato in the diet was used. They fed 2 groups of 30 rats including both sexes with a diet containing 72% potato, irradiated or not irradiated with 10 krad, for 1 yr. No differences in growth and protein efficiency between the groups were observed. Also, in the other short-term studies, no adverse effects due to irradiation of potatoes were observed.

In the 2 long-term studies, Okuneva (1958) fed rats with a diet containing potato irradiated with 46.5 krad, for 13–14 months; and Burns et al. (1960) fed rats with a diet containing 35% dried potato irradiated with 13.5–40 krad, for 4 generations over a period of 2 years. In each study, no abnormal findings ascribable to irradiation were observed for growth, food efficiency, mortality, hematological or pathological examinations, or reproductive performance.

In 1969, the Joint Committee classified the results for the evaluation of the safety of irradiated foods into 3 categories: unconditional, conditional, and temporary acceptance. After considering the results of the experimental studies listed in Table 2, the Committee placed irradiated potatoes in the category "temporary acceptance", since insufficient data were available to establish safety fully even though there was no evidence

TABLE 2. Toxicological data available in 1969 for irradiated potatoes

Animal	No. of animals/group	Irradiation dose (krad)	Duration of feeding	Ref.
Short-term studies				
Rat	10	9.3	45–50 days	Okuneva, 1958
Dog	3	46.5	8 months	Okuneva, 1958
Pig	5, 1	10	13 weeks	Horne & Hickman, 1959
Dog	2, 2	7 and 14	101 weeks	McCay & Rumsey, 1961
Rat	14, 14	200	40 days	Jaarma & Henricson, 1964
Pig	1, 1	14–15	4 months	Jaarma & Henricson, 1964
Rat		10	12 months	Lang & Bässler, 1966
Rat		8	43 days	Verela & Moreira-Verela, 1966
Pig	2, 4	14–15	until the offspring reached 90 kg live-weight	Jaarma & Bengtsson, 1966
Pig	7, 8	14–15	until the animals fattened from 25 kg to 90 kg live-weight	Jaarma & Bengtsson, 1966
Long-term studies				
Rat	20	46.5	13–14 months	Okuneva, 1958
Rat	25, 25	13.5–20.0 and 27.0–40.0	4 generations	Burns et al., 1960

that irradiated potatoes were harmful, and recommended reproduction studies in mice and rats with adequate numbers of animals, as well as carcinogenicity studies in another species, for example the mouse, as additional necessary work.

Table 3 summarizes the details of toxicological studies reported after 1969. The 4 studies by Ikeda *et al.* (1971), in which the present author took part, included a short-term study on a small number of monkeys, long-term studies in mice and rats, and a reproduction study over 4 generations in mice, including teratogenicity tests. In these studies, irradiated or non-irradiated potatoes were incorporated into an ordinary diet at a concentration of 35%. Except in the long-term study on rats, no adverse effects ascribable to irradiation were observed for ordinary toxicological parameters, or for carcinogenicity, teratogenicity and reproductive performance.

Figure. 1 shows growth curves for the female groups in the long-term study in rats. Significant growth depression was apparent in those groups fed with potato irradiated at 30 and 60 krad, in the later stages of the experiment. Table 4 lists the ovary weights of rats examined after 3, 6, 12, and 24 months. In the 60-krad group, both the absolute and relative weights decreased significantly compared to those in the 2 respective control groups at 6 months, and a similar trend (though not significant) was noted at 12 months. On the other hand, a trend towards increasing ovary weight was observed at 3 and 24 months. No abnormal histopathological findings were noted in these ovaries.

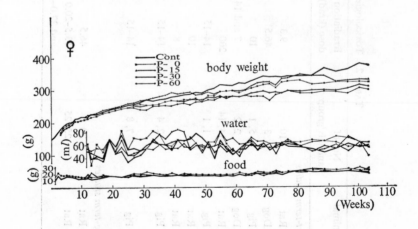

FIG. 1.   Curves for growth, water and food consumption of rats fed with irradiated and nonirradiated potatoes.

TABLE 3. Toxicological data on irradiated potatoes after 1969

Animal	No. of animals/ group	Irradiation dose (krad)	Duration/kind of test	Ref.
Monkey	2–3	60	6 months	Ikeda et al., 1971
Mouse	40, 40	15, 30, and 60	21 months carcinogenicity	Ikeda et al., 1971
Rat	30, 30	15, 30, and 60	24 months	Ikeda et al., 1971
Mouse		60	4 generations teratogenicity and reproduction	Ikeda et al., 1971
Mouse	45, 45	10–12	24 months reproduction and carcinogenicity	Coquet et al., 1974
Rat	70, 70	12 and 50	reproduction, teratogenicity and dominant lethal	Palmer et al., 1975

TABLE 4. Ovary weights in rats fed with irradiated or non-irradiated potatoes

		Time of examinations (months)			
		3	6	12	24
Cont.	absol.	77.5 ± 25.70	67.7 ± 8.10	56.5 ± 28.31	92.1 ± 61.76
	relat.	34.56 ± 13.13	26.96 ± 3.58	21.38 ± 9.81	26.56 ± 14.89
P-0	absol.	75.9 ± 23.31	68.2 ± 18.16	60.7 ± 25.51	115.8 ± 41.30
	relat.	33.80 ± 12.06	25.99 ± 6.37	22.71 ± 9.73	36.56 ± 16.48
P-15	absol.	102.7 ± 19.48	69.5 ± 16.12	73.2 ± 55.35	100.6 ± 45.20
	relat.	46.40 ± 11.51	28.34 ± 6.06	25.11 ± 18.07	29.63 ± 16.23
P-30	absol.	89.8 ± 46.81	66.8 ± 24.61	49.2 ± 11.14	89.9 ± 35.85
	relat.	41.53 ± 21.53	26.26 ± 10.66	18.08 ± 3.44	33.54 ± 13.98
P-60	absol.	96.1 ± 29.89	44.8 ± 7.64**(*)†	43.7 ± 3.74	124.5 ± 44.23
	relat.	42.62 ± 12.31	17.74 ± 2.75**(*)†	16.42 ± 2.56	42.25 ± 13.19

† Levels of significance; ** $P < 0.01$ when compared to the control; (*) $P < 0.05$ when compared to P-0.

Coquet *et al.* (1974) carried out 24–month toxicity and reproduction studies over 4 generations in mice using potato irradiated with 10–12 krad. No adverse effects due to the irradiation were noted in the case of carcinogenicity or reproductive performance.

Palmer *et al.* (1975) carried out a reproduction study for 3 generations in rats with a diet containing 35% potato, irradiated or non-irradiated with 12 krad. Teratogenicity tests, including observation of internal organs by Wilson's method, were also conducted in F_2 animals. In this study, some differences between the groups were noted in certain findings of the offspring. However, the observed variations were either within the background data of the authors' institute, or had no biological significance. No adverse effects due to the irradiation were apparent in the mother animals.

Recently, a new type of toxicity, genetic toxicity, has attracted wide concern in addition to the conventional general and special toxicity for the evaluation of the safety of chemical substances. In Japan, this toxicity caused particular concern in connection with the proved high mutagenicity of AF-2 (a food preservative) in microbes. In 1974, a guideline for evaluation of the genetic safety of food additives and other substances was prepared by the Food Sanitation Council (Table 5). As the first screening, mutagenicity tests in more than 2 assay systems in microbes having respectively different characteristics, were recommended. It was also suggested that susceptibility and metabolic activation tests were desirable at this stage. As the second screening, *in vitro* cytogenetic assay in cultured mammalian cells and/or recessive lethal assay in vinegar fly or specific loci assay in silkworms were recommended.

TABLE 5. Guideline for evaluation of the genetic safety of food additives and other substances (Food Sanitation Study Council, 1974)

1) First screening
   Mutagenicity tests in more than 2 assay systems in microbes.
   (Susceptibility and metabolic activation tests also desirable.)
2) Second screening
   a) *In vitro* cytogenetic assay in mammalian cells
                                 and/or
   b) Recessive lethal assay in vinegar fly, or specific loci assay in silkworms.
3) *In vivo* assay in mammals
   a) Host-mediated assay
   b) *In vivo* cytogenetic assay
   c) Dominant lethal assay
   d) Specific loci assay in mice

Greater importance was placed on *in vivo* assays in mammals, including those host-mediated, *in vivo* cytogenetic and dominant lethal assays in more than 2 animal species. The guideline suggested that specific loci assay in mice, which detects recessive mutagenesis, might not be practical in view of the very large number of animals and heavy expenses required to carry out this assay, although it could be considered in certain very special and important cases.

It is rather difficult to answer the question "To what extent should genetic safety be taken into consideration when evaluating the safety of irradiated foods in man?", due to the specificity of irradiated foods as well as the relative novelty of genetic toxicity. It may therefore be constructive to review some of the experimental work which has been done on the genetic toxicity of irradiated food.

Table 6 summarizes the details of studies so far carried out on the mutagenicity of irradiated potatoes. Kopylov *et al.* (1972) performed a dominant lethal assay in mice after oral administration of acid-alcohol extract of irradiated potato (10 krad) prepared at 24 hr after the irradiation. They obtained a positive result. In order to confirm these findings, Levinsky *et al.* (1973) performed another study under identical experimental conditions except for the irradiation dose (12 krad). The test material was given orally to male mice twice daily for 1 week, and then the mice were mated with female mice for 1 week. The same procedure was applied to the male mice at 1, 2, 3, and 4 weeks after the end of administration of the test material. Pregnant animals were sacrificed on day 14 and the ratio of early deaths to total implants (mutagenic index) was measured. No effects of irradiation on male fertility or the mutagenic index were observed at any of the weeks tested.

Zajcev *et al.* (1975) carried out dominant lethal assays in mice and rats using alcohol extracts prepared at 40 to 90 days after irradiation. No difference between irradiated and non-irradiated potatoes was found.

TABLE 6.   Mutagenicity of irradiated potatoes in mammals

Animal	Irradiation dose (krad)	Test	Ref.
Mouse	10	dominant lethal	Kopylov *et al.*, 1972
Mouse	12	dominant lethal	Levinsky *et al.*, 1973
Mouse	10	chromosome	Osipova *et al.*, 1975
Mouse	10	dominant lethal	Zajcev *et al.*, 1975
Rat	10	dominant lethal	Zajcev *et al.*, 1975
Rat	10 (MeV electrons)	micronucleus	Hossain *et al.*, 1976

Osipova *et al.* (1975) studied the incidence of chromosomal aberration in bone marrow cells of mice given potato extract preserved for 4 months after irradiation. The incidence of chromosomal rearrangement was 8% in the case of the irradiated potato and 3% in the control.

Hossain *et al.* (1976) failed to observe any mutagenic activity in extracts prepared either just after or at 24 hr after irradiation in a micronucleus test using bone marrow cells of rats.

In 1976, the FAO/IAEA/WHO Joint Committee on the wholesomeness of irradiated foods evaluated the results of studies on irradiated potatoes reported after 1969, and placed potatoes in the category of "unconditional acceptance". This suggests that adequate biological data exist to establish the safety of irradiated potatoes, as required under the conditions of unconditional acceptance proposed by the Joint Committee in 1969. Irradiated wheat, wheat flour, chicken, papaya and strawberries were also placed in the category "unconditional acceptance" by the Joint Committee in 1976.

Trials to elucidate the safety of food itself, not foreign substances such as intentional additives or food pollutants, have been made on irradiated foods for the first time. Various problems remain to be studied in connection with the safety evaluation methods to be used for irradiated foods, and modifications will inevitably become necessary with the development of sciences related to safety evaluation. The present author considers it important that the various problems inherent in the methodology of safety evaluation be established first, and that efforts then be made to solve these problems so as to ensure the safety of irradiated foods.

REFERENCES

Burns, C. H., Abrams, G. D. and Brownell, L. E. (1960), *Toxicol. Appl. Pharmacol.*, **2**, 111.

Coquet, B., Guyot, D., Galland, L., Fouillet, X. and Rouaud, J. L. (1974), Technical Report Series-IFIP-R18.

Horne, T. and Hickman, J. R. (1959), *Int. J. Appl. Radiat.*, **6**, 255

Hossain, M., Huismans, J. W. and Diehl, J. F. (1976), *Toxicology*, **6**, 243.

Ikeda, Y., *et al.* (1971), Final Report to the Japan Atomic Energy Committee

Jaarma, M. and Bengtsson, G. (1966), *Nutr. et Dieta*, **3**, 109.

Jaarma, M. and Henricson, B. (1964), *Acta vet. scand.*, **5**, 238.

Kopylov, V. A., Osipova, I. N. and Kuzin, A. M. (1972), *Radiobiologiya*, **12**, 524.

Lang, K. and Bässler, K. H. (1966), *Food Irradiation-Proceedings of a Symposium, Karlsruhe*, 6–10 June 1966, IAEA, Vienna

Levinsky, H. V., Wilson, M. and MacFarland, H. N. (1973), Technical Report Series-IFIP-R9.

McCay, C. M. and Rumsey, G. L. (1961), Unpublished report submitted by the U. S. Army.

Okuneva, L. A. (1958), *Voprosy Pitaniya*, **17**, 49.

Osipova, I. N., Shillinger, Yu. I. and Zajcev, A. N. (1975), *Voprosy Pitaniya*, **4**, 54.

Palmer, A. K., Cozens, D. D., Prentice, D. W., Richardson, J. C. and Christopher, D. H. (1975), Technical Report Series-IFIP-R25.

Zajcev, A. N., Shillinger, J. I., Kamaldinova, Z. M. and Osipova, I. N. (1975), *Toxicology*, **4**, 267.

1.5 Chemical Contaminants of Foods

D.E. Coffin* and W.P. McKinley*

The problem of the presence of chemicals in foods is one of the major concerns of food regulatory agencies. Most of these agencies have concentrated their efforts on compliance programs to ensure that regulatory restrictions on chemical contaminants were not exceeded. Within this type of activity, sampling is invariably biased towards the portion of the food supply suspected of containing higher than normal levels of the specific chemicals. These programs do not provide data on the incidence and levels of contaminants representative of the overall food supply. The data produced by properly biased compliance programs is much closer to representing the worst possible situation than the normal situation.

To permit reasonable assessments of the likely human effects of chemicals, information is required on the effects of chemicals and on the exposure to these chemicals from all sources. This paper will report on some efforts to obtain information relating to the human exposure to a few chemicals through the food supply. Because of the time limitations, it will not be possible to discuss any of the work in detail. Rather, some of the results will be presented in a summary form to illustrate the types of information which may be derived from such studies. Much of the Canadian data to be presented has not yet been published in the scientific literature.

To obtain information on such exposure, programs based on random sampling of the food supply or of specific portions of the food supply have been used in several countries. The results of these programs may be applied to determine the background levels and detect changes in the chemical contamination of foods; to determine the sources and geographical distribution of food contaminants; to determine the effects of storage and processing on food contaminants; to determine the dietary exposure of human populations or population segments to food contaminants in relation to established toxicologically acceptable levels of exposure; to permit the establishment of meaningful mechanisms for the control of food contaminants and to determine the effectiveness of control actions.

* Food Directorate, Health Protection Branch, Department of National Health and Welfare, Tunney's Pasture, Ottawa, Canada K1A OL2

In North America, programs of random sample food monitoring have been concerned primarily with pesticide residues, chlorinated hydrocarbon contaminants, mycotoxins, nitrosamines, monomers of polymeric packaging materials and polyaromatic hydrocarbons in a variety of agricultural commodities, fish, foods (including human milk) and complete diets. Programs of this nature have provided information necessary to make informed decisions regarding the safety of foods and the necessity for and effectiveness of control actions.

Recent toxicological findings and the illustration of some instances of excessive levels of metals in the environment or the food supply have stimulated interest in the degree of trace element contamination of foods. It is of particular importance to determine the background levels of these elements in specific foods before adequate but realistic limits for specific foods can be established. The average levels of cadimum and lead in some Canadian agricultural commodities and related processed foods and some comparative data reported from United States studies[1] are shown in Table 1. This table illustrates that cadmiun and lead are present in a wide variety of agricultural commodities and foods. The average levels of cadmium were less than 0.10 mg/kg except for 0.10 to 0.18 mg/kg for pork and beef liver, and 0.26 and 0.61 mg/kg for pork and beef kidney. Most of the commodities contained average levels of lead less than 0.10 mg/kg. Except for beef kidney at 0.26 mg/kg, the average lead content did not exceed 0.20 mg/kg for any of the 16 agricultural commodities examined. There was no evidence of significant changes in the levels of these contaminants in the Canadian agricultural commodities over the 5 year period. An effect of food processing technique is illustrated by the higher levels of lead in canned products than in the corresponding raw commodities. Relative lead contents of milk and canned condensed milks changed dramatically between 1974 and 1975.

Particularly high lead levels have been found in some canned baby food products. To avoid high lead exposures to young children, most Canadian and United States baby foods have for the past few years been packed in glass jars. In a survey of Canadian baby foods conducted in 1975, the levels of cadmium averaged 0.02 mg/kg or less in all types of products except the high solids content dry cereals at 0.06 mg/kg. The three types of products packed exclusively in glass, (meat and meat dinners, vegetables and fruits and desserts) had lead levels averaging from 0.02 to 0.04 mg/kg. Infant formulae packed in a variety of containers and dry cereals had average lead levels of 0.07 and 0.10 mg/kg respectively. The only two types of products packed exclusively in cans were evaporated and condensed milks and juices and drinks with average lead levels of 0.06 and 0.26 mg/kg.

Data on the total dietary exposure to cadmium, mercury and lead are

TABLE 1. Mean cadmium and lead contents

Commodity	Cadmium (mg/kg)		Lead (mg/kg)	
	Canada (1971–75)	United States (1974)	Canada (1971–75)	United States (1974)
Agricultural Commodities				
apples	.01		.16	
cabbage	.02		.06	
carrots	.03	.05	.07	.20
flour	.04	.06	.12	.05
potatoes	.04	.06	.04	.05
tomatoes	.02		.04	
milk	.02	.01	.04	.02
eggs	.03	.07	.08	.17
beef	.03	.04	.09	.07
pork	.03		.09	
poultry	.02	.04	.08	.13
beef liver	.15	.18	.14	.09
pork liver	.10		.13	
poultry liver	.07		.06	
beef kidney	.61		.26	
pork kidney	.26		.09	
Canned Foods				
apple juice			.22	
tomatoes			.31	
tomato juice			.30	
condensed milk—1974			.18 (.10)	
condensed milk—1975			.10 (.05)	

Figures in parentheses represent the calculated contribution of lead from the milk in the concentrated product.

available for both the United States and Canada[2–6]. The average dietary contributions of cadmium, lead and mercury in Canada for the period 1969 to 1972 were 67, 115 and 12 μg/person/day. The corresponding average dietary exposures in the United States were 36 μg/person/day of cadmium from 1968 to 1975, 64 μg/person/day of lead from 1972 to 1975 and 3 μg/person/day of mercury from 1972 to 1975. The relatively high cadmium content of the Canadian diet is supported by other data which indicate significantly higher cadmium levels in human kidney cortex in Canada than in the United States[8].

The FAO/WHO provisional tolerable weekly intakes for cadmium, lead and mercury are equivalent to daily intakes of 0.95–1.19, 7.15 and 0.72

μg/kg body weight of cadmium, lead and mercury respectively[7]. Based on the results of total diet studies, the daily intake by Canadian adults was 1.12, 1.92 and 0.20 μg/kg body weight for cadmium, lead and mercury respectively. Based on the results of the 1975 survey of baby foods the cadmium and lead intakes for 1-month-old infants were 1.51 and 4.37 μg/kg body weight and 3.27 and 8.11 μg/kg at 12 months. These figures point out the much greater exposure to lead and cadmium of infants than the adult population.

A survey of agricultural commodities on the Canadian market in the years 1972 to 1975 gives some indication of the levels of pesticides during this brief time period. Table 2 lists the average levels of the most commonly occurring pesticides in these commodities. Residues in products of animal origin were primarily DDT, dieldrin and HCH (BHC) with only occasional occurrence of other residues such as heptachlor epoxide, chlordane and toxaphene and of the two industrial contaminants HCB and PCBs. Generally much lower levels of these pesticides were detected in plant materials. However, it is interesting to note the high levels of DDT and dieldrin in carrots. Residues of endosulfan appeared only in fruit and vegetables and significant dicofol residues were found in apples and oranges.

Table 2. Mean pesticide contents of agricultural commodities on the Canadian market, 1972–75

Commodity	Pesticide Content (μg/kg)					
	DDT[†]	Dieldrin	HCH	Endosulfan	Dicofol	Total organo-phosphates
milk & butter (fat)	34	15	16			
beef (fat)	13	6	17			
pork (fat)	44	1	3			
poultry (fat)	60	12	5			
eggs	5	<1				
flour	1	<1	7			5
potatoes	4	<1				<1
carrots	39	4	1			5
cabbage	<1	<1		3		
beans	1		<1	1		
tomatoes	1		1	7		
vegetable oils	1	<1	6			43
apples	1			1	5	112
oranges	1	<1		<1	52	58

† Total of DDT, DDE and TDE.

Organophosphorus pesticide residues were detected only in plant commodities with the major residues being found in vegetable oils, apples and oranges. While 14 different organophosphates were detected, the residues consisted primarily of malathion in flour and vegetable oils, diazinon in carrots, ethion and parathion in oranges, and phosalone and imidan in apples. Over this 4-year time period no trends in the concentration of pesticides in any of the 14 agricultural commodities were evident. This survey did point out some regional differences in the levels of organochlorine pesticide residues in the Canadian food supply. The predominant feature was relatively low levels of DDT, dieldrin and HCH in the food supply in the Prairie provinces of Canada.

Total diet studies in the United States since 1965[3,9–13] and in Canada since 1969[14–17] have shown marked decreases in the normal dietary exposure to organochlorine pesticides. Dietary intakes of total DDT (DDT + DDE + TDE) of greater than 50 μg/person/day in the United States from 1965 to 1967 decreased to less than 10 μg/person/day since 1972. Similarly dietary intakes in Canada decreased from approximately 20 μg/person/day in 1969 to less than 5 μg/person/day since 1974. Much lower levels of other organochlorine pesticides were found in these studies and the daily intake has decreased markedly in recent years. Dietary intake of organophosphate pesticides in the United States has varied from 4 to 18 μg/person/day but no trends in dietary intake were evident from 1966 to 1975. In Canada, no trends were in evidence with the dietary intakes varying from 1 to 5 μg/person/day between 1969 and 1976.

Another source of food for a very important segment of the population is human milk. The levels of organochlorine pesticides in human milk are much greater than those found in cow's milk. The mean levels of DDT in human milk in Canada from surveys conducted on 1967, 1970 and 1975 were approximately 140, 80 and 45 μg/kg of whole milk (18). The levels of other organochlorine pesticide residues in human milk were much lower and decreased significantly over this period. However, the average level of PCBs was 6 μg/kg in 1970 and 12 μg/kg in 1975. Because of improvements in methodology within this time, it is not known whether or not this is a significant increase. Confirmation of the changing exposure of humans to DDT is shown by corresponding significant decreases in the level of DDT in human adipose tissue in both Canada and the United States[19,20].

The differences in exposure of different segments of a population is illustrated by the dietary exposure of infants and adults in Canada in 1974-75 to some chlorinated hydrocarbon compounds. In no instance did the adult dietary intake of pesticides approach the ADI. The highest relative intake was that of dieldrin at 12% of the ADI. For 1-month-old infants fed on cow's milk, the levels were somewhat higher because of the greater food intake in relation to body weight. Again the only significant intake was that of dieldrin at 90% of the ADI. Nursing infants were exposed to much higher levels of all organochlorine compounds through human milk, with the exposure to DDT and dieldrin at 1 month being somewhat greater than the ADI. The exposure of nursing infants to PCBs was much greater than that of the other groups.

Trace quantities of N-nitrosamines occur in cured meats as the result of reaction of the nitrite curing agent with amines present in the meat or other ingredients. One particular problem has been the formation of nitrosopyrrolidine during the frying of bacon. In practise and by regulation the level of curing salts used in bacon production has changed over the past decade. The general use of either ascorbates or erythorbates in bacon production may also have had some effect in reducing the formation of nitrosopyrrolidine during the frying of bacon. In the United States there has been a steady decline in the average levels of nitrosopyrrolidine in fried bacon from 71 μg/kg in 1971–72 to 11 μg/kg in 1977[22,23]. In Canada, a similar decline from 29 μg/kg in 1972 to 9 μg/kg in 1978 occurred[21].

The effects of control actions are illustrated by the results of surveys showing the complete elimination of nitrosopyrrolidine and nitrosopiperidine from mettwurst and thuringer liver sausages by discontinuing the use of premixed curing salts and spices[24], and by an 80% or greater reduction in the vinyl chloride content of vegetable oils and vinegar after the introduction of regulations to control the vinyl chloride content of foods.

The data presented have been almost entirely averages obtained from a number of individual samples. The pattern of distribution of the individual sample results is also very important in determining the range of probable exposure to chemical contaminants via foods. It is also important to remember that average levels of food intake are not sufficient to determine the exposure of any population to chemical contaminants. Differences in individual food consumption and dietary composition must also be considered to realistically determine the pattern of human exposure to chemicals in foods.

Some of the data collected on chemical contaminants in foods in Canada and United States has been presented in summary form and some of the applications of this data in determining human exposure to chemicals and to the development and evaluation of control mechanisms have been illustrated.

REFERENCES

1. Compliance Program Evaluation: FY 1974. Heavy Metals in Food Survey. Bureau of Foods. U.S. Food and Drug Administration. 1975.
2. Mahaffey, K. R., Corneliussen, P. E., Jelinek C. F., and Fiorino, J. A., *Environ. Health Perspectives*, **12**: 63–69, 1975.
3. Johnson, R. D. and Manske, D. D., *Pest. Monit. J.,* **11**: 116–131, 1977.
4. Meranger, J. C. and Smith, D. C. *Can. J. Public Health,* **63**: 53, 1972.
5. Kirkpatrick, D. C. and Coffin, D. E. *Can. Inst. Food Sci. & Technol. J.* **7**: 56–58., 1974.
6. Kirkpatrick, D. C. and Coffin, D. E., *Can. J. Public Health*, **68**: 162–164, 1977.
7. List of Maximum Levels Recommended for Contaminants by the Joint FAO/WHO Codex Alimentarius Commission CAC/FAL2-1973. Joint FAO/WHO Food Standards Programme, FAO, Rome.
8. Hammer, D. I., Calocci, A. V., Hasselblad, V., Williams M. E., and Pinkerson, C., *J. Occup. Medicine*, **1**: 956–964, 1973.
9. Duggan, R. E. and Corneliussen, P. E., *Pest. Monit. J.,* **5**: 331–341, 1972.
10. Manske, D. D. and Corneliussen, P. E., *Pest. Monit. J.,* **8**: 110–124, 1974.
11. Manske, D. D. and Johnson, R. D., *Pest. Monit. J.,* **9**: 94–105, 1975.
12. Johnson, R. D. and Manske, D. D. *Pest. Monit. J.* **9**: 157–169, 1975.
13. Manske, D. D. and Johnson, R. D., *Pest. Monit. J.,* **10**: 134–148, 1977.
14. Smith, D. C., *Pest. Sci.,* **2**: 92–95, 1971.
15. Smith, D. C., Sandi E., and Leduc, R., *Pest. Sci.,* **3**: 207–210, 1972.
16. Smith, D. C., Leduc R., and Charbonneau, C., *Pest. Sci.,* **4**: 211–214, 1973.
17. Smith, D. C., Leduc R., and Tremblay, L., *Pest. Sci.,* **6**: 75–82, 1975.
18. Mes. J. and Davies, D. J., *Bull. Environ. Contam. Toxicol.,* 1979 (In Press).
19. Mes. J., Campbell, D. S., Robinson, R. N., and Davies, D. J. A., *Bull. Environ. Contam. Toxicol.,* **17**: 196–203, 1977.
20. Kutz, F. W., Yobs, A. R., Strassman, S. C., and Viar, Jr. J. F., *Pest. Monit. J.* **11**: 61–63, 1977.
21. Sen, N. P., Donaldson, B., Seaman, S., Collins B., and Iyengar, J. R., *Can. Inst. Food Sci. Technol. J.,* **10**: A13–A15, 1977.
22. Greenberg, R. A., *Proc. 2nd Int. Symp. Nitrite Meat Prod.,* pp. 203–210. Zeist, 1976. Pudoc, Wageningen.
23. Havery, D. C., Kline, D. A., Miletta, E. M., Joe, F. L., and Fazio, T., *J. A. O. A. C.* **59**: 540–546, 1976.
24. Sen, N. P. and McKinley, W. P., *Proc. IV Int. Congress Food Sci. Technol.,* III. 476–482, 1974.
25. Williams, D. T. and Miles, W. F., *J. A. O. A. C.* **58**: 272–275, 1975.

2. Nutritional Aspects of Food Processing

2.1 Effects of Processing on the Nutritional Value of Foods: an Overview

J. Claude Cheftel*

Most treatments to which foods are submitted have an overall beneficial effect; however, in a number of cases, industrial processing and commercial storage reduce the level of nutrients and lower the original nutritional value. A survey, even superficial, of the subject would imply that the following 3 questions be discussed : (1) what are the nature, extent, cause, and mechanisms of the losses in nutrients, or changes in nutrient availability? (2) are such losses or changes of major nutritional or toxicological concern, or of commercial significance? and (3) could something be done to improve the situation? Such questions can hardly be answered in general terms and should be considered case by case. However, because of the large amount of individual and unconnected data, we have no other course but to attempt to determine any common denominators which may exist.

2.1.1 Losses of Nutrients or Changes in Nutrient Availability

Relevant data can be found in a few recent books and reviews[3,4,15,17,18,22,27].

We will discuss briefly here 4 tables which summarize the main causes of losses or changes in vitamin, mineral, lipid and protein nutrients, respectively.

A. Vitamins (Table 1)[1,3,7,8,15,18,21]

Mention should first be made of the spontaneous post-harvest or post-mortem deteriorations due to enzymatic action[8] : there can be a two-fold

* Laboratoire de Biochimie et Technologie Alimentaires, Université des Sciences et Techniques, 34060 Montpellier, France

TABLE 1. Nutritional modifications of vitamins during food processing and storage

1. POST-HARVEST OR POST-MORTEM DETERIORATIONS
   Vit. C in market-fresh fruits and vegetables.
2. PHYSICAL REMOVAL OF FOOD PORTIONS
   Trimming, cereal refining (vit. B), etc.
3. WATER-LEACHING OF WATER-SOLUBLE VITAMINS
   Conveying, washing, cooking and blanching in water. Loss in liquid of canned
   foods. Thaw exudate.
4. OXIDATION: VIT. C, CAROTENES, VIT. A (O_2, METALS, ENZYMES,
   LIGHT, pH)
   Steam-blanching (vit. C), pasteurization (folic acid/milk), frying (vit. A), baking
   (folic acid/bread), catering (vit. C), dehydration, dehydrated and frozen storage,
   storage of canned foods.
5. LIGHT OR IRRADIATION: VIT. B_2 (milk), VIT. B_6, VIT. B_1
6. THERMAL DESTRUCTION: VIT. B_1, VIT. C (pH > 5). CAROTENE *cis*-ISO-
   MERIZATION
   Cooking, baking, sterilization (also vit. B_6), dehydration, catering, storage of
   canned and dehydrated foods (also vit. B_2), etc.
7. REACTION WITH FOOD CONSTITUENTS OR ADDITIVES
   SO_2 (vit. B_1), NO_2^- (vit. C, B_1, carotenes, folic acid), cysteine (pyridoxal), enzymes
   (B_1), alkalis (B_1, B_2, C, pantothenic acid), anthocyans (C).
8. INCREASED NUTRITIONAL AVAILABILITY OF VITAMINS
   Niacin, biotin, folic acid.
9. FOOD ENRICHMENT AND FORTIFICATION
   Vit. B_1, B_2, niacin (flour, bread, infant foods), vit. A (margarine, tea), vit. D (milk),
   vit. C (juices), etc.

difference in the ascorbic acid content of garden-fresh (and factory-fresh)
versus market-fresh fruits and vegetables, depending on the duration of
transport and commercial distribution. The physical removal of certain
edible portions, such as in cereal refining, results in what can be classified
as intentional losses of vitamins (and of minerals as well). The water-leaching of water-soluble vitamins (and minerals) during processing operations, including cooking, is one of the main causes of losses; it can be reduced through good manufacturing practices (less product fragmenta-
tion, small water/product ratio, etc.), but a certain degree of nutrient loss
is inevitable.

Many vitamins (vitamin C, carotenes, vitamins A and E, and folic acid)
are readily oxidized. Hot air drying, comminuting, and frying are clearly
detrimental. Oxidation reactions also occur during the storage of foods in
a dehydrated or frozen state. The pathway and kinetics of ascorbic acid

oxidation have been studied in detail (see ref. 1), together with the influence of pH, water activity, oxygen and metal concentrations, etc.

Thermal destruction occurs with many vitamins, especially ascorbic acid and thiamine at pH's above 5. The *cis*-isomerization of carotenes is enhanced below pH 5; it causes the production of two *cis* forms with 53 and 30%, respectively, of the vitamin activity of the all *trans* β-carotene.

There is at present increased interest in the precise description of the thermal destruction of vitamins in kinetic terms such as D values and activation energies[14,23]. HT-ST sterilization and aseptic canning reduce the destruction of nutrients, but can be used only for foods which heat rapidly. In the case of solid or pasty foods heating only by conduction, high temperature processes are detrimental. For example, the optimum heat treatment with respect to thiamine retention for green bean purée in a container was calculated to be 90 min at a (maximum) retort temperature of 120°C, which is very close to the commercial process. Such calculations are still restricted to the few nutrients for which D values and activation energies have been determined (as a function of pH, O_2 concentration, etc.).

Slow degradation of heat-sensitive vitamins occurs also in canned and dehydrated foods kept at room temperature, and in frozen foods. In the latter, the degradation of vit.C is 6 to 70 times faster at -7 than at -18°C,[8] and the vit.C level has been used as an index of the time-temperature tolerance of frozen foods. The hydrolysis of thiamine in canned foods is also a function of storage temperature and duration.

Vitamins may be present in various chemical forms with different nutritional availability. About 90% of the niacin in cereals is bound to polysaccharide-protein complexes, and unavailable; thermal or alkaline treatments will release it. The length of the polyglutamate side chain of folic acids influences intestinal absorption; thermal treatments probably break down this chain and increase the vitamin availability. Data on the specific stability and bioavailability of different vitamin forms are also of interest for the vitamin fortification of foods.

B. Minerals (Table 2)[27]

Mechanical loss of minerals through removal of certain food parts has already been mentioned. As with vitamins, water-leaching constitutes a major cause of loss of water-soluble minerals. The dissolution of mineral salts or complexes depends on the pH. Cooking fish in water removes some iodine. On the other hand, a recently suggested cooking process for tuna slices in acid water containing cysteine removes a large proportion of contaminating mercury. Blanching vegetables in water also removes undesirable pesticides and nitrates.

Gains in minerals during food processing are more likely to be detrimen-

TABLE 2.   Changes in mineral nutrients during food processing and storage

1. LOSSES
   1.1 MECHANICAL REMOVAL
   > Peeling of fruits and vegetables; refining of cereals (Ca, Fe, etc.); cheese preparation (Ca, K, Zn, Mg); ion exchange for drinking water (Ca, Mg).
   1.2 WATER-LEACHING
   > Cooking of vegetables in water: up to 60% loss in K, 40% Fe, 30% Ca, 50% Cu; water blanching of vegetables: 30–70% losses in K, Na, Mg, P; leaching in liquid of canned foods; cooking of fish in water: up to 80% loss in I.

2. GAINS
   2.1 PICK-UP
   > From water (Ca, Mg); from equipment (Fe, Cu, Zn, Mn, Cr, Ni); from cans and containers (Sn, Fe, Al, Pb, Cu, Zn); from lye peeling, brine grading (Na); from processing aids.
   2.2 INCREASED NUTRITIONAL AVAILABILITY
   > Size reduction (Fe); autoclaving (Fe in soy protein concentrates); baking (Zn phytate).
   2.3 ENRICHMENT AND FORTIFICATION
   > I to salt; F to drinking water; Ca, Fe, (Zn) to flour, bread, food analogs, infant foods, etc.

---

tal for texture, color and flavor than nutritionally favorable. The development of stainless steel machinery and the declining use of traditional metal cooking ware may however have contributed to a detrimental decrease in iron dietary uptake.

The nutritional availability of minerals such as iron depends on many factors, from the chemical form of the mineral (which determines its solubility and intestinal absorption) to the composition of the diet, and the physiological status of the individual[13,35]. Food processing influences mineral availability: breadmaking hydrolyzes zinc phytate, so releasing zinc; and autoclaving of soybean protein preparations increases iron availability, probably through an improved digestibility of protein-iron complexes.

Minerals added for the purpose of food fortification should be readily available. The most available iron salts, however, are also the most soluble and the best catalyzers of various deterioration reactions. Grinding elemental iron particles to a size below 15 μm greatly improves their availability.

C. Lipids (Table 3)

The chemical modifications of lipids during food processing and storage[2,28,30] consist mainly of changes in the double bonds of fatty acids and

TABLE 3. Nutritional modifications of lipids during food processing and storage

1. POSITION AND CONFIGURATIONAL CHANGES IN DOUBLE BONDS
   Hydrogenation causes the formation of conjugated and *trans*-isomers, with some
   loss of essential fatty acids; the metabolism of the isomers is similar to that of mono-
   enic or saturated fatty acid.

2. AUTOXIDATION REACTIONS
   Storage rancidity reactions result in the formation of free radicals, peroxides, volatiles, etc. Organoleptic changes predominate over nutritional damage.

3. THERMAL REACTIONS
   Deodorization (at 200–250°C) leads to the formation of cyclic monomers, various
   polymers (1–2%), volatiles, etc. Polymers are little absorbed.

4. THERMAL OXIDATION
   Oil or fat frying causes the formation of oxidized triglycerides, aromatic ring monomers (from linolenic acid), C–O–C esters, C–C and C–O–C polymers (30%), OH
   polar polymers, volatiles, etc. Biological effects include some loss of essential fatty
   acids, growth and organ toxicity of the aromatic ring monomers and oxidized dimers
   (only when given at high doses), but no carcinogenicity.

5. POSITIONAL CHANGES OF FATTY ACIDS IN TRIGLYCERIDES
   Interesterification increases the proportion of saturated fatty acids in the β position;
   this enhances their absorption.

6. TRIGLYCERIDE FRACTIONATION
   Winterization increases the polyunsaturated/saturated fatty acid ratio.

therefore cause some loss of essential fatty acids. It is only in the case of
frying in oil that "thermal oxidation reactions" give rise to some concern,
due to the formation of toxic derivatives. In practice, however, industrial
or domestic frying is unlikely to cause major detrimental effects, at least
when oils with a low linolenic acid content are used, and when frying conditions are not too severe.

D. Proteins (Table 4)[3,4,12,24]

Of the simple modifications of amino acid residues, thermal or alkaline
desulfuration of cysteine, and oxidation of sulfur amino acids are the most
frequent. Residues of methionine are readily oxidized to residues of methionine sulfoxide, while only severe oxidizing treatments lead to methionine sulfone, a derivative with no methionine activity. The PER and NPU
of casein containing all its methionine residues as methionine sulfoxide are
only 10% inferior to those of normal casein. This indicates that residues
of methionine sulfoxide are released from the protein, absorbed, and largely reduced back to methionine[5]. *In vivo* metabolic studies and *in vitro* rat
liver perfusions with free ^{14}C-methionine sulfoxide have also been carried
out[10].

TABLE 4. Nutritional modifications of proteins during food processing and storage

1. SIMPLE MODIFICATIONS OF AMINO ACID RESIDUES
   1.1 OXIDATION
   Bleaching, detoxifying or sterilizing with H_2O_2, and hot air drying, oxidize methionine residues to sulfoxide (90% methionine activity) and sulfone (O activity).
   1.2 DESULFURATION
   Heat and alkaline treatments degrade some cysteine (H_2S formation).
   1.3 ISOMERIZATION
   Severe heat, acid or alkaline treatments give unavailable D-amino acids.

2. PROTEIN "DENATURATION"
   Moderate heating of legume proteins (cooking, extrusion) increases starch and protein digestibility, and destroys antinutritional and toxic factors.

3. PROTEIN CROSS-LINKING
   3.1 "ISOPEPTIDE" CROSS-LINKS
   Severe heat treatments lead to ε-N-(γ-glutamyl)-lysine and ε-N-(β-aspartyl)-lysine residues, and cause a decrease in protein digestibility and in availability of all essential amino acids.
   3.2 LYSINOALANINE-TYPE CROSS-LINKS
   Severe heat treatments at pH $\geqslant$ 7 lead to lysinoalanine, lanthionine and ornithinoalanine residues, and cause decreased protein digestibility, partial loss of lysine and cysteine, and some kidney accumulation of lysinoalanine (rat).

4. BINDING OF NON-PROTEIN MOLECULES ONTO AMINO ACID RESIDUES
   4.1 REDUCING CARBOHYDRATES
   Most heat treatments and storage at $\geqslant 20°C$ lead to deoxyketosamines, premelanoidins and brown pigments, and cause unavailability of substituted lysine, reduced protein digestibility, and some toxic effects (rat).
   4.2 OXIDIZING LIPIDS
   Free radical and carbonylamine reactions cause some amino acid destruction and protein cross-linking.
   4.3 ALDEHYDES ex. "tanning" of animal feeds.
   4.4 INTENTIONAL ACYLATION
   Leads to changes in functional properties, protection against Maillard reactions, fixation of methionine; availability of ε-N-acylated lysine residues depends on acyl group.
   4.5 OTHER MOLECULES: QUINONES, NITRITES, SULFITES, CHLORINATED MOLECULES, ETC.

Two types of processing have been shown to reduce the overall digestibility of food proteins through the formation of intra- and interchain cross-links between amino acid residues[12]. These are (1) severe heat processing of protein foods low in carbohydrate, such as meat and fish[10,19], and (2) severe alkaline processing of food proteins, as may occur during the purification and spinning of vegetable proteins[6,9,10,26]. In the first case, there is a predominance of "isopeptide" cross-links between the ε-amino group of lysine residues and the side chain of glutamine or asparagine. These cross-links partially resist proteolytic breakdown during digestion and therefore reduce the digestibility of the protein and the availability of many amino acids. In the second case, there is a predominance of acid and protease-resistant lysinoalanine and lanthionine cross-links. These derivatives form through desulfuration of cysteine into residues of dehydroalanine which then cross-link with residues of lysine or of cysteine. The nutritional effects are similar to those observed in the case of isopeptide cross-links.

The metabolism of free ε-N-(γ-glutamyl)-lysine and of lysinoalanine has been thoroughly studied in rats[10]. Some accumulation of lysinoalanine occurs in the kidney, and this may explain the fact that free lysinoalanine is nephrotoxic to some strains of rats (but not to 5 other animal species)[6].

It is unlikely that such cross-links form to a nutritionally significant extent during the cooking or sterilization of protein foods. The practical nutritional importance of such data is probably limited to the manufacture of fish or meat meals. However, it certainly remains of interest to confirm further that these newly discovered amino acid derivatives have no toxic effects.

Various food constituents or food additives may react with and bind to amino acid residues. Carbonyl compounds such as reducing sugars are specially reactive and readily bind to the ε-amino group of lysine residues, which then become nutritionally unavailable. These "Maillard" reactions take place even at ordinary temperatures. They are greatly enhanced at higher temperatures and lead to protein polymerization through nonprotein cross-links. They occur extensively in baked goods, fried potatoes, drum-dried milk, etc. Maillard reactions have been intensively studied from the chemical, nutritional and toxicological standpoints[10,11]. Although they significantly reduce the availability of lysine (a nutritionally limiting factor of cereal diets), and even the protein digestibility of some foods, they also contribute to desirable colors, flavors and textures in foods. The fact that "premelanoidins" of intermediate molecular weight are partially absorbed and induce some toxic effects in rats certainly deserves further investigation.

2.1.2 PRACTICAL SIGNIFICANCE OF NUTRIENT CHANGES

Apart from rare and remote risks of toxic effects, several other factors must be considered in order to assess the practical nutritional significance of the nutrient changes reviewed above. First, the vitamin and mineral content of raw foods may vary widely with genetic and environmental factors: 5-fold variations in the natural ascorbic acid content of tomatoes, and 12-fold variations in the original carotene content of carrots have been observed. Even more significant is the relative importance of a given food as a source of a specific nutrient in the "average" diet: e.g. loss of vit. C is of nutritional concern in processed potato products, but not in milk. It can also be argued that no nutrient modification during processing or storage is of any practical significance so long as the diet provides an adequate daily intake of that nutrient.

While overt deficiencies of calories and of nutrients such as vit. A, B_1, D and C, niacin, calcium, iron, iodine, fluorine, zinc, and protein (mainly lysine) exist in many underdeveloped regions, marginal deficiencies may also occur even in industrialized countries, for some of the above nutrients plus vit. B_2, B_6, folic acid, magnesium, manganese, chromium, silicon. The existence of these deficiencies (due to undernutrition, excessive dependence on staple foods, inconsiderate changes in diet, vulnerable groups, etc.) not only justifies special care during food processing but also dictates that some categories of foods be nutritionally enriched.

The recent introduction in the USA of optional nutrition labeling regulations[31,33,34] has created a strong commercial incentive for manufacturers to pay more attention to the nutrient quality of foods, and to its preservation during processing and distribution.

2.1.3 POSSIBLE IMPROVEMENTS

Systematic knowledge from well-controlled experiments could lead to the establishment of a data bank for the nutrient content of foods at different stages of processing. Actual food composition tables[29,32] may not be sufficiently reliable for some vitamins and trace elements, and do not provide sufficient information about variations around average values[25] or availability. Better knowledge of the kinetic parameters of nutrient destruction, together with results of accelerated storage test, would permit the computer prediction of nutrient losses as a function of various processing or storage conditions and therefore facilitate process optimization[16,20].

Nutrient destruction can often be minimized by a better adherence to good manufacturing practices (i.e. proper control of process and storage parameters, exclusion of air, etc.).

Specific steps to reduce nutrient destruction include improvements in thermal treatments, such as HT-ST sterilization and aseptic canning for liquid and agitated fluid foods, and hot fill and thin containers (such as pouches) for the sterilization of slow conduction heating foods. These techniques, which are primarily used for improving organoleptic quality, may however require a refrigerated storage if the advantage in quality is to be maintained for more than a few months. Other specific steps bear precisely on storage conditions. The maximum acceptable storage temperature of various processed foods in order to secure a 90% vitamin retention after 12 months has been determined (see ref. 21). Although it would certainly be costly, for example, to store canned spinach at 8°C, such an approach may be acceptable for some products, and may also become necessary if nutrition labeling regulations are made mandatory. The other alternative is to supervise and shorten commercial distribution.

Since institutional feeding is expanding, catering techniques should be improved (e.g. foods should not be kept warm for hours before serving).

As to specific nutrient enrichment of selected foods, this may be used more widely against deficiencies, both in developing and in industrialized countries. In the latter case, the primary targets should include infant foods and fabricated new foods such as meal replacers, meat analogs, and snacks.

As a general conclusion, it may be said that a certain degree of nutrient loss should be considered in a cost/benefit perspective: it represents the price that one must pay for the well-known advantages of processing, first among which comes the wider availability of a variety of foods.

References

1. Archer, M. C. and Tannenbaum, S. R., Vitamins, *Nutritional and Safety Aspects of Food Processing* (ed. S. R. Tannenbaum), Marcel Dekker (1979). In press.
2. Artman, N., The chemical and biological properties of heated and oxidized fats, *Adv. Lip. Res.*, **7**, 245 (1969).
3. Bender, A. E., *Food Processing and Nutrition*, Academic Press (1978).
4. Cheftel, J. C., Chemical and nutritional modifications of food proteins due to processing and storage, *Food Proteins* (ed. J. R. Whitaker and S. R. Tannenbaum), AVI, Westport, Conn. (1977).
5. Cuq, J. L., Besançon, P., Chartier L., and Cheftel, C., Oxidation of methionine residues of food proteins and nutritional availability of protein-bound methionine sulphoxide, *Food Chem.*, **3**, 85 (1978).
6. De Groot, A. P., Slump, P., Feron V. J., and Van Beek, L., Effects of alkali-treated proteins: feeding studies with free and protein-bound lysinoalanine in rats and other animals, *J. Nutr.*, **106**, 1527 (1976).

7. De Ritter, E., Stability characteristics of vitamins in processed foods, *Food Technol.*, **30**, 48 (1976).

8. Fennema, O., Loss of vitamins in fresh and frozen foods, *Food Technol.*, **31**, 32 (1977).

9. Finot, P. A., Bujard, E., and Arnaud, M., Metabolic transit of lysinoalanine bound to protein and of free radioactive ^{14}C-lysinoalanine, *Protein Cross-linking B* (ed. M. Friedman), p. 51, Plenum Press (1977).

10. Finot, P. A., Magnenat, E., Mottu, F., and Bujard, E., Disponibilité biologique et transit métabolique des acides aminés modifiés par les traitements technologiques, *Ann. Nutr. Alim.*,**32**, 325 (1978).

11. Finot, P. A., Bujard, E., Mottu, F., and Mauron, J., Availability of the true Schiff's bases of lysine, Chemical evaluation of the Schiff's base between lysine and lactose in milk, *Protein Crosslinking B* (ed. M. Friedman), p. 343, Plenum Press (1977).

12. Friedman, M. (ed.), *Protein Crosslinking, Nutritional and Medical Consequences*. Plenum Press (1977).

13. Fritz, J. C., Bioavailability of mineral nutrients, *Chemtech.*, **6**, 643 (1976).

14. Hamm, D. J. and Lund, D. B., Kinetic parameters for thermal inactivation of pantothenic acid, *J. Food Sci.*, **43**, 631 (1978).

15. Harris, R. S. and Karmas, E., (ed.), *Nutritional Evaluation of Food Processing*, 2nd ed., AVI, Westport, Conn. (1975).

16. Hayakawa, K. I., Review on computerized prediction of nutrients in thermally processed canned foods, *J. Ass. Off. Anal. Chem.*, **60**, 1243 (1977).

17. Hollingsworth, D. F. and Martin, P. E., Some aspects of the effects of different methods of production and of processing on the nutritive value of food, *World Rev. Nutr. Diet.*, **15**, 1 (1972).

18. Høyem, T. and Kvåle, O., (ed.), *Physical, Chemical and Biological Changes in Food Caused by Thermal Processing*, Applied Sci. Pub., Barking (1977).

19. Hurrell, R. F., Carpenter, K. J., Sinclair, W. J., Otterburn, M. S., and Asquith, R. S., Mechanisms of heat damage in proteins, 7. The significance of lysine-containing isopeptides and of lanthionine in heated proteins, *Brit. J. Nutr.*, **35**, 383 (1976).

20. Karel, M., Prediction of nutrient losses and optimization of processing conditions, *Nutritional and Safety Aspects of Food Processing* (ed. S. R. Tannenbaum), Marcel Dekker (1979). In press.

21. Kramer, A., Storage retention of nutrients, *Food Technol.*, **28**, 50 (1974).

22. Labuza, T. P., Nutrient losses during drying and storage of dehydrated foods, *Critical Reviews in Food Technology*, **3**, 217 (1972).

23. Lund, D., Design of thermal processes for maximizing nutrient retention, *Food Technol.*, **31**, 71 (1977).

24. Mauron, J., General principles involved in measuring specific damage of food components during thermal processes, *Physical, Chemical and Biological Changes in Food Caused by Thermal Processing* (ed. T. Hyem and O. Kvale), p. 328, Applied Sci. Pub., Barking (1977).

25. McCarthy, M. A., Murphy, E. W., Ritchey, S. J., and Washburn, P. C., Mineral content of legumes as related to nutrition labeling, *Food Technol.*, **31**, 86 (1977).

26. O'Donovan, C. J., Recent studies of lysinoalanine in alkali-treated proteins, *Food Cosmet. Toxicol.*, **14**, 483 (1976).

27. Tannenbaum, S. R. and Young, V. R., Minerals, *Nutritional and Safety Aspects of Food Processing* (ed. S. R. Tannenbaum), Marcel Dekker (1979). In press.

28. Vles, R. O. and Houtsmuller, U. M. T., Connaissances actuelles sur les graisses alimentaires: leur importance en nutrition humaine, *Rev. Franç. Corps Gras.*, **11**, 523 (1977).

29. Watt, B. K. and Merrill, A. L., Composition of foods: raw, processed, prepared, *Agriculture Handbook* No. 8, U.S.D.A. (1963).

30. Witting, L. A., Perkins E. G., and Kummerow F. A., Lipids, *Nutritional and Safety Aspects of Food Processing* (ed. S. R. Tannenbaum), Marcel Dekker (1979). In press.

31. Anon., *Compliance Procedures for Nutrition Labeling*, F.D.A., Washington, D. C. (1973).

32. Anon., *Composition of Foods*, 2nd ed., Medical Research Council., London (1978).

33. Anon., Nutrition labeling, *Federal Register*, 38: 6951, F.D.A., Washington, D. C., Mar. 14, 1973.

34. Anon., Nutrition labeling, *Food Technol.*, **28**, 43 (1974).

35. Anon., Physical acceptability and bioavailability of iron-fortified food, *Nutr. Rev.*, **5**, 298 (1976).

2.2 Design of Thermal Processes for Minimizing Nutrient Loss

Daryl B. Lund*

It is a matter of record that generally food processes have been designed from the consideration of cost and quality of product. "Quality of product" refers generally to organoleptic quality factors such as texture, flavor and color. Within the last ten years, however, other characteristics of food processing operations have been used to judge adequacy of food processes. These, of course, are waste generation and energy utilization, two bases upon which to evaluate food processes which have developed because of consumer concern on the one hand (waste generation) and self-survival of the industry (energy utilization) on the other hand. Now the industry, prompted again by consumer concern, has added nutrient content as a basis upon which to evaluate suitability of food processes.

The food industry has in general been concerned about retention of nutrients but usually there was insufficient data upon which to quantify the effect of various processes on nutrients. Also, there has been the intuitive feeling that food quality characteristics such as color, flavor and texture were more important in the sense that if the consumer did not accept or eat the product then it did not make any difference what the nutrient content of the food was. There are several examples of situations in which products contained all or most of the required nutrients but was not acceptable to the consuming public.

Although the data base quantifying the effect of processing on nutrients is insufficient and much more research work must be completed in this area, some generalizations and conclusions can be made on the effects of processing on nutrients. Consequently, now and more so in the future, evaluation of food processes will be made using several bases (for example, nutrients, cost, energy, waste, and quality factors). Obviously there are trade-offs in which some conscientious decision-making and prioritizing will need to be made. At least we are coming closer to a full definition of food processes.

The objective of this paper is to review progress in the assessment of thermal processes applied to food with regard to nutrient retention. Some

*Department of Food Science, University of Wisconsin, Madison, Wisconsin, USA

data already exist upon which to base the nutritional evaluation of food processes[1,2]. This is particularly true for the quantitative description of the effects of thermal processes on well-studied nutrients.

For our purposes, a thermal process is defined broadly as a process in which the temperature of the product is elevated above ambient temperature for short periods of time and subsequently the temperature is reduced to ambient or lower temperatures for storage.

The first function of a thermal process might be to increase palatability such as in precooked foods. A second function might be to change the characteristics of the product to increase product desirability. Examples include gelatinization of starches to increase viscosity or heating maple sap to induce caramelization. A third and certainly more widely applied function is to increase product stability through the inactivation of enzymes or microorganisms or through the removal of oxygen from the product.

Lund[3] recently reviewed the basis of thermal processes applied to foods to increase shelf-life. The processes and their respective basis are: (1) blanching—enzymes or removal of tissue gas, (2) pasteurization—vegetative cells or pathogenic organisms and (3) commercial sterilization—spores of anaerobic sporeformers.

The dependence of the destruction rates of these bases on temperature can be compared to the dependence of the destruction rates of nutrients and other quality factors by considering the generalized data in Table 1.

TABLE 1.   Thermal resistance of various food constituents[†]

Constituent	z (°F)	E_a (kcal/mole)	D_{121} (min)
Vitamins	45–55	20–30	100–1000
Color, Texture, Flavor	45–80	10–30	5–500
Enzymes	12–100	12–100	1–10
Vegetative Cells	8–12	100–120	0.002–0.02
Spores	12–22	53–83	0.1–0.5

† from Lund[3]

With these values it is now possible to compare the relative values for the basis of the process to those of nutrients to assess if optimum processes exist. Obviously if the basis of the process and nutrients exhibit the same temperature dependence then optimization of the process for nutrient retention must be based on factors other than thermal history. Several important observations can be made by examining the table. First, nutrients and quality factors exhibit similar temperature dependence. This is important because it suggests that processes which were designed to maximize quality factor retention would also maximize nutrient retention. Second, the reaction rate constants (D_{121}-values) for nutrients and quality factors are several orders of magnitude larger than for enzymes, vegetative cells or spores. This is important because frequently processes are designed to reduce vegetative and spore populations by 10^5 to 10^{12} and if nutrients were not significantly more resistant, the food would be nutritionally worthless following the thermal process. The third observation from the table is that reaction rates for nutrients and quality factors are much less dependent on temperature than are those for vegetative cells and spores. This suggests that there may be an opportunity to optimize thermal processes for nutrient retention.

For blanching, a comparison of the z-value for heat resistant enzymes (usually relatively large z-values) and nutrients suggests that the thermal process per se does not dictate the process of choice for retention of nutrients. Optimization of the blanching process should be based on factors other than the thermal history of the product. For example leaching losses and oxidative losses may be significantly different between processes.

For pasteurization processes, it can be seen that the basis of the process (vegetative cells) exhibits a greater dependence on temperature than do nutrients. Under these circumstances it would appear that application of high temperature-short time (HTST) processes would be less detrimental to nutrients than low temperature-long time processes.

Optimization of commercial sterilization processes initially may appear as straightforward as that for blanching and pasteurization. Examination of thermal death time plots such as that produced by Feliciotti and Esselen[4] would seem to clearly indicate that the best process is a high temperature-short time process. This principle has been used in designing thermal processes for fluids which utilize temperature in excess of 175°C (350°F) for residence times on the order of fractions of a second. One precaution that must be noted when processing fluids containing enzymes is that enzymes may survive these ultra high temperature treatments. Another consideration in ultra high temperature processes is the degree of "cook" which a product receives. Generally characteristics which describe "cookness" of products exhibit a temperature dependence similar to those for nutrients and heat resistance enzymes[5]. Thus under some circumstances ultra high temperature processes may result in undercooked products and it may be necessary to use degree of cooking as the basis of the process.

The conclusion that HTST processes are best for retention of nutrients applies only when one other important assumption applies. That assumption is that each volume element of the food experiences the same thermal history as every other volume element. This assumption certainly applies for products which heat very rapidly and consequently most of the thermal process occurs at or near the heating medium temperature.

However, for conduction heating foods which would include large particles which are not sterile in the interior, much of the thermal process occurs during the heating and cooling phases and thus the assumption does not hold. Hence one must examine the potential for optimization of commercial sterilization processes for nutrient retention based upon the characteristics of the thermal history. Lund[3] summarized the available approaches to optimization of thermal processes for conduction heating foods and pointed out that because of the distribution of thermal histories within a solid or viscous food system, HTST processes were not the optimum for retention of nutrients. Recently Thijssen et al.[6] confirmed the earlier studies which concluded that process optimization for nutrient retention in conduction heating foods was not HTST and that process improvement would depend on increasing heat transfer characteristics of the product or decreasing critical distances for heat transfer (i.e. thin packages).

In summary, optimization of blanching processes must be based on other routes of nutrient loss than thermal processing itself. For pasteurization, HTST processes are generally superior for nutrient retention unless heat resistant enzymes are present. The same conclusion applies to commercial sterilization processes applied to foods which heat primarily by convection and contain particulates sterile at the center. For conduction heating foods, the optimum thermal process is dependent on the heat transfer characteristics of the product and container geometry. In general, a definite optimum does exist. Finally it is important to note that for conventional geometries employed in the canning industry, the heating medium temperatures currently used for processing conduction heating foods are generally those which, in fact, result in maximum retention of nutrients.

ACKNOWLEDGEMENT: Contribution from the College of Agricultural and Life Sciences, University of Wisconsin-Madison, Madison, Wisconsin.

References

1. Harris, R. S. and Karmas, E. (Eds)., *Nutritional Evaluation of Food Processing*, The AVI Publ. Co., Inc. Westport, Conn., USA. (1975).
2. Høyem, T. and Kvale, O., *Physical, Chemical and Biological Changes in Food Caused by Thermal Processing*, Applied Science Publ. Ltd., London, (1977).

3. Lund, D. B., Design of thermal processes for nutrient retention. *Food Technol.*, **31(2)**: 71–78, (1977).
4. Feliciotti, E. and Esselen, W. B., Thermal destruction rates of thiamin in pureed meats and vegetables, *Food Technol.*, **11**: 77–84, (1957).
5. Dagerskog, M., Time-temperature relationships in industrial cooking and frying. Chapt. 6 in *Physical, Chemical and Biological Changes in Food Caused by Thermal Processing*, T. Høyem and O. Kvale (Eds). Applied Science Publ. Ltd., London, (1977).
6. Thijssen, H. A. C., Kerkhof, P. J. A. M., and Liefkens, A. A. A. Short-cut method for the calculation of sterilization conditions yielding optimum quality retention for conduction-type heating of packaged foods, *J. Food Sci.*, **43**: 1096–1101, (1978).

2.3　Toxic Effects of Oxidized Lipids

Fred A. Kummerow*

Oxidized lipids, which I will define as oxidized polyunsaturated fatty acids (PUFA), and oxidized sterols present two major problems to the food industry. One, the oxidized PUFA cause undesirable odors and flavors in a food product[1,2]. Two, the oxidized sterols cause an increase in smooth muscle cell degeneration in the intima[3,4], a key factor in the development of arterio- and atherosclerosis, the underlying cause for cerebral strokes (CVE) and coronary heart disease (CHD)[5]. Japanese have 2 1/2 times more cerebral strokes, but less heart disease than Americans[6]. I believe that both types of arterial damage are related to the foods we eat.

2.3.1 OXIDIZED POLYUNSATURATED FATTY ACIDS

The odor and flavor problem is time and polyunsaturated fatty acid (PUFA)-dependent. Its deterioration could be greatly accelerated by exposure to heat[7]. The peroxidized or "rancid" fat which can form at freezing or room temperature is believed to destroy the riboflavin, thiamin, and vitamin A in food products[8]. Rancid foods have such undesirable flavor and odor characteristics that such foods are usually rejected by the consumer and, as they are not consumed, they present no nutritional or biological problem. On the other hand, the PUFA in frying fats do not develop objectionable odors or flavors; in fact, they develop flavors which are considered desirable by hundreds of millions of consumers all over the world.

If deep fat fried food items are not carefully protected against the development of rancidity by antioxidants, air-tight packaging or consumed immediately after frying, they will rapidly become rancid and are rejected by the consumer. Deep fat fried foods present another problem which may have biological significance to the consumer. If these foods are fried in a fat or an oil which contains polyunsaturated fatty acids (PUFA), the frying medium gradually accumulates hydroxy acids, aldehydes, ketones, epoxides, alkoxy substituted unsaturated esters and cyclic acids more rapidly than

---

*The Burnsides Research Laboratory, University of Illinois, Urbana, Illinois 61801, USA

PUFA-free frying fat. Over 95 recognizable volatile and more than 20 nonvolatile oxidation products have been found in heated oil[9]. These volatile and nonvolatile compounds are formed from the PUFA during heating in the presence of air[10,11]. The nonvolatile products that remain in the oil are of most concern to the biological significance of heated fats[12,13].

These residual nonvolatile products contribute to the pleasing taste of potato chips, french fries, fried noodles and doughnuts[4]. They have been extracted from these fried food items[15] and have been found to have the same chemical characteristics as the frying oil that they had been prepared in. If protected from contact with air, the peroxide value of such food items are too low to provide an organoleptically unacceptable product. Yet, the presence of nonvolatile oxidation products in frying oils has stimulated a great interest in their possible biological significance.

When rats which were kept on diets marginal in protein and vitamin content were fed used frying fat, they developed diarrhea and enlarged livers, they had an unkept appearance, and they did not gain as much weight as rats fed the fresh unheated fat[16]. Approximately 60% of the nonvolatile oxidation products of heated corn oil has been reported to be excreted in the feces, 20% was metabolized, and the remainder was found in the gastrointestinal tract, carcass, and liver[17]. The cyclic acids which were isolated from heated fat have been reported to be present in the lymph of rats which had been fed such cyclic acids[9]. Rats fed a diet which contained 8% casein and a synthetically prepared cyclic acid, similar in structure to those in heated fats, gained less weight and contained significantly more liver lipid[18,19] than those not fed cyclic acids. A higher level of protein (15% casein) counteracted the influence of the cyclic acids.

The many studies[20-32] on the biological significance of heated fats had an impact on the fat and oil industry. Soybean oil was, therefore, hydrogenated in such a way as to produce a low dienoic (C18:2) and high monoenoic (C18:1) fat with approximately 50% of the C18:1 in the *trans* configuration[33]. Such a frying oil is still liquid enough at body temperature to provide for a good "mouth-feel" and yet is relatively heat stable. Unfortunately, the *trans* elaidic (C18:1) acid has metabolic properties which differ from the natural oleic (C18:1) acid. It is recognized as a saturated rather than an unsaturated fatty acid by acyl-glycerol-3-phosphoryl-choline transferase[34,35] and acyl-CoA-cholesterol-O-acyl transferase[36-40]. Moreover, under conditions involving less than an optimum intake of linoleic acid, *trans* fatty acids substitute for essential fatty acids (EFA) in biological systems[41-44]. As many studies have shown that the fatty acids in the phospholipid and cholesterol esters in cell membranes influence the properties of membranes[45-49], intensive studies on the biological significance of the *trans* fatty acids in frying fats are currently in progress.

2.3.2 Oxidized Sterols

Oxidized sterols, such as 25-hydroxy cholesterol, have been shown to accelerate smooth muscle degeneration in the intima layer of arteries. This derivative of oxidized cholesterol was found in supposedly pure crystalline cholesterol[3,4]. As millions of pounds of fat are used in frying operations each year, the potential for forming oxidized cholesterol in the frying of fish, poultry or potatoes exists if the potatoes are fried in beef tallow. Data provided by McDonald's, Inc. for french fries indicate that they contain 12 mg of cholesterol/100 g of fries[50]. The fat in which chickens are fried in commercial establishments contains 214 mg of cholesterol/100 g of fat[51]. The fat which has been used to fry fish contains similar levels of cholesterol.

We first noticed the influence of cholecalciferol (the oxidized sterol with vitamin D activity) in a routine study on the use of commercial swine as an animal model[52–56]. More cellular debris was noted in the diseased areas as compared with the nondiseased areas of the same aorta from the swine which had been fed a commercial ration of corn and soybean meal. A comparison of vitamin D contents of swine and human tissues indicated that both assayed for substantial amounts of vitamin D. The amounts were greater in tissues from subjects given therapeutic vitamin D. The serum, fat, muscle, and liver from human subjects assayed for higher levels of vitamin D than these tissue from the swine which had been fed a regular corn and soybean commercial ration[52] (Table 1).

Table 1.   Comparison of vitamin D content of swine and human tissue
IU vitamin D/pound of tissue

| | Swine | | Human | |
	Normal	Fed vitamin D₃[†1]	Normal	Fed vitamin D₃[†2]
Muscle	360[†3]	5,765[†3]	454[†4]	18,160[†3]
Liver	600	2,270	0–1860	2,043
Fat	380	—	544–1770	4,540
Serum	386/100 ml	4,360/100 ml	500–1800/100 ml	

[†1]Piglet fed 100,000 IU/lb. ration for 6 weeks.
[†2]Treated for osteomalacia. [†3]Muscle. [†4]Diaphragm.

Raised lesions could be found in the thoracic aorta of weanling piglets after only one month of feeding 25,000 IU of vitamin D₃/pound of feed/day; this level of vitamin D is approximately the therapeutic doses of vitamin D₃ that are used in the treatment of osteomalacia in humans[57]. Electron microscopy indicated that the grossly normal areas of the aorta from weanling swine that had been fed only 6 times more vitamin D than in the commercial ration for 6 weeks and sacrificed at 6 months of age had a higher frequency of degenerated smooth muscle cells than the grossly normal areas of the aorta of swine fed the initial D-unsupplemented commercial ration. The plaques, observed by scanning microscopy, were ele-

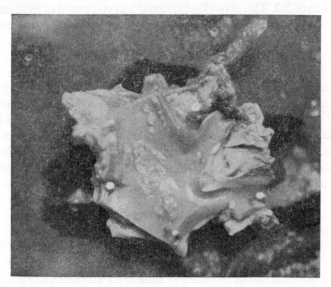

FIG. 1a—Aortic arch of 3-month-old swine fed cholecaliferol for 1 month (12x normal level)

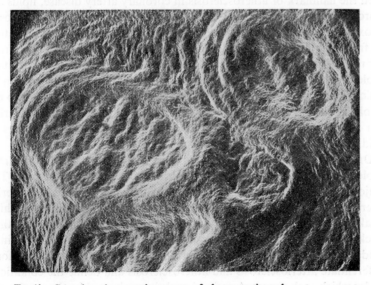

FIG.1b—Scanning electronmicroscopy of above aortic arch.

vated with a central depression. Histologically, these plaques consisted of intimal thickening located above the calcified elastica in the shallow media. The crystalline materials from the plaques were calcium and phosphorus with a ratio of 5:3. This crystalline material was composed of 99 % purified hydroxy apatite $(3Ca_3(PO_4)_2 \cdot Ca(OH)_2)$ and 1 % minor components (Fig. 1a, 1b).

One can conclude from these data that an oxidized sterol, such as vitamin D, has a very disruptive influence on the integrity of the smooth muscle cell in the coronary artery. Furthermore, the disruptive influence cannot be reversed once the integrity of the cell has been disrupted. The removal of vitamin D from the diet of weanling swine after only six weeks of supplementation with six times more vitamin D than the level ordinarily found in swine ration did not prevent the accumulation of lipid droplets and thickening of the coronary arteries at six months of age. Vitamin D was more disruptive of the smooth muscle cells in the coronary arteries than in the smooth muscle cells in the aorta. Furthermore, its removal from the diet allowed for more lipid infiltration than its continued presence in the diet[58-63].

It seems significant that the lipid-laden cells that were found in the thoracic aortas of three-year-old swine kept on cholesterol-free diets, devoid of saturated fat or those fed vitamin D for six weeks, duplicated the electron microscopy of human thoracic tissue that was obtained as a by-product of coronary bypass surgery. Although lipid deposits have usually been the hallmark of atherosclerosis in coronary artery disease, lipids are scarce in cerebral arteriosclerosis in Japanese[64]. Japanese are also exposed to oxidized fat; a large fraction of the frying fat is used in the preparation of fried noodles, a favorite Japanese food. This fat is prepared from hydrogenated fish oils, whale oil, and beef tallow, all of which contain cholesterol. In addition, fish oil contains substantial amounts of vitamin D, which is not deactivated by the hydrogenation process. Japanese also eat smoked fish and salt-dried fish in quantity. Both processes of preparing fish for human consumption would provide for substantial amounts of oxidized fatty acids and oxidized cholesterol.

On a low fat diet, such as the Japanese diet, the presence of oxidized cholesterol may cause intimal thickening without lipid accumulation. The major cause of death is due to cerebral hemorrhage rather than arteriosclerosis. Because of the high blood pressure which is caused by the high intake of salt, the hardened cerebral arteries are ruptured rather than thickened to the point at which blood flow is impeded. Studies with animal models and comparison of the diets of population groups, therefore, differentiate arteriosclerosis and atherosclerosis and define the conditions under which each occurs. Arteriosclerosis is accelerated by the continuous presence of oxidized sterols in the diet of population groups on low fat diets. In population groups on low fat diets, a high salt intake may act as an added "risk factor". In populations on high fat diets, intermittent oxidized sterol intake and excessive fat calories may act as a "risk factor" and provide for the development of atherosclerosis by providing an over-abundance of acetyl CoA for fat synthesis in the artery tissue (Fig. 2).

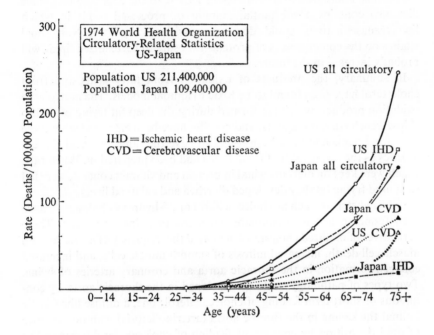

FIG. 2

Hydrogenation has made is possible to convert billions of pounds of fish and marine oils and soybean oil into acceptable products. It is now possible to hydrogenate in such a way as to minimize *trans* fatty acid formation which I believe should be minimized. It may be impossible to hydrogenate fish oil so as to remove all *trans* acids because of the high melting point of completely saturated C_{20} and C_{22} acids. Therefore, it would be better to substitute soybean, palm, and coconut oil for fish oils and use the fish oils in nonedible products such as paint oils[65,66]. The rearrangement process with sodium ethoxide catalyst has made it possible to rearrange completely hydrogenated soybean oil so as to produce a *trans*-free margarine such as the Becel margarine produced by Unilever in Europe. It is also possible to use a combination of micro ovens and fat frying so as to minimize oxidized

PUFA and oxidized sterol formation. I believe it would produce a more stable product and result in a more healthful food item. The Japanese fat industry has a special interest in oxidized lipids as 80,800 metric tons of hydrogenated fish oil were used in the production of 269,500 metric tons of Japanese margarines and shortenings in 1976. These hydrogenated fish oils have the potential to add vitamin D, oxidized cholesterol, isomeric *trans* fatty acids, and oxidized derivatives of PUFA to the Japanese diet. This diet also contains a substantial amount of processed foods in which lipoxygenase activity could decrease nutritive value[67-78]. Nutritional studies on the consequences of proteins exposure to peroxidized lipids will probably increase in the future.

In summary, the products of oxidation from fatty acids and from cholesterol have been found to be toxic to animal models. The nonvolatile oxidation products which are formed during the deep fat frying of potato chips, french fries, doughnuts, and noodles have been extracted from these fried food items and have been found to have the same chemical charac-teristics as the frying fat that these foods had been prepared in. When rats, which were kept on diets marginal in protein and vitamin content, were fed such used frying fat they developed diarrhea and enlarged livers.

Oxidized sterols, such as cholecalciferol or 25-hydroxy cholesterol, have been found to act as angiotoxins when fed to swine or rabbits. These derivatives of oxidized cholesterol increased the frequency of aortic smooth muscle cell death, increased mitosis of smooth muscle cells, and increased collagen formation in the thoracic aorta and coronary arteries of swine. Two types of pathology could be developed in the thoracic aorta by con-tinuous or short term feeding of cholecalciferol: one, a diffuse fibroelastic intimal thickening in the thoraic aorta (arteriosclerosis) with no evidence of lipid deposition by continuous feeding of cholecalciferol (vitamin D_3) or two, an intimal thickening in the thoracic aorta and intimal thickening with foam cells and extracellular lipid deposits (atherosclerosis) in the coronary arteries after a short period of supplemental cholecalciferol fol-lowed by 3–4 months of supplement-free diets. These two types of arterial damage were identical to that in the plugs of thoracic aorta obtained as a by-product of elective coronary bypass surgery. Since population groups which consume less cholecalciferol-supplemented foods and less deep fat fried cholesterol containing foods have a lower incidence of coronary heart disease, it seems judicious for food processors to reduce these pre-viously unconsidered "risk factors" to a minimum.

REFERENCES

1. Kummerow, F. A., *Lipid and Their Oxidation*. Schultz, H. (Ed.). Avi Publishing Company, Chapter 16, (1964).
2. Perkins, E. G., Rao, M. K. G. and Kummerow, F. A., *Intern. Symp. Deterioration Lipids*, 177–182, (1973).
3. Imai, J., Werthessen, N. T., Taylor, C. B. and Lee, K. T., *Arch. Pathol. Laboratory Medicine*, **100**, 565, (1976).
4. Kummerow, F. A. *Am. J. Clin. Nutr.*, **32**, 58–88 (1979).
5. Imai, H. and Thomas, W. A., *Exp. Mol. Pathol.*, **8**, 830, (1968).
6. World Health Organization, Circulatory-Related Statistics, Japan vs. U.S., (1974).
7. Chang, S. S. and Kummerow, F. A., *J. Am. Oil Chemists' Soc.*, **30**, 403–407, (1953).
8. Quackenbush, F. W., *Oil Soap*, **22**, 366, (1945).
9. Artman, N. R., *Advances in Lipid Research.*, R. Paoletti and D. Kritchevsky (Eds.). Academic Press, New York, New York, vol. 7, p. 245, 1969.
10. Johnson, O. C., Sakuragi, T., and Kummerow, F. A., *J. Am. Oil Chemists' Soc.*, **33**, 433–435, (1956).
11. Johnson, O. C. and Kummerow, F. A., *J. Am. Oil Chemists' Soc.*, **34**, 407–409, (1957).
12. Perkins, E. G. and Kummerow, F. A., *J. Nutr.*, **68**, 101–108, (1959).
13. Sugai, M., Witting, L. A., Tsuchiyama, H., and Kummerow, F. A., *Cancer Res.*, **22**, 510–519, (1962).
14. Mookherjee, B. D., Deck, R. E., and Chang, S. S., *J. Agr. Food Chem.*, **13**, 131–134, (1965).
15. Perkins, E. G., *Food Technol.*, **21**, 125–139, (1967).
16. Perkins, E. G. and Kummerow, F. A., *J. Am. Oil Chemists' Soc.*, **36**, 371–375, (1959).
17. Perkins, E. G., Vachha, S. M., and Kummerow, F. A., *J. Nutr.*, **100**, 725–731, (1970).
18. Iwaoka, W. I., and Perkins, E. G., *Lipids*, **11**, 349–353, (1976).
19. Anonymous, *Nutri. Rev.*, **26**, 210–212, (1968).
20. Keane, K. W., Jacobson, G. A., and Krieger, C. H., *J. Nutr.*, **68**, 57–74, (1959).
21. Nolen, G. A., Alexander, J. C., and Artman, N. R., *J. Nutr.*, **93**, 337–348, (1967).
22. Warner, W.D., Abell, F. N., Mone, P. E., Poling, C. E. and Rice, E. E., *J. Am. Dietet. Assoc.*, **40**, 422–426 (1962).
23. Poling, C. E., Eagle, E., Rice, E. E., Durand, M. A. and Fishen, M., *Lipids*, **5**, 128–136 (1970).
24. Govind Rao, M. K., Hemans, C., and Perkins, E. G., *Lipids*, **8**, 342–347, (1973).
25. Witting, L. A., Nishida, T., Johnson, O. C., and Kummerow, F. A., *J. Am. Oil Chemists' Soc.*, **34**, 421–424, (1957).

26. Friedman, L., Horwitz, W., Shue, G., and Firestone, D., *J. Nutr.*, **73**, 85–93, (1961).
27. Shue, G. M. *et al.*, *J. Nutr.*, **94**, 171–177, (1968).
28. Kaunitz, H., *Food Technol.*, **21**, 60–64, (1967).
29. Hermans, C. Kummerow, F. A. and Perkins, E. G., *J. Nutr.*, **103**, 1665–1672, (1973).
30. Endres, J., Bhalerao, V., and Kummerow, F. A., *J. Am. Oil Chemists' Soc.*, **39**, 118–121, (1962).
31. Endres, J. G., Bhalerao, V. R., and Kummerow, F. A., *J. the American Oil Chemists' Society*, **39**, 159–162, (1962).
32. Lundberg, W. O. (Ed.), *Autoxidation and Antioxidants*, vols. 1 and 2. Wiley, New York, (1961–1962).
33. Zalewski, S., and Kummerow, F. A., *J. Am. Oil Chemists' Soc.*, **45**, 87–92, (1968).
34. Lands, W. E. M., Blank, M. L., Nutter, L. J., and Privett, O. S., *Lipids*, **1**, 224–229, (1966).
35. Lands, W. E. M., *J. Am. Oil Chemists' Soc.*, **42**, 465–467, (1968).
36. Goller, H. J., Sgoutas, D. S., Ismail, I. A., and Gunstone, F. D., *Biochemistry* **9**, 3072–3076, (1970).
37. Sgoutas, D. S., *Biochimica et Biophysica Acta*, **164**, 317–326, (1968).
38. Sgoutas, D. S., and Kummerow, F. A., *Am. J. Clin. Nutr.*, **23**, 1111–1119, (1970).
39. Sgoutas, D. S., *Biochemistry*, **9**, 1826–1833, (1970).
40. Sgoutas, D. S., Jones, R., and Lieght, M., *Intern. J. Biochemistry*, **4**, 437, (1973).
41. Egwim, P. O. and Sgoutas, D. S., *J. Nutr.*, **101**, 307–314, (1971).
42. Egwim, P. O. and Sgoutas, D. S. *J. Nutr.*, **101**, 315–322, (1971).
43. Egwim, P. O. and Kummerow, F. A., *J. Nutr.*, **102**, 783–792, (1972).
44. Egwim, P. O. and Kummerow, F. A., *Lipids*, **7**, 567–571, (1972).
45. De Kruyff, B. Demel, R. A., Slotboom, A. J., Van Deenen, L. L. M., and Rosenthal, A. F., *Biochimica et Biophysica Acta*, **307**, 1–19, (1973).
46. Demel, R. A., Brockdorfer, K. R., and Van Deenen, L. L. M., *Biochimica et Biophysica Acta*, **152**, 694–703, (1972).
47. Van Den Bosch, H., Slotboom, A. J., and Van Deenen, L. L. M., *Biochimica et Biophysica Acta*, **176**, 632, (1969).
48. Van Den Bosch, H., Van Golde, L. M. C., Slotboom, A. J., and Van Deenen, L. L. M., *Biochimica et Biophysica Acta*, **152**, 694–703, (1968).
49. Hoelzl Wallach, D. F., *The Plasma Membrane: Dynamic Perspectives Genetics and Pathology*, The English Universities Press, Ltd., London, 1972.
50. Nutritional Analysis of Food Served at McDonald's Restaurants. 1977. WARF Inst. Inc, Madison, Wisconsin, McDonald Systems Inc.
51. Kummerow, F. A. J. Food Sci., **40**, 12, (1975).
52. Kummerow, F. A., Cho, B. H. S., Huang, W. Y. T., Imai, H., Deutsch, M. H., and Hooper, W. M., *Am. J. Clin. Nutr.*, **29**, 579, (1976).
53. Committee on Animal Nutrition. *Nutrient Requirements of Swine*, National Research Council, Washington, D.C., *Nat. Acad. Sci.*, **30**, (1973).

54. Committee on Animal Nutrition, National Research Council. *Nutrient Requirements of Poultry*. Washington, D.C., *Nat. Acad. Sci.*, (1971).
55. Committee on Animal Nutrition, National Research Council. *Nutrient Requirements of Beef Cattle*. Washington, D.C., *Nat. Acad. Sci.*, (1971).
56. Horowitz, W. 1975. *Official Methods of Analysis*. Washington, D.C. Association of Official Analytical Chemists, 851.
57. Fleischman, A. I., Bierenaum, M. L., Baichelson, R., Hayton, T. and Watson, P., *Vitamin D and Hypercholesterolemia in Adult Humans. Atherosclerosis*, 468, (1970).
58. Taura, S., Taura, M., Imai, H. and Kummerow, F. A., *Artery*, 4, 395–407 (1978)
59. Jackson, R. L., Morrisett, J. D., Pownall, H. J., Gotto, A. M., Kamio, A., Imai, H., Tracy, R. and Kummerow, F. A., J. Lipid Res., 18: 182–190, (1977).
60. Taura, S., Taura, M., and Kummerow, F. A., *Artery*, 4: 100–106, (1978).
61. Taura, S., Taura, M., Imai, H., Kummerow, F. A., Takuyasu, K. and Cho, S. B. H., *Arterial Wall*, 4, 245–257 (1978).
62. Huang, W. Y., Kamio, A., Yeh, S-J. C., and Kummerow, F. A., *Artery* 3: 439–455, (1977).
63. Taura, S., Taura, M., Takuyasu, K., Kamio, K., Kummerow, F. A. and Cleveland, J. C., *Artery*, 3, 529–541 (1977).
64. Kamio, A., Huang, W. Y., Imai, H. and Kummerow, F. A., *J. Electronmicroscopy*, 26, 29–40 (1977).
65. Chang, S. S., and Kummerow, F. A., *J. Am. Oil Chemists' Soc.*, 31: 324, (1954).
66. Chang, S. S. and Kummerow, F. A., *Am. J. Oil Chemists' Soc.*, 30, 403, (1953).
67. Narayan, K. A. and Kummerow, F. A., *J. Am. Oil Chemists' Soc.*, 40, 339, (1963).
68. Tappel, A. L., *Federation Proc.*, 32, 1870, (1973).
69. Roubal, W. T., *J. Am. Oil Chemists' Soc.*, 47, 141, (1970).
70. Schaieh, K. M. and Karel, M., *Lipids*, 11, 392, (1976).
71. Gardner, H. W. and Kleiman, R., *Lipids*, 12, 941, (1977).
72. Gardner, H. W., Weisleder, D. and Inglett, G. E., *Lipids*, 12, 655, (1977).
73. Tannenbaum, S., Barth, R. H. and Le Roux, J. P., *J. Agr. Food Chem.*, 17, 1353, (1969).
74. Yong, S. H. and Karel, M., *Lipids*, 13, 1, (1978).
75. Gardner, H. W., Kleiman, R., Weisleder, D. and Inglett, G. E., *Lipids*, 12, 655, (1977).
76. Trombly, R. and Tappel, A. L., *Lipids*, 10, 441, (1975).
77. Gardner, H. W. and Kleiman, R., *Lipids*, 12, 941, (1977).
78. Ohfuji, T. and Kaneda, T., *Lipids*, 8, 353, (1973).

2.4 Nutritive Value of Diet in Actual Consumption

Carmen Ll. Intengan*

Surveys of food consumption have been undertaken in many countries to assess the national food situation and the nutritional status of the population. This kind of survey is usually carried out by collecting food intake data from statistically sampled households. The method of data collection may vary from one country to another depending on how food is managed in the household. Thus, in well developed countries where purchases of food may be made in bulk or on a weekly basis, it may be possible to estimate food consumed in the household by the inventory method, i.e., by taking stock of food available at the beginning and end of the week and adding whatever additional food items may have been purchased during the week. It may also be possible for a houswife to recall the food served to family members since recipes and portions served tend to be fairly well standardized in well developed countries. In developing countries such as the Philippines where most households purchase food on a daily basis, recipes are usually mixed and very varied, and weights and/or measures are usually only approximated, the food consumed is best measured by actually weighing the amount of food consumed, either individually or in groups such as households.

In countries where food consumption surveys have not been undertaken the food balance sheet, which is usually prepared annually, presents estimates of the food supply available for human consumption. This is obtained from the total foodstuffs produced in the country and the amount of foodstuffs imported. Deductions are made for the amounts exported, for animal feed, for amounts used as seeds, for amounts used in the manufacture of nonfood products, and losses due to various causes.

The estimated amounts of food consumed by the people, collected either from household surveys or from food balance sheets, are then evaluated for their nutritive value. The nutrient values of raw foods as published in most Food Composition Tables (FCT) are used for estimating the nutrients contained in the foods consumed. In most reports, however, no corrections

*Food and Nutrition Research Institute, National Science Development Board, Pedro Gil Street Taft Avenue corner, Ermita, Metro Manila, The Philippines

196

are made for losses of nutrients during the preparation and/or cooking of food.

Nutrient losses as reported in the literature vary considerably. New methods of processing are now being applied which may minimize losses. In this paper, food losses will be discussed using the traditional methods of cooking as practiced in the Philippines.

The FCT published in the Philippines[1] presents data on the nutritive value of fresh raw foods usually selected at their optimum maturity and not wilted or decayed. The corresponding values for cooked foods most commonly used in the Filipino diet are likewise given. The percentage retention of vitamins and minerals after cooking by boiling with a minimal amount of water averaged about 80% for minerals, niacin and carotene, and about 70% for other vitamins (see Table 1).

TABLE 1. Percentage retention of vitamins in some individually boiled vegetables in the Philippines (cooking fluid included)

Vegetable group	Ca	Fe	Caro-tene	Thia-mine	Ribo-flavin	Niacin	Ascor-bic acid
Leafy greens (10)	83	61	72	68	71	75	65
Dried beans (3)	76	39	—	69	46	56	—
Tubers (5)	80	94	—	62	67	89	85
Other vegetables (13)	85	82	85	77	72	90	66

It is fortunate that in most Filipino dishes, the cooking water is usually consumed. This is because most vegetables are pan fried or sauteed with garlic, onions, tomatoes and with either pork or shrimps. The cooking water therefore has the most flavor and, as shown by Krehl and Winters[2] contains a large percentage of the vitamins.

To obtain a better estimate of the loss in nutrients in the preparation and cooking of Philippine foods, some 35 recipes popularly used in various regions of the country were studied by Lontoc *et al.*[3,4] These recipes calculated for 6 servings each, were prepared in the test kitchen of the Food and Nutrition Research Institute. All food items used for each recipe were doubled in amount. The duplicate amount was analyzed in the fresh state. The cooking procedures simulated the methods commonly employed by housewives in the particular region where the recipe originated. The cooked sample was slurried and analyzed in the same manner as the fresh sample. Table 2 shows the percentage retention of vitamins and minerals in various Philippine recipes.

In general, the greatest loss was in ascorbic acid followed by thiamine, riboflavin and niacin. Vitamin A/carotene was found to be the most stable.

TABLE 2. Percentage retention of vitamins and minerals
in Philippine recipes

Recipes	Ca	Fe	Vit. A value	Thia- mine	Ribo- flavin	Niacin	Ascor- bic acid
Vegetable dishes (7)†	69	64	83	59	62	69	50
Fish/shellfish with vegetables (14)	61	61	75	55	53	66	50
Meat with vegetables (9)	29	38	48	25	32	38	38
Meat dishes (3)	49	53	53	42	49	46	—
Fish (2)	20	34	14	20	28	27	—

†Figures in parentheses indicate numbers of recipes analyzed.

Vegetable dishes showed a relatively higher percentage retention of vitamins and minerals than other recipes. The cooking methods generally employed are either boiling or sauteing in a small amount of oil, garlic, tomatoes and onions. It takes at most 10 min to cook foods by these vegetable recipes. However, the losses (except for carotene) tend to be somewhat higher than when single food items were simply boiled, as shown in Table 1.

The nutrient retention in fish/shellfish recipes cooked with some vegetables simply followed that found with vegetable dishes. The methods of cooking used in preparing these recipes were sauteing, frying or boiling. A little more time was needed to prepare these recipes. More handling of the food was necessary prior to its cooking; for example, crab meat had to be removed from its shell, fish was flaked and made into balls, and vegetables were diced or cut into pieces depending on the recipe.

The meat dishes and meat with vegetable recipes showed the least retention of vitamins and minerals among the recipes studied, apart from fish-only dishes. Several factors contribute to this lower retention of nutrients. First, it takes a far longer time to cook meat. Many of the recipes used several methods of stewing. In some recipes, sufficient water was used to provide enough sauce after cooking to be served with the meal. In other recipes, more water was added to provide sufficient broth. The temperature of cooking also varied. Although a "simmering" temperature is desirable, it is quite difficult to keep the temperature below boiling point, especially when a native stove using firewood is employed.

The greatest loss of nutrients was shown by two recipes for fish alone. One recipe used vinegar when cooking the fish, and the other used tomato sauce. An acid pH and the temperature and length of cooking time were apparently factors which contributed to the higher loss of nutrients.

Except in coastal areas in the Philippines, fresh fish is not readily available. Most people, especially in rural areas, unless they are near rivers and lakes, rely on dried fish as a protein dish to be eaten with rice. However, the process of drying fish currently practiced in the country entails a large percentage loss of several nutrients, as shown in Table 3.

TABLE 3. Percentage retention of protein and vitamins in dried catfish and anchovy

	Catfish	Anchovy
Protein	83	87
Thiamine	4	50
Riboflavin	10	53
Niacin	19	—

Rice is the main staple of most Asian diets. In the Philippines, milled rice dominates as the major cereal consumed. Corn grits average about 1/4 of the total cereal consumed. Wheat, although consumed least, is showing an increasing trend. Cereals contribute on average about 1/2 of the per capita protein intake of the Filipino diet. However, rice protein, although of better quality than corn or wheat has a lower percentage of nitrogen absorption. Tanaka *et al.*[5] have reported that about 15% of undigested protein particles are excreted in the human feces. This is an important consideration in view of the minimal intake of protein in the Filipino diet.

The primary function of cooking is to prepare foods in an edible form. Different methods of cooking may be employed for variety, consumer acceptability and improvement in palatability. Since losses are bound to occur, it is important for the nutritionist to evaluate the effects that different methods of cooking have on the retention of vitamins and minerals, so that (1) proper modifications can be applied to the cooking procedures to minimize as far as possible the loss of essential nutrients, and (2) information on actual nutrient losses can be incorporated into better planning and evaluation of diets.

From the data presented here, it is apparent that evaluation of the nutritional quality of diet on the basis of data obtained on a fresh basis is subject to overestimation. Considerable variation has been shown in the cooking losses tested. Also, until more definite data can be obtained, the present assessment should be regarded as only a rough estimate of the cooking losses in Philippine foods. The estimates given were based on preliminary data, on the preparation and cooking methods currently practiced in the country and on the proportional amount consumed in each food group. These estimates did not include nutrient loss which occurs when foods are improperly stored, which is probably extant in most developing countries and hence, a contributory factor to the total nutrient losses.

Table 4 summarizes the *per capita* nutrient intake per day when corrected for percentage losses in the preparation and cooking of Philippine foods. The loss in protein is computed only for rice: 20% for cooking and 15% for digestibility. Of note are the cooking losses for ascorbic acid which were the lowest among the nutrients studied. This is due to the fact that fruits, besides containing more ascorbic acid, are eaten raw and are therefore subject to 100% retention in terms of estimated total ascorbic acid actually consumed. For other vitamins and minerals, the estimated amount lost in the total food consumed averaged about 30% for calcium, iron and vitamin A; 35% for riboflavin and niacin; and 40% for thiamine.

TABLE 4.   Mean one-day *per capita* nutrient intake actually consumed

Nutrients	*Per capita* intake/ day	Cooking losses (%)	Corrected nutrient intake
Protein (g)	47.4	32†	40.9
Calcium (g)	0.36	30.6	0.25
Iron (mg)	10.5	29.5	7.4
Vitamin A (IU)	2063	29.3	1459
Thiamine (mg)	0.74	40.5	0.44
Riboflavin (mg)	0.54	35.2	0.35
Niacin (mg)	14.4	36.3	9.2
Ascorbic acid (mg)	62.2	26.2	45.9

†Losses applied only to 276 g *per capita* intake of rice.

Data on food and nutrient intake are relevant indicators of the actual food and nutriture of the people and they have been used as basic factors in policy decisions by development planners in nutrition, agriculture, health, economics, education and other related fields. Considering that development projects and programs are generated from information provided by survey data and food balance sheets, it behooves our food processors, dieticians and nutrition educators to take positive action to control and/or minimize losses of nutrients in food preparation and for nutrition evaluators to allow for unavoidable losses in nutrients when estimates are made of actual consumption.

REFERENCES

1. Food and Nutrition Research Institute, NSDB, Philippines, *Food Composition Table Recommended for Use in the Philippines*, 1968 Revision.
2. Krehl, W. A. and Winters, R. W., Effect of cooking methods on retention of vitamins and minerals in vegetables, *JADA*, **26**, 966 (1950).
3. Lontoc, A. V., Abdon, I. C., Soriano, M. R., Palad, J. G., Eusebio, E. C., Morga, N. S., Soriano, E. R., Tanchuco, R. H., Alejandro L. A., and Roldan, S. C., Vitamin and mineral retention in some regional recipes, *Philip. J. Nutr.*, **28**, 27 (1975).
4. Lontoc, A. V., Abdon I. C., and Alabastro, V. Q., Vitamin and mineral retention in thirty-two regional recipes, Part II, in press.
5. Tanaka, Y., Resurreccion A. P. and Juliano B. O., Some properties of undigested protein, IRRI Seminar, Chemistry Dept., Feb. 11, 1978.

Subplenary Sessions

Main Topic III: Preservation and Processing of Food

1. Food Preservation
2. Enzymes in Food Processing
3. Fermentation

1. Food Preservation

1.1 Food Preservation by Irradiation

Karoly Vas*

Geographically and geopolitically, food needs and food supplies display a highly variable ratio. In some countries production greatly exceeds man's physiological needs, while in many others the reverse is true. The latter situation usually results in malnutrition, which at present affects about one third of the world's population.

Several experts consider that world food production, if evenly distributed, should be adequate to ensure decent feeding of the whole of mankind. However, in view of the present social and political difficulties related to even distribution and the widening gap between the growth rates of population and food, increasing the food supplies appears to be the only realistic way of remedying the situation. This again involves boosting agricultural production and preserving the produce more effectively. As the average annual increase in agricultural production can, at best, reach only a few percent, and yearly food losses are several times higher, preservation appears to represent the immediate goal for world action.

To achieve this purpose, a wide variety of existing preservation techniques are available. However, for either technical or economic reasons, none of these is universally applicable, so that a search for new methods of preservation is thoroughly justified and actively being pursued in many countries. One of the new methods consists of exposing the food to ionizing radiations, and is called food irradiation. This technique involves the use of radiation sources such as encapsulated γ-ray-emitting isotopes (^{60}Co or ^{137}Cs) or electron-ray-emitting electrical machines (accelerators).

1.1.1 SCOPE OF APPLICATION

This new physical process is applicable to a number of problems, some of which can be solved by irradiation in a unique way.

*Central Food Research Institute, H-1525 Budapest, Herman Ottó ut 15, Hungary

A number of undesirable *physiological changes* in foods of plant origin may be prevented by low doses of ionizing radiation. Sprouting of potatoes, onions, garlic and yams is irreversibly prevented by irradiation, while over-ripening and concomitant deteriorative changes can be retarded in several fruits such as papayas, mangoes, litchies, avocados, etc.

Microbial spoilage of quickly perishable foods such as fruits, vegetables, meat, poultry, fish and other marine products, can be slowed down by medium doses of radiation. Microbial decontamination of less perishable foods, of food ingredients and processing aids (e.g. spices, starch, protein and enzyme preparations), as well as sterilization of meat and animal feedstuffs can be achieved by doses in the higher range.

Microbial infections of significance to public health (e.g. salmonellosis) can be prevented by ionizing radiations applied to products such as fish, meat, feedstuffs, etc.

Infestation with agents of *animal origin* (e.g. insects and parasites) can be combatted with low doses of ionizing radiation in foods as diverse as dried dates, fish, meat and grain. In this way, not only public health hazards (trichinella, cysticercus, etc.) but also economically important animal infestations (insect damage, problems in plant quarantine, etc.), can be controlled.

1.1.2 Special Advantages

Any new method of food preservation can justify its existence only if it is able to offer specific technological and/or economic advantages over existing methods. One of the special features of the present method is that it is a "cold" method of preservation, i.e., it does not cause any appreciable temperature increase in the product (1–4° C at maximum). It can therefore be applied to heat sensitive products, to frozen goods (such as frozen egg pulp or poultry) and to viscous materials (such as dried dates), without affecting their consistency.

A further important and unique feature of the method is that the applied radiations are able to penetrate into the middle of even bulky goods, thereby facilitating treatment in the *ready-packaged* state, so preventing post-treatment re-infestation or recontamination by microorganisms. Also, destruction of insects and their eggs in the *center* of a kernel (e.g. grain) or of a large piece of food such as of a large fruit, can be effected. The requirements of plant quarantine in fruits having the size of a mango or even in larger fruits or vegetables, can thus be met.

The *energy requirements* of the process are low. This is of special significance at a time of the severe energy crisis which now faces the majority of developing countries where the need for improved food preservation is most acute. Reduction of the energy requirements also has another advantageous side-effect, in that it can contribute towards overall *reduction of the pollution* caused by the combustion products of traditional fuels as normally applied in present-day techniques for food preservation. Furthermore, being a physical method, the new process does *not impart chemical residues* to the treated product and, by *lowering the need for chemicals*, as used in fumigation, other types of insect control or food preservation, it again represents a potential tool for achieving a cleaner environment.

Among the special assets of food irradiation, its contribution to the *improvement of food quality* must also be mentioned. It facilitates (1) the creation of new types of shelf-stable convenience foods which can be stored at room temperature, as well as (2) improvement of the technological quality (texture, nutrition) and the microbiological safety of foods, and (3) reduction of the need for the chemicals used in controlling food poisoning (e.g. nitrite, sodium chloride, etc.).

1.1.3 LIMITATIONS

In view of the above advantages of food irradiation, it may appear difficult to understand why the new process has not yet been introduced on a world-wide scale. The first large-scale application has been its use in Japan for the prevention of sprouting in potatoes. The second-largest industrial application will soon be established in Italy. However, regardless of the fact that 58 pilot plants were operational in 30 countries in 1975, the rate of actual large-scale industrial introduction can, at best, be termed sluggish.

Investigations into the reasons for this situation have revealed two major problems. One is the very fact that the new process is a physical one. While this is of great advantage from the viewpoint of wholesomeness and environmental considerations, it suffers from the disadvantage common to all physical methods of food preservation, viz. it cannot be applied profitably on a small scale. In view of the relatively high costs of establishing an irradiation plant, as in the case of canning, refrigeration, freezing, etc., no economical operation is conceivable below a certain threshold value of plant throughput capacity. This, of course, requires rather concentrated production, in sufficient total quantity, of the product(s) to be treated, preferably in the vicinity of the plant. Economic calculations so far performed have shown that, once this threshold is reached, the unit cost of irradiation amounts to only a few percent of the value of the food product treated and is of the same order of magnitude as that of traditional preservation methods (Atomic Energy of Canada, 1975) (Fig. 1).

The second factor hindering the practical introduction of food irradiation is basically a psychological one. For a long time, the safety for human

Dose (kGy)	Utili-zation (h a⁻¹)	Through-put (kta⁻¹)	Cost ($ t⁻¹)	Process cost (% of wholesale price of product)	Product
0.05	2000	42	1.5	0.9—1.1%	Potatoes
0.05	2000	42	1.5	0.4—0.6%	Onions
0.2	8400	1092	0.23	0.13%	Wheat, Maize
0.2	8400	1092	0.23	0.04%	Rice
2	2000	5	21	7.7—10.6%	Oranges
3	6000	9	10	1.2—1.9%	Chicken
3	6000	9	10	1.1%	Turkey
45	6000	6	76	4.8—5.1%	Beef
0.75	1500	1.2	50	4.0%	Fish

Fig. 1. h: hour, a: annum, t: tonne

consumption ("wholesomeness") of an irradiated product has been questioned. Suspicions arose from an unwarranted association of food irradiation with the atomic bomb. This bias has tended to cause public health officials to hesitate over approving application of the irradiation process. Prior to granting permission, use of the process has to be proved to be harmless for each individual food item separately. This is in contrast to the approach adopted with all traditional processes, e.g. heat treatment (cooking, frying, canning), heat removal (refrigeration, quick-freezing), and even some of the newer processes such as irradiation with infrared or high-frequency waves. Most of these have never been tested for their public health safety prior to use, or indeed, for the most part, at any subsequent time. Due to this scientifically unjustifiable and psychologically motivated status of food irradiation, extensive testing on safety for consumption has long been carried out. It is now being continued in many countries and, in the last decade, at the international level (International Project in the Field of Food Irradiation (IFIP), Karlsruhe, F.R.G.).

1.1.4 Prospects

Given the advantages and limitations of the food irradiation process, the overall outlook is rather encouraging since the former by far outweigh the latter. Much will depend on the results of international attempts to achieve harmonization among the widely differing national legislations concerning the topic. International agencies (FAO, IAEA, WHO, OECD) are now in the process of devising a common regulatory approach to the

Product \ Country	BUL.	CAN.	CHI.	CZE.	DEN.	FRA.	F.R.G.	HUN.	ISR.	ITA.	JPN.	NET.	PHI.	S.A.F.	SPA.	THA.	U.K.	URU.	U.S.A.	U.S.S.R.
Shallot					77															
Fresh, tinned and liquid food												72								
Deep frozen meals (hosp.)						72						69								
Food for hospital patients																	69			
Dry food concentrates	72																			**66**
Cod and haddock fillets		73																		
Shrimps												70								
Culinary prepared meat																				67
Poultry (eviscerated)		73										71/**76**								66
Semi prepared meat																				64
Wheat flour and whole wheat flour		59																		
Wheat and wheat flour																			**63**	
Grain	72																			**59**
Spices and condiments						74						71								
Endive												75								
Powdered batter mix												74								
Vegetable filling												74								
Cocoa beans												69								
Mangoes													76							
Strawberries						73						69								
Asparagus												69								
Mushrooms				76								**69**								
Fresh fruits and vegetables	72																			64
Dried fruits	72																			66
Garlic	72				77					73										
Onions	72	65		76	77			73	68	73		71/**75**			75	73				67/73
Potatoes	72	60	74	76	**70**	72	74	69	**67**	73	72	70	72	77	69			70	64	58

Fig. 2. Dates of approval (19 . .) of irradiated foods in various countries (unconditional approval dates in bold face).

subject which could then be recommended to member states for adoption in their specific national food law systems. A first attempt has in fact recently been completed at the recommendation of an FAO/IAEA/WHO Advisory Group on the International Acceptance of Irradiated Food (November 1977, Wageningen, Netherlands).

A second important task to be achieved at the international level is the elaboration of international standards for food irradiation. On the basis of the evaluation of wholesomeness data by a Joint FAO/IAEA/WHO Expert Committee on the Wholesomeness of Irradiated Food (August-September 1976, Geneva, Switzerland), a draft General Standard for Irradiated Foods and a draft Code of Practice for the Operation of Radiation Facilities used for the Treatment of Foods were prepared and submitted to the Codex Committee on Food Additives (CXFA), the subsidiary body of the Codex Alimentarius Commission of the Joint FAO/WHO Food Standards Programme, designated by the Commission to deal with food irradiation. After their acceptance by the CXFA, the drafts were recently approved (May 1978, Rome, Italy) by the Codex Alimentarius Commission at step 6 in the 9-step procedure of the Codex. The drafts now go before the October 1978 meeting of the CXFA for further processing*. If the Codex procedure is successfully completed, a recommended international standard and a code of practice will be put before the 116 member states of the Codex for their acceptance. This will then facilitate the entrance of irradiated foods into international trade.

However, the situation is at present handicapped by the fact that national clearances, although available in a total of 20 countries for a total of 26 commodities (Fig. 2), show a rather scattered pattern. This inevitably gives rise to uncertainties for industrial enterprises entering the field of food irradiation. Very few, if any, entrepreneurs are actually willing to take the risk without being assured that the irradiated product can be safely marketed over a wide area. It is hoped that harmonization of the regulatory system and the eventual establishment of international standards will contribute towards further progress, and will ultimately lead to a breakthrough in the practical application of this promising and much-needed technique of food preservation.

---

*At its 12th Session (10–16 October, 1978), the CXFA promoted the drafts to step 8.

REFERENCES

1. Anon., *Aspects of the Introduction of Food Irradiation in Developing Countries*, International Atomic Energy Agency, Vienna, p. 97–108 (1973).
2. Atomic Energy of Canada Ltd., *Food Irradiation 1975*, Ottawa (1975).
3. Balázs-Sprincz, V., Evaluation of the economic feasibility of radiation preservation of selected food commodities, *Atomic Energy Rev.*, **15** (3), 407 (1977).
4. Brynjolfsson, A., Energy and food irradiation, *Food Preservation by Irradiation*, Proc. Symp., Wageningen, 1977, IAEA, Vienna, vol. 2, 285 (1978).
5. Diehl, J. F., Lebensmittelbestrahlung—ein Fortschrittsbericht, *Kerntechnik*, **19**, 494 (1977).
6. Goresline, H. E., The potentials of ionising radiation for food preservation, *Food Irradiation Information*, IFIP, Karlsruhe, No. 2., 20 (1973).
7. Josephson, E. J., Overview of prospects for food irradiation, 36th Ann. Mtg. Inst. Food Technologists, Anaheim, California (1976).
8. Libby, W. F. and E. F. Black, Food irradiation: an unused weapon against hunger, *Bulletin of the Atomic Scientist*, p. 51–55, Feb. 1978.
9. Sundaram, K., Food irradiation: contributions to public health in developing countries, *Nuclear India*, p. 3–6, Aug. 1977.
10. Thomas, A. C. and Basson, R. A., Food for keeps, *Nuclear Active*, No. 14, 26, Jan. 1976.
11. Vas, K., A besugárzásos élelmiszertartósítás nemzetközi helyzete, *Élelmezési Ipar (Budapest)*, **30**, 325 (1976).
12. Vas, K., Recent advances in the preservation of food by irradiation, *IAEA Bull.*, **18**, (3–4), 2 (1976).
13. Vas K., Food irradiation: technical and legal aspects, *Food and Nutrition*, **3** (3), 2 (1977)
14. Vidal, P., L'irradiation, nouveau procédé de conservation, *Industries alimentaires et agricoles*, **90** (9–10) (1973).

1.2 Influence of Controlled Atmospheres on Quality Stability in Food Storage

José A. Muñoz-Delgado*

The favorable effects of low temperature in food preservation can in some cases be improved by additional treatments, i.e. so-called supplements or aids to refrigeration. Modification of the normal composition of the air in contact with foods resulting in a modified atmosphere is one of the most effective ways of extending quality life. The terms "modified atmosphere" (MA) and "controlled atmosphere" (CA) are often used interchangeably to define atmospheres where the proportions of the components of normal air are deliberately changed. While in MA storage there is no attempt to control the atmosphere components at specific concentrations, in CA storage the atmosphere is not only modified but its composition is precisely adjusted according to specific requirements.

1.2.1 CONVENTIONAL USE OF CA STORAGE FOR FRUITS AND VEGETABLES

This technique has been discussed in several reports and reviews[26,37] [38,41,42] and in various books [16,18-20,29,33,34]. It has been applied mainly to apples and pears. Storage of fruits and vegetables in CA leads either to an extension of storage life as compared with conventional refrigeration or to better retention of quality attributes. The reasons for this[10,38] may be summarized as follows: metabolic processes, especially respiration and overmaturity are retarded; the rate of production of ethylene and other oxidizable volatiles is reduced; losses by rotting are also reduced either because the resistance of the host to the attack is better maintained due to retardation of maturity or because there is a direct fungistatic effect on fungi in produce which can tolerate CO_2 concentrations in excess of 10%; better retention of chlorophyll, firmness and of certain constituents such as sugars and carotenoids, and of some substances responsible for flavor, especially organic acids; better appearance after storage during whole and retail sale because the increased CO_2 concentration and reduced O_2 in the tissues exert a strong residual effect, and, for example, fruits after removal

---

*Instituto del Frío, Ciudad Universitaria, Madrid 3, Spain

of CA storage ripen more slowly so that they have a longer shelf-life than normal air-stored fruit.

Misuse of CA is easy because even closely related vegetables or fruits, and even different varieties of the same fruits, have specific and so far un-predictable tolerances for low O_2 and/or high CO_2 concentrations.

A decrease of O_2 concentration to levels up to 1.5–3% is not generally a major problem for most fruits and vegetables which have a longer storage life and retain a better quality at these conditions. The susceptibility to CO_2 is the most important problem and the effect of CO_2 on the produce does not depend merely upon species and variety but also on the degree of maturity, time, temperature and O_2 concentration. It is generally found that susceptibility to CO_2 increases when the O_2 level in the storage atmos-phere decreases.

1.2.2 NEW TRENDS IN CA STORAGE

A. CA Application to Crops Other than Apples and Pears

New developments and applications of CA to crops other than apples and pears have been made to determine the practical and economical feasibility of applying this technique to certain fruits and vegetables whose nature, seasonal production or price may justify such studies. Examples of foodstuffs which have recently been tested in this way include avocados (2% O_2, 10% CO_2) peaches and nectarines (1% O_2, 5% CO_2), mangoes (5% O_2, 5% CO_2), oranges (10–15% O_2, 0% CO_2), mandarins (10% O_2, 0–2% CO_2), persimmons (2% O_2, 8% CO_2, or 3% O_2, 0–3% CO_2, depend-ing on astringency), bananas (3% O_2, 5% CO_2), potatoes (2% O_2, 12–15% CO_2), and tomatoes (3% O_2, 0% CO_2). However, further research is need-ed to determine the real potential for their preservation in CA conditions on a commercial scale.

B. New Techniques in CA Application

a. Initial Anaerobic Storage

It is well known[30] that the nature of the product and the time of initial storage in 100% N_2 exert a strong influence on the maintenance of quality and ripening of certain fruits and vegetables, e.g. green bananas and strawberries. Several apple and pear cultivars stored for 1 week in a 100% N_2 atmosphere[11] at 0°C and –1°C, respectively, after harvesting and subsequently stored at 0°C and –1°C by replacing the oxygen-free atmos-phere by CA conditions (2.5% O_2, 5% CO_2 for apples; 14% O_2, 7% CO_2 for pears) were firmer, retained higher acid levels after 180 days storage and ripening for 1 week at 21°C, and developed less scald injury and fungal rot when post-harvest anaerobiosis storage was used than when only

CA storage was employed. Pears also showed a lower rating for both scald injury and breakdown.

b. Short-term High CO_2 Treatment

The benefits obtained from high CO_2 treatment of apples include retainment of firmness, reduction of loss of malic acid, retardation of ethylene production, delay of climacteric rise in respiration, suppression of increase in protein nitrogen and improvement of quality. CO_2-treated pears have higher contents of total sugars and organic acids which may contribute to higher quality[27]. The lower amount of soluble pectin found may be associated with the firmer tissues in the treated pears.

A 10-day exposure of Golden Delicious apples to CO_2 levels of about 20% and 10% O_2 at the beginning of CA storage delays softening and loss of titrable acidity during subsequent CA storage (2.5% O_2, 1% CO_2)[7] at $-1°C$ for 8 months. Flavor is better and differences in color from untreated fruits are small and not consistent. No off-flavors or internal browning are produced.

The difference in behavior of different varieties of apples demonstrates how difficult it is to generalize about the application of a specific, determined treatment and how important it is to bear in mind the different factors which may influence the keepability and tolerance of fruits and vegetables to different gases and concentrations.

c. Short-term High O_2 Treatment

In the case of apple cultivars susceptible to scald, such as Granny Smith, attempts have recently been made[25] to reduce the disease by treating the fruit during storage with atmospheres enriched in O_2 (about 50%). The most efficient treatments were those applied at the very beginning of cold storage and after 98 days of storage.

d. Low O_2 Storage

For this method of CA storage, the current recommendation is to maintain the CO_2 below 1% and the O_2 between 1.8 and 2.5%. Several apple cultivars susceptible to core flush can be stored in this way with excellent results as regards reduction of the incidence of the disease[13]. The presence of CO_2 increases losses from core flush and from rotting and the incidence of these disorders falls as the CO_2 concentration is reduced. The low O_2 method can be also used for pears.

e. CO_2 Shocks

French studies[24] on CO_2 shocks (10–30%) for 1–3 days, applied periodically during storage of certain fruits and vegetables in normal air, have given encouraging results with pears, bananas, asparagus and peppers. Such storage resulted in less rotting and physiological disorders (scald or internal breakdown of pears), and better quality of the other products than in a conventional controlled atmosphere. However, further research is needed before this technique can be applied on a commercial scale.

f. CA with Intermittent Warming

Progress has recently been made in the intermittent warming of peaches and nectarines, for example, as well as of mangoes[26] both in air and CA for controlling decay. Combining CA with intermittent warming permitted the longest storage.

g. Delayed CA

Recent studies have shown that for certain pear cultivars a delayed CA gives better results than a continuous CA established from the first moment of storage. This is the case of Spanish experience with Blanquilla pears[32] and French experience[22] with Passa Crassana pears.

h. Hypobaric Storage

This is a form of storage in which the pressure exerted on the produce is reduced. The method not only reduces the O_2 concentration in the storage atmosphere but also increases the diffusion of ethylene in fruits and vegetables by evacuation from the tissues of the product, leading to an extension of storage life.

Since the process involves continuous evacuation, mold growth is also retarded by the constant air flow. However, desiccation must be prevented by proper humidification[35].

The first American experience[2] in this field resulted in a significant increase in the storage life of several varieties of fruit, apricots, cherries, peaches, pears, tomatoes, and avocados, by holding the material at a pressure of 0.25 to 0.5 atm. Some data[3,4,9,43,44] on the comparative storage life of produce stored in refrigeration and under hypobaric conditions have recently been compiled[5]. In general, firmness is better retained, while chlorophyll and starch degradation, losses of sugars and titrable acidity, and formation of carotenoids are delayed by subatmospheric pressure treatment.

i. Stabilization of the Barometric Air Pressure

Recent experiments in Switzerland[39] have shown that CA storage of 6 varieties of apples at 2° C, 92 % relative humidity, 2–3 % O_2, 3 % CO_2 and a stable hyperbaric condition (10 mm water column) gave better results than storage without pressure control. The fruits were more healthy, had less scald of the senescence type, displayed higher penetrometric values, were more acid, less yellow, more crisp and gave higher values on degustation tests.

j. Use of Gases Lethal to Enzymes and Microorganisms

It has been attempted[21] to replace the normal atmosphere surrounding and within fresh food tissues with gases that were specifically lethal to enzymes and microorganisms, in the hope of producing a biostatic condition in fresh tissues whereby their fresh-like quality could be fixed.

Quality can be maintained even at room temperature if practically all the O_2 is evacuated from fresh food tissues which are then flushed with a gas such as CO which exerts a lethal effect on the oxidative enzymes causing oxidative browning, and a bactericidal gas such as ethylene oxide (EO), in that order. This technique has been applied to peeled, diced or sliced potatoes, apples and peaches, whole and sliced mushrooms and fresh ground beef patties (Table 1).

C. CA Applications to Other Fresh Produce

a. Meat

In addition to chilling, modification of the atmosphere in which meat is stored or packaged has attracted growing attention in the search for optimal conditions to delay quality changes and to stabilize the color which is governed by reactions between the muscle pigment myoglobin and oxygen depending on the oxygen partial pressure. The gas composition of the environment can also influence the rate and type of microbiological spoilage.

The inhibitory effect of CO_2 on aerobic psychorphilic organisms responsible for spoilage in chilled meat is well known. Many studies have involved the use of CO_2, generally at high concentrations, with modified levels of oxygen[17,31]. However, darkening of meat is accelerated[23,36].

Other investigations[40] have shown that fresh meat packed at O_2 and CO_2 concentrations substantially higher than atmospheric remained red longer than meat packed in air. Successful application of this technique depends on producing a layer of oxymyoglobin which is sufficiently thick to obscure the metmyoglobin developing underneath, and ensuring that the environmental volume is sufficiently large to accommodate reduction by tissue respiration and prevent the oxygen pressure falling to an ineffective level during storage.

Very recent experiments[1] have shown that success in storage of meat prepacked in an atmosphere of 80% O_2 and 20% CO_2 depends not only on the composition of the atmosphere but also on the initial bacterial load and storage temperature ranging from 2 to 7°C (Table 2).

Continuous exposure of beef to atmospheres containing CO[6,12,14] at a minimum concentration of 1% extends both the color and odor shelf life. Samples can be stored at a temperature ranging from 0 to 2°C for 2 weeks.

The beneficial effects of CO on meat color and of high concentrations of CO_2 on microbial growth have been combined by the application of an atmosphere containing 1% CO and 50% CO_2 plus 49% air[15] to improve the microbiological and color shelf lives of ground beef patties stored at 2°C.

b. Fish

A limited amount of research has been carried out on the storage of fish

TABLE 1. Quality changes in several foodstuffs stored in different atmospheres

Product	Evacuation (inches)	Gas treatment		Storage temp. (°C)	Shelf life (days)	Sensory quality			Appear.[3]
		Flush	Storage			Discol.[1]	Text.[2]	Flav.	
Potato disks	30	Control	Air	room temp.	30	6	7	putrid	3
		CO	CO	room temp.	30	4	5	putrid	3
		EO	N₂	room temp.	30	7	2	normal	4
		CO-EO	N₂	room temp.	30	3	2	normal	3
Apple disks	30	Control	Air	room temp.	30	5	5	alcoholic	3
		CO	CO	room temp.	30	4	4	alcoholic	3
		EO	N₂	room temp.	30	6	2	normal	3
		CO-EO	N₂	room temp.	30	4	2	normal	
Peach slices	27	Control	Open container	+ 3	2				3
		Control	Sealed container	+ 3	31				3
		CO	N₂	+ 3	62				4
		CO-EO	N₂	+ 3	13				3
Mushrooms	15	Control	Air	− 2	9				3
		N₂	N₂	− 2	12				3
		CO	N₂	− 2	20				3
Raw beef patties		Air	Sealed container	− 2	50				3
		N₂	N₂	− 2	20				3
		CO	N₂	− 2	75				3
				+ 3	75				4

†1 1 = White; 2 = normal; 3 = trace brown; 4 = slight brown; 6 = dark brown; 7 = black.

†2 1 = Whole, firm; 2 = softer, normal; 3 = soft; 4 = mushy; 5 = mushy, partly liquef.; 6 = mostly liquef.; 7 = entirely liquef.

†3 5 = Fresh-like quality; 4 = slightly poorer than fresh; 3 = decidedly poorer but acceptable; 2 = questionable acceptability; 1 = unacceptable.

Source: Ref. 21. Data compiled into one table by the present author.

Table 2.   Storage life of beef packed in a mixture of 80% O_2 and 20% CO_2

Initial bacterial load (log/g)	Shelf life (days)		
	2°C	5°C	7°C
7.2	2	1	1
6.9	3	2	1.5
5.3	6	5	3.3
5.0	7	6	3.8
4.2	11	8	6.0
3.5	13	10	7.5

Source: Ref. 1.

in gas mixtures other than air, and different responses have been obtained. Atmospheres containing 25%, 40–60%, and 50% CO_2 have been reported to extend the storage life of fish due to the effects of this gas on psychrophilic microorganisms.

CO_2 has been used to extend by 5–7 days the refrigerated sea water (RSW) normal storage life of salmon, halibut, rockfish and shrimps. Recent experiments have shown that RSW at $-1°C$ saturated with CO_2, results in a pH change to the acid side which alters the conditions for growth of spoilage bacteria. An atmosphere of approximately 11.5% CO_2 1.5% O_2 and 87% N_2[28] extends by at least 4–7 days the storage life of fresh dressed salmon packed in flake ice in a ratio of 1:1 to provide a constant temperature of $+ 0.5°C$ and to maintain the surfaces of the fish moist in such a way that the gas used comes in contact with them.

1.2.3 Conclusions

Regarding the influence of MA on fruit and vegetable quality during and after refrigerated storage, some benefit appears, generally speaking, when this type of atmosphere is applied. However, further research is needed to determine the tolerance of different species and varieties to each gas, gas mixtures, gas concentrations and exposure times, in order that only beneficial effects may occur.

Hypobaric storage represents a feasible technique for prolongating the storage life of fruits and vegetables compared to storage in atmospheric conditions. However, more research is again needed.

In the case of meat and fish, MA with high CO_2 concentrations appears to exert a marked influence on microbial growth, but more studies on the application of CA to the storage of fresh fish are required.

In the special case of fresh meat, application of MA with low CO and high CO_2 concentrations, use of high O_2 and CO_2 atmospheres, and packaging in O_2-enriched environments appear to represent a good supplement to refrigeration for extending storage life.

REFERENCES

1. Albertsen, B., Unpublished data, personal communication (1978).
2. Burg, S. P. and Burg, E. A., *Science*, **153**, 314 (1966).
3. Burg, S. P. and Burg, E. A., *Plant Physiol.*, **42**, 144 (1967).
4. Burg, S. P., *Hort. Sci.*, **8**, 202 (1973).
5. Burg, S. P., *Postharvest Biology and Handling of Fruits and Vegetables* (Haard, N. S. and Salunkhe, D. K., ed.), p. 172–188, AVI Publishing Co. (1975).
6. Clark, D. S., Lentz, C. P. and Roth, L. A., *Can. Inst. Food Sci. Technol. J.*, **9**, 114 (1976).
7. Couey, H. M. and Olsen, K. L., *J. Am. Hort. Sci.*, **100** (2) 148 (1975).
8. Ohace, Jr., W. C. Davis, P. C. and Smoot, J. J., Proc. XIIth Int. Congr. Refrig., Madrid (Centro Experimental del Frío, ed.), 383 (1969).
9. Dilley, D. A., *102nd Ann. Rept. Mich. State Hort. Soc.*, **82** (1972).
10. Do, J. Y. and Salunkhe, D. K., *Postharvest Physiology, Handling and Utilization of Tropical and Subtropical Fruits and Vegetables* (Pantastico, Er. B., ed.), p. 175–185, AVI Publishing Co. (1975).
11. Eaves, C. A., Forsyth, F. R. and Lockhard, C. L., Proc. XIIth Int. Congr. Refrig., Madrid (Centro Experimental del Frío, ed.), vol. III, 307 (1969).
12. El-Badawi, A. A., Cain, R. F., Samuels, C. E. and Anglemeier, A. F., *Food Technol.*, **18**, 159 (1964).
13. Fidler, J. C. and North, C. J., Atti Congr. Int. Conserv. Distr. Prod. Ortofrutticoli, Bologna, vol. I, 303 (1963).
14. Garcia-Matamoros, E. and Moral, A., Proc. XIXth Réunion Europ. des Chercheurs en Viande, 1, 317 (1973).
15. Gee, D. L. and Brown, W. D., *J. Agric. Food Chem.*, **26**, 1, 274 (1978).
16. Haard, N. S. and Salunkhe, D. K., *Postharvest Biology and Handling of Fruits and Vegetables*, AVI Publishing Co. (1975).
17. Huffman, D. L., *J. Food Sci.*, **39**, 723 (1974).
18. Hulme, A. C., *The Biochemistry of Fruits and Their Products*, vol. 1, Academic Press (1970).
19. Hulme, A. C., *The Biochemistry of Fruits and Their Products*, vol. 2, Academic Press (1971).
20. International Institute of Refrigeration, *Packing Stations for Fruits and Vegetables* (IIR, ed.), Paris (1973).
21. Kramer, A., Kaffexakis, J. G. and Bresser, T., *Bull. I. I. R., Annex*, **3**, 121 (1973).
22. Leblond, C., 2nd Int. Symp. Pear Growing, *Acta Hort.*, **69**, 275 (1977).

23. Ledward, D. A., Nicol, D. J. and Shaw, M. K., *Food Technol. Austr.*, **23**, 30 (1971).
24. Marcellin, P., *Bull. I. I. F.*, **5**, 1151 (1977).
25. Marcellin, P., Blondeau, J. P., Dessaux, C. and Pouliquen, J., XIVth Int. Congr. Refrig., Moscow, Publ. No. C2. 45 (1975).
26. Marcellin, P. and Kane, D., Coll. Int. CENECA, Le Froid en Agriculture, Publ. No. 5214, Paris (1977).
27. Mellenthin, W. M. and Wang, C. Y., 2nd Int. Symp. Pear Growing, *Acta Hort.*, **69**, 323 (1977).
28. Nelson, R. W. and Tretsven, W. I., XIVth. Int. Congr. Refr., Moscow, Publ. No. C2. 48 (1975).
29. Pantastico, Er. B., *Postharvest Physiology, Handling and Utilization of Tropical and Subtropical Fruits and Vegetables*, AVI Publishing, Co. (1975).
30. Parsons, C. S., Gates, J. E. and Spalding, D. H., *Proc. Am. Soc. Hort, Sci.*, **84**, 549 (1964).
31. Partmann, W., Frank, H. and Gutschmidt, J., *Fleischwirtschaft*, **8**, 1967; **9**, 1205 (1970).
32. de la Plaza, J. L., 2nd Int. Symp. Pear Growing, *Acta Hort.*, **69**, 261 (1977).
33. Ryall, A. L. and Lipton, W. J., *Handling, Transportation and Storage of Fruits and Vegetables*, vol. 1, AVI Publishing Co. (1972).
34. Ryall, A. L. and Pentzer, V. T., *Handling, Transportation and Storage of Fruits and Vegetables*, vol. 2, AVI Publishing Col. (1974).
35. Salunkhe, D. K. and Wu, M. T., *Postharvest Biology and Handling of Fruits and Vegetables* (Haard, N. S. and Salunke, D. K., ed.), p. 153–171, AVI Publishing Co. (1975).
36. Silliker, J. H., Woodruff, R. E., Lugg, J. R., Wolfe, S. K. and Brown, W. D., *Meat Sci.*, 1, 195 (1977).
37. Stoll, K., Mitteil. Eidg. Forshungsanstalt für Obst, Wein und Gartenbau, Wädenswil, Flugschrift Nr. 78, 38 (1973).
38. Stoll, K. *Bull. I. I. F.*, **6**, 1302 (1974).
39. Stoll, K. XIVth Int. Congr. Refrig., Moscow, Pub. No. C2. 44, (1975).
40. Taylor, A. A. and MacDougall, D. B., *J. Food Technol.*, **8**, 453 (1973).
41. Ulrich, R., Proc. XIIth Int. Congr. Refrig., Madrid (Centro Experimental del Frío, ed.), vol. 3, 37 (1967).
42. Ulrich, R., *Postharvest Physiology, Handling and Utilization of Tropical and Subtropical Fruits and Vegetables* (Pantastico, Er. B., ed.), p. 186–200, AVI Publishing Co. (1975).
43. Wu, M. T., Jadhav, S. J. and Salunkhe, D. K., *Food Sci.*, **37**, 952 (1972).
44. Wu, M. T. and Salunkhe, D. K. *Experientia*, **28**, 866 (1972).

1.3 Cereal Preservation under Hermetic Conditions

Hisateru Mitsuda*

1.3.1 CURRENT TRENDS IN STUDIES OF CEREAL PRESERVATION THROUGHOUT THE WORLD

Traditionally, people have stored cereal grain in such places as caves, underground pits and wooden cribs in order to protect it from animals, birds, rodents and insects. Even now there is no established technique for the safe preservation of harvested grain which can be adapted to conditions all over the world.

Generally speaking, the principle of regulating the temperature and moisture content of grain has been considered the most important among the various environmental factors influencing quality. Grain is usually dried to a moisture content of between 10 and 15% prior to storage. Aeration with naturally-cold air or refrigeration is employed to regulate the temperature and thus lower the activities of insects and fungi[1].

In contrast, hermetic preservation works on the basic principle of restricting the oxygen supply by placing the grain in an airtight container. This technique itself is by no means a new one for preserving grain, and many pioneering experiments in such areas as entomology and the ecology of microflora, have been conducted in various countries. However, new developments in the use of inert gases open further interesting possibilities. A change from open type preservation of grain to a hermetic one seems to be one of the clear world-wide trends in cereal preservation.

Strange as it may seem, hermetic conditions have been produced simply by making grain containers airtight. The respiration of any insect that may be present, together with that of grain embryos, consumes the oxygen and produces carbon dioxide. Many experiments on the airtight storage of dry and high moisture grains have been undertaken in the United Kingdom[2]. The units used for these experiments ranged from relatively small pits to large 1000-ton structures made of vapor-proof concrete or butyl rubber and other flexible materials. Silos of butyl rubber bags supported by metal

*Laboratory of Food Science and Technology, Research Institute for Production Development, 15 Morimoto-cho, Shimogamo, Sakyo-ku, Kyoto 606, Japan

mesh were used to store damp grain. Many experiments have also been carried out on trial storage in tropical countries. The conclusion reached was that airtight storage provided a useful method for preserving dry grain in good condition.

Most grain-exporting nations have so far relied on chemicals to meet the strict conditions imposed. In Australia an organophosphorus compound called Malathion has played a vital role since the early 1960's. However, resistance to it and the residue problem have prompted investigations into replacement insecticides. It has become necessary to examine the possibility of producing lethal atmospheres by other means including the purging of silos with nitrogen or carbon dioxide gas and the use of oxygen-free atmospheres produced by burners or catalytic generators. In the 1970's, Bailey et al. at the Stored Grain Research Laboratory of CSIRO began to investigate so-called "Controlled Atmosphere Storage" as opposed to simple airtight storage[3]. In many subsequent storage experiments, they have continued to examine the most adequate composition of gases for grain to be stored.

In Italy, Snamprogetti, an ENI petrochemical research and development company, has been working for a number of years on the use of nitrogen in grain storage. Experimental work was carried out using mini silos, and later a 25-ton capacity silo[4]. They are now developing the hermetic storage method with nitrogen on a commercial scale.

1.3.2 Studies on the Hermetic Preservation of Cereals in Japan

There have been few scientific studies on cereal preservation under hermetic conditions in Japan. On the basis of data obtained in studies on the respiration of hibernating cold-blooded animals in our laboratory at Kyoto University in 1952, the authors introduced the principle of hermetic preservation of cereal grain in naturally cold places. This is based on lowering the respiration in the grain by using both carbon dioxide-enriched air and a low temperature, thus retaining the original freshness of the grain even after prolonged preservation[5] (Fig. 1). The new skin-packaging technique, the so-called Carbon Dioxide Exchange Method (CEM), which is characterized by packaging grain in plastic laminated film bags with carbon dioxide-enriched air, also contributed to the development of the present method. In this technique, head space gases in the package can be effectively eliminated by the ability of grain to adsorb the carbon dioxide gas[6]. The mechanism of such carbon dioxide gas adsorption has been investigated in detail[7]. Long-term preservation tests were carried out by this new technique from 1967 to 1972, both underwater in man-made pools, ponds and a lake, and underground in caves and abandoned mines. Unlike conventional open-type preservation, using bags made of straw,

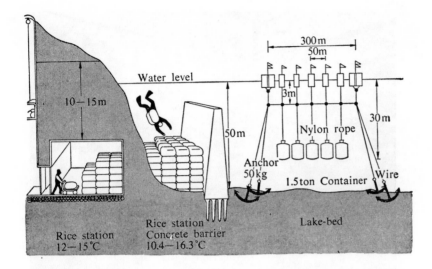

FIG. 1. Theoretical scheme for the underwater and underground storage of cereals.

kraft paper or jute, this new technique proved to be effective in preventing quality changes of grains and in inhibiting the growth of harmful insects and fungi in the bag. For example, the germination capacity of paddy rice retained its original value even after 3 years of storage. Considerably higher enzyme activities were also detected in grain stored underwater than in that stored under natural conditions. The amount of stale flavor as determined from the amount of pentanal and hexanal, indicated that deterioration proceeded at a considerably lower rate in grain stored underwater than in that kept in atmospheric storage.

A new type of fully-automatic packaging machine using carbon dioxide gas was constructed in 1972 which permitted a large-scale packaging test and transportation tests from granary areas to urban areas in Japan to be carried out[8]. After accumulating basic data concerning the practical feasibility of this technique in cooperation with agricultural government offices, agricultural auxiliary organizations and some private companies, the technique has been adopted by the industry for the preservation of polished rice since July 1973 (Fig. 2).

The merits of CEM skin-packaging are as follows: (1) the packages are easy to produce, (2) permeation of moisture and gas is almost completely prevented, (3) deterioration caused by aerobic microorganisms, insects and oxygen is effectively prevented, (4) breakage and slipping down of bags do not occur in loading, (5) the packages are reshapable even after sealing, and (6) the technique can be used widely in food packaging and

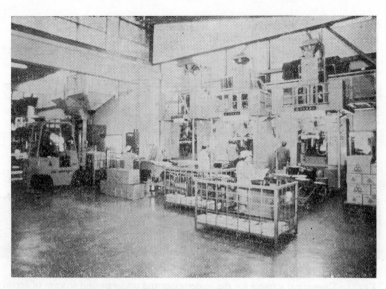

FIG. 2. One of the large-scale central polishing factories in which CEM skin-packages are being produced.

safe preservation because it eliminates the need for chemical food additives. Skin-packaging of polished rice has also been accepted by various types of consumers. For example, many Japanese who live abroad as well as people engaged in deep sea fishing and mountain climbing have reported success in retaining flavor in rice stored in CEM packages.

Although hermetic preservation of polished rice by the CEM technique has been steadily developing in Japan, the open-type preservation of paddy and brown rice at an ambient temperature still prevails in most warehouses. The introduction of bulk preservation of cereals and legumes under hermetic conditions would be most valuable to ensure future famine reserves of grain in Japan.

For reaching an ultimate solution to the food preservation problems of the world, it seems imperative that food scientists and technologists contribute more actively to the field of hermetic preservation, and that they promote an international exchange of useful ideas for safely preserving post-harvest grains in general.

REFERENCES

1. Burrel, N. J., *Storage of Cereal Grains and Their Products* (ed. C. M. Christensen), chap. 11–12, p. 420, American Association of Cereal Chemists (1974).
2. Hyde, M. B., *ibid.*, chap. 10, p. 383, American Association of Cereal Chemists (1974).
3. Bailey, S. W. and Banks, H. J., Proc. 1st Int. Working Conf. Stored-Product Entomology, Savannah, Georgia, U.S.A., Oct. 7–11, 1974, p. 362 (1975).
4. Shejbal, J., Tonolo, A., and Careri, G., *Ann. Technol. Agric.*, **22**, 773 (1973).
5. Mitsuda, H., *Food Technol.*, **23**, 64 (1969).
6. Mitsuda, H., Kawai, F., and Yamamoto, A., *Food Technol.*, **26**, 50 (1972).
7. Mitsuda, H., Yamamoto, A., Suzuki, F., Nakajima, K., Yasumoto, K., and Kawai, F., *J. Nutr. Sci. Vitaminol.*, **23**, 145 (1977).
8. Mitsuda, H., Kawai, F., Kuga, M., and Yamamoto, A., Proc. IV Int. Congr. Food Sci. Technol, vol. IV, p. 100 (1974).

1.4 Preservation of Fruit Juices and Storage Stability

Robert E. Berry*

1.4.1 PRESERVATION METHODS

Fruit juices may generally be preserved by canning and sterilization, as heat stabilized concentrate, as frozen concentrate or by dehydration. Products thus preserved may avoid microbial spoilage but are subject to continuous flavor and nutrient deterioration. The rates of these changes are related to temperatures at which these products are stored. Juices may be generally preserved by "hot-pack" and "cold-fill" methods. For a typical high-temperature, long-time process (hot-pack) juices are usually heated to around 85–95° C for 30 sec or longer to destroy yeast, bacteria and most thermal resistant molds. In such systems, the juices are canned or bottled while hot and the containers allowed to cool slowly, using the residual heat for additional sterility assurance.

Some juices such as citrus may be microbially stabilized at lower temperatures (around 70–75° C), but require exposures near 100° C to de-activate pectinesterase enzymes to avoid loss of "cloud" and a consequential undesirable appearance caused by settling of insolubles. In juices with temperature-sensitive flavor a "cold-fill" process may be used. The product may be heated as high as 115° C for a very short time (2–5 sec) and then cooled immediately as low as −1° C. The cold product is filled into containers (usually glass) which have been rinsed with a solution of chemical sterilant such as sodium hypochlorite or an iodophore.

Another method of preserving juices is partial removal of water, i.e., concentration. For most juices, the higher the solids the more stable the product. Removal of water may be achieved by low-temperature, long-time methods, usually under vacuum, (20–60° C for 10–30 min). Over the past 15 years, high-temperature, short-time methods have been developed which usually result in less deterioration in quality. The temperature accelerated short-time evaporator (widely known as the TASTE evaporator) has been used on many types of juices for this purpose. These evaporators

*U.S. Citrus and Subtropical Products Laboratory, P. O. Box 1909, Winter Haven, Florida 33880, USA

226

have 4 to 6 effects and the product temperature may increase during the first 2 or 3 effects to 96° C after which it gradually decreases through remaining effects to about 16° C at the exit. Total time at elevated temperatures usually does not exceed 1 or 2 min. Such juice concentrates, prepared at about 50–65° Brix require frozen storage for optimum quality. Concentrates have been prepared as high as 80–90° Brix, and while microbially stable at room temperature, they are often affected by nonenzymic browning.

1.4.2 DEHYDRATION

Another preservation method used for fruit juices is dehydration. While almost every conceivable type of drying has been used for preparation of fruit juice powders, none have been adopted commercially to any significant extent. The reasons are probably more economic than technological. It is technologically feasible to dry fruit juices by any of several methods including freeze-drying, foam-mat drying, drum drying and certain types of spray drying (Berry and Veldhuis, 1977). However, the dehydration does not improve the quality and may only slightly improve convenience. On the other hand it will also increase cost. Also, reduced storage stability has been reported on dried whole juices, and studies by Shaw and Berry (1976) showed this was due to the residual moisture content. Synthetic dried juice drinks had good storage stability because of low moisture content rather than discrete separation of individual components, which had been previously suspected as being responsible for their stability. Both dried whole juices and synthetic drink mixes stored well when kept cool (21° or below).

Of all the preservation methods described, canning is the simplest but concentration is probably the most economical. The removal of water, which requires some expenditure of energy, saves on cost of storage and transportation as well as cost of containers. The further removal of water to a dehydration product does not warrant the extra cost, except in very special situations (e.g., export, specialty products, and unrefrigerated storage).

1.4.3 VITAMIN C STABILITY

A principal nutrient often provided by fruit juice products is vitamin C and storage stability is often judged by stability of this vitamin. Because of its susceptibility to oxidation, it is greatly affected by the packaging material as well as time and temperature of storage. When orange juice was stored in different type containers at temperatures shown in Table 1, polystyrene, polyethylene and wax cardboard carbons were relatively poor containers for protecting vitamin C from oxidation, but crown-capped glass bottles were satisfactory (Bissett and Berry, 1975). For frozen concentrated orange juice there appeared to be little effect so long as the product remained frozen.

TABLE 1.   Retention of 90% or more ascorbic acid in orange juice
in different containers at different temperatures.

	Temp. °C	Days
Single strength		
Crown capped glass	25	45
Crown capped glass	16	60
Crown capped glass	10	90
Polyethylene	1 to 10	21
Polystyrene	1 to 10	8
Waxed cardboard	10	6
Waxed cardboard	1	10
Waxed cardboard	−7	21
Frozen concentrated		
Foil-lined fiberboard	1 or less	>100
Foil-lined fiberboard	−20	>365
Polyethylene lined	1	30
Polyethylene lined	−7	50
Polyethylene lined	−20	>365

From Bissett and Berry (1975).

Effects of higher temperatures on percent reduction of the U. S. Recommended Dietary Allowance (RDA) of vitamin C were studied by Nagy and Smoot (1977). Some of their findings are shown in Table 2. At below 40°C, samples retained 100% or more U.S. RDA per six-ounce (180 ml) serving for 12 weeks or longer. At 49°C or above only a very small percentage was provided by a serving of juice after 12 weeks. They also found the percent of retained vitamin C plotted against storage time at elevated temperatures followed a logrithmic curve. An Arrhenius plot showed two distinct slopes.

TABLE 2.   Effect of high temperatures on percent U.S. RDA of vitamin C
in canned single-strength orange juice after 12 weeks storage.

Seasonal type oranges	% U.S. RDA (per 180 ml)				
	Orig.	32°C	38°C	43°C	49°C
Early	144	132	117	95	6
Mid	164	146	131	103	3
Early-	140	120	106	83	3
Valencia	144	130	114	92	14
Late-	92	85	75	59	7
Valencia	122	110	96	75	3

From Nagy and Smoot (1977).

Above a temperature of about 21°C, a much higher reaction rate evolved. They concluded it is misleading to assume a mean storage temperature determined by averaging could be used for prediction of vitamin C retention in SSOJ stored at fluctuating elevated warehouse temperatures over an extended period.

1.4.4 FLAVOR STABILITY

A common indicator of storage stability of juice products is furfural. Nagy and Randall (1973) determined citrus juices at elevated temperatures developed a detectable change in flavor when furfural had increased from an initial value of 5 $\mu g/l$ or less to the range of 25–50. This level of furfural build-up and onset of flavor change occurred well after 1.5 years at 5°C but in less than 2 weeks at 30°C. Orange and grapefruit juices from 3 different plants, stored at a range of temperatures, showed flavor changes after about 8–10 weeks at 16°C, and after 2–4 days at 35°C (Nagy and Dinsmore, 1974).

Additional compositional studies indicated a number of other degradation products which form in canned single-strength orange juice stored for 12 weeks at 35°C. These included mostly furanoid compounds which could form from carbohydrates, especially monosaccharides. A list of such compounds is shown in Table 3 (Tatum *et al.*, 1975). Three of these compounds contributed greatly to off-flavor development: α-terpineol, 2,5-dimethyl-4-hydroxy-3(2H) furanone, and 4-vinyl guaiacol. The first has a turpentine-like flavor, the second the flavor of cooked pineapple and the third the flavor of burnt sugar. Another study by Tatum *et al.* (1969) showed many of these compounds could be formed from ascorbic acid. Table 4 lists ascorbic acid degradation products isolated and identified from the storage of instant (dehydrated) orange juice, as well as those formed in fructose

TABLE 3. Some degradation products found in canned single-strength orange juice after 12 wk at 35°C.

Furfural

α-Terpineol

3-Hydroxy-2-pyrone

2-Hydroxyacetyl furan

2,5-Dimethyl-4-hydroxy-3(2H)-furanone

cis-1,8-p-Menthanediol

trans-1,8-p-Menthanediol

4-Vinyl guaiacol

Benzoic acid

5-Hydroxymethyl furfural

From Tatum *et al.* (1975).

TABLE 4. Compounds isolated from ascorbic acid degradation.

Acetic acid[a,b,c]	D-Hydroxy-2-pyrone[a]
Furfural[a,b]	2-Hydroxyacetylfuran[a,b]
2-Acetylfuran[a]	2,5-Dihydrofurioc acid
2,2'-Difurylmethane	Deoxyfuroin
Furfuryl alcohol[a,c]	2–Furoic acid
γ-Butyrolactone[a,c]	Furoin
γ-Crotonolactone[a,c]	Furil
Methylcyclopentenolone[a,c]	

From Shaw *et al.* (1977).
[a]Also present in stored instant orange juice.
[b]Also identified in a fructose-acid model study.
[c]Also identified in a fructose-base model study.

model studies (Shaw *et al.*, 1977). Generally, juice products should be stored at lowest practicable temperatures to assure optimum flavor stability.

REFERENCES

Berry, R. E., and Veldhuis, M. K., Citrus Science and Technology, Nagy, S., Shaw, P. E. and Veldhuis, M. K., eds., p. 229, 1977.

Bissett, O. W., and Berry, R. E., *J. Food Sci.*, **40**, 178–180, (1975).

Nagy, S., and Dinsmore, H. L., *J. Food Sci.*, **39**, 1116–1119, (1974).

Nagy, S., and Randall, V., *J. Agr. Food Chem.*, **21**, 272–275, (1973).

Nagy, S., and Smoot, J. M., *J. Agr. Food Chem.*, **25**, 135–138, (1977).

Shaw, P. E., and Berry, R. E., *J. Food Sci.*, **41**, 711–712, (1976).

Shaw, P. E., Tatum, J. H., and Berry, R. E., Development in Food Carbohydrate —1, G. G. Birch and R. S. Shallenberger, eds., Applied Science Publishers, Ltd., London, Chapter 6, pp. 91–111, 1977.

Tatum, J. H., Nagy, S., and Berry, R. E., *J. Food Sci.*, **40**, 707–709, (1975).

Tatum, J. H., Shaw, P. E., and Berry, R. E., *J. Agr. Food Chem.*, **17**, 38–40, (1969).

1.5 Pasteurization and Sterilization of Meat and Fishery Products

1.5.1 PRESENTATION AND QUALITY

Traditionally, both pasteurized and fully cooked meat and fishery products have been packed in tin plate or aluminum cans. However, considering the widespread use of refrigeration equipment in the industrialized
countries, Dr. C. Olin Ball predicted as early as the mid-50's that meat
products would be sold to an increasing extent in a semiperishable form
from refrigerated display cabinets. For meat products that are hardly ever
seasonal, a long keeping time is not necessary, and the various plastic
pouches, etc. used for refrigerated foods seem to be more convenient and
appealing to the consumer.

The above prediction appears now to have been fulfilled. Fully cooked
canned meat and fishery products have become more or less stabilized,
while the sale of refrigerated products is increasing very rapidly. The container manufacturing industry has attempted to counteract this in many
ways. Easy-open cans were introduced; so were low-profile cans, i.e. cans
that are very flat and therefore permit rapid heat penetrations. Such cans
may be prepared both for retail sales and for the catering trade. Low-
profile containers for the retail trade may also be made of rigid plastic with
the lid sealed to the bottom, as opposed to the use of the double seam
known from the sanitary can.

A number of pasteurized and fully cooked products are also packed in
plastic pouches, a development which occurred more rapidly in Japan and
Europe than in the USA, where extreme caution regarding migration at
heat processing temperatures held back approval by the health authorities.

A considerable market for pasteurized or fully cooked meat and fishery
products may exist in low-income, often tropical, countries, where the
need for fully preserved products is considerable and where the use of
refrigeration is still not widespread. Surprisingly, industry has so far not
experienced much success in its attempts to fill this need.

---

*Danish Meat Products Laboratory, Howitzvej 13, DK-2000, Copenhagen F, Denmark

1.5.2 Keeping Quality and Safety

A. Fully-staple Products

Sterile products. Such products as tuna fish and sardines are often cooked to complete sterility. They are packed with the bones in, and require a heat process that will render the bones unnoticeable when the product is consumed. The heat process that will achieve this normally also results in complete sterility.

Fully-cooked products. It is normally accepted that, for example, normal canned products are not cooked to sterility, but to so-called "commercial sterility" or better "commercial stability". They are cooked to such a temperature that all harmful organisms which might develop in the product are destroyed by the heat. These products may not necessarily be sterile. They frequently contain spores, e.g. of thermophilic organisms that will not develop at usual storage and distribution temperatures or organisms that cannot develop in the particular product because of its pH, salt, low water activity, etc.

The heat processes, which such products are normally required and assumed to undergo, are often termed 12 D cooks, i.e. any part of the content of the can should have received heat treatment equivalent to 12 times the decimal destruction time for *Clostridium botulinum*, type A. The maximum decimal destruction time for *Clostridium botulinum*, type A, is normally considered to be not more than 0.20 min at 250°F (121.1°C). Thus, a 12 D cook would be a heat treatment equivalent to 2.4 min at 121.1°C (the so-called F_0 value). Some meat and fishery products fall into this category. Some may even be cooked more than called for by the classical consideration, i.e. they are often cooked to F_0 values of 6 to 12 min since it is necessary to attain an extremely high degree of safety with regard to *Clostridium botulinum* and a reasonably high degree of assured keeping quality. Some spore-forming spoilage organisms are very heat resistant. For example, *Bac. stearothermophilus* has a decimal destruction time of 6 min at 121.1°C. A cook to $F_0 = 12$ min thus assures only a reduction of the number of spores present of that organism from 10^2 to 10^0 or the equivalent. According to Lechowich et al.[1], some cured products such as canned corned beef are also fully cooked in accordance with the 12 D concept. Here, however, F_0 values only sufficient for the destruction of *Clostridium botulinum* are achieved, since the salt and nitrite in the product prevent the outgrowth of spoilage organisms and product quality would suffer if a more severe heat treatment was used. Considering the very large number cans of these types of products sold annually, they exhibit a remarkable degree of safety, although in recent years 4 cases of botulism have been encountered with such products.

B. Shelf-staple Products and "Dreiviertel Konserven" (3/4 Canned)

Heat process. The largest turnover in shelf-stable meat products involves products which have been cooked even to nearly what is considered a safe heat process in accordance with classical theory. Luncheon meat, hams in small cans, etc. are often cooked to F_0 values of 0.2 to 0.8. Even so, these products have never been implicated in any case of food poisoning which could be attributed to insufficient heat treatment. These products belong to the cured meat category, and it is easily demonstrated that their safety and keeping quality are contingent to the presence of salt and nitrite. Pivnick[2] has expressed the protection (P) against harmful organisms by the formula $P = D + I$, where D and I represent the log values of thermal destruction and the inhibitory effect of the product. However, only products with a reasonably low initial count can be bacteriologically safe and staple. It is suggested, therefore, that the parameter LC for low count be included in the formula, such that $P = LC + D + I$.

Low initial count. The number of bacteria and especially sporeformers is very low in meat and fishery products. Moreover, these products are almost all manufactured under conditions where low temperatures are maintained throughout most of the preparation of the product, etc. Simonsen[3] has quoted many tests on raw material used for these products. They rarely show more than about 10^2 *Clostridia* or *Bacilli* per g and less than 20 spores. Thus, there is hardly any need to work at the degree of safety prescribed for in the so-called 12–D safe process. On the other hand, it is well established that maintenance of low spore numbers is necessary. Whenever massive artificial inoculations have been tried, growth, and even toxin formation, can occur in products otherwise treated in the manner of those normally sold in the trade.

The traditional safe heat processes are calculated on the basis of their equivalent at 121.1°C, the F_0 value. However, in the calculation, it is assumed that the inclination, *z*, of the decimal reduction time curve is 10°C. Many data suggest that *z*-values often are lower, especially for spoilage organisms and particularly in salty substrates, e.g. 8°C instead of 10°C. This may represent a further explanation of the inapplicability of the classical calculation. The products here considered are normally heat processed to maximum product temperatures of 95–105°C. If for such a process an F_0 value of 1.0 is calculated on the basis of $z = 10°C$, the F_0 value would be 2.0 when the *z*-value was 8°C. Thus, what are registered as extremely low F_0 values may often in part arise from the use of an incorrect *z*-value in the calculations.

Inhibition. As mentioned above, salt exercises some inhibitory effect on outgrowth, especially in the case of heat-damaged spores. Results vary from 4.5% to 10% salt-in-brine (salt to salt plus water ratio) as the concentration sufficient for inhibition of *Clostridium botulinum*. Similar concentrations are required for the inhibition of *Bacillus* species.

Nitrite, which is used in the manufacture of all these products, exercises a considerable inhibitory effect. It is well known that nitrite gradually disappears during heat processing and storage. Even so, the ingoing amount of nitrite has a decisive effect on the inhibition of both growth and toxin formation. At low initial counts, about 150 ppm of ingoing nitrite seems to be sufficient to prevent formation of botulinum toxin. At very high spore numbers obtained by artificial inoculation, even 400 ppm is not sufficient.

pH also has a marked effect on inhibition. However, the pH effects are particularly noticeable below values of 6.2. In the normal pH range of the products considered here, only small variations are found.

Since the inhibitory effects in shelf-stable cured meat derive mainly from the combination of salt and ingoing nitrite, it is disconcerting to note that regulatory efforts have recently been made to reduce the amount of nitrite used in these products or to exclude it altogether. Extensive experiments carried out in the Netherlands[4], Denmark[5] and Canada[6] over several generations of experimental animals have failed to demonstrate an increase in evidence of cancer, even at very high doses of ingoing nitrite. One very recent experiment by Newberne[7] used extremely high amounts of nitrite (250 to 1000 ppm) which were added directly to the feed of experimental animals. In this case, a small increase in carcinogenic symptoms appeared to be detectable in the nitrite group. However, it is difficult to accept that experiments employing such extraordinarily high doses have any real relevance to the use of the very low doses employed in meat products, especially when several experiments involving quite large doses have failed to demonstrate any adverse effects.

A tentative proposal has been made in the USA that the amount of ingoing nitrite in these products be reduced to 40 ppm and the addition of 500 ppm sorbate be made mandatory, since this is considered sufficient for the inhibition of toxin formation. However, the data to justify this proposal are still insufficient.

Ingredient control. Due to the reliance on salt, nitrite, water activity, and possibly even pH for stability in these products, it is clear that great care should be exercised to ensure that the specified levels of these factors are attained during manufacture.

Pasteurized products. A wide range of products are packed in either tin cans or plastic pouches in heat pasteurized form. These products are normally only cooked sufficiently to destroy viable bacteria, i.e. to center temperatures of 65–80°C. Stability is ensured by low storage temperatures, normally below 5°C. Where temperature abuse occurs, protection is found mainly in the fact that a varied flora of spoilage organisms exists unharmed in the product, so that it becomes inedible due to spoilage long before any toxin can be formed. Examples of these products are cans with cured cooked ham, various comminuted cured meat products, which are hot filled into casings, and ready-prepared dishes, which are hot filled into plastic pouches.

C. Heat Processing

A considerable disparity often exists between the care exercised in safe heat process calculations and actual manufacturing conditions. For example, when instituting a control system for heat processing of canned meats in Denmark, many sources of error were encountered. Some of the more important are summarized below. Even small variations in either vacuum in the can or counter pressure in the retort can result in slight bulging of the cans, leading to much slower heat penetration than assumed. It is obvious that thermometers and thermographs should be accurately calibrated and so placed that they indicate the actual temperature in the retort among the products. Nevertheless, cases were observed where temperature readings were as much as 10°C off the actual temperature between the containers.

Steam retorts. It is common knowledge that all air must normally be vented from the heating chamber in a steam retort. However, surprisingly often this principle is not adhered to as strictly as necessary, resulting in considerable temperature differences between various parts of the retort.

Water-filled retorts. In Denmark, the meat industry makes wide use of water-filled retorts because strict maintenance of uniform temperatures is then more easily achieved. However, sources of error exist. The retorts are often equipped with an external centrifugal pump for water circulation. To ensure that water actually circulates in the retort, a flow meter is mandatory. Also, the circulating water needs to cover all cans, so that a water level indicator is required.

Rotation. Many different systems of can-rotation during heat processing have been introduced. The retorts often show an uneven temperature distribution. For example, increased heat penetration into the can may result in a need for larger dimensions of steam supply pipes than anticipated, and the resulting insufficient steam supply leads to a very uneven temperature distribution. In Denmark, a case was also observed of a smaller rotator retort where all cans were placed inside a rotating cylinder. However, since the cylinder had only a few perforations for water circulation, the water circulated mainly around the cylinder, not in between the cans. Increasing the number of perforations rectified the situation.

There are reasons to believe that the very serious defects in heat processing equipment observed in uncontrolled systems in Denmark are not unique to that country, especially since several of the defective retorts encountered were very modern equipment from highly recognized foreign manufacturers.

The high degree of safety which is assumed to be obtained by a 12 D cook has proved sufficient, possibly not because excessively high contaminations of very heat resistant *Clostridium botulinum* spores, e.g. 10^{11} per g, are ever present, but rather because considerable deviations from the calculated F_0 value often occur.

D. After-processing Infection

The best known source of contamination of the contents of a container after heat processing is that of penetration of spoilage organisms or pathogens into the can through the seal during cooling of the hot cans in unsterile water. Also, can-handling requires care: one case is known of food poisoning following handling of wet cans by a worker with a *Staphylocci*-infected hand. Wet cans should therefore preferably not be handled at all.

Less well known than the above cases are situations where canned or pasteurized products are removed from the can or casing, sliced and used directly for consumption after, for instance, an overnight storage period. These pasteurized products remain free of most ordinary spoilage organisms, and thus of most potentially antagonistic organisms. If, however, the product is subject to some infection with pathogens such as *Staphylocci* after the container is opened, serious outbreaks may occur. One such outbreak has been reported which affected all passengers aboard a jumbo jet aircraft, due to consumption of ham which was sliced and then used for airline catering.

REFERENCES

1. Lechowich, R. V., Brown, W. L., Deibel R. H., and Somers, I. I., *The Role of Nitrite in The Production of Canned-Cured Meat Products*, Aut. 1977. (Mimeographed)
2. Pivnick, H., Symp. on the Microbiology of Semi-Preserved Foods, Prague, Oct. 1970.
3. Simonsen, B., **92** *sider (om bakterier og saltet kodkonserves)*, Slagteri—og Konserveslaboratoriet, København (1972). (Mimeographed)
4. Van Logten, M. J., den Tonkelaar, E. M., Kroes, R., Berkvens Johanna M., and van Esch, G. J., *Fd. Cosmet. Toxicol.*, **10**, 475 (1972).

5. Knudsen, I. and Meyer, O. A., *Mutation Res.*, **56**, 177 (1977).
6. Procter, B. G. and G. Rona, *Research Report*, Bio-Research Laboratories, Ltd., Ottawa, Canada (1977).
7. Newberne, P. M., Final report on contract FDA 74/181, *Dietary Nitrite in the Rat*, Dept. of Nutrition and Food Science, MIT, Cambridge, Mass. (1978).

2. Enzymes in Food Processing

2.1 Amylase in Food Processing: the Subsite Theory and Its Applications

Keitaro Hiromi*

Amylase is the best used enzyme in industry. Its use in food processing can be summarized as follows. Bacterial liquefying α-amylase is widely employed for liquefaction in starch processing for various purposes, mostly in conjunction with other amylases. Mold α-amylase is used in the baking industry, due to its heat instability. Mold glucoamylase is an important enzyme in the production of glucose and glucose syrup, and in various kinds of alcohol fermentation. Plant and bacterial β-amylase is utilized in the production of maltose and maltose syrup. In this case, bacterial de-branching amylase is employed to facilitate the action of β-amylase.

These amylases display their own characteristic action patterns, which must in some way be related to the structure of their active sites. In view of the large variety of amylases and action patterns, it seems important to systematize these action patterns into a unified theory. In this paper, *the subsite theory* which has been developed to correlate the action pattern and active site structure of amylase systematically[1-4] will be introduced. It is expected to have useful application in the utilization of amylase in food processing.

The action patterns of amylases may be classified as follows: (1) cleavage of α-1,4 and/or α-1,6 glucosidic linkage, (2) exo- or endo-type degradation, (3) dependency of hydrolysis rate on the degree of polymerization (DP) (designated by n) of the substrate, (4) cleavage pattern of oligosaccharides, (5) transglycosylation and condensation activity (apart from hydrolysis, and (6) tendency for multiple attack. In the case of linear substrates, it is possible to correlate the action patterns 3 and 4 quantitatively with *the subsite structure* of amylase, as will be seen later. Fig. 1 shows the DP-

*Department of Food Science and Technology, Faculty of Agriculture, Kyoto University, Kyoto 606, Japan

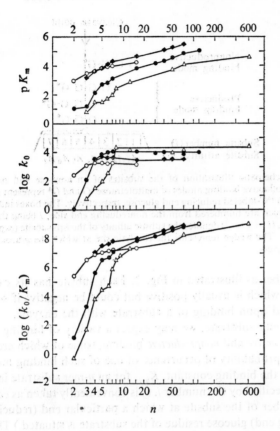

FIG. 1. Dependency of rate parameters on the degree of polymerization (*n*) of linear substrates. K_m, Michaelis constant (in molar concentration of substrate molecule); k_0, molecular activity (maximum velocity/molar concentration of enzyme) (sec^{-1}). ◯, Glucoamylase from *Rhizopus delemar*; ●, Taka-amylase A from *Aspergillus oryzae*; △, liquefying α-amylase from *Bacillus subtilis*; ◆, saccharifying α-amylase from *Bacillus subtilis*. (After K. Hiromi, *Denpun Kagaku* (Japanese), **21**, 190 (1974))

dependency of rate parameters for hydrolysis, the Michaelis constant K_m and the molecular activity k_0, for several amylases.

2.1.1 THE SUBSITE THEORY

The active site of amylase is assumed to consist of a certain number (*m* in total) of subsites, each of which specifically interacts with a glucose residue of the substrate, through hydrogen bonding, for example. The strength of interaction will be called the *subsite affinity*. It is denoted by A_i, which is expressed in free energy units (kcal/mole), where *i* is the

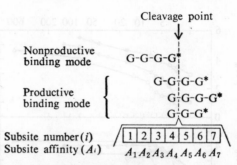

FIG. 2. Schematic illustration of the subsites of an amylase and productive and nonproductive binding modes of maltotetraose. G and G^* represent a glucose residue and ^{14}C-labeled reducing end glucose, respectively. The boxes indicate the subsites which are numbered from the nonreducing end side, i being the subsite number. A_i ($i = 1 \sim 7$) denotes the subsite affinity of the i-th subsite (expressed in kcal/mole). The wedge represents the catalytic site at which the glucosidic link-sage is cleaved.

subsite number as illustrated in Fig. 2. Each subsite has its own subsite affinity, A_i, which is usually positive but could be negative if some strain were induced upon binding of a substrate with the enzyme.

For an n-mer substrate, we may expect a variety of binding modes including *productive* and *nonproductive* binding, some of which are shown in Fig. 2. The probability of occurrence of one of such binding modes is determined by the binding constant, $K_{n,j}$, for an n-mer substrate in the binding mode specified by the number j. (j is conveniently taken as equal to the subsite number of the subsite at which a particular end (reducing and/or nonreducing end) glucose residue of the substrate is situated.) The binding constant $K_{n,j}$ can be expressed in terms of the subsite affinities A_i's of the subsites which are occupied by the substrate molecule in the relevant mode of binding as follows:

$$K_{n,j} = 0.018(\overset{cov.}{\underset{i}{\sum}} A_i/RT)_{n,j} \tag{1}$$

where $\overset{cov.}{\underset{i}{\sum}}$ indicates that the sum is to be taken for all the covered (occupied) subsites, and R and T denote the gas constant and absolute temperature, respectively.

When there are multiple binding modes of a substrate, the rate parameters K_m and k_0 are given in terms of the productive binding constant, $K_{n,p'}$ and nonproductive binding constant, $K_{n,q'}$ and an intrinsic rate constant k_{int} for the hydrolysis of glucosidic bond in the productive complexes, which is assumed constant irrespective of the DP of the substrate or the binding mode. Thus we have

$$1/K_\mathrm{m} = \sum_j K_{n,J} = \sum_p K_{n,p} + \sum_q K_{n,q} \tag{2}$$

$$k_0 = k_\mathrm{int} \sum_p K_{n,p} / (\sum_p K_{n,p} + \sum_q K_{n,q}) \tag{3}$$

$$k_0/K_\mathrm{m} = k_\mathrm{int} \sum_p K_{n,p} \tag{4}$$

where the suffixes p and q refer to the numbers specifying the productive and nonproductive binding modes, respectively, and j signifies both p and q. Substitution of Eq. 1 into Eqs. 2–4 gives the expressions for the rate parameters (K_m and k_0) obtainable from experiments, in terms of $(m + 1)$ subsite parameters, the m subsite affinities, A_i's, and one rate constant, k_int. Thus, it is possible to determine the subsite parameters, A_i's and k_int, from the DP-dependence of the rate parameters, K_m and k_0, and *vice versa*[1-3].

The cleavage pattern of maltooligosaccharides is also closely related to the arrangement of subsite affinities, as seen from Fig. 2, where typical modes of cleavage of reducing end-labeled maltooligosaccharide are shown as an example. The rates of formation of end-labeled maltose (G–G*) and end-labeled maltotriose (G–G–G*) from end-labeled maltotetraose (G–G–G–G*) (v_I and v_II, respectively) are proportional to the probabilities of the corresponding binding modes, I and II, and hence the corresponding binding constants, K_I and K_II, respectively. Thus, using Eq. 1, we have

$$\frac{v_\mathrm{I}}{v_\mathrm{II}} = \frac{K_\mathrm{I}}{K_\mathrm{II}} = \frac{\exp[(A_3 + A_4 + A_5 + A_6)/RT]}{\exp[(A_4 + A_5 + A_6 + A_7)/RT]} = \exp[(A_3 - A_7)/RT] \tag{5}$$

By measuring the ratio of v_I to v_II, the relative magnitude of the subsite affinities can so be determined[4]. If the rate of formation of end-labeled maltose produced from end-labeled maltotriose, v_III, is measured and compared with v_I, the subsite affinity A_3 can be obtained[5], as may be readily seen from analogous considerations (*cf.* Fig. 2). In this way, from the quantitative analysis of products formed from end-labeled substrates, the subsite affinities of the subsites other than the two adjacent to the catalytic site (the wedge in Fig. 2) can be determined. This method is also useful for studying the transglycosylation and condensation, as well as hydrolysis, in amylase-catalyzed reactions.

Thus, we have two methods for evaluating the subsite affinities, A_i's. The first is the kinetic method based on the dependency of rate parameters on the DP of linear substrates[1-3], and the second is the product analysis method utilizing the cleavage pattern of end-labeled maltooligosaccharides[4,5]. The former method is especially useful for exo-amylase[1], whereas the latter is useful for endo-amylase[4]. The two methods are also complementary in many respects. Once the subsite affinities for an amylase are determined, the rate parameters, K_m and k_0, can be predicted theoretically for any linear substrate (of arbitrary chain length), as can all the cleavage patterns (the probabilities of cleavage at respective linkages), for reactions catalyzed by this amylase.

Using these methods, we have determined the subsite structures of several amylases. The results are shown in Fig. 3 in the form of histograms[1-6]. The negative or zero affinity of the subsite adjacent to the catalytic site may well be due to strain induced in the enzyme-substrate complex, which could be distortion in the pyranose ring facilitating hydrolysis as proposed in lysozyme. It is noteworthy that there is a great variety of subsite structures, reflecting the various characteristic action patterns of individual amylases.

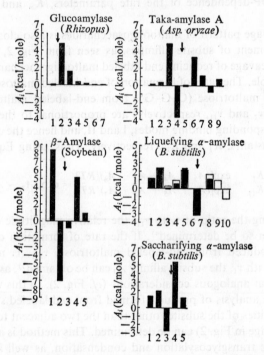

Fig. 3. Subsite structure of amylases. The subsite affinities (black or white pillars) were obtained by the kinetic method and/or the product analysis method.[1-4] The numbers on the abscissa are the subsite numbers, and the arrow shows the cleavage point. The white pillars for bacterial liquefying α-amylase represent values obtained by Thoma et al.[4] using reducing end-labeled α-methyl maltodextrins.[4] The black pillars show data obtained by the author and his colleagues.

2.1.2 PRACTICAL APPLICATION OF THE SUBSITE THEORY

The subsite theory is practically applicable for various purposes. First, it is useful for giving a molecular interpretation of substrate specificity. For example, the difference in relative rates of hydrolysis (the ratio of k_0 values) for maltose and amylose of *Rhizopus* glucoamylase and buckwheat α-glucosidase can be attributed to a difference in relative magnitudes of the first and the third subsite affinities[7]. In contrast to glucoamylase (Fig. 3), buckwheat α-glucosidase has a higher first subsite affinity than third ($A_1 > A_3$). This makes productive binding predominant for all the substrates, leading to a flat DP-dependence of k_0 (*cf.* the DP-dependence of k_0 for glucoamylase in Fig. 1). Second, the subsite theory, which can predict the binding modes of various substrates and analogs, permits studies to be made on the location of specific amino acid residues, e.g. tryptophan, in the active site of amylase, by means of chemical modification and spectroscopic methods. Thus, a tryptophan residue at the first subsite of *Rhizopus* glucoamylase has been located by difference spectrophotometry[8]. Third, prediction of the time courses of amylase reactions, including product distribution, can be made with a computer by using a small number of parameters, i.e. A_i's and at most 3 basic rate constants

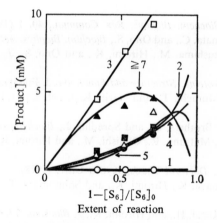

FIG. 4. Degradation of reducing end-labeled maltohexaose (S_6) by Taka-amylase A[9]. Concentrations of reducing end-labeled *n*-mer products ($n = 1 \sim 7$) are plotted against extent of reaction (expressed as the fraction of remaining initial substrate, S_6). The numbers in the figure represent the DP (n) of products. The solid lines are theoretical curves obtained by computer simulation, and the symbols (open circles, etc.) show actual experimental results obtained by product analysis. The curve for $n \geq 7$ indicates the formation of linear substrates longer than the initial substrate, which has been confirmed to be due mainly to transglycosylation.[5]

for hydrolysis, transglycosylation and condensation[5]. A typical example of the calculations is shown in Fig. 4 for Taka-amylase A-catalyzed degradation of maltohexaose, based on a general reaction scheme involving hydrolysis, transglycosylation and condensation[9]. Calculations along this line have been made for the degradation of amylose with DP = 20 catalyzed by several amylases and buckwheat α-glucosidase, in a single enzyme system and in combinations of two enzymes, e.g. one of the two endo-amylases (Taka-amylase A and bacterial liquefying α-amylase) and one of the two exo-enzymes (*Rhizopus* glucoamylase and buckwheat α-glucosidase)[10]. The results indicate that appreciable differences occur in product distribution and in yield of glucose, depending on the kind of enzymes used and on whether they are employed simultaneously or consecutively. Such studies are important and useful for the practical application of amylases in food processing. Further development of the subsite theory will include branched substrates and rapid reaction kinetics, and investigations along these lines are now in progress.

References

1. Hiromi, K., *Biochem. Biophys. Res. Commun.*, **40**, 1 (1970); Hiromi, K., Nitta, Y., Numata, C., and Ono, S., *Biochim. Biophys. Acta*, **302**, 362 (1973).
2. Nitta, Y., Mizushima, M., Hiromi, K., and Ono, S., *J. Biochem.*, **69**, 567 (1971).
3. Hiromi, K., *Proteins: Structure and Function* (ed. Funatsu, M., Hiromi, K., Imahori, K., Murachi, T., and Narita K.,), vol. 2, p. 1, Kodansha-Halsted Press (1972).
4. Thoma, J. A., Brothers, C., and Spradlin, J., *Biochemistry*, **9**, 1768 (1970).
5. Suganuma, T., Matsuno, R., Ohnishi, M., and Hiromi, K., *J. Biochem.*, **84**, 293 (1978).
6. Suganuma, T., *Doctoral Thesis*, Kyoto Univ. (1978).
7. Chiba, S., Kanaya, K., Hiromi, K., and Shimomura, T., *Agr. Biol. Chem.*, **43**, 237 (1979).
8. Ohnishi, M., Kegai, H., and Hiromi, K., *J. Biochem.*, **77**, 695 (1975).
9. Matsuno, R., Suganuma, T., Fujimori, H., Nakanishi, K., Hiromi, K., and Kamikubo, T., *J. Biochem.*, **83**, 385 (1978).
10. Kondo, H., Nakatani, H., Matsuno, R., and Hiromi, K., in preparation.

2.2 Development of the Technique of Glucose Isomerization

Yoshiyuki Takasaki*

The technique of isomerizing glucose to fructose is now being developed on a world-wide scale, and is expected to be improved further in the future.

Almost the entire sugar consumption of Japan is dependent on imports. Techniques for the production of such sweetenings as millet jelly and glucose from locally obtained starch, have thus long been developed. Since the saccharification of starch by enzymes was introduced in 1959 and glucose of good quality could be mass-produced, isomerization of glucose to fructose has been seriously studied for new applications.

Research on the isomerization of glucose to fructose has a long history. Various methods have so far been designed: (1) the alkali isomerization method, (2) the ion exchange resin method, (3) chemical reduction of glucose to sorbitol and microbial oxidation of the sorbitol to fructose, and (4) the direct isomerization method with enzymes. Detailed explanations of methods (1)–(3) are not included in this paper, since none has actually been industrialized. Method (4) was first industrialized in Japan in 1966 and has been successfully used up to the present.

The isomerization of glucose by enzymes is considered to present the following advantages: (1) it causes no side reactions, (2) there is no loss sugar by destruction, (3) almost no color is introduced, (4) the finished product has a good taste, (5) the inversion from glucose to fructose is highly efficient, and (6) the reaction can proceed at high concentrations.

2.2.1 PRODUCTION OF GLUCOSE ISOMERASE.

Research has long been carried out on enzymes which catalyze reactions between free aldose and free ketose. In 1952, Akabori et al.[1] discovered an enzyme which catalyzes a reaction between D-erythrose and D-erythrulose, and later, enzymes such as D-xylose isomerase[2] and D-arabinose isomerase[3] which isomerize the pentoses, D-xylose and D-arabinose, respectively, to the corresponding ketoses were also found. In 1955, Palleroni et al.[4] showed that mannose isomerase, a hexose-isomerizing enzyme,

Fermentation Research Institute, Agency of Industrial Science and Technology, Ministry of International Trade and Industry, 5–8–1, Inage-Higashi, Chiba 280, Japan

245

catalyzes a reaction between mannose and fructose. Then, in 1957, Marshall *et al*[5] discovered that *Pseudomonas hydrophila* cultivated in a medium containing D-xylose contained an enzyme which isomerized glucose to fructose in the presence of arsenate. This discovery inspired research on glucose-fructose isomerization by enzymes throughout the world. Thus, as shown in Table 1, various microorganisms including yeasts, bacteria, actinomycetes, etc., but not fungi, were found to contain enzymes which isomerize glucose to fructose. The basic properties of the major enzymes are listed in Table 2. They may be classified into 3 broad groups, as follows.

TABLE 1. Microorganisms producing glucose-isomerizing enzymes

Bacteria	Actinomycetes	Yeasts
Pseudomonas, Aerobacter, Bacillus, Lactobacillus, Paracolobactrum, Escherichia, Leuconostoc, Micrococcus, Flavobacterium, Brevibacterium (Curutobacterium), Arthrobacter	*Streptomyces, Thermoactinomyces,* thermophilic *Streptomyces, Thermomonospora, Nocardia, Thermopolyspora, Microbispora, Pseudonocardia, Micromonospora, Microellobospora, Actinoplanes*	*Saccharomyces, Pullularia*

TABLE 2. Enzymatic properties of glucose-isomerizing enzymes

Microorganism	Optimum pH	Optimum temp. (°C)	Requirement	Substrate
Ps. hydrophila	8.5	42–43	Arsenate, Mg	Glu, Xyl
Aer. cloacae	7.6	50	Arsenate, Mg	Glu, Xyl
Lact. brevis	6–7	60	Mn	Glu, Xyl, Rib
B. megaterium	7.7	35	NAD	Glu
Aer. aerogenes	6.5–7.0		Arsenate	Glu, Xyl, Man
Esch. intermedia	7.0	40	Arsenate	Glu, Glu-6-p
Paracolo. aerogenes	7.0	40	NAD, Mg	Glu, Man
St. phaeochromogenes	93.–9.5	80	Mg	Glu, Xyl, Ara
Streptomyces sp.	7.0	80	Mg	Glu, Xyl
Streptomyces sp. YT-6	7.0	85–90	Mg	Glu, Xyl, Rib
B. coagulans	7.0	70	Co	Glu, Xyl
Arthrobacter sp.	8.0	60–65	Mg	Glu, Xyl
Brev. pentosoaminoacidicum	8.0–8.5	70	Co	Glu, Xyl

Glu: glucose, Xyl: D-xylose, Rib: D-ribose, Man: mannose
Glu-6-p; glucose-6-phosphate, Ara; L-arabinose

(1) *NAD-linked glucose-isomerizing enzyme.* This enzyme isomerizes glucose to fructose or glucose and mannose to fructose, requiring NAD as a cofactor at the time of the reaction. This enzyme is produced by

Bacillus megaterium[6] and *Paracolobactrum aerogenoides*[7].

(2) *Phosphoglucose isomerase.* This enzyme isomerizes glucose to fructose in the presence of arsenate, in addition to the isomerization of glucose-6-phosphate to fructose-6-phosphate. Natake[8] clarified that this enzymatic activity originates from phosphoglucose isomerase[8]. This enzyme is produced by *Aerobacter cloacae*,[9] *Escherichia intermedia*,[8,10] etc. The enzymatic isomerization of glucose to fructose by *Ps. hydrophila* reported by Marshall *et al.*[5] is considered to include this sort of enzyme since it requires arsenate.

(3) *Xylose isomerase.* In addition to catalyzing the conversion of glucose and fructose, this enzyme also catalyzes the conversion of D-xylose to D-xylulose, and a certain enzyme of this type further catalyzes the conversion of D-ribose to D-ribulose. At present, the enzymes utilized in industry are of this type. Yamanaka[11] clarified that the glucose-isomerzing activity and D-xylose-isomerizing activity of *Lactobacillus brevis* originated from the same enzyme. This enzyme is generally termed glucose isomerase. The K_m for D-xylose is usually smaller than that for glucose, i.e. the affinity of substrate against enzyme is larger for D-xylose than for glucose, so that the enzyme may be termed D-xylose isomerase. However, enzymes with almost equal levels of affinity are known[12], and sometimes the affinity for D-ribose exceeds those for D-xylose and glucose[13]. It is known that the enzyme is also induced by D-ribose[14]. Furthermore, some xylose isomerases[15] are reported to act only on D-xylose, not on glucose. Hereafter, this enzyme is called glucose isomerase.

When studies on the isomerization of glucose by enzymatic methods were first begun, it was necessary to find (1) an enzyme which did not require arsenate for the reaction, (2) a microorganism which did not require expensive D-xylose as an inducer, and (3) an enzyme with excellent properties which was sufficiently stable for industrial use. The author began his research to develop an enzymatic production process without using D-xylose as an inducer, and reported glucose-isomerizing enzymes from *Bacillus megaterium*[6] and *Paracolobactrum aerogenoides.*[7] However, these enzymes were insufficiently stable for industrialization. Subsequent studies on *Streptomyces* which was able to assimilate xylan, revealed that the organism produced glucose isomerase upon cultivation in a medium containing xylan[16]. Since xylan is present in all land plants as a major component, it appeared possible that glucose isomerase could be prepared very economically using xylan-containing materials such as wheat bran, corn cobs, etc. After establishment of such an enzyme production process, commercial production of fructose was first begun in 1966.

This *Streptomyces* strain produces xylanase which hydrolyzes xylan, but the main product of the hydrolysis by the xylanase is xylobiose, and little D-xylose is produced[17]. Detailed studies were carried out on the production of glucose isomerase by this *Streptomyces* strain, and it was found that xylobiose was a far superior inducer than D-xylose for the production of glucose isomerase and when both xylobiose and D-xylose were present together in the medium, more glucose isomerase was produced than in the case of the single presence of either of these substances (Fig. 1)[17]. Further studies on inducers for the production of glucose isomerase are still required, and some current work aims to develop microorganisms without any special inducer requirement[18]. Recently, glucose isomerase has been employed as an immobilized enzyme, and the life of the enzyme has been prolonged. As a whole, the amount of enzyme used is thus being reduced, although the production of fructose syrup by glucose isomerization is expected to increase in the future.

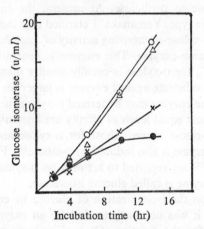

FIG. 1. Time course of induction of glucose isomerase in *Streptomyces* sp.
-x- X_2 0.5%, -●- X_1 0.5%, -○- X_2 0.2% + X_1 0.3%, -△- X_2 0.1% + X_1 0.4%
X_1; D-xylose, X_2; xylobiose

For the production of glucose isomerase, in addition to inducer, corn steep liquor[16] and a metal ion such as Co^{2+} are usually added. Co^{2+} exerts a marked accelerating effect on the production of this enzyme. Addition of about 1×10^{-3} M $CoCl_2$ to the medium, increases the production of glucose isomerase 1.5 to 2 times[16]. Cultivation is usually carried out aerobically at a temperature of about 30°C for 25–30 hr. Glucose isomerase is an intracellular enzyme, and its extraction from the microbial cell is performed by autolysis[19].

2.2.2. Properties of Glucose Isomerase

The glucose isomerase of *Lactobacillus brevis*,[11] *Streptomyces* sp.,[20] and *Bacillus coagulans*[21] has been purified and crystallized. The molecular weight of the enzyme is assumed to be about 160,000[20-22] and the molecule is thought to have a structure with subunits[21],[22]. At the time of crystallization of glucose isomerase from *Streptomyces* sp., Co[2+] and Mg[2+] are added, and the resultant enzyme crystals contain about 4 atoms of Co and about 33 atoms of Mg per molecule[20]. Crystallographic studies[23] of glucose isomerase and studies on its binding with metals and substrates[24] are now in progress.

The optimum temperature for glucose isomerase at a reaction time of about 30 min, is usually found to lie within the range of 60–80° C. However, the glucose isomerases of thermophilic Actinomycetales such as thermophilic *Streptomyces* sp[22]. and *Actinoplanes* sp[26]. have a far superior heat stability with an optimum temperature of 85–90° C. Fig. 2 compares the effect of temperature on the glucose isomerase reactions of *Streptomyces* sp.[20] and thermophilic *Streptomyces* sp.[25]

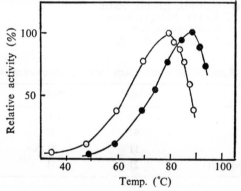

FIG. 2.   Effect of temperature on the glucose isomerase reaction.
–○– *Streptomyces* sp.
–●– Thermophilic *Streptomyces* sp.

The optimum pH is usually around 6–8, although that for glucose isomerase from *Streptomyces phaeochromogenes* is on the alkaline side at 9.3–9.5[27]. Fig. 3 illustrates the effect of pH on the glucose isomerase reaction of *Streptomyces* sp.[20]

At the time of reaction, glucose isomerase requires Mg[2+], Mn[2+] or Co[2+]. As shown in Table 3, such requirements differ markedly according to the kind of enzyme. The enzyme used at present in industry is an Mg[2+] requiring glucose isomerase.

Glucose isomerase is an SH-enzyme and is inhibited by pCMB, Ag[+], Hg[2+] and Cu[2+][20]. The inhibition by pCMB is restored by the addition of cystein[20]. Ca[2+] also inhibits glucose isomerase[20], but such inhibition is said to be reduced by increasing the concentration of Mg[2+][28]. Sugar alcohols such as xylitol and sorbitol inhibit glucose isomerase competitively.[11],[16]

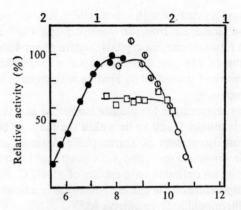

FIG. 3. Effect of pH on the glucose isomerase reaction.
-●- Na_2HPO_4-KH_2PO_4 buffer
-◐- Na_2CO_3-$NaHCO_3$ buffer
-□- NaOH-glycine buffer
-○- Na_2HPO_4-NaOH buffer

TABLE 3.   Requirement of metal ions for the glucose isomerase reaction

Origin of enzyme	Mg^{2+}	Mn^{2+}	Co^{2+}
Lact. brevis	5	100	32
Streptomyces sp.	97	27	100
B. coagulans	11	11	100
Brev. pentosoaminoacidicum	21	11	100

The K_m value of the enzyme for glucose is large, and the reaction is barely inhibited by a high concentration of glucose. The reaction can therefore be conducted in highly concentrated glucose.

Glucose isomerase generally catalyzes the conversion of D-xylose to D-xylulose in addition to the reaction between glucose and fructose. Moreover, certain enzymes of *Lactobacillus* sp.[11], *Streptomyces* sp.[13], *Bacillus* sp.[22], etc. also catalyze the reaction between D-ribose and D-ribulose (Table 4).

TABLE 4.   Substrate specificity and K_m values

Origin of enzyme	K_m for xylose	K_m for glucose	K_m for ribose
Lactobacillus brevis	0.005	0.92	0.67
Streptomyces sp.	0.032	0.16	No action
Streptomyces albus	0.20	0.20	No action
Streptomyces sp. YT-6	0.30	0.20	0.14

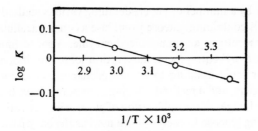

FIG. 4. Plots of log *K vs.* 1/*T*.
K = (Fructose)/(glucose)
Temp. 25–75°C

The reaction between glucose and fructose by glucose isomerase is reversible. As is clearly seen from Fig. 4, which illustrates the effect of temperature on the equilibrium constant, *K*, the reaction of glucose to fructose is endothermic[29], and the amount of fructose produced increases with increasing reaction temperature. At about 50°C, the ratio of glucose to fructose approaches 1:1, and at the usual reaction temperature of 70°C, the reaction proceeds with about 55% fructose and 45% glucose. If more fructose than this is required, steps must be taken to shift the equilibrium. For this purpose, various methods using borate[30], borate-form anion exchange resin[31], water-insoluble polymer with dihydroboronyl base[32], and oxyanion compounds of Ge, Sn, Mo and W[33] have been discussed. For example, if the reaction is carried out in the presence of borate, the isomerization ratio can be improved up to 88–90% at maximum[30]. The concentrations of substrate and borate to attain the highest isomerization ratio are 1 mole of sodium tetraborate against 4 moles of glucose[30].

Another technique for shifting the reaction further to the fructose side is to utilize an enzyme with a better heat resistance and to carry out the reaction at as high a temperature as possible. However, since fructose in particular decomposes on vigorous heating, suitable precautions or counter measures must be taken. The equilibrium of the glucose isomerase reaction represents an important problem for future study.

2.2.3 IMMOBILIZATION OF GLUCOSE ISOMERASE

Recently, active research has been carried out on enzyme immobilization. Since (1) glucose isomerase is an intracellular enzyme, (2) its production yield is rather limited, (3) its price is high even though demand is large, (4) its reaction is simple and easily analyzable, and (5) the enzyme is stable, glucose isomerase represents a very suitable subject for study as an immobilized enzyme. Thus, several papers and patent applications have appeared. These studies on the immobilization of glucose isomerase are characterized by a number of papers detailing various methods for treating microbial cells containing glucose isomerase as an intracellular enzyme to obtain better results as an immobilized enzyme. Also, techniques such as immobilization by entrapment, adsorption onto an inorganic carrier, adsorption or ionic bonding to an ion exchanger, covalent bonding to inorganic carriers, and a method utilizing membranes have been described.

In the initial stages of the application of glucose isomerization, microbial cells containing glucose isomerase were used as the enzymatic source, and the enzyme was employed only once in a batch process. However, in 1968, the method of immobilizing glucose isomerase by heat-treatment of the microbial cells containing the enzyme for a short period at 60–80° C was developed, so preventing autolysis and avoiding the release of glucose isomerase from the cells[19,34]. Thus, reuse of the enzyme in the batch process and continual isomerization[19,34] became possible. This method is thought to represent the first case where an immobilized enzyme has been used on a large scale.

Subsequently, due to increased demand for glucose isomerase, an enzyme having long-term stability, physical intensity and ease of utilization was sought. Currently desired attributes for the immobilized enzyme used in industry are (1) that it have a high activity per unit volume (to complete the isomerization at SV 0.5–1), (2) that the half life of activity exceed 1000 hr, and (3) that it be packed in a column to allow the highly concentrated glucose solution to pass through easily and uniformly[28]. Methods now employed in industry include shaping treatment of microbial cells containing glucose isomerase, and immobilization onto an ion exchanger (DEAE-cellulose[36] or anion exchange resin[36-38]) or an inorganic carrier such as alumina[39]. Each method has its merits and demerits, and unification into a single method is not feasible. Immobilization by shaping treatment of microbial cells containing glucose isomerase, which utilizes the advantage that the glucose isomerase is an intracellular enzyme, is considered to represent the major current technique with the best prospects.

2.2.4 Characteristics of the Product

The fructose syrup obtained by glucose isomerization was not standardized in Japan for a long time. However, in 1976, it was placed under the control of a Japan Agricultural Standard[40]. Table 5 summarizes the details, and also gives analytical results for typical products currently available on the market.

2.2.5 Isolation of Fructose

It is now possible to produce fructose syrup by glucose isomerization with an enzyme, whereby the glucose is equivalent to the fructose, i.e. the

TABLE 5.   Characteristics of fructose syrup

(1) Japan Agricultural Standard (June 25, 1976)

Item	Glucose-fructose syrup	Glucose-fructose syrup cont. sucrose
Water	<30%	<30%
Sugar	>70%	>70%
Glucose	>45%	
Fructose	>42%	
Sucrose	0%	10–50%
Other sugars	8%	
pH	4.5–5.5	4.0–6.0
Color	<0.250	<0.250
Ash	<0.1%	<0.1%
Turbidity	<0.200	<0.200

(2) Typical Products

Product	Fructose (%)	Glucose (%)	Maltose (%)	Sucrose (%)	Other (%)	Water (%)
A	30	35	—	0	10	25
B	33	39	—	0	3	25
C	15	31	22	0	7	25
D	22	26	—	20	7	25

one is completely the same as the invert sugar obtained by sugar inversion. However, at this level of fructose content the product is liquid so that it cannot be pulverized, and during storage, the product solidifies by the isolation of glucose. Also, the sweetness does not exceed that of sugar. Development of a product with a higher content of fructose is therefore greatly needed. The most suitable way of producing material with higher fructose is, as mentioned above, to shift the equilibrium of the reaction to the fructose side in some way or other. However, several technical problems still remain unsolved. Another method would be to isolate the fructose from the mixture of glucose and fructose. The following techniques are known: (1) formation of a CaO-fructose complex, (2) formation of a $CaCl_2$-fructose complex, (3) formation of an NaCl-glucose complex, (4) fractionation with an organic solvent, (5) oxidation of the glucose to gluconic acid, and (6) column chromatography using an ion exchange resin, etc. Among these, separation by chromatography is recommended for economical and bulkd prouction of fructose as a food. The most popular method is to use a calcium-form cation exchange resin, as actually applied

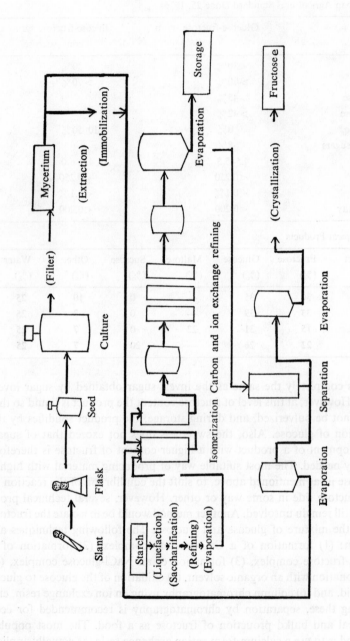

FIG. 5. Manufacturing process of glucose isomerase and fructose.

in Europe and the USA. In Japan, also, a separation process for obtaining fructose with an ion exchange resin has recently been developed (Fig. 5), and products with higher fructose contents have been manufactured and sold on the market.

The present author has investigated the isolation of fructose with a bisulfite-form anion exchange resin, and obtained results superior to those for calcium-form cation exchange resin insofar as degree of separation was concerned[41].

2.2.6 CONCLUSION

The technique of glucose isomerization with enzymes explained above continues to be developed. It is difficult to estimate the future demand for fructose syrup, but according to separate estimates by Wardrip[42] and Kolodry[43] in the USA, 20–30% of the total sugar consumption of the USA will probably derive from fructose syrup in 1980. In Japan, the present production of fructose syrup amounts to only several percent of the total sugar consumption; however, this proportion is likely to increase in future.

REFERENCES

1. Akabori, S. *et al.*, *Proc. Japan Acad.*, **28**, 39 (1952).
2. Mitsuhashi, S. *et al.*, *J. Biol. Chem.*, **204**, 1011 (1953).
3. Cohen, S. S., *ibid.*, **201**, 71 (1955).
4. Palleroni, H. J. *et al.*, *ibid.*, **218**, 535 (1956).
5. Marshall, R. O. *et al.*, *Science*, **125**, 648 (1957).
6. Takasaki, Y. *et al.*, *J. Agr. Chem. Soc. Japan*, **36**, 1010 (1962).
7. Takasaki, Y., *Agr. Biol. Chem.*, **28**, 740 (1964).
8. Natake, M., *ibid.*, **32**, 303 (1968).
9. Tsumura, N. *et al.*, *ibid.*, **25**, 616 (1961).
10. Natake, M. *et al.*, *ibid.*, **28**, 510 (1964).
11. Yamanaka, K., *ibid.*, **27**, 271 (1963).
12. Takasaki, Y., *Ann. Mtg. Agr. Biol. Chem. Soc. Japan*, 210 (1965).
13. Takasaki, Y., Japanese Patent Appl. Kokoku, 49–81007 (1974).
14. TzuYuan Hsu *et al.*, *Wu Hua Hsueh Yu Sheng Wu Wu Li Hsueh Pao* (*China*), **4**, 342 (1964); *Chem. Abstr.* **62**, 6728 (1965).
15. Slein, M. W. *J. Am. Chem. Soc.*, **77**, 1663 (1966).
16. Takasaki, Y., *Agr. Biol. Chem.*, **30**, 1247 (1966).
17. Takasaki, Y., *ibid.*, **38**, 667 (1974).
18. Lee, C. K., *et al.*, US Patent 3,645,848 (1972).

19. Takasaki, Y., *Fermentation Advances*, p.561, Academic Press (1969); *Rept. Ferment. Res. Inst.*, **37**, 23 (1970); Japanese Patent 585,185 (1970).
20. Takasaki, Y., *Agr. Biol. Chem.*, **30**, 1247 (1966).
21. Hogue-Angeletti, R. A., *J. Biol. Chem.*, **250**, 7814 (1975).
22. Danno, G., *Agr. Biol. Chem.*, **34**, 1795 (1970).
23. Berman, H. M. *et al.*, *J. Biol. Chem.*, **249**, 3983 (1974).
24. Schray, K. J. *et al.*, *ibid.*, **247**, 2034 (1972).
25. Takasaki, Y., Japanese Patent 775,785 (1975).
26. Japanese Patent Appl. Kokai 49–132,287 (1975).
27. Tsumura, N. *et al.*, *Agr. Biol. Chem.*, **29**, 1129 (1965).
28. Yoritomi, K., *Food Industry*, **19**(22), 20 (1976).
29. Takasaki, Y., *Agr. Biol. Chem.*, **31**, 309 (1967).
30. Takasaki, Y., *ibid.*, **35**, 1371 (1971).
31. Takasaki, Y., US Patent 3,689,362 (1970).
32. Kobayashi, T., Japanese Patent Appl. Kokai. 52–1090 (1977).
33. Japanese Patent Appl. Kokai 53–20440 (1978).
34. Takasaki, Y., *Rept. Ferment. Res. Inst.*, **37**, 31 (1970).
35. Mermelstein, N. H., *Food Technol.*, 20, June 1975.
36. Schnyder, B. J., *Die Stärke*, **26**, Jahrg, Nr. 12, 409 (1974).
37. Samejima, H., *et al.*, *Enzyme Engineering*, vol. 2, 131, Plenum Press, (1974); Japanese Patent Appl. Kokai 48–56770 (1973).
38. Fujita, Y., *et al.*, Japanese Patent Appl. Kokai 50–94187 (1975).
39. Japanese Patent Appl. Kokai 49–110889 (1974).
40. Ministry of Agriculture and Forestry, Official Announcement No. 6095, June 25, 1976.
41. Takasaki, Y., *Agr. Biol. Chem.*, **36**, 2575 (1972).
42. Wadrip, E. K. Symp. Sugar and Other Sweeteners in Food Processing, Michigan State Univ., March 10–11, 1975; *Food Technol.*, 20, June 1975.
43. Kolodry, S., *Chem. Eng. News*, **54** (17), 13 (1976).

2.3 Enzymes Involved in the Generation of Glucose from Cellulose

T. M. Wood* and S. I. McCrae*

Although there are many examples of microorganisms that can attack native cellulose, cell-free culture filtrates that are capable of extensively degrading highly ordered cellulose in the manner of the intact living microorganism can be prepared from only a few fungi. The most notable examples of such cell-free culture filtrates are those from *Trichoderma viride*[1], *T. koningii*[2], *Fusarium solani*[3], and *Penicillium funiculosum*[4]. Culture filtrates of most other cellulolytic fungi can hydrolyse soluble derivatives of cellulose (carboxymethylcellulose) or partially degraded cellulose (H_3PO_4-swollen cellulose), but hydrolysis of highly ordered cellulose (cotton fibre) is minimal.

Fractionation studies performed in our laboratory on the cellulase of *T. koningii*[5], *F. solani*[6], and *P. funiculosum*[7], have shown that the synergistic action of three types of enzyme can account for the activity towards highly ordered cellulose. These are (a) cellobiohydrolase (also called C_1)[5] which can solubilize partially degraded cellulose, but is unable to hydrolyse either soluble derivatives of cellulose or highly ordered cellulose, (b) endo-$(1 \rightarrow 4)$-β-glucanase (also called Cx) which can hydrolyse soluble derivatives of cellulose or partially degraded cellulose, but which show little capacity for attacking highly ordered cellulose; (c) cellobiase or β-glucosidase. These components, which when acting together can completely solubilize native cellulose, lose this ability when separated and recover it when recombined in their original proportions (Table 1).

In some other cellulase systems that manifest a capacity for hydrolysing crystalline cellulose, enzymic activities other than the ones already mentioned have been found. However, it would appear from published data, that while the presence of these enzymes clearly increases the rate of hydrolysis of cellulose, their presence is not essential for extensive hydrolysis. Notable in this respect are the oxidase synthesized by the fungus *Sporotrichum pulverulentum*[8] and the $(1 \rightarrow 4)$-β-D-glucanglucohydrolase of *T. viride*[9]. A suggestion that an essential feature of a cellulase that can

Department of Carbohydrate Biochemistry, Rowett Research Institute, Bucksburn, Aberdeen AB2 9SB, Scotland, U.K.

TABLE 1.   Cellulase (cotton solubilizing) activity of cellobiohydrolase, endo-(1 → 4)-β-glucanase and β-glucosidase of *T. koningii* and *F. solani*, when acting alone and in combination.

Enzyme	Cotton solubilization (%)	
	T. koningii	*F. solani*
Cellobiohydrolase	1	2
Endo-(1 → 4)-β-glucanase	1	1
β-glucosidase	NIL	1
Endo-(1 → 4)-β-glucanase + β-glucosidase	6	4
Cellobiohydrolase + endo-(1 → 4)-β-glucanase	53	58
Cellobiohydrolase + β-glucosidase	20	18
Cellobiohydrolase + endo-(1 → 4)-β-glucanase + β-glucosidase	72	71
Original unfractionated enzyme system	71	71

All enzymes were present in the same proportions in which they were present in the original cell-free culture filtrate. Incubations were for 7 days at 37°C[14].

hydrolyse highly ordered cellulose is a non-hyrolytic enzyme that produces some localized disruption of the hydrogen bonds as a preliminary to hydrolysis by the endo-(1 → 4)-β-glucanases[10], has never been substantiated.

On the basis of the evidence presently available then, it would appear that the mechanism of cellulase action can be discussed in terms of the hydrolytic enzymes, endo-(1 → 4)-β-glucanase, cellobiohydrolase and β-glucosidase. For the first phase of the reaction, a logical explanation of the synergistic action between cellobiohydrolase and endo-(1 → 4)-β-glucanase on crystalline cellulose is that the new chain ends generated by the endo-(1 → 4)-β-glucanase are attacked by the cellobiohydrolase; and this hypothesis now enjoys wide support. Clearly, however, such a hypothesis does not define the mechanism completely. It still does not explain why it is that endo-(1 → 4)-β-glucanase and cellobiohydrolase are individually both capable of degrading H_3PO_4-swollen cellulose, and not highly ordered cellulose, yet when acting in concert can hydrolyse highly ordered cellulose with comparative ease. In other words, the precise mechanism of synergistic action between endo-(1 → 4)-β-glucanase and cellobiohydrolase at the site of attack still requires elucidation.

In terms of the mechanism of action and the production of glucose, some other properties of the enzymes are of interest. Particularly significant in this regard is the control of the rate of hydrolysis which is effected by the inhibitory properties of the products of hydrolysis.

Glucose and cellobiose are the principal products of the hydrolysis, and both have been found to be potent inhibitors of the synergism shown by cellobiohydrolase and endo-(1 → 4)-β-glucanases, even at low concentrations[11]. Indeed, in the case of cellobiose, a concentration of 0.01 % is sufficient, under certain conditions[11], to effect 79 % inhibition of the cotton solubilizing activity shown by a reconstituted mixture of cellobiohydrolase and endo-(1 → 4)-β-glucaanse of *T. koningii*: glucose at the same concentration produces 45 % inhibition.

Since cellobiose has been shown to be a potent inhibitor of the action of cellobiohydrolase on the more easily accessible H_3PO_4-swollen cellulose[12], the effect of this sugar on the ability of the mixture of cellobiohydrolase-endoglucanase to solubilize cotton cellulose is easily understood. No such rationalisation is possible, however, to explain the inhibition manifested by glucose on the cotton solubilizing activity of the same enzyme mixture, for glucose, even at a concentration of 1 %, had no effect on the capacity of the individual enzymes to solubilize H_3PO_4-swollen cellulose. Thus, glucose is inhibitory in some, as yet, unexplained way only to the combined action of cellobiohydrolase and endoglucanase on a highly ordered substrate.

The relative proportions of the various enzymes present in the incubation mixtures are important for maximum rate of hydrolysis of cellulose. This has been established by measuring the cellulase (cotton solubilizing) activity shown when endo-(1 → 4)-β-glucanase and cellobiohydrolase were mixed in different proportions. It was found possible to 'saturate' endoglucanase with cellobiohydrolase, or conversely[13]. Clearly, both enzymes must be present in the correct proportions for maximum efficiency in terms of cotton solubilizing activity; and, of course, there must be an excess of β-glucosidase to prevent the accumulation of the inhibitor, cellobiose.

Another property which may be of interest in an industrial context is that the endo-(1 → 4)-β-glucanase synthesised by one fungus can act synergistically with the cellobiohydrolase of another[13]. The degree of synergism shown by mixtures of these enzymes varies widely, however. In the case of enzyme components from the cellulases of *F. solani*, *T. koningii* and *P. funiculosum*, a high degree of synergism, resulting in the extensive solubilization of highly ordered cellulose, is observed[7] (Table 2). In contrast, when cellobiohydrolase from *T. koningii*, *F. solani* or *P. funiculosum* cellulase is added to endoglucanase from culture filtrates of the fungi *Myrothecium verrucaria* or *Stachybotrys atra*, only a small potentiation in activity is observed.

Why is it that all endo-(1 → 4)-β-glucanases cannot co-operate with cellobiohydrolase to the same extent? Clearly, there are several possible reasons. Firstly, if, as seems likely, it is the endo-(1 → 4)-β-glucanases that

Table 2. Synergistic effects on cellulase activity shown by combinations
of cellobiohydrolase, endo-(1 → 4)-β-glucanase and β-glucosidase
from various fungal sources.

Source of cellobiohydrolase	Source of endo-(1 → 4)-β-glucanase and β-glucosidase	Solubilization of cotton (%)
T. koningii	T. koningii	54
T. koningii	F. solani	79
F. solani	F. solani	59
F. solani	T. koningii	51
P. funiculosum	P. funiculosum	72
P. funiculosum	T. koningii	51
T. koningii	M. verrucaria	20
T. koningii	S. atra	21
P. funiculosum	M. verrucaria	20
P. funiculosum	M. verrucaria	11

All assays contained equal amounts of cellobiohydrolase, endo-(1–4)-β-glucanase
and β-glucosidase activities. Neither of the components showed a significant capacity for solubilizing cotton fibre when acting individually.

initiate the attack, it may be that the endoglucanases in some culture
filtrates produce fragments of chain that are too small or too large to be
accommodated by the active site of the cellobiohydrolase. Alternatively, it
is possible that some fungi may use completely different mechanisms from
the one discussed here. But a third possibility, and one which we favour, is
that the cellobiohydrolases and endoglucanases must interact in some way
to form a complete cellulase complex. Some recent results obtained in our
laboratory may be relevant in this regard.

Six endo-(1 → 4)-β-glucanases have been isolated from *T. koningii* cellulase using a series of chromatographic and electrophoretic fractionation
procedures[7] (Fig. 1). Of the six endo-(1 → 4)-β-glucanases isolated, only
four were major components (E_1, E_{3a}, E_{3b} and E_4 in Fig. 1). One of the
components (E_1) had a molecular weight very much smaller (13,000) than
the other three (E_{3a} and E_{3b}, 38,000; E_4, 31,000), but all four were similar
in that they could hydrolyse CM-cellulose or H_3PO_4-swollen cellulose.
The pattern of attack differed, but there was a definite relationship in the
mode of action on each of these substrates. The low molecular weight
endo-(1 → 4)-β-glucanase (E_1) was the 'most random' in its attack on
CM-cellulose in that it could effect the greatest change in viscosity per
unit increase in reducing power: by the same criterion E_{3b} was the least
'random'. Since viscosity is a parameter related to chain length, then
clearly one can conclude that the low molecular weight endoglucanase was
generating the most end groups, and E_{3b} the least.

The pattern of attack was the same when the insoluble H_3PO_4-swollen

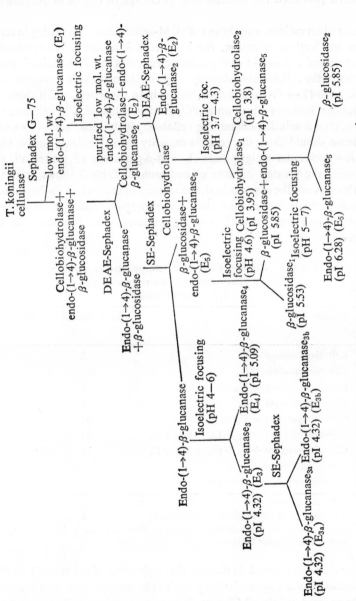

Fig. 1. Fraction of *T. koningii* cellulase. Endo-(1→4)-glucanases$_{2and4}$ were present in trace amounts only. Cellobiohydrolase$_{1and2}$ and β-glucosidase$_{1and2}$ were isoenzymes.

cellulose was used as substrate; the low molecular weight endo-$(1 \rightarrow 4)$-β-glucanase produced the greatest rate of change of degree of polymerisation.

These observations, and those with CM-cellulose are interesting in terms of the mechanism of action, for if synergistic action between cellobiohydrolase and endo-$(1 \rightarrow 4)$-β-glucanase enzymes can be explained simply in terms of the cellobiohydrolase hydrolysing the new chain ends generated by the endo-$(1 \rightarrow 4)$-β-glucanases, as has been suggested, and if there is a relationship between attack on H_3PO_4-swollen cellulose, CM-cellulose and cotton, then a solution containing cellobiohydrolase and endo-$(1 \rightarrow 4)$-β-glucanase should show the greatest capacity for solubilizing cotton fibre. The low molecular weight endo-$(1 \rightarrow 4)$-β-glucanase (E_1) after all, was producing the greatest number of end groups. Table 3 shows, however, that this was not the case. Indeed, the mixture of endo-$(1 \rightarrow 4)$-β-glucanase and cellobiohydrolase did not show any synergism, and a mixture of cellobiohydrolase and endo-$(1 \rightarrow 4)$-β-glucanase$_{3b}$ was the same in this respect.

Table 3.   Cellulase (cotton solubilizing) activity shown by reconstituted mixtures of the components of *T. koningii* cellulase.

Enzyme	Solubilization of cotton (%)
Cellobiohydrolase + E_1	2
Cellobiohydrolase + E_{3a}	34
Cellobiohydrolase + E_{3b}	2
Cellobiohydrolase + E_4	51
Cellobiohydrolase + E_{3a} + E_4	53
Cellobiohydrolase + E_1 + E_{3a} + E_{3b} + E_4	53
Cellobiohydrolase + E_1 + E_{3a} + E_{3b} + E_4 + β-glucosidase	72
Original unfractionated enzyme	71

All components were recombined in the same proportions in which they were present in the original unfractionated enzyme. E_1, E_{3a}, E_{3b} and E_4 were endo-$(1 \rightarrow 4)$-β-glucanases isolated as shown in Fig. 1. Incubations were carried out for 7 days at $37°C$[14].

How then can we explain the fact that only some of the endo-$(1 \rightarrow 4)$-β-glucanases can act synergistically with cellobiohydrolase in solubilizing highly ordered cellulose? Clearly, there are several possible explanations. It seems reasonable to suggest, however, that the solubilization of the more crystalline areas is effected only by those pairs of cellobiohydrolase and endo-$(1 \rightarrow 4)$-β-glucanase enzymes that can form a 'loose' physical complex on the surface of the cellulose crystallite. In the case of *T. koningii* cellulase this would be between cellobiohydrolase and endo-$(1 \rightarrow 4)$-β-glucanase$_{3a}$, or cellobiohydrolase and endo-$(1 \rightarrow 4)$-β-glucanase$_4$.

In essence, then, we consider that the enzymatic hydrolysis of cellulose involves sequential action, where the endo-$(1 \rightarrow 4)$-β-glucanases initiate the attack and the new chain ends that are generated are then hydrolysed by the cellobiohydrolase. This type of attack may operate on amorphous as well as crystalline areas, but in the latter case we would suggest that the second stage of the hydrolysis (i.e. the removal of cellobiose by the cellobiohydrolase) must follow the first instantly in order to prevent the reformation of the glucosidic linkage between two glucose residues which are held rigidly in position by intermolecular hydrogen bonds: an enzyme-enzyme complex of the type described would be an efficient catalyst in the circumstances.

Clearly, no adventitious aggregate of enzymes can constitute an enzyme system that is capable of hydrolysing highly ordered cellulose: only a carefully balanced system of enzymes capable of acting together and in sequence can accomplish the efficient generation of glucose.

LITERATURE CITED

1. Mandels, M. and Reese, E. T., *Develop. Ind. Microbiol.* **5**, 5 (1964).
2. Wood, T. M., *Biochem. J.* **109**, 217 (1968).
3. Wood, T. M. and Phillips, D. R., *Nature* **222**, 986 (1969).
4. Selby, K., *Adv. Chem. Ser.*, **95**, 34 (1969).
5. Wood, T. M. and McCrae, S. I., *Biochem. J.* **128**, 1183 (1972).
6. Wood, T. M. and McCrae, S. I., *Carbohydrate Research*, **57**, 117 (1977).
7. Wood, T. M. & McCrae, S. I., *Proc. Bioconversion Symp.* I.I.T. Delhi, India, 111 (1977).
8. Eriksson, K-E., Pettersson, B. & Westermark, U., *FEBS Letters*, **49**, 282 (1974).
9. Li, L. M., Flora, R. M. & King, K. W., *Arch. Biochem. Biophys.* 129, 416 (1965).
10. Reese, E. T., Siu, R. G. H. & Levinson, H. S., *J. Bacteriol.* **59**, 485 (1950).
11. Wood, T. M. and McCrae, S. I., *Biochem. J.* **171**, 61 (1978).
12. Wood, T. M. & McCrae, S. I., *Proc. Symp. on Enzymatic Hydrolysis of Cellulose*, Aulanko, Finland, 231 (1975).
13. Wood, T. M. & McCrae, S. I., *Biotechnol. & Bioeng. Symp.* No. 5, 111 (1975).
14. Wood, T. M. *Biochem. J.* **115**, 457 (1969).

2.4 Coagulation of Casein Micelles with Immobilized Proteases

N. F. Olson* and T. Richardson*

2.4.1 CASEIN AND CASEIN MICELLES

Bovine caseins are a heterogenous mixture of protein fractions which are usually distinguished by their electrophoretic mobility (Woodward, 1976). They are considered to be unique because the three major, non-identical fractions, α_s-, β- and κ-caseins, form spheres or micelles of greatly different sizes by a self-assembly mechanism (Slattery, 1976). Several models that have been proposed to describe casein micelle structure were reviewed by Thompson and Farrell (1973) and Slattery (1976). These models differ primarily in the position of κ-casein and whether micelles consist of subunits. Presence of κ-casein is critical since α_s- and β-caseins are insoluble in the presence of Ca^{2+} concentrations found in milk but are stabilized in micellar form by κ-casein. Distribution of casein fractions in micelles is unresolved but treatment of micelles with immobilized papain or immobilized carboxypeptidase indicated that all major fractions were available on the micelle surface (Ashoor *et al.*, 1971; Cheryan *et al.*, 1975c). This sustains those micelle models possessing a relatively uniform distribution of fractions but not models in which κ-casein is in the center of the micelle or forms a coat on the surface.

2.4.2 CLOTTING OF CASEIN MICELLES

Most proteases are able to modify casein micelles and cause clotting of milk but commercial enzymes are selected for their high clotting activity and low proteolytic activity. Coagulation of milk by milk-clotting enzymes occurs in two phases, a primary or enzymatic phase and a secondary or clotting phase (Ernstorm and Wong, 1974; Green, 1977). During the primary phase, a single peptide (phe-met) bond of κ-casein is cleaved to form a soluble, acidic peptide and the remainder of the molecule, called para-κ-casein, which apparently remains associated with casein micelles. This slight modification lowers stability of micelles in milk and causes their aggregation. The mechanism of aggregation is not completely elucidated

---

*Department of Food Science, University of Wisconsin, Madison, Wisconsin 53706, USA

but the negative charge on micelles is reduced by loss of the peptides allowing further interaction of micelles (Green and Crutchfield, 1971; Green and Marshall, 1977; Kirchmeier, 1972; Payens, 1966; Pearce, 1976). Proteolysis of κ-casein during the primary phase follows a typical rapid release of peptides to a maximum. The extent of proteolysis necessary to induce aggregation of micelles and clotting of milk is in dispute. Green and Marshall (1977) found that visible clotting of milk did not occur until a minimum level of proteolysis occurred but Guthy and Novak (1977) detected aggregation of particles (micelle-clumps) in milk during the primary phase before visible clotting. Treating milk with immobilized pepsin, which allowed separation of the two phases, indicated that clotting time varied inversely and exponentially with the amount of nonprotein-nitrogen released within limits of treatments used (Hicks *et al.*, 1975). This suggested that aggregation of micelles, in which only some of the κ-casein molecules are modified, is possible if there is sufficient time for orientation of micelles to allow interaction of para-κ-casein and negatively charged groups on micelles as suggested by Green and Marshall (1977).

Rate of coagulation of casein micelles is influenced by temperature, pH, presence and concentration of cations, carbohydrate composition of κ-casein, and concentration of enzyme. Experiments with soluble milk-clotting enzymes suggested that pH adjustment affected both phases of milk-clotting (Pyne, 1955) but the secondary phase was influenced to a greater extent by pH modification when immobilized pepsin was used as a mechanism to separate the two phases (Cheryan *et al.*, 1975a). The indirect relationship between concentration of milk-clotting enzyme and clotting time is well-known. However, the ratio of $\alpha_s:\kappa$-casein may be a critical factor in determining initial velocity of chymosin action in milk-clotting (Castle and Wheelock, 1973). Various commercial milk-clotting enzymes differ in some kinetic properties but the mechanism of aggregation of the para-κ-casein and electrophoretic patterns of peptides releases were similar (Itoh, 1972; Kovács-Proszt and Sanner, 1973). These factors have allowed successful interchange of appropriate proteases as soluble or immobilized milk-clotting enzymes.

2.4.3 IMMOBILIZED MILK-CLOTTING ENZYMES

Several proteases have been immobilized and used to clot milk (Green, 1977; Taylor *et al.*, 1976). Immobilized porcine pepsin appeared to be the most suitable even though the soluble form has a low pH optimum and is not very active or stable at the normal pH of milk. The altered and improved characteristics upon immobilization may have resulted from the charge density on the support which creates a microenvironment of low pH as compared to that in the bulk fluid. A number of supports and methods of immobilizing proteases have been evaluated but covalent attachment and adsorption have been used most commonly (Taylor *et al.*, 1976). Physical adsorption is the simplest but desorption is likely when treating milk which has a high ionic strength. Covalent attachment can eliminate enzyme desorption but it is a more complicated procedure. The type of support is dictated in part by the configuration of reactor used. Milk-clotting enzymes have been coupled *via* glutaraldehyde to alkylamine porous glass particles or glass particles coated with zirconia to increase their stability (Ferrier *et al.*, 1972; Cheryan *et al.*, 1975a, 1975b, 1976). Stability of the linkage during use was increased also by treatment with borohydride which reduces the more labile imino linkage between glutaraldehyde and the enzyme (Cheryan *et al.*, 1975b, 1976).

The ability to coagulate milk with immobilized milk-clotting enzymes results from unique characteristics of casein and different responses of the two phases of clotting to temperature (Berridge, 1942; Cheryan *et al.*, 1975). The markedly higher temperature coefficient of the secondary phase ($Q_{10} = 12 - 15$) allows completion of the primary phase at low temperature before clotting occurs. Milk at 5 to 15° C is usually pumped at controlled rates through a reactor containing sufficient immobilized enzyme to obtain adequate enzymatic action. Milk emerging from the column is warmed and clots within a few seconds or minutes depending upon extent of proteolysis.

As expected, the contact time between immobilized protease and milk affected the rate of the secondary phase of milk clotting. A direct relationship was observed between space-time in the reactor and logarithm of clotting activity which is the reciprocal of clotting time (Cheryan *et al.*, 1975b). A fluidized-bed reactor was superior to a packed-bed reactor under almost all conditions used by Cheryan *et al.* (1975b). Clotting activity of the fluidized-bed reactor was greater at each space-time value presumably from improved mass transfer from movement and turbulence in the fluidized-bed reactor and the tendency for channeling in the packed-bed ractor. Operating at lower space-time values by increasing milk flow rates reduced efficiency of the fluidized-bed reactor more extensively, probably from excessive turbulence and back-mixing. Fewer problems with plugging and buildup of contaminants occurred during use of the fluidized-bed reactor.

Continuous treatment of skimmilk resulted in very rapid losses in enzymatic activity during initial stages of treatment and a slower but exponential loss during subsequent operation of the reactor (Cheryan *et al.*, 1975b, 1976; Ferrier *et al.*, 1972). Inactivation was not caused by desorption of enzyme but appeared to be caused in part by deposition of proteins and peptides on the immobilized enzyme (Cheryan *et al.*, 1975b; Ferrier *et al.*, 1972). The pH of milk was important since immobilized rennet or pepsin lost activity more rapidly when milk was treated at pH 5.6 as compared to pH 6.6 (Cheryan *et al.*, 1975b).

Loss of activity was partially reversed and minimized by regeneration and modification of the surface of the support. Washing immobilized pepsin with water restored some activity but maximum regeneration was obtained by washing with dilute hydrochloric acid or urea at pH 3.5 (Cheryan *et al.*, 1975b; Taylor *et al.*, 1977). However, subsequent treatment of milk caused an extremely rapid loss in activity with the clotting time reaching a plateau equivalent to the level before regeneration. This remarkable memory effect has been observed routinely with porous glass and alumina as enzyme supports. Reasons for the effect have not been defined. Inactivation during continuous usage was minimized by precoating the support with proteins and coupling pepsin to the proteins (Cheryan *et al.*, 1976). Effectiveness of stabilizing enzymatic activity during use varied with the type of protein; a protein coat with a higher pI and/or greater hydrophilicity improved enzyme stability.

Immobilized proteases were used to study the mechanism of milk clotting and the structure of casein micelles. Several studies have demonstrated the ability of skimmilk and skimmilk fractions which have been treated with immobilized pepsin to coagulate untreated skimmilk and casein micelles (Cheryan *et al.*, 1975a; Hicks *et al.*, 1975; Lee *et al.*, 1977). Treating skimmilk and mixing with an equal volume of untreated skimmilk resulted in complete clotting of the mixture but at a slower rate than the treated skimmilk. Clotting rate of the mixture was slower than predicted by dilution effects suggesting that clotting was inhibited by unmodified casein micelles or by a lack of sufficient modified micelles to act as foci for clotting (Cheryan *et al.*, 1975a; Lee *et al.*, 1977). In another study, skimmilk from which casein micelles were removed by centrifugation and then treated with immobilized pepsin caused clotting of untreated casein micelles or skimmilk (Hicks *et al.*, 1975). Since the skimmilk used to prepare the serum had not been cooled, it appeared that para-κ-casein formed from κ-casein in the serum phase of skimmilk was capable of bridging between casein micelles to cause clotting. However, treatment of both micelles and serum increased the rate of clotting indicating that interaction between micelles also occurred. Characteristics of clotting and rheological properties of curd formed by immobilized proteases appears to be similar to those formed by soluble milk-clotting enzymes (Olson and Bottazzi, 1977).

Immobilized proteases have been useful and could have potential in basic studies on milk clotting and chemistry of bovine casein. They may also have application in continuous cheese manufacturing if the economics of the system are improved. This would require more complete immobilization of enzyme, less expensive enzyme supports and better stability or means of regenerating the enzymatic activity.

References

Ashoor, S. H., Sair, R. A., Olson, N. F. and Richardson, T. (1971). *Biochim. Biophys. Acta*, **229**, 423–430 (1971).

Berridge, N. J., *Nature*, **149**, 194 (1942).

Castle, A. V. and Wheelock, J. V., *J. Dairy Res.* **40**, 77–84, (1973).

Cheryan, M., Van Wyk, P. J., Olson, N. F. and Richardson, T., *J. Dairy Sci.* **58**, 477–481 (1975a).

Cheryan, M., Van Wyk, P. J., Olson, N. F. and Richardson, T., *Biotechnol. Bioeng.*, **17**, 585–598, (1975b).

Cheryan, M., Richardson, T. and Olson, N. F., *J. Dairy Sci.*, **58**, 651–657, (1975c).

Cheryan, M., Van Wyk, P. J., Richardson, T. and Olson, N. F., *Biotechnol. Bioeng.* **18**, 273–279, (1976).

Ernstrom, C. A. and Wong, N. P. Milk-Clotting Enzymes and Cheese Chemistry. In "Fundamentals of Dairy Chemistry," AVI Publ. Co., Westport, Conn., (1974).

Farrell, H. M., Jr., *J. Dairy Sci.*, **56**, 1195–1206, (1973).

Ferrier, L. K., Richardson, T., Olson, N. F. and Hicks, C. L., *J. Dairy Sci.*, **55**, 726–734 (1972).

Green, Margaret L., *J. Dairy Res.*, **44**, 159–188, (1977).

Green, Margaret L. and Crutchfield, G. *J. Dairy Res.*, **38**, 151, (1971).

Hicks, C. L., Ferrier, L. K., Olson, N. F. and Richardson, T., *J. Dairy Sci.*, **58**, 19–24, (1975).

Itoh, T. *Milchwiss.*, **27**, 470–473, (1972).

Kirchmeier, O., *Zeitschrift für Lebensmittel-Untersuchung und Forschung*, **149**, 211–217, (1972).

Kovács-Proszt, Gizella and Sanner, T., *J. Dairy Res.*, **40**, 263–272, (1973).

Lee, H. J., Olson, N. F. and Richardson, T., *J. Dairy Sci.*, **60**, 1683–1688, (1977).

Olson, N. F. and Bottazzi, V., *J. Food Sci.*, **42**, 669–673, (1977).

Payens, T. A. J., *J. Dairy Sci.*, **49**, 1317, (1966).

Green, Margaret L. and Marshall, R. J., *J. Dairy Res.*, **44**, 521–531, (1977).

Pearce, K. N., *J. Dairy Res.*, **43**, 27, (1976).

Pyne, G. T., *Dairy Sci. Abstr.*, **17**, 532, (1955).

Slattery, C. W., *J. Dairy Sci.*, **59**, 1547–1555, (1976).

Taylor, M. J., Cheryan, M., Richardson, T. and Olson, N. F., *Biotechnol. Bioeng.*, **19**, 683–700, (1977).

Taylor, M. J., Richardson, T. and Olson, N. F., *J. Milk Food Technol.*, **39**, 864–871, (1976).

Thompson, M. P. and Farrell, H. M., Jr., *Neth. Milk Dairy J.*, **27**, 220–239, (1973).

Woodward, D. R., *Dairy Sci. Abstr.*, **38**, 137–150, (1976).

2.5   Utilization of Pectic Enzymes in Food Production

Walter Pilnik* and Franciscus M. Rombouts*

Pectic enzymes occur in higher plants and are synthesized by micro-organisms. Their substrate is a variety of pectic substances which occur as structural polysaccharides in the middle lamella and the primary cell wall of higher plants. Native pectic enzymes can therefore produce important texture changes in fruits and vegetables during storage and processing operations. Microbial pectic enzymes are important in plant pathology; they are also produced on a large scale as a processing aid for the food industry.

2.5.1 PECTIC SUBSTANCES AND PECTIC ENZYMES

A simplified presentation of the structure of pectic substances or "pectin" consists of a chain of α–1,4 linked D-galacturonic acids, partly esterified with methanol (Fig. 1). The complicated chemical structure and physical properties of pectic substances are described by Doesburg (1965), Pilnik and Voragen (1970) and Kawabata (1977). It is usual to speak of pectin if more than half of the monomers are esterified. If less than ca 10 % is esterified one speaks of pectic acid (pectate) and the group in-between is referred to as low methoxyl pectin. This model is commonly used to characterize pectic enzymes. For a detailed description of pectic enzymes we refer to Rombouts and Pilnik (1972), Macmillan and Sheiman (1974), Fogarty and Ward (1974) and Rexová-Benková and Markovic (1976).

Pectinesterases (PE; EC 3.1.1.11) transform pectin into low methoxyl pectin and finally pectic acid (pectate) by hydrolyzing the ester bonds (Fig. 1). PEs appear in many higher plants and are also produced by molds and bacteria. They attack the pectin chain from the reducing end or next to a free carboxyl group and then act along the molecule. In this way blocks of free carboxyl groups are formed which make the pectate extremely calcium sensitive.

Polygalacturonases (PG) hydrolyze glycosidic linkages next to a free carboxyl group. Their best substrate is pectic acid. PGs are produced by

---

Agricultural University, Dept. of Food Science De Dreijen 12, 6703 BC Wageningen, The Netherlands

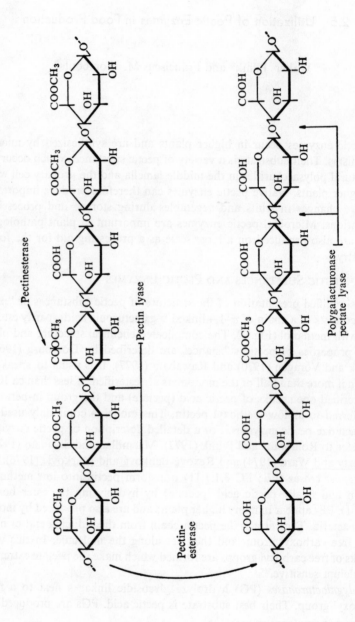

Fig. 1. Fragment of pectin molecule with points of attack of pectic enzymes

most fungi, including some yeasts, by some bacteria and are frequently found in higher plants. There are endo PGs (EC 3.2.1.15) and exo PGs (EC 3.2.1.67).

Pectate lyases (PAL) split glycosidic linkages next to a free carboxyl group by β-elimination. PALs are mainly bacterial enzymes; they are made by only a few molds and have not been found in higher plants. There are endo PALs (EC 4.2.2.2) and exo PALs (EC 4.2.2.9). The preferred substrates are pectic acid and low methoxyl pectin.

Pectin lyases (PL; EC 4.2.2.10) split glycosidic linkages next to a methylated carboxyl group by β-elimination. Only endo PLs are known for which highly esterified pectin is the best substrate. PL is produced by fungi only.

2.5.2 COMMERCIAL PECTINASES

Such products are based on surface or submerged cultures of *Aspergillus niger* and contain PE, PG and PL. They can therefore fulfill their technical function of degradation of highly esterified pectic substances by two pathways, i.e. deesterification by PE and hydrolysis by PG or direct depolymerization by eliminative splitting of the glycosidic linkages. Special preparations with mainly PG activity or PL activity are also on the market. It should be noted that apart from pectolytic activities all commercial pectinases contain varying amounts of other enzymes: cellulases, xylanases, arabanases, galactanases, glycosidases, proteases, esterases and oxidoreductases. Some manufacturers also add amylases from other sources to degrade starch in apple products. It is estimated that enzyme production for food uses in the western world amounts to 45 million US$ p.a. (Beck and Scott, 1974), one fourth of which relates to pectic enzymes.

2.5.3 FUNCTIONS OF PECTIC ENZYMES

A. Plant physiology.

Consistency changes during ripening and storage of fruit and vegetables are often linked to pectic changes which in turn can be ascribed to pectic enzymes (Doesburg, 1965; Pilnik and Voragen, 1970). There are indeed many changes in pectolytic activity accompanying or causing such changes but "the actual mechanism of cell wall softening of fruit is still a matter of conjecture" (Fogarty and Ward, 1974).

B. Microbiology

Phytopathological phenomena like post harvest decay and rotting of fruit and vegetables can in most instances be linked to the pectic enzyme production of the organisms concerned (Albersheim *et al.*, 1969; Bateman and Miller, 1966; Lund, 1971). The food technologist knows that softening of cucumbers and olives in brine is due to yeast PG and bacterial PAL. Pectic enzymes from the heat resistant mold *Byssochlamys fulva* can cause decay of strawberries in syrup or in jam (Eckardt, 1976). Highly heat resistant PG from *Rhizopus* spp. appears to be responsible for texture breakdown in canned apricots (Luh *et al.*, 1978). There are also desirable aspects: Pectic enzymes are said to play an important role in coffee and cocoa fermentation. The same is true for "Edelfäule" or *Botrytis cinerea* rot of grapes. The fungus grows through the skin; as a result of water evaporation higher sugar concentrations are obtained and the wine then has a higher alcohol content. The metabolic products of the mould also give it a special flavour (Drawert and Krefft, 1977).

C. Native enzymes in fruit and vegetable processing

The presence of PE in citrus fruits is responsible for one of the best studied enzymic phenomena in food technology: The cloud loss in citrus juices (Joslyn and Pilnik, 1961; Krop, 1974). All citrus juices display strong PE activity. If this is not inhibited by heat inactivation or by freezing, the native pectin will be deesterified and will coagulate with the calcium ions of the juice. As a consequence loss of cloud occurs: On standing the juice separates into a clear supernatant and a layer of sediment. In the case of concentrates formation of a calcium pectate gel occurs, from which no juice can be reconstituted. These are serious quality defects. Unfortunately citrus juices are extremely heat sensitive and other alternatives to the expensive frozen product than hot pack juices are sought. Some commercial clarifying enzymes will act as stabilizing enzymes (Baker and Bruemmer, 1972), apparently by rapidly degrading pectate, so that calcium pectate coagulation cannot occur (Krop, 1974). The same effect can be obtained by chelation of calcium ions, but this creates legal problems. Another approach is based on the fact that PE displays end product (pectate) inhibition. Addition of pectate clarifies the juice (Baker, 1976; Krop and Pilnik, 1974), producing thus the phenomenon one wants to prevent. However, we have been able to establish that by degrading pectate a degree of polymerization can be found (8–10) which has the inhibitory effect of the high polymer preparation, but does not coagulate with calcium. Because of the competitive nature of the inhibition, the addition of such preparations will not prevent, but delay clarification (Thermote *et al.*, 1977). More recent work in our laboratory has shown that there may be another reason for incomplete inhibition: There are at least two forms of PE in orange juice. One of these is inhibited more strongly by the oligomers than the other (Versteeg *et al.*, 1978). So far we have only investigated one variety of oranges. Other varieties may have distributions of these fractions which may allow a more complete inhibition or none at all. The addition of a galacturonide oligomer seems less of an additive problem than the addition of calcium sequestrants. Enzymatic self clarification of citrus juices is not only a negative point. It is made use of in the manufacture of clarified lemon and lime juices which are simply left standing under preservation, although they may now be clarified rapidly with enzymes and filter-aid (Uhlig, 1978).

In tomato juices high PE and PG activities can be found. The tomato industry therefore knows the cold-break and the hot-break process (McColloch *et al.*, 1950). In the first instance there is a holding time between disintegration and pasteurization in which PE converts the highly esterified tomato pectin into a low methoxyl form which then is degraded by the PG. In this way quite thin products are obtained which can be concentrated for uses in tomato-ketchup, sauces, etc. In the hot-break process the juice is heat treated as quickly as possible to preserve its highly viscous character which the consumer expects in single strength tomato juice.

2.5.4 USE OF COMMERCIAL PECTINASE PREPARATIONS

A. Fruit juice clarification

This is the oldest and still largest use of pectinases, applied mainly to apple juice but also to pear and grape juices. The pressing operation gives juices which are viscous from dissolved pectin and have a persistent turbidity. Through the addition of a pectinase preparation the viscosity drops and a "break" of the turbidity can be observed: Cloud particles coagulate to larger units and settle down. Clear juice can then be easily obtained by centrifuging and/or filtration, in many cases after addition of gelatin to precipitate polyphenols. The bulky precipitate not only removes astringency but also enrobes cloud particles. There are even pectinase preparations which are combined with gelatin. This process dates back to the early thirties but more than 35 years passed before Japanese workers (Endo, 1965; Yamasaki *et al.*, 1967) explained its mechanism. Apple juice which contains highly esterified pectin (>90%), may be clarified by a combination of PE and endo PG, or by PL alone, whereas in the case of grape juice, containing pectin with degrees of esterification between 44 and 65%, PL alone does not perform so well (Ishii and Yokotsuka, 1973). The clarification of juices by pectin degradation is also important in the manufacture of high solids concentrates to avoid jelling and development of haze (Heatherbell, 1976). A hot clarification process for apple juice concentrate saving enzyme and time and avoiding microbiological problems has recently been described (Grampp, 1977).

B. Juice extraction

Enzyme treatment of pulp is a time honoured process for black currants and other soft and stone fruits. The partial destruction of pectin releases juice and allows the anthocyanins to diffuse from the skins into the juice (Charley, 1969; Pilnik and Rombouts, 1978). This process has also caught the interest of red wine manufacturers. It allows for good yields of red grape juice especially in combination with a moderate heat treatment which can be directly fermented as is the case for white wines; a simpler technique than fermentation on the skins. In the European apple juice industry mechanized and automatized pressing equipment was introduced at the same time that the pressing quality of the apples decreased because of variety (*Golden Delicious*) and prolonged storage. In this situation the pulp enzyming process became in many instances a necessity and was shown to increase also the yield of apples of good pressing quality (Rombouts and Pilnik, 1978). In this process, enzyme inhibition by apple polyphenols could be largely diminished by preoxidation or by a small addition of polyvinylpyrrolidon. In the case of apples we were able to show that enzyme preparations which depolymerize highly esterified pectin (>90%) can be successfully used. The juice obtained from enzyme treated pulp has a higher methanol content than that obtained by purely mechanical pressing; in apple juice, e.g. 100 to 300 ppm as compared to 30 to 100 ppm in normal juices. It is difficult to say whether this constitutes a hazard as little is known about the subacute toxicity of methanol. At any rate methanol can be "lost" by concentrating. In the case of apple juice the possibility then exists to recover low methanol aroma from peels (Guadagni *et al.*, 1971).

C. Maceration and liquefaction

These processes can be seen as first and final steps of pulp enzyming. For maceration the enzyme treatment is meant only to degrade the middle lamella pectin so that plant tissue becomes a suspension of free but intact cells. There are claims that this can be achieved by using, e.g. only PG, assuming that the degree of esterification of the middle lamella pectin is much lower than that of cell wall pectin. This may not be true in all cases and in fact for carrots a macerating effect is claimed for pure PG as well as for pure PL (Grampp, 1972; Ishii and Yokotsuka, 1975; Zetelaki-Horváth and Gátai, 1977). Whether maceration only occurs or whether the process goes further to bring about the effects of pulp enzyming with cell destruction may be simply a question of intensity of enzyme action. There are many descriptions of macerating fruit for nectar bases (Strübi *et al.*, 1978) and vegetables for baby food preparations (Charley, 1969), but it is unknown to what extent this is used industrially.

Enzyming of pulp can be carried through to an almost complete liquefaction of fruit and vegetables if cellulase is used together with pectolytic enzymes (Pilnik *et al.*, 1975). Slightly viscous, clear or turbid juices, containing enzyme resistant tissue, skin particles and eventually pits are obtained which can be centrifuged or sieved or filtered to give juices in 90 to 98 % yield. This process reduces waste and seems especially suited for products for which no juice extraction equipment has been developed (tropical fruit) or where important constituents would be lost with the pulp fraction (carotene in carrots).

D. Applications in citrus technology

There is quite a large use of pectinase preparations in the citrus industry: When washing the pulp discarded during juice extraction to recover solids the yield is improved. Such pulp-wash juices then also have a low viscosity and can be concentrated (Braddock and Kesterson, 1976). Albedo is easily removed from peels to be used in marmalade or for confections (Villadsen and Möller, 1967). Citrus essential oils are usually obtained as an emulsion in peel juice. The enzymatic break down of pectin facilitates separation operations like creaming-up and centrifugation (Platt and Poston, 1962). A very important development is the manufacture of clouding agents from citrus peel. These are strongly turbid low viscosity preparations, suitable for concentration, obtained by a combination of mechanical comminution and enzyme action (Larsen, 1969). All these uses are entirely empirical so far and no studies have been published yet to show the rôle of the various pectolytic activities.

2.5.5 NUTRITIONAL ASPECTS

Most of the processes described so far are based on partial or complete enzymatic break-down of pectic substances. However, from the nutritional point of view, pectin is a valuable food constituent: Its physiological significance as dietary fiber is well documented (Truswell, 1976; Chenoweth and Leveille, 1975). It is therefore worthwhile to pay attention to processes in which pectin is saved as much as possible, e.g. by limiting the period of enzyme treatment (Krebs, 1968), or by clarification of fruit juices using fungal or plant proteases (Meurens, 1973).

REFERENCES

Albersheim, P., Jones, T. and English, P. D., *Ann. Rev. Phytopathol.*, 7, 171–194 (1969).
Baker, R. A., *J. Food Sci.*, 41, 1198–1200 (1976).

Baker, R. A. and Bruemmer, J. H., *J. Agric. Food Chem.*, **20** (6), 1169–1173 (1972).

Bateman, D. F. and Millar, R. L., *Ann. Rev. Phytopathol.*, **4**, 119–146 (1966).

Beck, C. I. and Scott, D., Enzymes in foods-for better or worse, 1974. In: Food Related Enzymes (J. R. Whitaker, ed.). Advances in Chemistry Series 136, pp. 1–30. American Chemical Society, Washington, D. C.

Braddock, R. J. and Kesterson, J. W., *J. Food Sci.*, **41**, 82–85 (1976).

Charley, V. L. S., *Chem. Ind.*, 635–641, 1969.

Chenoweth, Wanda, L. and Leveille, G. A., Metabolism and physiological effects of pectins, 1975. In: Physiological effects of food carbohydrates (A. Jeanes and J. Hodge, eds). ACS Symposium Series 15, pp. 312–324. American Chemical Society, Washington, D. C.

Doesburg, J. J., Pectic substances in fresh and preserved fruits and vegetables (1965). IBVT-Communication No. 25. Sprenger Institute, Wageningen, The Netherlands.

Drawert, F. and Krefft, M., *Chem. Mikrob. Technol. Lebensm.*, **5**, 105–112 (1977).

Eckardt, Christiane, 1976. Untersuchung über Vorkommen, Entwicklung und Hitzeresistenz von *Byssochlamys fulva* und *Paecilomyces*-Arten als potentiellen Verderbniserregern in Erdbeerenkonserven. Diss. Justus von Liebig-Universität, Giessen, Fed. Rep. of Germany.

Endo, A., *Agric. Biol. Chem.*, **29**, 229–233 (1965).

Fogarty, W. M. and Ward, O. P., Pectinases and pectic polysaccharides, 1974. In: Progress in Industrial Microbiology (D. J. D. Hockenhull, ed.), **13**, 59–119. Churchill Livingstone, Edinburgh.

Grampp, E., *Dechema Monographien*, **70**, 175–186 (1972).

Grampp, E., *Food Technol.*, **31** (11), 38–41, (1977).

Guadagni, D. G., Bomben, J. L. and Harris, J. G. *J. Sci. Food Agr.*, **22**, 115–119 (1971).

Heatherbell, D. A., *Alimenta*, **15**, 151–154. (1976).

Ishii, S. and Yokotsuka, T., *J. Agr. Food Chem.*, **21** (2), 269–272 (1973).

Ishii, S. and Yokotsuka, T., *Agr. Biol. Chem.*, **39**, 313–321 (1975).

Joslyn, M. A. and Pilnik, W., Enzymes and enzyme activity, 1961. In: The Orange, Its Biochemistry and Physiology (W. B. Sinclair, ed.), pp. 373–435. University of California Press, Berkeley, Calif.

Kawabata, A., *Memoirs Tokyo Univ. Agr.* **19**, 115–200. (1977).

Krebs, J., Fed. Rep. of Germany Patent 1792064, 1968.

Krop, J. J. P., The mechanism of cloud loss phenomena in orange juice, 1974. Doctoral Thesis, Agricultural University, Wageningen, The Netherlands.

Krop, J. J. P. and Pilnik, W. *Lebensm. -Wiss. u. Technol*, **7** (1), 62–63 (1974).

Larsen, S., *Ber. Wiss. Techn. Komm. IFU* **9**, 109–135, (1969).

Luh, B. S., Ozbilgin, S., and Liu, Y. K., *J. Food Sci.*, **43**, 713–720. (1978).

Lund, Barbara M., *J. Appl. Bacteriol.*, **34**, 9–20 (1971).

Macmillan, J. D. and Sheiman, M. I. Pectic enzymes, 1974. In: Food Related Enzymes (J. R. Whitaker, ed.), pp. 101–130. American Chem. Society, Washington, D. C.

McColloch, R. J., Nielsen, B. W. and Beavans, E. A., *Food Technol.*, **4** (9) 339–343 (1950).

Meurens, M. J. G. G., Belg. Patent 807407, 1973.

Pilnik, W. and Rombouts, F. M., Pectic Enzymes, 1978. In: Polysaccharides in Food. (J. M. V. Blanshard and J. R. Mitchell, eds.) pp. 109–126, Butterworths, London

Pilnik, W. and Voragen, A. G. J. Pectic substances and other uronides, 1970. In: The Biochemistry of Fruits and Their Products (A. C. Hulme, ed.), **1**, 53–87.

Pilnik, W., Voragen A. G. J., and de Vos, L., *Flüssiges Obst*, **42** (11), 448–451 (1975).

Platt, W. C. and Poston, A. L., US Patent 3058887, 1962.

Rexová-Benková, Lubomïra and Markovic, O., Pectic enzymes, 1976. In: Advances in Carbohydrate Chemistry and Biochemistry (R. S. Tipson and D. Horton, eds.), **33**, 323–385. Academic Press, New York.

Rombouts, F. M. and Pilnik, W., *CRC Crit. Rev. Food Technol.*, **3**, 1–26. (1972).

Rombouts, F. M. and Pilnik, W., *Process Biochem.*, **13** (8), 9–13 (1978).

Strübi, P., Escher, F., and Neukom, H., *J. Food Sci.*, **43**, 260–263 (1978).

Termote, F., Rombouts, F. M. and Pilnik, W., *J. Food Biochem.*, **1**, 15–34 (1977).

Truswell, A. S., *Näringsforskning* **20**, Supplement No. 14, Marabou Symposium "Food and Fibre", p. 51–54, 1976.

Uhlig, H., *Röhm Spektrum*, **20**, 44–45 (1978).

Versteeg, C., Rombouts, F. M., and Pilnik, W., *Lebeusm-Wiss. u.-Technol.*, **11**, 267–274 (1978).

Villadsen, K. J. S. and Möller, K. J., US Patent 3347678, 1967.

Yamasaki, M., Kato, A., Chu, S. -Y., and Arima, K., *Agric. Biol. Chem.*, **31** (5), 552–560 (1967).

Zetelaki-Horváth, K. and Gátai, K., *Acta Alimentaria*, **6** (3), 227–240 (1977).

3. Fermentation

3.1 Production of Amino Acids and Nucleotides by Fermentation

Kô Aida*

Monosodium glutamate, inosine 5′-monophosphate and guanosine 5′-monophosphate are widely used as flavor enhancers throughout the world. All were first industrialized in Japan. The present paper describes modern aspects of the microbial production of amino acids and nucleotides in Japan.

3.1.1 PRODUCTION OF AMINO ACIDS

The Japanese annual production of amino acids has already reached a level equivalent to more than 300 million dollars. The market ranges widely from food seasonings and feed additives to pharmaceuticals. The present situation of the amino acid industry in Japan is summarized in Table 1. As can be seen, it is now possible to produce most amino acids by microbial processes.

The most important amino acid is L-glutamic acid, whose fermentative production was first developed by Kinoshita and Udaka et al. in 1957 when they succeeded in isolating *Micrococcus glutamicus* (later designated *Corynebacterium glutamicum*). Following their publication, L-glutamic acid fermentation has always been the most intensively investigated of the various amino acid fermentations. Many L-glutamate producing strains have been reported. Glucose and molasses are the principal raw materials, although considerable efforts have been made to replace these materials with carbon sources such as acetic acid, ethanol, *n*-paraffin and other petrochemicals.

Glutamic acid fermentation provides a typical example of a case in which cell permeability represents a vital factor in regulating the outcome. Based

*Institute of Applied Microbiology, University of Tokyo, Bunkyo-ku, Tokyo 113, Japan

TABLE 1. Production of amino acids in Japan

Amino acid	Method	Amount (tons/yr)
L-Alanine	E, C	10–50
DL-Alanine	C	150–200
L-Arginine	F	200–300
L-Aspartic acid	E	500–1,000
L-Asparagine	Ex	10–50
L-Citrulline	F	10–50
L-Cysteine	Ex	100–200
L-Cystine	Ex	100–200
L-DOPA	F, C	80–200
Glycine	C	5,000–6,000
L-Glutamic acid	F	100,000
L-Histidine	F	100–200
L-Homoserine	F	10–50
L-Hydroxyproline	Ex	10–50
L-Glutamine	F	200–300
L-Isoleucine	F, Ex	10–50
L-Leucine	F, Ex	50–100
L-Lysine	F	15,000
DL-Methionine	C	60,000–70,000
L-Methionine	F, C	100–200
L-Ornithine	F	10–50
L-Phenylalanine	F, C	50–100
L-Proline	F	10–50
L-Serine	I, C	10–50
L-Threonine	F	50–100
L-Tryptophan	E, C	10–50
DL-Tryptophan	C	50–100
L-Valine	F	50–100

E, Enzymatic synthesis; C, chemical synthesis; F, fermentative production; Ex, extraction; I, microbial production from intermediate.

on numerous experimental results for the production of L-glutamic acid from carbohydrates, a biotin requirement was substantiated in almost all glutamate-producing bacteria. Moreover, it was found that a large amount of glutamate accumulated with a limited supply of biotin or oleic acid, or on addition of penicillin or surfactants. On the other hand, the process of L-glutamic acid production from *n*-paraffins involved a limited supply of thiamin or the addition of penicillin. In the case of glycerol-requiring mutants, a limited supply of glycerol resulted in the accumulation of glutamate from both carbohydrates and *n*-paraffins.

Results obtained using a glycerol auxotroph or the addition of penicillin suggested the involvement of phospholipids in the permeability of L-glutamic acid in the cell membrane. Penicillin or other β-lactam antibiotics caused excretion of UDP-*N*-acetylhexosamine derivatives and phospholipids as well as excretion of L-glutamic acid. Indispensable factors for over accumulation of L-glutamic acid were (1) that the cell membrane be composed of an incomplete phospholipid layer, formed by the regulation of phospholipid synthesis or the addition of penicillin, and (2) that the cells contain a very active biosynthetic system for L-glutamic acid formation.

The biosynthesis of amino acids in bacterial cells remains under the severe control of metabolic regulation. To accumulate a large quantity of particular amino acids, it is necessary to release the regulation mechanism. For this purpose, many auxotrophic mutants, analog-resistant mutants and combinations of both such mutations have been induced. In the case of auxotrophic mutants, the feedback inhibition or repression can be released by the addition of a suboptimal amount of the amino acid required by the mutant for growth. On the other hand, analog-resistant mutants can avoid the feedback control mechanism by its insensitivity to feedback inhibition or repression.

Fig. 1 shows the control mechanism of L-lysine biosynthesis and the breeding of L-lysine-producing strains of *Brevibacterium flavum*. Both as-

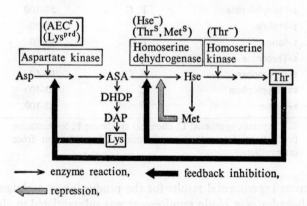

Fig. 1. Control of lysine biosynthesis and lysine-producing mutants.

ASA, Aspartate semialdehyde; DHDP, dihydrodipicolinate; DAP, diamino-pimelate; Hse, homoserine; AEC[r], *S*-(2-aminoethyl)-L-cysteine resistant; Lys[pr], lysine producer; Thr[s]Met[s], threonine- and methionine-sensitive; Hse[-], homoserine auxotroph.

partate kinase and homoserine dehydrogenase are under the control of concerted feedback inhibition with L-lysine and L-threonine, and homoserine dehydrogenase is repressed with L-threonine. S-(2-aminoethyl)-L-cysteine-resistant mutants, homoserine-requiring mutants and threonine- and methionine-sensitive mutants are known to produce large amounts of L-lysine in the culture broth.

Fig. 2 shows the control mechanism of aromatic amino acid biosynthesis in *Corynebacterium glutamicum*. Phenylalanine- and tyrosine-requiring mutants of this bacterium, KY 9456, were found to produce 0.15 mg/ml L-tryptophan. After several treatments, mutant PX-115-97 derived from it was able to produce 12 mg/ml L-tryptophan.

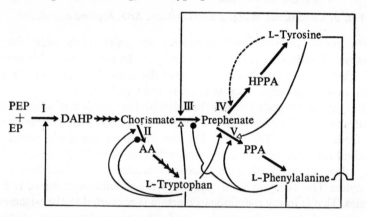

FIG. 2. Control of aromatic amino acid biosynthesis in *Corynebacterium glutamicum*.
◀— feedback inhibition (◀—partial inhibition), ◁—activation, ●—repression.
   I, DAHP synthetase; II, anthranilate synthetase; III, chorismate mutase; IV, prephenate dehydrogenase; V, prephenate dehydratase.

Transduction can also be applied for the construction of amino acid-accumulating strains of *Serratia marcescens* combined with regulatory mutation. Production of L-arginine, L-histidine and urocanoic acid are examples of this method. Fig. 3 shows the breeding procedure of an arginine-accumulating strain of *Serratia marcescens*. Mutant RA3179 was derepressed in the biosynthesis of L-arginine, and mutant RA4246 was desensitized from feedback inhibition with L-arginine. Arginine accumulators must have both these properties. This was successfully accomplished by co-transduction. Since *arg A* was found to be situated close to *lys A* in *Serratia marcescens* by genetic analysis, co-transduction of *arg A* was effected using lysine requirement as a selection marker. The transductant AT 404 was feedback inhibition resistant and derepressed in the arginine biosynthetic pathway. It could accumulate 25.5 mg/ml L-arginine. Another

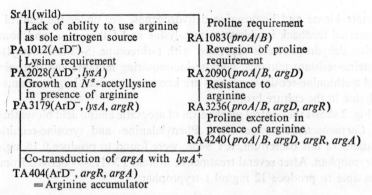

FIG. 3. Construction of arginine accumulator. ArD, Arginine degradation.

useful method to avoid feedback control mechanisms is the microbial production of amino acids from intermediates. In some cases, this method is highly effective and has been successfully applied to the industrial production of amino acids such as L-serine and L-isoleucine.

Enzymatic methods include the microbial conversion of suitable substrates to desired amino acids with intact cell or microbial enzymes extracted from the cells. Toray Co. has developed an enzymatic production method for L-lysine. DL-Amino-ε-caprolactam or cyclic lysine anhydride is synthesized chemically from chlorocyclohexane obtained as a by-product of nylon. The Toray method consists of the simultaneous use of two enzymes. That is to say D-aminocaprolactam is converted to the L-isomer by racemase of *Achromobacter obae*, and L-aminocaprolactam is converted to L-lysine by hydrolase of *Cryptococcus laurentii*. Both enzymes are induced by the addition of DL-caprolactam and isolated cells are directly used in the enzymatic process. A 20% L-lysine solution can be obtained which is easily purified to a high purity product.

3.1.2. PRODUCTION OF NUCLEOTIDES

In 1913, Kodama found that the flavor of *katsuobushi* (dried bonito) was due to IMP. In 1959, Kuninaka and Sakaguchi demonstrated for the first time that an enzyme of *Penicillium citrinum* can decompose RNA to 5'-nucleotides, and Omura and Ogata subsequently reported that *Streptomyces aureus* produced the same type of enzyme. Following these discoveries, a wide range of research on new methods for the industrial production of nucleotides and related substances was initiated.

At present, the total industrial production of 5'-IMP and 5'-GMP by the hydrolyzing and fermentative methods exceeds 3000 tons per year. These 5'-nucleotides are now competitively produced by 4 different methods in Japan: (1) enzymic hydrolysis of RNA to 5'-nucleotides (from 1961), (2) fermentative production of nucleosides and their phosphorylation to 5'-nucleotides (from 1964), (3) direct fermentative production of 5'-nucleotides (from 1966), and (4) chemical decomposition of RNA to nucleosides and their phosphorylation (from 1967). Inosine, AICAR and guanosine are produced by fermentation, and they are converted chemically to 5'-IMP or 5'-GMP.

Investigations aiming to develop a fermentative method for inosine production resulted in the establishment of an industrial process. The industrial production of 5'-IMP was effected by chemical or enzymatic phosphorylation of inosine. Inosine is also used in the medical field as a drug for treating hepatic diseases. Most inosine producers are adenine-requiring mutants.

Direct fermentative production of 5'-IMP is likely to be the most advantageous procedure, if a reasonable accumulation of 5'-IMP can be obtained. At present, industrial production of 5'-IMP by direct fermentation is being carried out with a mutant induced in *Brevibacterium ammoniagenes*. The characteristics features of 5'-IMP accumulation by *Brevibacterium ammoniagenes* KY13102, an adenine leaky mutant, are (1) that hypoxanthine accumulation is observed at an early stage of cultivation and (2) that abrupt accumulation of 5'-IMP occurs after 3 days accompanied by a decrease in hypoxanthine.

A model for a direct 5'-IMP accumulation mechanism has been presented. The characteristic features of this model are (1) that by limitation of Mn^{+2}, abnormal swollen cells are induced in a later stage of cultivation, and (2) that 5'-IMP accumulation occurs extracellularly by salvage biosynthesis, mainly due to breakdown of the permeability barrier.

TABLE 2.   Fermentative production of nuclic acid-related compounds.

Product	Yield	Microorganism[†]	Company	Ref.
Adenosine	16 g/l	*Bacillus* sp. (xanthine⁻)	Asahi	Haneda *et al.* (1971)
ATP	1.5 g/l	*B. ammoniagenes*	Kyowa	Tanaka *et al.* (1968)
CDP-choline	35 μmoles/ml	*S. carlsbergensis*		Tochikura *et al.* (1971)
FAD	1 g/l	*Sa. lutea*	Tanabe	Chibata *et al.* (1970)
NAD	1.9 g/l	*B. ammoniagenes*	Kyowa	Nakayama *et al.* (1968)
Orotic acid	20 g/l	*A. paraffineus* (uracil⁻)	Kyowa	Kawamoto *et al.* (1970)
c-AMP	8 g/l	*Microbacterium* sp.	Kikkoman	Ishiyama *et al.* (1976)

[†]*A.* = *Arthrobacter*; *B.* = *Brevibacterium*; *S.* = *Saccharomyces*; *Sa.* = *Sarcina*.

It has been found 3–5 mg of CoA can be accumulated in culture broth of *Brevibacterium ammoniagenes* by the addition of pantothenic acid, cysteine and the cationic surfactant, CPC, after being cultured for 3 days in an AMP-containing medium. Using the fermentation of sugars by dried cells of a variety of yeasts, a new method for producing sugar nucleotides such as UDP-glucose, GDP-mannose, UDP-galactose and UDP-GlcNAc, has been established. This method has been termed "coupled fermentation with double or multiple energy transfer". Fermentative production of CDP-choline, CDP-ethanolamine and their derivatives has also been developed using an almost identical method to that for sugar nucleotide production.

As shown in Table 2, various nucleotide-related compounds are currently being produced by fermentation for medical or reagent use. Further expansion of the areas of application of these compounds is strongly anticipated.

3.2 Extracellular Production of Proteins by Bacteria

Shigezo Udaka*

Enzymes of microbial origin have a long history of utilization throughout the world. The kinds and amounts of such enzyme proteins have rapidly increased in recent years, and most are extracellular products. Although the enzymatic activity of extracellular enzymes so produced is very high, the amount of enzyme protein is usually small. These well-known facts clearly demonstrate the ability of many microorganisms to excrete certain proteins and accumulate them in their extracellular culture fluid. We have therefore investigated the possibility of producing large amounts of extracellular proteins by fermentative processes.

As a result of a screening program, we found several excellent protein-producing bacteria[1]. Employing such bacteria, we are now able to carry out protein production in a very high yield from carbohydrate and ammonia. The present paper describes the fermentation conditions for the extracellular production of proteins, some of the properties of the product, and the mechanism of protein excretion.

Bacillus brevis No. 47 strain was found to be one of the best protein-producing bacteria isolated from nature. We therefore utilized this strain throughout the present study. A large amount of protein can be produced relatively easily in a nutrient rich medium. However, the efficiency of protein production varied greatly dependent on the actual composition of the culture medium. *B. brevis* cells grow well in a medium containing nutrients such as yeast extract or meat extract, but significant amounts of protein are not accumulated. Polypepton, which is a commercial product and equivalent to peptone, was found to be a suitable nutrient for both bacterial growth and the production of protein. It appeared to contain factor(s) which stimulated protein excretion, since it exerted a marked stimulatory effect on protein production but little effect on growth when added to a medium containing other nutrients. We attempted to characterize these stimulatory factors, and found that it presumably consisted of polypeptide with a molecular weight of a few thousand. We tested the effect of various

---

*Department of Food Science and Technology, Faculty of Agriculture Nagoya University, Chikusa-ku, Nagoya 464, Japan

amino acids on protein production in a nutrient rich medium. Only glycine and isoleucine caused any increase in protein production. When these amino acids were added together in appropriate concentrations, the amount of protein accumulated was about twice that obtained without addition of these amino acids. Under these conditions, the yield of protein was 12 g/l (Fig. 1).

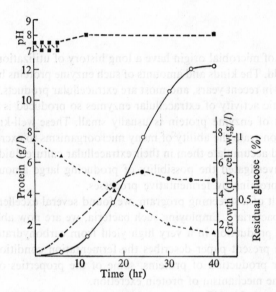

FIG. 1. Time course of protein production in a nutrient rich medium. *B. brevis* No. 47 was aerobically cultivated in a medium containing 1% glucose, 1% polypepton, 0.2% yeast extract, 0.5% meat extract, 0.25% glycine, 0.5% isoleucine, pH 7. The pH of the culture was controlled at 8. ○, extracellular protein; ●, growth; ▲, residual glucose; ■, pH.

Next, we attempted to determine the cultural conditions suitable for protein production with a simple synthetic medium containing sufficient carbohydrate and inorganic nitrogen source. Although the efficiency of protein production was low, about 2 g/l of protein was produced by *B. brevis*[2] from 4% glucose, 1% ammonium sulfate and a mixture of inorganic salts. It was found that the low yield of protein with synthetic minimal medium was not due to inefficiency of the protein biosynthesis itself. The reason for the low yield appeared to be related rather to the efficiency of protein excretion; i.e., the problem concerned the structure and function of the cell envelope. Such an hypothesis was supported by the fact that antibiotics known as inhibitors of cell wall synthesis were quite effective in increasing the protein yield. As shown in Fig. 2, addition of an appropriate amount of bacitracin brought about protein production that was several fold greater than that without the drug. The time of addition of the drug was also important. Under these conditions, about 10 g/l of protein (1% solution) were obtained by culturing the bacteria in a simple medium containing sufficient carbon and nitrogen source[3]. This result indicated an extraordinary capability of the bacteria. That is to say, they were able first to synthesize 20 kinds of natural amino acids, then build up certain proteins from these amino acids and excrete them into the medium.

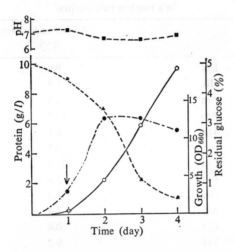

FIG. 2. Time course of protein production in a synthetic medium. *B. brevis* was cultivated in a synthetic medium containing 5% glucose, 1% ammonium sulfate, and a mixture of inorganic salts, with 2% CaCO$_3$.[3] Bacitracin was added at the time indicated by arrow. For symbols, see Fig. 1.

During the period of protein production, the increase in cell mass as well as amount of intracellular protein was about the same regardless of whether bacitracin was added or not. Thus, the increases in protein formation with bacitracin was restricted to extracellular protein formation. This is interpreted to mean that the excretion of proteins was specifically stimulated by bacitracin. Cells grown in a nutrient rich production medium appear to have little barrier to protein excretion, but cells grown in a synthetic medium without drug addition have a considerable barrier.

The trichloroacetic acid-precipitable substance of the excretion product of this fermentation was exclusively a mixture of proteins. Analysis by SDS-polyacrylamide gel electrophoresis revealed several protein bands as the major excretion product. The molecular weight of the major proteins produced with nutrient rich medium ranged between 100,000 and 140,000.

The proteins produced with synthetic medium had a lower molecular weight than the extracellular proteins formed with rich medium. Table 1 shows an example of the amino acid composition of the protein product. The content of lysine was rather high and that of half-cystine was low. The amino acid composition was not so different from ordinary bacterial proteins.

TABLE 1.   Example of the amino acid composition of
the extracellular protein product of *B. brevis* grown
in a nutrient rich medium

	Amino acid content (%)
Lys	9.6
His	1.5
Arg	4.3
Asp	13.5
Thr	6.3
Ser	3.8
Glu	11.8
Pro	3.6
Gly	4.8
Ala	6.4
Cys	0.4
Val	9.2
Met	2.5
Ile	5.3
Leu	7.4
Tyr	4.5
Phe	5.1
Trp	0.7

Some progress has been made in elucidating the mechanism of protein excretion by this organism[4]. The following experiments strongly support the view that *B. brevis* cells excreted proteins and the accumulation of extracellular protein was not the result of cellular autolysis. Apart from the extracellular protein, other cellular macromolecules such as DNA or RNA could not be found in significant amounts in the culture supernatant. We failed to detect any significant amount of prelabeled radioactive nucleic acid in the supernatant of the fermentation broth, and found only a little of the radioactivity of prelabeled cellular proteins. Second, enzyme activities of cellular anabolic metabolism were observed only in the intracellular extract, and not in the extracellular culture fluid. Third, analysis of the protein band pattern obtained by SDS-polyacrylamide gel electrophoresis revealed a large difference between the intracellular and extracellular proteins. These data cannot be explained if protein production is accompanied by autolysis.

The time course of extracellular protein excretion and the results of certain immunological studies indicated that the extracellular proteins were synthesized near the cell surface and excreted without time lag towards the extracellular fluid as they were formed. mRNA for extracellular proteins was found to be unstable, like that for intracellular proteins.

In conclusion, it can be said that we succeeded in developing a novel procedure for the efficient production of protein by a fermentative process.

ACKNOWLEDGEMENT: The author wishes to thank his colleagues for their efforts in accomplishing the work described here.

REFERENCES

1. Udaka, S., *Agric. Biol. Chem.*, **40**, 523 (1976).
2. Tsuchida, T., S. Miyashiro, H. Enei and S. Udaka, Abstr. Ann. Mtg. Agr. Chem. Soc. Japan, Tokyo, 207 (1977).
3. Miyashiro, S., Enei, H., Takinami, K., Hirose, Y., Tsuchida, T., and Udaka, S., Abstr. Ann. Mtg. Agr. Chem. Soc. Japan, Tokyo, 207 (1977).
4. Udaka, S., Yamaoka, T., and Tsuchida, T., Abstr. Ann. Mtg. Agr. Chem. Soc. Japan, Nagoya, 549 (1978).

3.3 Recent Progress in Beer Production

Lüdwig W. Narziß*

Beer consumption in the world is still increasing. In the traditional "Beer Countries", however, a saturation of the market enforced by traffic legislation and changes in consumer drinking habits is apparent. In countries with a steadily rising output, it is the primary aim of the breweries to meet demand, either by extending existing capacity or by optimizing or accelerating the process. Advances in brewing research have led to improvement of the individual steps of the brewing process. An increasingly detailed knowledge of raw materials permits better utilization as well as avoidance of production difficulties and shortcomings. Recent developments enable the brewer to utilize units of large capacity in brewing fermentation and storage. By thoughtful adjustment of the fermentation parameters, production time can be reduced without changes in the character of the individual beer.

In Japan, like Germany, very strict regulations exist regarding beer production. The German Purity Law (Reinheitsgebot) means that only malt, hops, water and yeast can be used. In Japan, although certain amounts of adjuncts such as maize or rice are permitted, no further additives are allowed and even for stabilization of the beer a limited range of strictly defined means only can be applied. This ensures the consumer of a highly pure and sound product. On the other hand, it represents a challenge to both brewer and scientist to control a natural process by natural methods.

3.3.1 MALTING

Malt quality exercises a dominating influence on the brewing process as well as on the beer properties. Today's barley varieties are the result of careful selection and breeding. They combine a high extract level and high enzymic capacity with good agricultural properties[1-3]. However, they hardly attain the yield of feeding or winter barley, which are rich in protein.

Along with improved malting barley, thoughtful application of individual germination parameters enables the maltster to influence the

*Lehrstuhl und Laboratorium für Technologie der Brauerei I, Technische Universität, D-8050 Freising-Weihenstephan, München, FRG

development and action of hydrolytic enzymes. For example, higher temperatures of 16–20° C at the start of germination as well as a stepwise increase of moisture up to 48–50% favor synthesis of the various enzymes and modification of the endosperm[4–6]. An increase in α-amylase for instance allows reduction of the germination time by *ca.* 3 days. One limiting factor, however, is the degradation of the endosperm walls. It is often difficult to modify the insoluble hemicelluloses and to break down the long chains of β-glucan.

The use of exogenous gibberellic acid offers a possibility to accelerate the process further. However, some varieties with poor malting performance show differences in the modification of the dorsal and the furrowed side of the kernel[7]. Abrasion achieves a better and more equal penetration of the gibberellic acid and thus a more effective stimulation of the aleuron layer[8,9]. This method is also favorable without any application of G.A. Furthermore, the husk content is diminished, and a more even germination and better modification are attained[10].

During kilning, i.e. under the conditions of the drying process at temperatures of 50–65° C, an increase in the level of certain enzymes can be observed. This compensates to some extent for the inevitable losses at high kilning temperatures[11,12]. The enzymic degradation of malt constituents proceeds during the drying process, thus forming sugars and amino acids which react to the various products of the Maillard reaction. Kilning temperatures above 80° C promote a stronger color pick-up during the individual steps of brewing[13,14].

3.3.2 BREWHOUSE PROCEDURES

The mashing procedure must consider the optimal conditions of individual enzymes in order to obtain the desired wort composition. α- and β-amylases are rapidly inactivated during the optimal temperatures. Their effects depend broadly on the preparation (dissolution, gelatinization) of the starchy material[15,16]. Peptidases are less sensitive, although they show a superior capacity within a temperature range of 45–55° C. The action of carboxypeptidases is clearly limited by the more susceptible endopeptidases. Pronounced rests as well as a low pH of 5.4–5.6 provide the desirable distribution of nitrogenous material, in particular the amount of α-amino-nitrogen (*ca.* 22% of the total nitrogen)[17,18]. These rests may promote the dissolution of zinc, which is, however, precipitated at higher temperatures[19,20].

The degradation of hemicelluloses and gums is a limiting factor in any reduction of mashing time. In particular, if poorly modified malts are processed, the majority of the β-glucan is released along with the gelatinization of starch at *ca.* 60–65° C. As there is hardly any detectable β-glucanase activity at these temperatures, the full amount of this viscous material remains unaltered and leads to filtration difficulties in wort and beer[21-23]. Thus, malt modification is of paramount importance.

A favorable wort composition as obtained by a well-adjusted mashing process can be subject to deterioration by secondary effects. Uncontrolled oxygen uptake during mashing or lautering achieves an oxidation of polyphenols and affects the color of the wort and beer[24,25]. Insufficient separation of mash and wort causes a release of significant amounts of fatty acids into the wort and so a detrimental effect on the flavor stability of the beer[26,27].

Wort boiling has remained unaltered for the last 50 years, the different processes concerned requiring a time of 90–120 min. More vigorous boiling and better protein precipitation were obtained by using external cookers suggesting a reduction of boiling time by 30%. However, isomerization of hop bitter substances did not improve in the same way, unless higher temperatures of 108–110°C were applied[28,29]. It was then possible to reduce the boiling time to 50–60 min and to attain at least equal wort properties. A dramatic reduction in boiling time is feasible by higher temperatures of 120–150°C[29,30]. Within 5–2 min, the individual reactions are satisfactorily achieved without any adverse effect on wort composition or beer quality. Concurrently, the physical stability of beers is improved.

During wort boiling a certain increase in color by 3–5 EBC units is inevitable[31,32]. This depends largely on the preexisting coloring substances formed during the preceding processes such as kilning and mashing (melanoidins) or extracted during mashing, lautering and wort boiling (polyphenols). The ensuing steps of wort treatment and wort cooling lead to further alterations. As the wort is exposed to temperatures of 90–95°C for at least 2 hr, another increase in color, a post-isomerization of hop bitter substances by 15–25%, and a further polymerization of polyphenols occur[33-35]. Hot break separation must be achieved thoroughly, since residues affect fermentation and maturation of the beer and cause a breakdown of flavor stability[36,37].

3.3.3 FERMENTATION AND MATURATION

Although the majority of breweries still achieve a conventional fermentation (7 days), maturation and storage (4–10 weeks), accelerated processes have been developed throughout the world. The most perfect appears to be the continuous system devised by Coutts et al.[38] In a similarly short time, a bioreactor succeeded in fermenting and maturing a beer of good quality but this process was never used on a fully commercial scale[39].

The fermentation velocity is increased by higher fermentation temperatures of 12–20°C, but greater amounts of higher alcohols and esters are produced[40,41]. The application of pressure (t/10 bar) inhibits the formation of these by-products by controlling yeast growth[41,42]. Acetolactic acid, the precursor of diacetyl, is formed earlier and in greater amounts with increasing fermentation temperatures[41,43,44]. However, its reduction via diacetyl, acetoin and butanediol during the second phase of fermentation is markedly promoted by higher temperatures and additionally supported by pressure. The limited yeast growth leads to an overaging of the yeasts, unless the procedures of yeast cultivation and propagation make allowance for this fact.

Maturation of beers fermented at high temperatures is fairly rapid, if the fermentation temperatures are maintained until the flavor threshold of the vicinal diketones and their precursors is attained. The total time for fermentation, maturation and cold storage (2 days) amounts to 14–17 days[45]. Acetaldehyde and dimethylsulfide[46] fall rapidly at higher temperatures; the higher alcohols and esters undergo a further increase. By means of pressure, however, it is possible to obtain a pattern of by-products which resembles in general that of conventional processes[47,48]. Only β-phenylethanol and its ester always remain at a higher level. Additionally, the content of hexanoic, octanoic and decanoic acids and their esters may be markedly higher[49], causing a deterioration of head retention[50]. The precipitation of bitter substances due to the rapid fall in pH is considerable; however, the beer bitterness is somewhat harsher, so that a lower level of bitter substances is preferable anyway[51]. Such beers frequently show a "yeasty" note, which can be avoided by rejecting yeast after 2 or 3 fermentations.

Conventional primary fermentation at a low temperature of 8.5–9.5°C followed by maturation at higher temperatures of 15–30°C may offer some advantages. Whereas the low fermentation temperature ensures a normal pattern of by-products, the high maturation temperatures along with 10–12% krausen hardly affect this. The amount of extract fermented in this phase was far too low to alter the levels of esters and alcohols significantly. Also, the fatty acids and their esters exhibited even more favorable figures than conventionally matured beers[45,51]. On providing a threshold of "total diacetyl" of 0.1 mg/l, it took 2–4 days at 30°C, 4–6 days at 20°C, and 6–9 days at 15°C to obtain a fully matured beer. After a storage time of 2 days at 0°C, the beers showed normal head retention and the usual level of bitter substances. The original character of the beers could be reproduced. Even the typical hoppy flavor was noticeable. This method permits reuse of the pitching yeast several times; the basic character of the beer is preserved; the maturation is adjusted to the individual wort, including some space for security; yeast is removed after each stage; maturation is achieved by sound, active yeast cells which guarantee low levels of fatty acids; and the production time is 14–17 days. This is comparable with other accelerated processes[45,52].

3.3.4 CONCLUSION

The above examples show that the production of beer can be steadily improved to optimize the individual processes involved and to augment the economy. However, each step must be carefully considered to determine whether the beer quality can be maintained and whether further alterations are possible. The factors involved include the flavor, foam and stability as well as the flavor stability of the final product.

REFERENCES

1. Barley Varieties EBC, E. B. C., P. O. B. 510,2380 Zoeterwoude (NL).
2. Barley Trials EBC, E. B. C., P. O. B. 510,2380 Zoeterwoude (NL).
3. *Braugerstenjahrbuch*, Arbeitsgemeinschaft zur Förderung des Qualitätsgerstenanbaues im Bundesgebiet (1977).
4. MacLeod, A. M., E. B. C. Proc.. 63 (1977).
5. Narziß, L. and Friedrich, G., *Brauwiss.*, **23**, 229, 265 (1970).
6. Narziß, L., Monograph-II E. B. C. Barley and Malting Symposium, 62 (1975).
7. Palmer, H. G., E. B. C. Proc., 59 (1971).
8. Baxter, E. D., Booer, C. D. and Palmer, G. H., *J. Inst. Brew.*, **80**, 549 (1974).
9. Palmer, G. H., Barett, J. and Kirshop, B. H., *J. Inst. Brew.*, **78**, 81 (1972).
10. Kieninger, H., *Brauwelt*, **116**, 1317 (1976).
11. Narziß, L. and Rusitzka, P., *Brauwiss.*, **30**, 1, 105 (1977).
12. Narziß, L., Reicheneder, E., Ishikawa, T. and Mohr, J., *Brauwiss.*, **28**, 160 (1975).
13. Yoshida, T., Horie, Y. and Kuroiwa, J., *Rept. Res. Lab. Kirin Brewery Co.*, No. 15, 45 (1972).
14. Narziß, L. and Stippler, K., *Brauwiss.*, **29**, 276, 289 (1976).
15. Schur, F., Pfenninger, H. and Narziß, L., *Schweiz. Br. Rdsch.*, **85**, 220 (1974); **86**, 57, 153 (1975).
16. Narziß, L., *Brauwelt*, **112**, 1027 (1972).
17. Jones, M. and Pierce, J. S., E. B. C. Proc. 128, (1963).
18. Narziß, L. and Lintz, B., *Brauwiss.*, **28**, 305 (1978).
19. Mändl, B., *Brauwelt*, **116**, 657 (1976).
20. Narziß, L., Barth, D., Yamagishi, N. and Heyse, U., in press.
21. Schuster, K., Narziß, L. and Kumada, J., *Brauwiss.*, **20**, 185, 280 (1967).
22. Narziß, L. and Litzenburger, K., *Brauwiss.*, **30**, 264, 314 (1977).
23. Bathgate, G. N., Monograph-I E. B. C.-Wortsymposium, 198 (1974).
24. Vancraenenbroeck, R., Monograph-I E. B. C.-Wortsymposium, 313 (1974).

25. Narziß, L. and Bellmer, H. G., *Brauwelt*, **115**, 285 (1975).
26. Drost, B. W., van Eerde, P., Hoekstra, S. F. and Strating, J., E. B. C. Proc. 451 (1971).
27. Hoekstra, S. F., E. B. C. Proc., 465 (1975).
28. Narziß, L., *Brauwelt*, **114**, 1763, 1793 (1974).
29. Narziß, L., *Brauwelt*, **117**, 1420 (1977).
30. Sommer, G. and Schilfarth, H., E. B. C. Proc., 233 (1975).
31. Silberhumer, H., *Brauwelt*, **113**, 819 (1973).
32. Narziß, L., *Brauwelt*, **114**, 355 (1974).
33. Krauß, G., *Mschr. f. Br.*, **24**, 304 (1971).
34. Narziß, L. and Bellmer, H. G., *Brauwiss.*, **29**, 233 (1976).
35. Narziß, L., *Brauwelt*, **118**, 44 (1978).
36. Nielsen, H., *Technical Quarterly MBAA*, **10** (1973).
37. Klopper, W. K., Tuning, B., and Vermeire, H. A., E. B. C. Proc., 659 (1975).
38. Coutts, M. W. and Ricketts, J., MBAA Proc. 68th Ann. Conv., 20 (1955).
39. Narziß, L. and Hellich, P., *Brauwelt*, **111**, 1491 (1971).
40. Krauß, G. and Sommer, G., *Mschr. f. Br.*, **20**, 51 (1967).
41. Miedaner, H., Narziß, L. and Wörner, G., *Brauwiss.*, **27**, 208 (1974).
42. Wellhoener, H. G., *Brauwelt*, **103**, 845 (1963).
43. Masschelein, Ch., *Brauwelt*, **115**, 608 (1975).
44. Inoue, T. and Yamamoto, Y., *Rept. Res. Lab. Kirin Brewery Co.*, **16**, 11 (1973).
45. Narziß, L. Miedaner, H., and Wörner, G., *Brauwiss.*, **27**, 233 (1974).
46. Nakajima, S. and Narziß, L., *Brauwiss.*, in press.
47. Wellhoener H., J., *Brauwelt*, **105**, 286 (1965).
48. Kumada, J. Nakajima S., Takahashi, T. and Narziß, L., E. B. C. Proc., 615 (1975).
49. Miedaner, H., *Brauwiss.*, in press.
50. Zürcher, Ch. and Krauß, G ,.*Mschr. f., Br.*, **24**, 230 (1971).
51. Narziß, L. and Neidhardt, W., *Brauwiss.*, **29**, 325 (1976).
52. Miedaner, H., Nakajima, S., and Narziß, L., E. B. C. Proc., 609 (1977).

3.4 Sake: History and Present Status

Kazuhide Kuriyama*

Sake is the traditional national beverage of Japan. It is inseparable from the daily life of the Japanese. Just as wine is a must with French cuisine, so is *sake* with Japanese food.

Today, however, the Japanese people's eating habits have become extremely diversified. As a result, almost all kinds of alcoholic beverages in the world are now produced, imported and consumed in the country.

The main alcoholic beverages in Japan are *sake* and beer. On comparing the total volumes of consumption, *sake* is found to be second only to beer, but in terms of absolute alcohol volume consumed, *sake* far exceeds beer.

At present, there are about 3000 *sake* breweries in Japan. These factories are on very different scales, producing from 500 to 20,000 kiloliters of *sake* per year. Fushimi in Kyoto and Nada in the suburbs of Kobe are especially renowned as *sake*-brewing centers. They may be likened to Bordeaux and Burgundy of French wine, or Rhine and Mosel of German wine.

3.4.1 HISTORY OF SAKE

Sake is made from rice. For more than 2000 years, from the beginning of rice cultivation in Japan, the methodology and techniques of *sake* brewing have been refined and mellowed through the ages. *Sake* was originally prepared as an offering to the gods. People drank it only on special occasions, such as at rituals and festivals. As time went by, however, the custom of drinking *sake* on ordinary occasions spread, first among nobles and then among the people at large.

In the 8th to 12th centuries, when the nobility with the emperor ruled the country, the government directly operated various industrial factories to meet its own needs, such as paper-making, weaving and dyeing shops. Another such factory was the *sake*-brewing factory. Thus, until around the 12th century, there were no privately operated *sake* breweries. The people at large either made *sake* for their own needs by a more primitive process or bought *sake* from shrines and temples which produced *sake* on a fairly large scale.

*Okura Shuzo Co., Ltd., Katahara-cho, Fushimi-ku, Kyoto 612, Japan

In the late 12th century, the governmental *sake*-brewing factory was abolished, and the brewing techniques established under the old system gradually spread among the people at large. In the 13th to 15th centuries, with the development of a barter economy, private *sake* brewers establish-ed themselves. Thus, at the beginning of the 15th century, according to available records, there were more than 300 *sake* breweries in Kyoto alone.

The basic brewing method used in Japan today was perfected in the 16th century. This method includes various excellent brewing techniques. Indeed, a low-temperature sterilization process very similar to pasteuri-zation was used 300 years before Pasteur was born.

3.4.2 CHARACTERISTICS OF *Sake* AND *Sake* BREWING

Sake is clear and pale yellow in color. It has a specific gravity of 1.0,

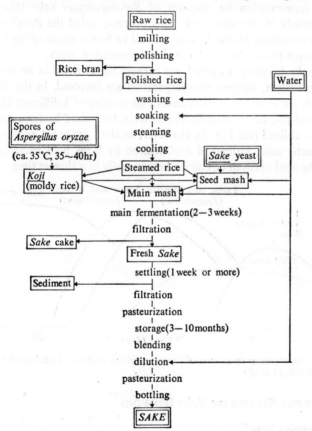

FIG. 1. Process chart of *sake* brewing.

an alcohol content of 15–16%, a characteristic aroma, little acidity, and a slight sweetness. It is often served warm in the cold season.

A process chart illustrating *sake* brewing in the modern factory is shown in Fig. 1. The methodology and techniques of *sake* brewing have some uniquely characteristic points when compared to the production methods of other alcoholic beverages in the world.

First, rice is used as the raw material and *koji*, a culture of *Aspergillus oryzae* grown on steamed rice, is employed to digest the rice enzymatically. The *koji* corresponds roughly to the malted barley used in the West. There are various kinds of molds grown on steamed rice, but *Asp. oryzae* possesses high α-amylase activity, so permitting fermentation in the presence of a high proportion of solid matter.

Second, the two reactions of saccarification by amylases of *Asp. oryzae* and fermentation by enzymes of *Saccharomyces sake* take place simultaneously in the same tank. This process, called the Parallel Combined Fermentation Method, is considered to be the cause of the high alcohol content (more than 20%) in the fermentation mash.

Since *sake* brewing is carried out without sterilization in an open fermentation system, various microorganisms are involved. In the classical seed mash, for example, a spontaneous succession of 3 different kinds of microorganisms, viz. nitric-reducing bacteria, lactic acid bacteria and *sake* yeast, was utilized (see Fig. 2). However, modern processes employ commercial lactic acid, instead of acidification by lactic acid bacteria. This enables the seed mash to be cultured more easily in a shorter time.

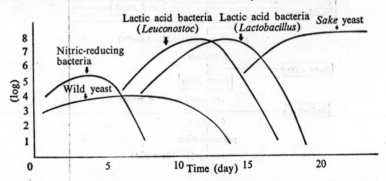

FIG. 2. Spontaneous succession of microorganisms in classical seed mash (after Saito, Kitahara *et al.*).

3.4.3 RECENT STUDIES ON *Sake* BREWING

A. Non-foaming Yeast[1]

Most *sake* yeasts form a high froth in the mash at the early stages of fermentation. Based on the relationship between the adsorption ability on the bubbles and foam productivity during the fermentation, certain kinds of non-foaming mutants have been isolated from the popular foaming strains. These non-foaming mutants are employed commercially, so permitting the use of smaller fermentation tanks.

B. Killer-resistant Yeast[2]

Contamination by wild yeasts often occurs during the fermentation of the main mash. It was found that some wild yeasts produced a factor which killed *sake* yeasts, and most of *sake* yeasts popularly used by *sake* breweries were sensitive to such killer strains. The isolation of killer-resistant mutants from popular sensitive *sake* yeasts has therefore been investigated, and attempts have been made to breed useful killer hybrids capable of producing good quality *sake* while preventing contamination by wild yeasts.

C. Alcohol-tolerant Yeast[3]

At the final stage of fermentation, the ratio of dead cells of *sake* yeasts tends to increase. This causes an increase in amount of amino acids and deep coloration of *sake*. Alcohol-tolerant mutants of *sake* yeast have therefore been isolated by the selection method from yeast cultures incubated in media containing 20% alcohol. The strains also show a resistance to the killer factor.

D. Hiochic Bacteria[4-6]

Sake sometimes becomes putrefied following invasion by certain kinds of lactic acid bacteria called hiochic bacteria during storage in bottles or tanks. This causes turbidity and a disagreeable off-flavor and taste. Most of the hiochic bacteria essentially require the presence of mevalonic acid (hiochic acid) for their growth. Since most of the mevalonic acid in *sake* derives from the *koji*, the isolation of *koji* mold mutants which do not produce mevalonic acid has been studied. Moreover, as a result of recent research on hiochic bacteria and the development of a technology of heat sterilization, *sake* is now sterilized completely and sold on the market without the addition of antiseptics.

E. Sake-protein Turbidity[7,8]

After heat pasteurization, *sake* sometimes becomes slightly turbid. This turbidity, so-called "*sake*-protein turbidity" if observed in bottled *sake*, causes the product to lose its market value. It has been shown that soluble proteins of saccharogenic enzymes derived from *koji* during fermentation form insoluble materials when denatured by heat and these gradually coagulate into particles to give *sake* a slight turbidity. The particles are too small to be removed by filtration alone. Either physical or enzymatic clarification methods can be employed to remove the turbidity by precipitation.

F. Deferriferrichrome Non-producing *Koji*[6,9]

Throughout the long history of *sake* brewing, the presence of iron in the water has been considered undesirable due to the tendency to cause deep coloration of *sake*. It has recently been found that the reddish-yellow color development in *sake* due to iron results from the formation of a reddish ferrichrome compound by reaction with the colorless deferriferrichrome produced by *Asp. oryzae* during *koji* making. It should be possible therefore to prevent excess color development in *sake* by brewing with a mutant strain of *Asp. oryzae* which produces a lesser amount of deferriferrichrome. Isolation of deferriferrichrome non-producing mutants has been investigated and applied in industrial production.

3.4.4 IMPROVEMENT OF EQUIPMENT AND MACHINERY[10-12]

Until quite recently, *sake* brewing was performed directly by hand during the coldest season of the year to prepare high quality *sake*. This was very arduous for the brewers.

Over the last 20 years, we have made studies on the equipment and machinery of *sake* brewing in order to develop labor-saving procedures. Although the principles of *sake* brewing are still based on the traditional methodology, a remarkably rapid switch from the classical to modern type of brewery has occurred.

A. Continuous Rice Polishing Apparatus

Polishing of rice is now carried out continuously and rapidly. This is done by connecting several mills in series in large factories.

B. Continuous Rice Steaming Machines

With the older batch-wise special wooden tubs, polished rice was long steamed for 60–90 min. However, steaming is now carried out for only 20–30 min, since enzymatic digestion of the steamed rice was found to be achieved even in rice steamed for only a short time. In modern large factories, a new automatic and continuous steaming machine as developed by us is widely used.

C. Cooling Machines for Steamed Rice

Cooling machines for steamed rice have come to be adopted in many factories. This has permitted operation within a smaller area.

D. Kasten System Apparatus for *Koji*-making

Koji was long cultured by using many small wooden trays placed in a warm incubation room. However, a large apparatus for *koji*-making with automatic control of temperature and moisture has now been introduced. This equipment is similar to the Kasten system used in beer production.

E. New Type of Tanks for Fermentation of the Mash

Previously, old Japanese cedar wood tanks were used. However, modern factories are now equipped with temperature-controlled metal tanks for fermentation of the mash.

F. New Type of Press of the Mash

Filtration of the mash has long been carried out by hydraulic pressure after distributing the mash into many small bags in a large wooden box. Recently, however, a new type of press which utilizes a flexible plastic wall and air pressure has been employed. Horizontal and vertical types of these new presses have been developed by us and are currently used not only for *sake* mash filtration but also for the filtration of hard separable substances in other industries.

G. Room-conditioning Systems

In smaller factories, *sake* is still brewed only in the winter because *sake* fermentation requires a low temperature. In large modern factories, however, artificial refrigeration and dehumidifying systems with bactericidal functions are employed to maintain a suitable brewing atmosphere. It is now possible therefore to produce *sake* of excellent quality throughout the year.

REFERENCES

1. Nunokawa, Y., Toba, H. and Ouchi, K., *J. Ferment. Technol.*, **49**, 959 (1971).
2. Imamura, T., Kawamoto, M. and Takaoka, Y., *J. Ferment. Technol.*, **52**, 293 (1974).
3. Hara, S., Sasaki, M., Oba, T., and Noshiro, K., *J. Soc. Brew. Japan*, **71**, 301 (1976).
4. Tamura, G., Nagura, A. and Suzuki, Y., *J. Agr. Chem. Soc. Japan*, **32**, 701, 707, 778, 783 (1958).
5. Kitahara, K., Kaneko, T. and Goto, O., *J. Agr. Chem. Soc. Japan*, **31**, 556 (1957).

6. Hara, S., Sugama, S., Hongo, K., Oba, T., Hasegawa, Y. and Murakami, H., *J. Ferment. Technol.*, **52**, 306 (1974).
7. Sugita, O. and Kageyama, K., *J. Ferment. Technol.*, **35**, 347 (1957); **36**, 63, 157 (1958).
8. Kuriyama, K., *Ann. Brew. Ass. Japan*, **14**, 11 (1959).
9. Tadenuma, M. and Sato, S., *Agr. Biol. Chem.*, **31**, 1482 (1967).
10. Kuriyama, K., Imayasu, S. and Ando, N., Abstr. Ann. Mtg. Agr. Chem. Soc. Japan, 423 (1968).
11. Kuriyama, K., Imayasu, S. and Ando, N., *J. Ferment. Technol.*, **41**, 254 (1963).
12. Imayasu, S., *J. Soc. Brew. Japan*, **61**, 106 (1966).

Subplenary Sessions

Main Topic IV: Physical, Chemical and Sensory Properties of Food

1. Physical Properties of Food
2. Chemical Aspects of Food Quality
3. Taste and Chemical Structure

1. Physical Properties of Food

1.1 Physical Parameters Attributing to the Mouthfeel of Liquid and Semi-Solid Foods

Chokyun Rha*

1.1.1. INTRODUCTION

Liquid and semi-solid foods constitute a major portion of our daily intake, and have a special importance due to their easily ingestible and digestible nature. Liquids and semi-solid solutions, suspensions, emulsions, pastes, gels and curds consititute a wide variety of numerous food products, and the present market volume of fluid and semi-fluid products in the United States alone is estimated to be well over 15 billion dollars.

In spite of their physical and commercial importance the studies on the sensory attributes of liquid or semi-liquid food has been very limited, especially regarding the mouthfeel.

1.1.2 TERMS DESCRIBING MOUTHFEEL

Recently Szczesniak (1978) made a study on the mouthfeel characteristics of beverages using a modified word association test to generate descriptive terms, and by deduction the terms were classified into various categories. There are many frequently used terms to describe the mouthfeel, and Szczesniak reported that among about 136 terms generated to describe the mouthfeel of beverages, 75 terms were mentioned approximately 3 or more times.

The most often used words referring to sensory perception are viscosity related. According to Szczesniak (1978), the *viscosity related terms*, thin, thick and viscous or viscosity, are followed by *feel on soft tissue* in frequen-

Food Material Science and Fabrication Laboratory, Department of Nutrition and Food Science, Massachusetts Institute of Technology, Cambridge, Massachusetts 02139, USA

cy of use. Among the eleven classified categories of terms, four; *viscosity related terms, feel on soft tissue, coating of oral cavity, resistance to tongue movement*, are primarily rheological attributes and comprise about 56% of the total references. Szczesniak (1978) reported that viscosity appeared to be the most conscious important single mouthfeel sensation, confirming again that the flow properties play an unquestionably important and dominant role in mouthfeel. However, in addition to rheological properties, other physical parameters contribute to the overall mouthfeel of the fluid semi-solid food. Surface characteristics as expressed by feel on soft tissue, residual mouthfeel, and also to some extent coating of the oral cavity, as well as moistness, density and temperature, contribute significantly to the mouthfeel both directly and indirectly by affecting the flow properties of the food.

1.1.3 Rheological Characteristics of Fluid and Semi-solid Foods

Beverages like milk and milk type drinks, coffee, tea, cocoa, juice, fruit and carbonated drinks, which are served in a glass or cup, have simple ideal flow behavior. Even beverages containing higher solid or particle content, if not Newtonain, still exhibit simple flow behavior within a narrow range under usual rheological measurements used today. Therefore rheological attributes to the mouthfeel of the beverage product under normal conditions are straightforward, and the attributes can be expressed with shear viscosity alone.

Semi-solid foods like yogurt, pudding, whipped cream, gels, curd and the like, which are eaten with a spoon, have more complex rheological properties. The rheological properties of these products are mostly non-ideal, due to the breakdown of quasi or non-permanent structure, and are dependent on shear rate and shearing time. Flow characteristics of fluid and semi-solid foods are summarized in Table 1 (Rha, 1978).

Yogurt, pudding, whipped cream and similar products theoretically can be considered to have a flow regime consisting of yield stress, a series of Newtonian, shear thinning, shear thickening regions representing specific structure formation or breakdown (Rha, 1978) interdispersed similar to the flow model in Figure 1. However, in actuality the number of regions may be greater than can be determined by instrumental measurements or phenomenological observation of structure formation or breakdown. On the other hand, some of these flow regions exist within only a very small range of shear rate and may not occur in practice or may not be recognized especially during the mastication and swallowing.

The single rheological behavior which best represents the general characteristics of these types of colloidal dispersions and many emulsions is

TABLE 1. Flow characteristics of fluid and semi-solid foods

Flow characteristics of fluids	Typical fluids having these flow characteristice	Consistency Index b	Flow behavior index s	Yield stress, C	Examples of food products
Newtonian	True solutions, dilute macromolecular solutions, emulsions, colloidal dispersions	Viscosity $b > 0$	$s = 1$	$c = 0$	Clarified juices, clear soup, oils, confectionary syrup, milk
Shear-thinning (Pseudoplastic)	Polymer solutions, pastes, emulsions, suspensions	Apparent viscosity $b > 0$	$0 < s < 1$	$c = 0$	Concentrated fruit or vegetable juice, purees, and paste, applesauce, starch and protein paste
Bingham plastic	Suspensions, colloids	Plasticity constant $b > 0$	$s = 1$	$c > 0$	Salad dressing such as French dressing, tomato catsup, fudge sauce
Mixed-type	Suspended particles of irregular shape in thick medium	Consistency index $b > 0$	$0 < s < 1$	$c > 0$	Sandwich spread, jelly, marmalade
Shear-thickening	Nearly saturated or concentrated suspensions, emulsions	Consistency index $b > 0$	$1 < s < \infty$	$c = 0$	Sausage slurry, homogenized peanut butter

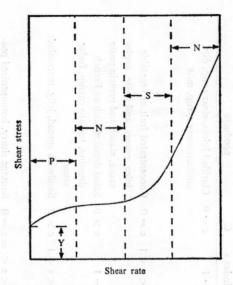

FIG. 1. General relationship between shear stress and shear rate. Y = yield stress, p = pseudoplastic region, N = Newtonian region, and S = shear-thickening region

shear thinning (pseudoplastic) properties. The shear thinning nature is often continuous and typical of the result of the structural nature of micro-suspensions, pastes and some emulsions. In contrast to this, gel and curd type products have a flow behavior of discontinuous nature with a distinct and prominent yield stress which is more likely non-linear visco-elastic in nature.

1.1.4 TEMPERATURE ATTRIBUTES TO THE MOUTHFEEL

Beverages are the product in which temperature attribute is the most critical. Cold or warm sensations generated in the mouth from direct contact with beverages is most likely responsible for the great demand enjoyed by the product. Most beverages and liquids are taken at extreme temperatures. The temperature of a hot drink, such as coffee, at the instant of drinking can be as high as 85° C and the temperature of a cold beverage for instance, a soft drink, ice tea or beer can only be a few degrees above the freezing point.

A beverage flows easily, is taken in large amounts, wets the surface of the oral cavity and soft tissue, does not form a thick boundary layer, and also gets mixed easily. Therefore, maximum contact occurs between the beverage and the inner surface of the mouth. Thus the beverage can accomplish the cooling or warming effect even with residence time in the mouth of one or less than one second. The maximum surface contact of the beverage in the oral cavity also allows maximum heat transfer. However, because of the short contact time, it is difficult to accurately estimate the heat transfer which takes place. In addition to the short contact time, because of the relatively low thermal conductivity and high heat capacity of the beverage, the amount of heat transferred is not likely to be significant.

The amount of heat transferred in the case of semi-solids would be even less. Although semi-solid foods tend to have longer resident time, up to a fraction of a minute in the oral cavity, more dependency on the conduction mode of heat transfer, and decreased contact area reduce the amount of heat transfer. Generally, the temperature attribute to the mouthfeel is not as significant in semi-solids or in solids as in liquids. Exceptions are when phase change occurs as in ice cream melting in the mouth.

The wide temperature range at which different beverages are consumed and effective contact between the beverage and the oral cavity accentuate the variation in viscosity in the wide temperature range. The variation in the viscosity of water, sucrose, alcohol solution, and honey at two extreme drinking temperatures 5°C and 85°C is given in Table 2. When the constituents and the arrangement in the fluid or semi-solid are relatively more complex, the changes in viscosity with temperature can be even more pronounced and it would be more difficult to make an accurate estimate as in the case of honey (Table 2).

TABLE 2.   The viscosity at cold and hot drink temperatures.

Temperature	Water	20% Sucrose Solution	Buckwheat Honey	20% Alcohol
Cold, 5°C	1.52	3.17	62,000	4.06
Hot, 85°C	0.34	0.55	1,500	1.55
			viscosity in cps	

1.1.5 RATE OF SHEAR RELATING TO MOUTHFEEL

Shama and Sherman (1973a) showed that the rate of shear applied to fluid foods in the mouth ranged from 10 to 1000 sec^{-1}. The tongue was considered primarily responsible for developing this shear. They estimated the physical stimulus in the sensory perception of viscosity in a low viscosity product at an approximately constant stress of 100 dynes/cm^2 or for the high viscosity product at an approximately constant shear rate of 10 sec^{-1}. Their subsequent work (1973b) indicated that the change in the oral stimulus from the shear rate to the shear stress occurred at a viscosity of about 70 cps.

Beverages exhibit viscosity lower than 70 cps. Therefore, it is reasonable as Szczesniak (1978) also stated that the rate of flow under a given force is the sensory measure of "viscosity" and is an outstanding and most clearly recognizable mouthfeel parameter of beverages. The rates of flow of the beverage into the mouth when sipped, while being mixed in the mouth and out into the throat when swallowed, under the given forces applied in these activities, are experienced as mouthfeel.

Assuming a Newtonian flow at the transition point, a beverage having 70 cps viscosity at constant stress of 100 dynes/cm^2 would experience a shear rate of approximately .14 sec^{-1}. This rate of shear is indeed a couple of orders of magnitude lower than the controlling shear rate of 10 sec^{-1} estimated for the evaluation of high viscosity products and indicates the limiting range of shear stress controlling mechanism.

The shear rate dependency of mouthfeel becomes more important, of course, with the material having a highly shear thinning nature. Hydrocolloids with apparent viscosity of a few hundred centipoise at a shear rate of sec^{-1} or in which shear stress developed was 100 dynes/cm^2 at 20 sec^{-1} was reported not to impart slimy mouthfeel but those with apparent viscosity about 400 cps at 10^{-1} or developed shear stress of 100 dynes/cm^2 at 50 sec^{-1} were considered slightly slimy (Szczesniak and Farkas, 1962).

Fig. 2 shows the general relationship between log apparent viscosity to shear rate of complex fluid. The numbers may represent concentration factors or any other factors which affect the apparent viscosity such as shape, factor, degree of aggregation, hydrodynamic volume, interparticle interaction, etc. The suspension of fruit cell wall material exhibits a more

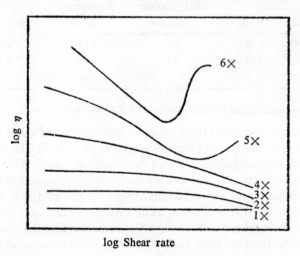

FIG. 2. Effect of shear rate on viscosity of a complex fluid; numbers represent concentration factors.

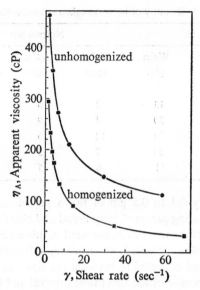

FIG. 3. Destruction of pocket-like structure decreases the apparent viscosity of a suspension of cranberry cell wall material (Holmes and Rha, 1978); the yield stress was 11.6 dynes/cm² for the unhomogenized suspension and 6.0 dynes/cm² for the homogenized suspension.

simple but sensitive nature and the decrease in apparent viscosity strongly depends on the rate of shear (Holmes and Rha, 1978). The apparent viscosity of more than four hundred centipoise at the shear rate near a few reciprocal seconds is high enough to be at the level where shear rate is controlling the apparent viscosity decrease rapidly to nearly 100 cps, which is nearly low enough to be shear stress controlling in at a shear rate of 60 sec^{-1}, as shown in Fig. 3. In the shear rate sensitive material like this and in material which encompass the transition region within very narrow shear rates, the physical stimulus in the sensory perception may shift from shear rate to shear stress controlling in practice.

1.1.6 OTHER CONSIDERATIONS

An individual produces one and one half liters of saliva in a day with the volume of secretion increasing when the strength of stimulus increases (Fenton, 1961). Ingested food is mixed with the saliva and food particles are reduced to a size convenient for swallowing. The secretion of saliva moistens food for bolus formation and lubricates bolus in preparation for deglutition.

The effect of mixing with saliva on the sensory perception has often been a concern of some workers. Pangborn and Lundgren (1977) determined

TABLE 3. Quantity of beverage taken in swallowing (gms)

Subject	Thirsty Drink	Normal Sip				
	Water (cold)	Water (26)	Water (hot)	Coffee (hot)	Coke (8–10°C)	Hot (choco-late)
A	27	13	2	6	16	9
B	69	30	4	9	16	18
C	76	29	12	16	30	37
D	47	19	7	5	20	
E	32	11	6	5	8	

that approximately 0.3 to 0.5 gm of saliva per minute was secreted in response to masticating pieces of crisp bread and also found the indication that salivary secretion increases as the need of lubricating food sufficiently to swallow the bolus increased. In drinking a beverage the amount of saliva generated and collected in between the sips can be estimated to be only several mg because of the short time interval and lack of need for lubrication. Table 3 shows the quantity of beverages taken in a preliminary study with five individuals. In a normal sip the quantity of beverage taken ranged from 2 gm for hot water to 37 gms for hot chocolate. Therefore, even at a low level of intake, dilution effect is not likely to be significant. However, more interesting effects of saliva would be the surface concentrating and surface active functions of mucous proteins rather than straight mixing and proportional changes in the colligative properties. Surface active properties of liquid and semi-solid food and those combined with saliva contribute to the spreading, adhesion, and diffusion thus partially to watery, juicy, sticky and creamy characteristics.

A sip is followed usually by a single swallowing. On the other hand, a drink may be completed with more than one subsequent swallowing. Semi-solids such as yogurt or pudding are directly, without chewing, swallowed resulting in a flow, similar to a plug flow aided by lubrication provided by saliva. Yogurt, although has flow behavior similar to water under the stress of 100 dynes/cm^2, mixing with saliva is minimum due to the short residence time. The consistency of custard is high enough that increased action of the tongue or the initiation of masticating action starts to take place. Curd and gel type foods with definite structure integrity and a significant yield value require, in most cases, mastication before swallowing. Gel which is more viscoelastic is subjected to slow rates but a higher number of mastications than curd which is harder but fractures without undergoing much elastic deformation. Curd and gel are masticated into small pieces, less than a fraction of an inch, before swallowing.

TABLE 4. Swallowing pressure†

	Swallowing pressure
Sipping water	74,000 dynes/cm²
Swallowing saliva	97,000 dynes/cm²
Drinking water	53,000 dynes/cm²
Spontaneous swallowing	41,000 dynes/cm²

†Adopted from Kydd and Toda (1962).

Extremely high pressure accompanies swallowing. The pressures exerted in swallowing exercise are given in Table 4 (Howell and Manly, 1948). The pressure applied in swallowing is higher than 400 times the stress at which sensory perception takes place in the oral evaluation. The swallowing is also high enough to overcome known yield stress of any semi-solid food. Further in the line of swallowing, esophagus pressure reaches approximately 125 dynes/cm² and the pressure increase to this point occurs within one second (Howell and Manly, 1948).

There are many physical parameters attributing to the mouthfeel. Individual preference or eating habits are also important parameters in the sensory attribute of mouthfeel. The deviation between individuals varies widely. For instance, the maximum temperature one can tolerate in sipping beverage can differ as much as 30°C between individuals. Possible deviation of these types should be evaluated and taken into consideration when the effect of temperature, rate of shear, applied motion and shear rates are studied in connection with the physical parameters attributing to the mouthfeel.

ACKNOWLEDGMENT: The author thanks Dr. Alina S. Szczesniak, General Foods Corporation, for providing information and cooperation in writing this artice.

REFERENCES

Fenton, P. F., The mouth and esphagus, Medical Physiology and Biophysics, Chapter 43, T. C. Ruth and J. F. Fulton, ed., 18th Edition, W. B. Saunders Co., Phil.

Glicksman, M., Gum Technology in the Food Industry, p. 59, Academic Press, New York and London, (1969).

Holmes, A. B. and Rha, Heat stability and contribution of polysaccharide constitutents to suspension properties of parenchyma cell suspensions, Paper

109 presented at 38th Ann. Meet., Inst. of Food Technologists, Dallas, June 4–7, (1978).

Howell, A. H. and Manly, R. S., *J. Dent. Res.*, **27**: 705–712 (1948).

Kydd, W. L. and Toda, J. M., Tongue pressures exerted on the hard palate during swallowing, *Am. Dent. Assoc.*, **40**, 319–330 (1962).

Pangborn, R. M. and Lundgren, B., Research note: salivary secretion in response to mastication of crisp bread, *J. of Texture Studies*, **8**: 4, 463–472.

Szczesniak, A. S. and Farkas, E. H., Objective characterization of the mouthfeel of gum solutions, *J. Food Sci.*, **27**, 381–385 (1962).

Szczesniak, A. S., Classification of mouthfeel characteristics of beverage, Food Texture and Rheology, (P. Sherman, ed.), Academic Press, N. Y. (1978).

Shama, F. and Sherman, P., Identification of stimuli controlling the sensory evaluation of viscosity, II. Oral methods, *J. Texture Studies*, **4**, 111–118 (1973a).

Shama, F. and Sherman, P., Variation in stimuli associated with oral evaluation of the viscosities of glucose solutions, *J. Texture Studies*, **4**, 254–262 (1973b).

1.2 Physics in Textural Properties of Foods

Philip Sherman*

1.2.1 INTRODUCTION

The so-called imitative and fundamental instrumental methods (Scott Blair, 1958) which are generally used to evaluate the textural properties of food do not accurately reflect the mechanical conditions operating during consumer evaluation of these properties by non-oral methods or by mastication. This presentation reviews possible mechanisms associated with sensory and instrumental evaluations of three textural properties, viscosity firmness and stickiness, as derived from information available on the behaviour of non-food materials under similar conditions. Viscosity and firmness are evaluated orally during the "first-bite phase of mastication," whereas stickiness takes a longer time (Brandt, *et al.*, 1963).

1.2.2 EVALUATION OF TEXTURAL PROPERTIES

A. Viscosity of fluid foods

The surface of the tongue and the roof of the mouth can be regarded as two flat parallel plates which are separated by only a small distance and which constitute a narrow gap through which the fluid food flows (Wood, 1968; Sharma and Sherman, 1973; Kokini *et al.*, 1978). When sensory panel ratings of the oral viscosities of a wide range of fluid foods are correlated with their viscometric flow data an approximately curvilinear relationship is obtained between the shear stresses and shear rates associated with oral viscosity evaluation (Shama and Sherman, 1975) with a rather flat region extending over shear rates in excess of about 100 sec^{-1}. These latter shear rates operate during the oral viscosity evaluation of very fluid foods which exhibit only slight, if any, non-Newtonian flow character. Many fluids exhibit turbulent flow at these shear rates, for example dilute glucose solution, and this results in an apparent increase in viscosity with increasing shear rate.

Viscosity is evaluated sensorily soon after a fluid food is introduced into

*Queen Elizabeth College (University of London), Campden Hill Road, London, W8 7AH, England

315

the mouth, so that its flow behaviour will not be modified to any degree, at this time, by secretion of saliva. Long chain polymer molecules reduce or inhibit turbulence during fluid flow (Gadd, 1965, 1966) so it is possible that the polymers present in saliva, including mucin, serum albumin and globulin, act in a similar way if there is any mixing of saliva with the fluid food.

Low shear rates are associated with the oral evaluation of more viscous fluid foods (Shama and Sherman, 1973a) which generally exhibit non-Newtonian flow. It has been suggested (Kokini et al. 1978) that when the non-Newtonian flow conforms to an Ostwald-de Waele type power law the viscous force on the tongue depends on the initial thickness (h) in the mouth of the food sample, the load or normal force (w) exerted by the tongue, the tongue's effective radius (R), the time (t) required for the evaluation and the power law constants (m and n) in accordance with the relationship viscous force on tongue $\propto$

$$mV^n\left[\frac{1}{h^{(n+1)/n}} + \left(\frac{w}{R^{n+3}} \cdot \frac{n+3}{2\pi m}\right)^{1/n} \left(\frac{n+1}{2n+1} \cdot t\right)\right]^{n2/n+1} \tag{1}$$

and

$$\tau = m\,(\dot{\gamma})^n \tag{2}$$

where $\dot{\gamma}$ is the operative shear rate.

Many viscous foods have an oil continuous phase, for example chocolate spread and peanut butter, while fluid foods such as milk and sugar solutions have an aqueous continuous phase. Under steady state spreading conditions flow velocity and spreadability are related by the relationship

$$\frac{dv}{dh} = -\frac{2S_c}{r\eta} \tag{3}$$

where dv/dh is the flow velocity gradient with respect to the h direction, S_c is the instantaneous spreading coefficient, η is the viscosity exhibited under the operative conditions and r is the direction in which the spreading force manifests itself (Yin, 1969). In addition,

$$S_c = \gamma_{s/a} - \gamma_{s/l} + \gamma_{l/a} \cos\theta \tag{4}$$

where $\gamma_{s/a}$, $\gamma_{s/l}$ and $\gamma_{l/a}$ are the surface tensions between the two oral surfaces (tongue and roof of mouth) and air, the oral surfaces and the food sample, and the food sample and air respectively and θ is the contact angle established by the food sample on the oral surfaces. The values of the parameters $\gamma_{s/l}$, $\gamma_{l/a}$ and θ will depend on the nature of the food and any possible influence exerted by saliva.

The shear stress-shear rate bounds associated with the sensory evaluation of viscosity by two non-oral methods, evaluation of the force required to stir the food in a glass beaker with a glass rod and of the rate at which the food flowed down the side of the beaker when it was tilted, do not exceed about 100 sec^{-1} (Parkinson, *et al.*, 1973). Neither evaluation procedure is likely, therefore, to involve turbulent flow. Viscosity evaluation by tilting the container may well involve the parameters listed in Equations (3) and (4).

B. Firmness of solid foods

Firmness is evaluated as the force required to compress a food sample to a given deformation (Szczesniak, 1963; Abbott, 1973).

Sensory evaluation of firmness, either in the mouth or by squeezing with the fingers, generally involves the application of a force which exceeds the yield stress of the food so that it exhibits a viscoelastic response. Furthermore, the viscoelastic response is non-linear with the compression increasing more than linearly as the applied force increases. The rate of compression also influences the force-compression behaviour (Shama and Sherman, 1973b, c).

When a cylinder shaped food sample is compressed during sensory or instrumental evaluation of firmness it assumes a barrel shape. Gouda cheese, for example, shows this behaviour in an Instron machine with the crosshead operating at 50 cm min^{-1} when the compression exceeds about 20%. Similar deformation behaviour occurs during sensory evaluation of firmness. At very high compression cracks appear in the samples.

Analysis of cine-film records of the Instron deformation of Gouda (Culioli and Sherman, 1976) and Leicester (Vernon Carter and Sherman, 1978) cheese samples indicate that the samples' upper and lower surfaces slowly increase in diameter during compression tests. The barrel deformation behaviour can be exaggerated by inserting sheets of emery paper between the samples' surfaces and the Instron plates before compression. However, if a thin film of lubricating mineral oil is spread over the upper and lower ends of the samples a different shape is assumed during compression. The sides of the samples now become concave and an hour-glass shape develops because the samples' surfaces now increase in diameter faster than the samples' central regions.

These observations suggest that surface friction influences lateral movement of the samples' surfaces during sensory and instrumental evaluation of firmness. The friction force is the product of the real area of contact (A) between the food's surfaces and the Instron plates and the shear strength of the junctions established between them and A is the ratio of w to the yield pressure of the food (Bowden and Tabor, 1958).

Photoelastic analysis of cylindrical samples undergoing uniaxial compression indicates a concentration of stress on the samples' surfaces (Hammerle and McClure, 1971). The restriction on surface expansion due to friction produces a transverse compressive stress which decreases with the distance inwards from the samples' two ends. This observation helps to explain the influence of sample height on the instrumental force-compression behaviour.

When allowance is made for the increase in surface area of samples during instrumental compression tests, and the data are plotted as true surface stress (ordinate) v. compression (abscissa) the resulting curve is much flatter than when the surface stress is calculated on the basis of the initial surface area of each sample. This means that lower surface stresses are developed than would be suggested by the usual method for calculating surface stress. With Gouda cheese a hump develops at about 50% compression (Culioli and Sherman, 1976), and this denotes the first appearance of microscopic size cracks. This level of compression is associated with firmness evaluation by squeezing the samples between the fingers whereas compression levels of 70% or more can be associated with the oral evaluation (Boyd and Sherman, 1975a). We may deduce, therefore, that firmness evaluation by squeezing samples between the fingers is mainly associated with sample compression, whereas oral evaluation is associated with compression and crack initiation and propagation.

It is apparent that this force on which sensory evaluation is based is the sum of the force required to overcome surface friction and the force required to compress the sample. Therefore, not all of the force identified is used to compress the sample. Unfortunately, it is not possible for the human senses to differentiate between these two force components, so that if a substantial part of the total force was required to overcome frictional effects then the reliability of sensory methods of firmness evaluation would be suspect. Similarly, the graphical representation of instrumental surface stress-compression behaviour should allow for surface friction effects when calculating the true surface stress.

C. Stickiness of Foods

Stickiness is usually evaluated instrumentally as the maximum force developed during adhesive or cohesive rupture between a flat circular metal plate and the food sample's surface. The maximum force developed prior to rupture depends on the instrumental test conditions employed (Jansen, 1961; Fukushima and Sone, 1968; Henry and Katz, 1969; Boyd, et al., 1974; Boyd and Sherman, 1975b).

The sensory evaluation of stickiness is based on the work which has to be done to overcome the attractive forces between the surface of the food and the surface of the tongue, teeth, palate, etc. (Szczesniak, 1963; Abbott, 1973). A similar definition could, of course, be applied to stickiness evaluated by withdrawing a finger from within the sample.

Most sticky foods exhibit cohesive rupture so that the surface of the food is very rapidly extended into filaments prior to rupture. At the high extension rates (U) involved cavitation may occur due to a reduced or even negative hydrostatic pressure in the sample.

In the mouth stickiness is not evaluated instantaneously so that one has to consider the influence that saliva may exert on the cavitation developed during sample extension. Polymers which reduce turbulence during the flow of liquids through pipes also reduce cavitation effects so saliva may reduce the cavitation effects associated with stickiness evaluation. Nevertheless, cavitation will not be completely eliminated so the evaluation of food stickiness in the mouth is not associated with the true maximum force developed during cohesive rupture, but rather with this force as modified by superimposed cavitation effects.

Cohesive rupture occurs when the magnitude of the cohesive forces within the food's microstructure is smaller than the adhesion forces between the food and the oral, non-oral or instrumental surface with which it is in contact. When the cohesive forces are greater adhesive rupture occurs. Therefore, several surface tension parameters are involved, as they are for both viscosity and firmness evaluations. The work of adhesion (W_A) between the sample and the surface with which it makes contact is given by

$$W_A = \gamma_s + \gamma_{LV} - \gamma_{SL} \tag{5}$$

where γ_s, γ_{LV} and γ_{SL} are respectively the surface tensions of the surface, the sample in equilibrium with its vapour and the interfacial tension between the surface and the sample (Salomon, 1965). For liquids this can be rewritten as

$$W_A = \gamma_{LV}(1 + \cos \theta) \tag{6}$$

where θ is the contact angle between the sample and surface.

In cohesive rupture two new surfaces are created, and the work of cohesion (W_C) is defined by

$$W_C = 2\gamma_{LV} \tag{7}$$

When $W_A > W_C$, cohesive rupture occurs, and when $W_C > W_A$ adhesive rupture occurs.

1.2.3 CONCLUSIONS

Hitherto it has been assumed that only one type of force is associated with the sensory or instrumental evaluation of each of the three textural parameters viscosity, firmness and stickiness. It now appears possible that the force identified in each case is not a unique force but rather the *net* force resulting from the simultaneous operation of two or more effects. When formulating instrumental test conditions it is essential that they simulate as closely as possible the comparable sensory evaluation situations so that these effects develop to the same degree in the former as in the latter situations.

REFERENCES

Abbott, J. A., in "Texture Measurements of Foods", A. Kramer and A. S. Szczesniak eds. (Reidels, Dordrecht, Holland), (1973).

Bowden, F. P. and Tabor, D., "The Friction and Lubrication of Solids" (Clarendon Press, Oxford, England), (1958).

Boyd, J. V., Parkinson, C. J. and Sherman, P., *Proc. IVth Int. Congr. Food Sci. Technol. Vol. II*, 121, (1974).

Boyd, J. V. and Sherman, P., *J. Texture Studies*, **6**, 507 (1975a).

Boyd, J. V. and Sherman, P., *Biorheology*, **12**, 317 (1975b).

Brandt, M. A., Skinner, E. Z. and Coleman, J. A., *J. Food Sci.*, **28**, 404 (1963).

Culioli, J. and Sherman, P., *J. Texture Studies*, **7**, 353 (1976).

Fukushima, M. and Sone, T., *J. Soc. Materials Sci. Japan*, **17**, 288 (1968).

Gadd, G. E., *Nature*, **206**, 463 (1965).

Gadd, G. E., *Nature*, **212**, 874 (1966).

Hammerle, J. R. and McClure, W. F., *J. Texture Studies*, **2**, 31 (1971).

Henry, W. F. and Katz, M. H., *Food Technol.*, **23**, 114 (1969).

Jansen, K., *J. Dairy Res.*, **28**, 15 (1961).

Kokini, J. L., Kadane, J. B. and Cussler, E. L., *J. Texture Studies*, **8**, 195 (1978).

Salomon, C., in "Adhesion and Adhesives" Vol. 1., R. Houwink end G. Salomon eds. (Elsevier, Amsterdam, Holland) (1965).

Scott Blair, G. W., *Adv. Food Research*, **8**, 1 (1958).

Shama, F., Parkinson, C. and Sherman, P., *J. Texture Studies*, **4**, 102 (1973).

Shama, F. and Sherman, P., *J. Texture Studies*, **4**, 111 (1973a).

Shama, F. and Sherman, P., *J. Texture Studies*, **4**, 344 (1973b).

Shama, F. and Sherman, P., *J. Texture Studies*, **4**, 353 (1973c).

Szczesniak, A. S., *J. Food Sci.*, **28**, 385 (1963).

Vernon-Carter, J. R. and Sherman, P., *J. Texture Studies*, **9**, 311 (1978).

Wood, F. W. in "Rheology and Texture of Foodstuffs" SCI Monograph No. 27, 40 (1968).

Yin, T. P., *J. Phys. Chem.* **73**, 2413 (1969).

1.3   Instrumental Methods of Food Texture Measurement

John M. deMan*

During the past few decades advances in texture test instrumentation have taken place in three main areas: mechanical, electronics, and test cells.

The mechanical requirements of a texture measuring system may be related to four basic test situations:

A. Stress as a function of strain

Stress can be measured by a variety of devices, such as simple springs or balances. Increasingly, with the more elaborate instruments, load cells or other force transducers with electronic amplification and measurement are used. The advantages include precision, wide range of force values, and possibility of recording of the results. Strain or deformation can be produced in the simplest case by hand operation, but more commonly by mechanical means. Basically two types of drive mechanisms have been used, hydraulic or mechanical. Examples of hydraulically operated instruments are the Kramer Shear Press (KS) and the testing machine developed by Mohsenin (1963). The KS was developed in an attempt to upgrade the pea tenderometer and make it into a more generally useful instrument. Some of the important improvements incorporated into the KS were the linear movement and the design and exchangeability of the test cell. The electronics of the KS are now obsolete although the general principle of the KS remains useful. Extensive work on modernization of the KS has been done by Voisey (1971). The use of hydraulically operated test instruments is declining in favor of mechanical systems.

The MIT Denture Tenderometer was the basis for the development of the texture profile. The G.F. Texturometer did not become very popular because it was found that similar results could be obtained by using a universal testing machine (UTM). The UTM combines the advantages of precision control of strain with precise measurement of stress. UTM's are now being used extensively in food texture studies. Through all of these developments it became clear that the best all-round texture test system should have a rugged and precise motor driven linear deformation mechanism,

*Department of Food Science, University of Guelph, Guelph, Ontario N1G 2W1,Canada

321

a modern force sensing system with troublefree electronics, and a versatile range of test cells. The Ottawa Texture Measuring System (OTMS) was developed by Voisey to satisfy these requirements. The universal test cell of the KS has several advantages but is extremely expensive. Voisey has developed a wide range of simple and cheap test cells for the OTMS which provide almost limitless opportunities for testing different types of foods.

B. Stress decay at constant strain

The measurement of time dependent properties of viscoelastic materials often involves measurement of relaxation. This can easily be done with some of the above-mentioned instruments by simply stopping the drive mechanism at a certain value of total deformation and continuing the recording of stress in the sample. UTM's are especially suitable for this purpose.

C. Strain change with time at constant stress

The measurement of creep, although very important in rheological studies has not been widely used in texture studies. An example of the use of this technique is the measurement of firmness of bread by gaseous compression (Willhoft, 1971). Commercially available equipment for creep testing is not as readily available as that for relaxation tests. The availability of reliable displacement transducers (LVDT) and suitable electronics has made the construction of this type of instrument much easier. The principle of construction of a creep testing apparatus for gels has been recently demonstrated by Rao *et al.* (1978). A creep testing apparatus used in our laboratory uses an LVDT and commonly utilized amplification and recording system.

D. Strain as a function of stress

This type of measurement is not commonly used in food texture studies. The equipment described under (C) could be used for this purpose. Some of the simpler traditional instruments would fall in this category, e.g. the cone penetrometer used for determining fat consistency.

Many of the test situations described in the above 4 categories require the preparation of a test sample of precisely known dimensions. This apparently simple technical problem constitutes one of the major difficulties in applying rheological analysis to data obtained by various instruments. Unfortunately, little emphasis has been placed in the past on this kind of auxiliary equipment. One of the tools used in our laboratories to prepare samples of well defined dimensions utilizes stretched steel wires to cut samples of different sizes.

It appears that much progress has been made in recent years in the development of texture measurement equipment. A major drawback of many instruments is the high cost. The use of interchangeable electronics would greatly reduce this problem. With the great improvements that have taken place in mass-produced electronic systems it is to be hoped that texture test systems will benefit from it. Not everybody needs or can afford a UTM, and simpler and cheaper alternatives should be available.

INTERPRETATION

Food texture studies have long suffered from the problem of uncritical use of numerical values obtained with various instruments. In recent years several authors have concerned themselves with this problem. The use of rotational viscometers to determine the "viscosity" of non-Newtonian liquids at one rate of shear is an example. Many researchers used the KS by placing a certain amount of sample in the universal test cell, and divided the sample weight by the maximum force or peak area. The assumption of a straight-line relationship was proved by Szczesniak *et al.* (1970) and others to be false in certain cases. The lack of a linear relationship between force and punch area in penetration tests has for many years remained a mystery. The pioneering work of Bourne (1966) established that the penetration force involves both compression and shear and the penetration force can be represented by the equation:

$$F = K_c A + K_s P + C$$

It was found by deMan (1969) that for certain foods there is a linear relationship between force and punch areas. Subsequent work by others has extended our knowledge on penetration forces to include different sizes and shapes of punches. For round punches the penetration force can be expressed (Kamel and deMan, 1975) by the equations:

$$F/A = K_c + 4K_s\, I/D + C/A \text{ and}$$
$$F/P = K_c\, D/4 + K_s + C/P$$

A recent study by Calzada and Peleg (1978) dealt with the mechanical interpretation of compressive stress-strain relationships of solid foods. It was found that the shape of the stress-strain curves and relaxation and compressibility data indicate the existence of two antagonistic mechanisms which regulate stress levels. Internal fractures decrease the mechanical strength and structural compaction increases it.

Often it is extremely informative to observe what happens to a sample during the deformation process. In many instruments the sample is not visible during the test. Much can be learned by observation in a specially constructed test cell. Voisey and Kloek (1978) studied the action taking place in a pea tenderometer by replacing the outside covers with transparent plastic.

A similar apparoach was used by Voisey (1977) in a study of interpretation of force-deformation curves obtained with different foods in the Kramer shear-compression cell. The cell was modified by replacing the front metal plate with one manufactured of clear acrylic plastic. This work demonstrated that the shear behaviour associated with the Kramer cell only occurs with certain products and at specific points in the deformation which do not necessarily coincide with the maximum force.

SYSTEMATIC INFORMATION

As our instruments improve and we have a better understanding of what the results mean, the accumulated knowledge will become more useful. Similarities or the lack of them between different foods will be noted and suggestions will be forthcoming for the use of the most appropriate methods. When the rheological properties of various types of foods have been systematically examined in basic studies, it will then be possible to select one or more parameters to be measured in routine test applications for quality control.

One of the best examples of systematic development of knowledge is the area of dough rheology. The availability of sophisticated test instruments (Brabender Farinograph, Extensigraph and Viscoamylograph) and their almost universal adoption by researchers have resulted in a very extensive body of information. This information is useful to all researchers using this equipment.

Another example is the extensive work done by Voisey and coworkers on pea tenderness. This work has involved careful and critical evaluation of the use of different instruments for measuring pea tenderness, evaluation of various factors affecting precision and repeatability of the tests and has led to important recommendations for improvement of pea tenderness evaluation as a quality control test in the vegetable processing industry.

STRUCTURE AND TEXTURE

Micro- and macrostructure are directly responsible for many of the textural attributes of foods. It is no wonder then that researchers have attempted to relate particular aspects of texture to the fine structure of foods. Methods of structure evaluation can be both physical and chemical. Physical evaluation of structure utilizes various kinds of microscopy, including light, transmitted electron microscopy and scanning electron microscopy (Stanley and Tung, 1976). Such methods used in conjunction with instrumental evaluation of texture assist in explaining the particular properties of many types of foods.

An example of this kind of study is given in a review of the texture of potatoes as related to pectin and starch (Reeve, 1977). The starch and pectin constituents of potatoes are determining factors in the textural quality of potatoes and structural changes involved in the cellular network can be followed by microscopy.

Such investigations are important for products with naturally occurring structure such as fruits and vegetables (cellular) and meats (fibrous). They are equally important for manufactured foods such as cheese, dough and bread, margarine and butter and many others.

INSTRUMENTAL AND SENSORY TESTS

The major objective of instrumental food texture analysis is to provide simple and rapid methods to supply data on the physical properties which can be related to sensory quality, as well as processing methods. This is now well recognized and of special value for this approach has been the development of the texture profile method (TMP) by a group of scientists at the General Foods Research Center in 1963. One of the originators of the TPM has reviewed the development of this technique during the 10 years following its first publication (Szczesniak, 1975). There is no doubt that the TPM has contributed greatly to the development of instrumental texture evaluation. The use of TPM has assisted in the interpretation of stress-strain curves obtained with various instruments and has provided a uniform basis for correlating instrumental and sensory evaluations.

An example of the usefulness of this approach is the study of Jeon and associates (1975) in evaluating the texture of cucumber pickles. In this work correlations were determined between TPM parameters of brittleness, hardness, total work of compression obtained instrumentally and sensory responses of firmness and crispness.

REFERENCES

Calzada, J. P. and Peleg, M., *J. Food Sci.*, **43**, 1087 (1978).
Jeon, I. J., Breene, W. M. and Munson, S. T., *J. Texture Studies*, **5**, 399 (1975).
Kamel, B. S. and deMan, J. M., *Lebensm. Wiss. Technol.*, **8**, 123 (1975).
Mohsenin, N., Penna. Agr. Expt. Sta. Bull. 701 (1963).
Reeve, R. M., *J. Texture Studies*, **8**, 1 (1977).
Stanley, D. W. and Tung, M. A., In: Rheology and Texture in Food Quality. AVI Publ. Comp. Inc., (1976).
Szczesniak, A. S., *J. Texture Studies*, **6**, 5 (1975).
Szczesniak, A. S., Humbaugh, P. R. and Block, H. W., *J. Texture Studies*, **1**, 356 (1970).

Voisey, P. W., *J. Texture Studies*, **2**, 129 (1971).
Voisey, P. W., *J. Texture Studies*, **8**, 19 (1977).
Voisey, P. W. and Kloek, M., *Can Inst. Food Sci. Technol. J.*, **11**, 87 (1978).

1.4 Interrelationship between Instrumental Methods and Sensory Assessment for Food Texture

John G. Kapsalis* and Howard R. Moskowitz**

1.4.1 INSTRUMENTAL MEASURES AND CORRELATIONS WITH SENSORY DATA

Well-defined measurements of the mechanical properties of food and the reduction of sensory attributes into fundamental primary entities, together with the functions which interrelate them, provide the basis for the eventual development of instruments calibrated in terms of human sensory response with high probability of prediction of the consumer reaction (Kapsalis and Moskowitz, 1977). Since mechanical measurements of most foods are time-dependent, the understanding of conditions prevailing during sensory testing (rate of shear, etc.) will aid in selecting the optimum conditions for instrumental testing (Sherman, 1975; Wood, 1968).

The development of a basic lexicon or irreducible language of sensory evaluation of food texture is a prerequisite for any successful method of profiling, of scaling and quantifying, and of correlating with rheological data (Szczesniak, 1977). Of particular benefit is the combined study of texture vocabulary with psychophysical measurements analyzed by simulation of mechanical processes involved in sensory testing (Cussler, Zlotnick and Shaw, 1977).

1.4.2 PSYCHOPHYSICS OF TEXTURE AND PRODUCT ENGINEERING

Psychophysicists search for relations between physical variables (e.g. modulus of elasticity), and sensory percepts (hardness, crunchiness, etc.). For many sensory attributes, perceived intensity(S) is a power function of physical intensity (I): $S = KI^n$. The exponent is unique and reproducible for each sensory attribute. Simple power functions no longer describe these experimental data. The researcher must use an *ad hoc* regression model to relate sensory perceptions to a combination of physical variables (Ii). The equation reads:

* *Food Sciences Laboratory, US Army Natick Research & Development Command, Natick, Massachusetts 01760, USA*
** *MPI Sensory Testing, Inc., 770 Lexington Avenue, New York, NY 10021, USA*

TABLE 1. Sequence of steps to optimize a snack product

a. Sensory Profile of Three Snack Food Items

	Physical Level				Magnitude Estimation Rating						
		Hunter				Total Purchase					
L		a	b	Shear	Baking Type	Interest	Softness	White-ness	Fluffi-ness	Firm-ness	Crunchi-ness
73.35		−2.40	12.75	85.80	1.00	58.8	64.6	67.1	71.0	59.2	22.8
71.05		−2.75	16.70	112.20	1.00	54.6	66.2	52.1	66.6	57.5	24.9
71.20		−3.05	17.50	103.40	1.00	69.3	54.6	38.6	54.9	53.2	19.6

b. Regression Equations Relating Sensory and Physical Measures

	Intercept	L	a	b	Shear	Type	Multiple R
Total Purchase							
Interest	−532.81	7.72	4.36	1.58	.31	−14.23	.80
Softness	−318.18	5.14	17.51	1.78	.45	−14.97	.94
Whiteness	−87.41	2.88	10.88	−3.84	.28	−6.20	.94
Fluffiness	−582.49	8.58	19.98	2.66	.59	−17.88	.94
Firmness	−82.68	1.85	−.06	−1.85	.47	−12.86	.95
Crunchiness	148.01	−1.61	−3.19	−2.00	.16	−3.34	.89

c. *Combination of Physical Parameters for Achieving a Pre-specified Sensory Profile*

Physical Variable	Highest Allowed	Lowest Allowed	Optimum Combination
Color Hunter L	74.25	69.90	74.16
a	– 2.3	– 3.45	– 2.3
b	11.4	17.5	11.4
Shear	129.8	85.8	129.4
Baking Type	2	1	1

	Softness	Whiteness	Fluffiness	Firmness	Crunchiness
Competitor's Sensory					
Profile to be Achieved	86.5	92.1	87.4	77.1	30.6
Product Should Generate	86.5	88.1	96.1	82.3	30.6

$$S = K_1I_1 + K_2I_2 \ldots K_nI_n + K_{n+1}$$

for the simplest model. Both the power rule and the linear regression equation *describe* the empirical relation between physical and perceptual variables, but *do not* allow manipulation of physical variables to produce a desired sensory percept except in the simplest cases. Non-linear regression equations model this relation.

Optimization-Profile Copying.   Pragmatic psychophysics provides a method for the product developer to combine ingredients or processes which produce a *desired* sensory profile. The approach can be best understood with a concrete, empirical example. The problem was to develop a potato snack product exhibiting the same sensory characteristics as a currently marketed snack product. The physical variables were color (Hunter L, a, b) and texture (shear press). The procedure follows: (1) Consumer (untrained) panelists profiled their perceptions of 12 systematically varied snack products, using several sensory attributes, and magnitude estimation, scaling (Table 1a). (2) A unique linear regression equation related each sensory attribute to a combination of physical variables (Table 1b). (3) The *target* sensory profile (current product) was specified by consumers, on the same attributes and scales. (4) Multiple objective ("goal") programming selected the physical variables that produced a sensory profile as statistically close as possible to that produced by the currently marketed product with the physical variables remaining within specified technological limits (Table 1c).

The technique coordinates the rheologist, food scientist and product developer so that each individual generates or is given actionable information. *Optimization-Maximization of Product Liking/Disliking.*   An alternative use of psychophysics is to select a combination of physical parameters which produces the most acceptable product. The same consumer and instrumental data were used, based upon the 12 products. The procedure

TABLE 2.   Non-linear model relating consumer's stated purchase interest in the snack product to physical variables

Purchase Interest = 2169 (L) −6.8(a) −1102.6(b) +1.01 (shear)
−15.4 (type of processing) +13.72(L)^2 +1.82(L)(a)
+15.6(L) (b) +84815 [R = 0.97]

Expected Purchase Interest = 100+

	L	a	b	Shear	Type
				Variables	
Upper Limit	74.25	−2.3	17.5	129.8	2
Lower Limit	68.9	−3.45	11.4	85.8	1
Optimal	69.9	−2.3	11.4	129.8	1

was to: (a) develop a non-linear model that relates purchase interest (buying intention) to physical variables; (b) account for the fact that purchase interest is related both to physical measures, and to *interactions* and non-linearities of these measures, and (c) maximize that non-linear equation, within constraints.

Table 2 shows the optimum physical formulation and the expected consumer purchase interest rating that would be given to this formulation. As a consequence, the equation is *actionable* in terms of guiding product developers towards a predesigned profile.

REFERENCES

Cussler, E. L., Zlotnick, S. J. and Shaw, M. C., Texture perceived with the fingers, *Perception & Psychophysics*, **21**, 504 (1977).

Kapsalis, J. G. and Moskowitz, H. R., The psychophysics and physics of food texture, *Food Technol.*, **31**, 91 (1977).

Sherman, P., Factors influencing the instrumental and sensory evaluation of food emulsions. In *Theory, Determination & Control of Physical Properties of Food Materials*, ChoKyun Rha (ed.), D. Reidel Publ. Co., Dordrecht-Holland, p. 251 (1975).

Szczesniak, A. S., Classification of mouthfeel chracteristics of beverages. Pres. IUoFST-sponsored Symp. "Food Texture and Rheology", Queen Elizabeth College, Univ. of London, 19–22 December (1977).

Wood, F. W., Psychophysical studies on the consistencies of liquid foods. In *Rheology and Texture of Foodstuffs*, Soc. Chem. Ind., London, p. 40 (1968).

1.5 Physicochemical Properties of Dairy Products

Toshimaro Sone*

Milk products have been produced mainly from cow's milk by physical, chemical and biochemical treatments such as heat pasteurization, separation of components, stirring or homogenization, addition of chemical detergents and microbiological or enzymatic fermentation. The physicochemical properties of the individual major milk components, such as milk fat, milk protein and sugar, thus contribute to the chracteristic properties of dairy products.

In the last decade, many physicochemical studies on dairy products have been made in an attempt to clarify the interrelationships between the physical structure, mechanical properties and chemical properties of milk protein and fat. The purpose of the present paper is to review certain interesting problems related to a number of dairy products arbitrarily selected from the veiwpoint of their physical structure, mechanical behavior and chemical properties.

1.5.1 MILK AND MILK PROTEIN

The primary product milk presents several basic problems. The casein micelle system which is a major protein in milk, is a hydrophilic colloid stabilized by electrokinetic potential and hydration. The conformation of the casein micelle is therefore drastically affected by variations in thermal conditions, ionic concentration and enzymatic action.

In recent years, detailed investigations on the structure of casein micelles have indicated that the micelle is in general roughly spherical in shape with an average diameter of $\sim$ 120 nm and is composed of spherical subunits of $10 \sim 20$ nm in diameter.[1] In the native micelle, these subunits are probably integrated by calcium caseinate phosphate with possible contributions from hydrogen and hydrophobic bonds. Demineralization of native skim milk by electrodialysis yields information about the conformation of the micelles and the role of Ca^{2+} in the integration of subunits. In the highest demineralized skim milk (Ca content, about 20 mg%), most casein micelles

* Technical Research Institute, Snow Brand Milk Products Co., Ltd., 1-2, Minamidai 1-chome, Kawagoe, Saitama 350, Japan

were found to be disintegrated into subunits, but rapid reformation of large casein micelles occurred on adding only calcium (5mg%)[2].

Milk is almost a Newtonian liquid, although its viscosity varies with temperature and the volume fraction of fat and solids not fat. Equations showing the influence of these factors have been given and confirmed experimentally[3,4].

1.5.2 RHEOLOGICAL BEHAVIOR OF RENNETED MILK

In the early phase of coagulation of renneted milk, two phases can be distinguished. These are a primary stage, which is a viscosity reduction in the renneted casein system according to zero-order kinetics, and a second stage involving first-order kinetics.

After decomposition of the protective colloid κ-casein, the para-casein forms cross-links with calcium ions and gelation of the milk starts. In the early stage of gelation, a few long-chain molecules join together mutually at some point. After this induction period, the process of coagulation begins to accelerate, and it extends towards the end of the process which is completed with the maximum rigidity, G_∞. The gelation curve should thus be sigmoid, so that Eq. (1) applies.[5]

$$\frac{dG}{dt} = G_\infty \ e^{-\tau/t}, \tag{1}$$

Where G is the rigidity modulus, and τ is the time taken by G to reach G_∞/e.

1.5.3 ANOMALOUS FLOW OF CREAM AND ITS WHIPPING PROPERTIES AS AFFECTED BY IONIC STRENGTH

In comparison with milk, cream constitutes a rather thick fat emulsion. It exhibits anomalous behavior, such as pseudoplastic age-thickening, and age-thinning, when the fat content exceeds 50% and especially the fat globule is in a solid state at temperatures below 40°C[6,7].

The milk fat-globule membrane consists of a lipoprotein complex whose thickness is about 4 nm and it plays a role in the stability of cream emulsions. Casein particles which aggregate on this membrane play a role in the flocculation of fat globules in cream due to physical or chemical adhesive forces.

Whipping cream is a highly elastic material. During the whipping of cream, most of the fat globules are arranged on the interfaces of air bubbles in the form of a coherent layer of stabilized whipped cream. Kieseker *et al.*[8] have published two observations regarding the whipping properties of cream: (1) that a decrease in pH or the addition of calcium salts caused clustering of the fat globules and shortened the whipping time, and (2) that the addition of a calcium sequestering agent resulted in fat globule dispersion and decreased the tendency for the cream to whip.

1.5.4 AGE-THICKENING OF CONDENSED MILK

Condensed milk, concentrated milk solid produced by water evaporation and sometimes with added sucrose, essentially consists of a suspension of lactose crystals, fat and colloidal proteins in a saturated solution of lactose or sucrose. Due to adsorption of aggregated casein on to the surface of the milk fat, the initial viscosity becomes very high during storage. This high initial viscosity is easily reduced by stirring and storage subsequent to stirring. Such age-thickening or development of thixotropic properties can be attributed to larger, more asymmetric units which account for the viscosity increase produced by natural or added polyvalent anions. Thus, addition of divalent cation to milk at the same level as anions, reduces the rate of age-thickening[9].

1.5.5 HYGROSCOPIC PROPERTIES OF POWDERED MILK

In dehydrated milk or skimmed milk powder, hygroscopicity should be considered as an important factor for preventing the powder from caking and from becoming insoluble. The sorption isotherm of milk powder obtained by the integral method is of the sigmoid type, but by the differential method it yields a quite different curve at a moisture increase of about 7%. This phenomenon can be attributed to the transformation of dehydrated amorphous lactose in milk powder into a crystallized form[10].

Adsorption isotherms indicate a combination of sorption by lactose in the glassy state and sorption on polar sites in proteins at relative vapor pressures of less than 0.4. At higher relative vapor pressures, moisture is absorbed only by the proteins, since lactose crystallization of lactose is completed. Increased preheat-treatment tends to increase the numbers of polar sites in dry milk proteins, resulting in increased water-binding properties. Increased fat content in dry milk reduces the numbers of moisture sorption sites per unit weight of product[11].

1.5.6 PHYSICAL STRUCTURE OF BUTTER AND ITS RELATION TO MECHANICAL PROPERTIES

Butter is manufactured from cream by churning and working, and consists of a complex water-in-oil emulsion. Its mechanical properties derive from the physical structure of the fat globules and enmeshed crystal fat in the continuous phase.

Basically, the consistency and spreadability of butter depend on the chemical components of the butter fat, as is expressed by the degree of unsaturation reflected in the iodine value. Strictly speaking, this shows how much linoleic acid is present in the butter fat. Wood *et al.*[12] have reported that the higher the content of linoleic acid of the milk fat, the softer is the butter. The next important factor is the thermal history of the cream used for making the butter. Sherbon *et al.*[13] have reported that the slow cooling of cream resulted in butter thermograms at 10 and 25° C which were similar to those from the Alnarp thermal treatment of cream (cooled to 4° C, held for 8 sec, then reheated to 19° C held for 6 hr, and slowly cooled in the vat overnight to 6° C), but they differed between 22 and 25° C. Shock-cooling resulted in a greater amount of crystallization than the other 2 treatments.

Butter also exhibits thixotropic properties due to breakdown of the weak interlinks of the fat crystals by mechanical working and their redevelopment on setting at the equilibrium temperature. The growth of the fat crystals during isothermal setting accords with Avrami's equation which describes the statistical crystal growth mechanism of soft metals. Increased butter fat crystallization corresponds to an increase in viscosity during setting.[14]

Shama and Sherman[15] have obtained a retardation spectrum for butter following working and setting. Butter shows a sharp, well-defined peak at around 10^4 sec before work softening. However, the peak remains at this value following working and aging. Work-softened butter showed the highest peak at immediately after working, but the peak height gradually recovered to the original value after aging for a long time. This indicates that only weak interlinked fat crystals are present in butter except for granular fats broken down by working.

1.5.7 FINE STRUCTURE OF PROCESSED CHEESE, AND THE VISCOELASTIC PROPERTIES OF GOUDA TYPE CHEESE AND PROCESSED CHEESE

Gouda cheese exhibits a box-type distribution spectrum of relaxation times based on measurements of the dynamic viscoelasticity (Fig. 1).

This distribution spectrum shifts to longer relaxation times with increase of maturation, probably as a result of the disintegraton of para-casein in the cheese during maturation.

The condensed sodium phosphate employed in making processed cheese plays an important role in the heat-melting of natural cheese, forming a characteristic texture due to binding with para-caseinate. When low molecular condensed sodium phosphate is used as melting salt for cheese, the casein particles become uniformly dispersed in the processed cheese, as shown in Fig. 2. The loosely compacted casein particles in processed cheeses are well hydrated and easy to melt reversibly by heat. On the other hand, in processed cheeses made with high molecular condensed sodium phosphate, the casein particles are linked in a pearl necklace-shaped man-

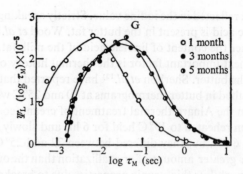

FIG. 1. Distribution of relaxation times of gouda cheese after various maturation Periods.

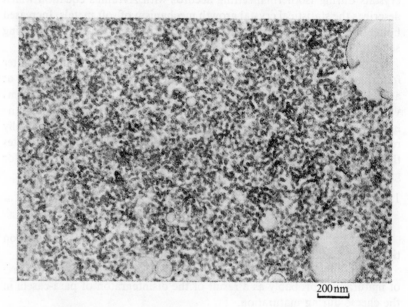

FIG. 2. Processed cheese (melting).

ner as shown in Fig. 3, and the final processed cheeses are irreversibly melted by heat[15]. Nakajima *et al*[17]. have reported that the addition of approximately 2% condensed sodium phosphate to cheese is the optimum for obtaining the softest well-hydrated processed cheeses.

Processed cheese has a relaxation spectrum with a wider relaxation time range than natural cheese[18]. This indicates that the attractive forces between the casein particles of processed cheese are weaker than those in

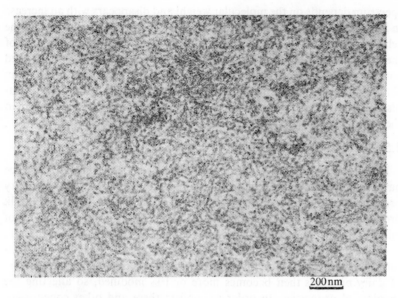

200 nm

FIG. 3. Processed cheese (non-melting).

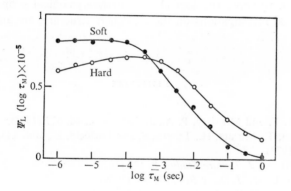

FIG. 4. Distribution of relaxation times of hard and soft type processed cheeses (after. Taneya, *et al.*, 1977).

natural cheese. Compared to the relaxation spectrum of heat-unmelted processed cheese, that of heat-melted cheese shifts to the shorter range of relaxation times (Fig. 4).

By analogy with the relaxation spectrum of high polymers, it has been concluded that the wedge-shaped relaxation spectrum is not influenced by the degree of polymerization or its concentration, but the box-shaped spectrum depends on the molecular weight and disappears with an increase in flowability. With an increase in degree of polymerization, the skirt of the relaxation spectrum extends to a longer time scale. From the view point of the mechanical interaction between long chain molecules, the box-shaped part of the relaxation spectrum depends on entanglement among long chain molecules and the wedge-shaped part is due to a relaxation mechanism in the interior of the molecules. This hypothesis can be applied to the relaxation mechanism of processed cheese discussed above.

1.5.8   CONCLUSION AND FUTURE PROSPECTS

In this review, only a few recent developments in the field of dairy science have been mentioned. More extensive physicochemical studies on dairy products are clearly necessary. The molecular conformation of milk protein (especially of the casein micelles), the crystal growing behavior of milk fat and lactose, and the structure of the fat-globule membranes are easily affected by thermal and mechanical treatments, variations in moisture, changes in ionic structure and enzymatic reactions. The fine structure of dairy products then becomes more or less modified, so affecting the rheological properties. In order to confirm these and other conclusions, combined physical and chemical studies such as on microstructure by electron microscopy, rheological and thermodynamical properties, and fundamental investigations on the molecular structure, are anticipated.

REFERENCES

1. Fox, P. F. and Morrisey, P. A., *J. Dairy Res.*, **44**, 627 (1977).
2. Kimura, T., Murata, H., Taneya, S. and Furuichi, E., 20th I.D.C. 2.1, 1.2, 238 (1978).
3. Rao, M. A., *J. Texture Studies*, **8**, 135 (1977).
4. Phipps, L. W., *J. Dairy Res.*, **36**, 417 (1969).
5. Scott Blair, G. W., *Biorheology*, **6**, 143 (1969).
6. Scott Blair, G. W., and Prentice, J. H., *Des Cahiers du Groupe Français de Rhéologie*, **2**, I 75 (1966).
7. Prentice, J. H., *J. Texture Studies*, **3**, 415 (1972).
8. Kieseker, F. G. and Zadow, J. G., *The Australian J. Dairy Technol.*, **28**, 108 (1973).
9. Samal, R. and Muers, M. M., *J. Dairy Res.*, **29**, 249, 259, 269 (1962).
10. Makino, T. and Sone, T., *Oyobutsuri* (Japanese), **30**, 475 (1961).
11. Heldman, D. R., Hall, C. W. and Hedrick, T. I., *J. Dairy Sci.*, **48**, 845 (1965).
12. Wood, F. M., Murphy, M. F., and Dunkley, W. L., *J. Dairy Sci.*, **58**, 839 (1975).

13. Sherbon, J. W., Dolby, R. M. and Russell, R. W., *J. Dairy Res.*, **39**, 325 (1972).
14. Sone, T., *J. Phys. Soc. Japan*, **16**, 961 (1961).
15. Shama, F. and Sherman, P., *J. Texture Studies*, **1**, 196 (1970).
16. Kimura, T. and Taneya, S., *J. Electroh Microscopy*, **24**, 115 (1975).
17. Nakajima, I., Tatsumi, K. and Furuichi, E., *Japan. J. Agr. Chem.*, **46**, 447 (1972).
18. Taneya, S., Izutsu, T. and Sone, T., Oral Presentation, IUOFST Symp. Food Texture and Rheology, London, Dec. 1977.

2. Chemical Aspects of Food Quality

2.1 Degradation of Casein Components during Cheese Maturation

Lawrence K. Creamer*

Cheesemaking is an important method for preserving the nutritive components of milk, and a great many different cheese varieties have been developed in various regions of the world. There are, however, only about 10–15 distinctly different varieties which are differentiated by moisture (or water) content, their pH, whether the curd was heated or not, and whether they were mould-ripened or not[1].

In the most general terms, cheese is made by coagulating milk and by acidifying and dehydrating the coagulum or curd until a compact mass is formed. Salt is usually added to the curd or diffused into the compact curd mass from a brine bath. The acid is almost always made using lactic acid bacteria in the milk. These become trapped in the curd and are important later in the cheese ripening. Coagulation is usually caused by the action of a proteolytic enzyme preparation known as rennet. A proportion of this enzyme remains in the cheese. The cheese is put aside to ripen at 4–10°C. It is often wrapped or waxed to prevent mould spoilage. The time taken to ripen depends on temperature, moisture, pH, salt concentration and whether or not the cheeses are mould-ripened.

The earliest studies of the proteolysis that occurs during cheese ripening involved the measurement of the increase in non-protein-nitrogen during the ripening period. It was found that non-protein-nitrogen increased continuously. Experiments involving the use of rennet and starter, another name for the lactic streptococci culture added to milk to make the lactic acid from the lactose, showed that the starter and moulds used in cheesemaking were more important than the rennet enzymes. After using more

---

* New Zealand Dairy Research Institute, Palmerston North, New Zealand

340

refined chemical assay methods it was concluded that the protein was degraded to non-protein-nitrogen via a series of peptides of ever-decreasing size[3].

The application of moving boundary electrophoresis to casein degradation in cheese and in solution by Lindquist and Storgards[2] demonstrated that the rennet enzymes were important in the initial stages of casein degradation in many cheese varieties. They used the electrophoresis patterns to describe three types of ripening: α-, β- and non-specific, in which α_s-casein, β-casein or both caseins were degraded rapidly.

The next important advance came in 1966 when Ledford and his colleagues[4] applied the technique of polyacrylamide gel electrophoresis in 4.5 molar urea solution to the problem of proteolysis during cheese ripening. In general terms their results supported those from the earlier electrophoresis studies with the important difference that α_{s1}-casein was always degraded more rapidly than β-casein in the earlier stages of cheese ripening, thus they were not able to find any examples of β-ripening. The reason for this disparity is most likely to be related to the method of analysis used by Lindquist and Storgards rather than to the cheese samples used.

Following this work, gel electrophoresis has proven to be a powerful tool in the study of casein proteolysis[5]. Subsequent studies[6-8] confirmed the earlier conclusion that the rennet enzyme was important in the initial degradation of α_{s1}-casein and these also showed that β-casein was not appreciably degraded by the rennet enzyme. This confirmation set in motion a number of studies on the action of chymosin, the active enzyme from calf vell rennet, and pepsin on casein in cheese and in solution. It was found that β-casein degradation in solution was almost as fast as that of α_{s1}-casein and β-casein hydrolysis gave rise to peptides that were rarely seen in cheese. It was finally realized that this phenomenon was caused by the high degree of β-casein self-association and the consequent inaccessibility of the chymosin-sensitive bonds of β-casein to the enzyme[9]. This can be simulated by the inclusion of salt in a casein solution because salt also causes extensive self-association of the protein.

Detailed study of the degradation of α_{s1}-casein by chymosin in cheese and in solution showed that bonds 23–24 and 24–25 were very sensitive[10]. However, comparison of most cheese electrophoresis patterns with those produced by the action of chymosin on casein show a number of additional bands near the origin. They are more intense in cheese matured at a higher pH. The peptides corresponding to these bands were isolated and identified as γ-, TS-and R-caseins, all of which are derived from β-casein by the cleavage of bonds 28–29, 105–106 and 107–108[11]. The almost universal occurrence of these peptides in all varieties of cheese, and especially in those in which the curd is heated to high temperatures, and the greater quantities in higher pH cheese led to the conclusion that plasmin or the alkaline milk protease[12] was the enzyme most likely to be responsible for this β-casein proteolysis[11].

In summary the enzymes responsible for specific proteolysis in cheese are chymosin and plasmin, whilst non-specific proteolysis is caused by the bacterial and mould enzymes. The first can be demonstrated using techniques such as gel electrophoresis while changes in non-protein-nitrogen, that is, small peptides, demonstrate the action of the latter enzymes[6,13,14].

Figure 1 shows some typical electrophoresis patterns from samples of different cheese varieties. In all cheeses α_{s1}-casein in initially converted into α_{s1}-I. The moderate moisture, high pH cheese, Gouda, shows pronounced

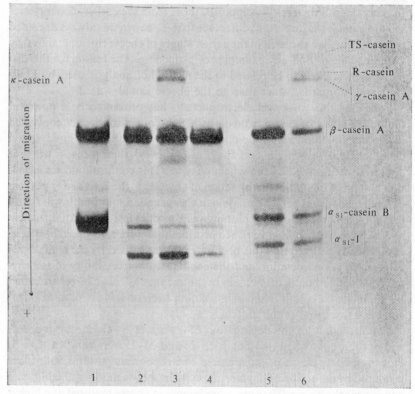

FIG. 1. Electrophoresis patterns of samples from several cheese varieties:
1. Whole casein.
2. Mozzarella, 90 days, pH 5.4, 50% moisture, heated curd.
3. Gouda, 90 days, pH 5.3, 43% moisture.
4. Cheddar, 90 days, pH 5.1, 35% moisture.
5. Camembert (central core) 40 days, pH 5.2, 52% moisture.
6. Camembert (outer edge) 40 days, pH 7.5, 52% moisture.

β-casein degradation to γ-, TS- and R-caseins. Camembert is interesting in that the neutral mould protease raises the pH in the outer shell of the cheese so that two distinct zones of degradation are observed. Chymosin activity predominates in the central zone whilst plasmin activity becomes important in the outer zone after the pH increases.

When milk of other ruminants is used, the same pattern of breakdown is observed with the α-caseins being degraded first[5].

In recent years there has been a large effort put into the finding of substitutes for chymosin for cheesemaking [15,16]. The major substitutes are pig pepsin, *Endothia parasitica* protease, *Mucor miehei* protease and *Mucor pusillus* protease. Extensive trials have been carried out with the result that large amounts of cheese are made with the *Mucor* proteases and with chymosin/pepsin mixtures. The electrophoretic patterns of breakdown are quite different from those obtained with chymosin[17]. Pepsin is less proteolytic than chymosin although it has a similar specificity. The two *Mucor* enzymes give similar patterns to one another and they appear to be more proteolytic than chymosin as well as having different specificities. These results confirm the earlier conclusion that the initial cleavage of the casein molecules is very dependent on the milk coagulant enzyme.

Bitterness is one of the most important of all protein-related defects in cheese. Early studies demonstrated that the relevant compound in bitter cheese was a peptide or peptides. Because of its economic importance, bitterness in cheese has been studied intensively for some tme[18-21]. One of the difficulties in early work was the apparently random nature of the occurrence of bitter cheese. Systematic studies using pasteurized milk, well-defined starter strains and rennet that was almost pure chymosin made it possible to produce non-bitter cheese at will and use it as a basis for comparative studies. These studies on Cheddar cheese showed that bitterness could be increased by increasing the rennet concentration or by carrying out the cheesemaking so that large numbers of actively growing lactic streptococci were present in the cheese curd after cooking and salting. Thus it seemed that a practical solution to the bitterness problem was in the choice of starter, rennet concentration, cooking temperature and salt addition[22].

Several studies have been carried out in which cheese was made and then the bitter component isolated and identified. In a study at our Institute[19], two cheeses, one bitter and the other non-bitter made on the same day but with different starters, were examined. It was found that the gel electrophoresis patterns were identical but the bitter cheese contained more peptides of moderately high molecular weight than the non-bitter cheese. A bitter fraction was isolated and found to contain three peptides from the region of α_{s1}-casein close to the chymosin cleavage point. An important finding was that the non-bitter cheese also had a bitter fraction, showing that bitterness in the cheese was related to the quantity of a bitter peptide or peptides present. Thus the concentration of bitter peptides had to exceed the flavour threshold for bitterness. This threshold is considered to increase with the age of a cheese because of the increase in the other flavour components. Studies by other groups identified a number of different peptides as being the bitter components in other cheeses, casein hydrolysates, etc.[e.g.20].

A study of a different type had been carried out by Ney, who showed that bitterness was related to hydrophobicity with the more hydrophobic peptides having a more intensely bitter flavour[23,24]. Peptides were more bitter than a mixture of their component amino acids. Caseins are hydrophobic proteins and it might be expected that they could give rise to a large number of bitter peptides. An examination of the sequence of α_{s1}- or β-casein and calculating the hydrophobicity of every possible nonapeptide, in-

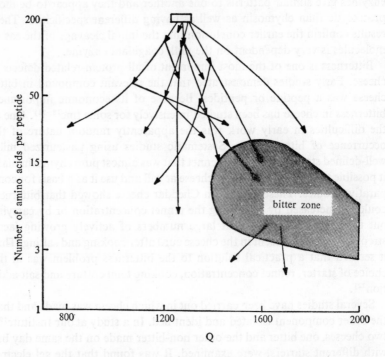

FIG. 2. Possible degradation pathway of casein during cheese maturation. The initial degradation is more likely to be caused by the rennet enzyme or plasmin, whilst later degradation is more likely to be caused by bacterial proteases. The zone of bitterness is bounded by solubility, hydrophobicity and peptide size.

dicated that there were a number of regions that could give rise to bitter peptides. Almost all of the identified bitter peptides come from these regions[19,25].

This type of calculation can be carried out for peptides of any size, and the results were essentially the same when it was done for pentapeptides, with regions of high hydrophobicity and regions of low hydrophobicity. The other criterion for bitter flavour in a peptide is solubility and thus only relatively small peptides have been found to be bitter[20,24,25].

With these factors, it is possible to make a diagrammatic representation of the origin of bitterness in cheese (Figure 2). The caseins, with a Q of about 1300, are hydrolysed through a number of intermediate steps to give a range of peptides, some bitter, some not. A cheese is bitter if it has too many peptides with the correct characteristics of size and hydrophobicity. Any factors which increase this number will increase bitterness and vice versa. Bitterness can thus be diminished by either preventing the formation of bitter peptides or by increasing their rate of hydrolysis to non-bitter peptides and amino acids. The generation of bitter peptides has been ascribed to bacterial proteases while the latter has been ascribed to bacterial peptidases. It seems likely, however, that because of the large number of different enzymatic pathways involved, the move from just below the flavour threshold to above it, that the explanation for the origin of bitterness in cheese is not simple, nor can the results obtained using one cheese variety with a particular milk coagulant, for example, be extrapolated to a different cheese variety or to cheese made with a different milk coagulant.

I acknowledge the advice and assistance I have had from Institute staff, Dr R. C. Lawrence and Mr J. Gilles in particular, during the course of this work.

REFERENCES

(The minimum number of possible references have been included.)
1. Kosikowski, F. V., "Cheese and Fermented Milk Foods", Michigan, Edwards Bros. (1977).
2. Lindquist, B., and Storgards, T., *Milchwissenschaft*, **12**, 462 (1957).
3. Schormuller, J., *Advan. Food Res.*, **16**, 231 (1968).
4. Ledford, R. A., O'Sullivan, A. C., and Nath, K. R., *J. Dairy Sci.*, **49**, 1098 (1966).

5. IDF Annual Bulletin, 1968, Doc. 44, "Use of Electrophoresis for the Identification of Mixtures of Cows', Ewes' and Goats' Milk in Dairy Products", Int. Dairy Fed., Brussells.
6. Desmazeaud, M. J., and Gripon, J.-C., *Milchwissenschaft*, **32**, 731 (1977).
7. Visser, F. M. W., *Neth. Milk Dairy J.*, **31**, 265 (1977).
8. Phelan, J. A., Guiney, J., and Fox, P. F., *J. Dairy Res.*, **40**, 105 (1973).
9. Creamer, L. K., *N. Z. J. Dairy Sci. Technol.*, **11**, 30 (1976).
10. Creamer L. K., and Richardson, B. C., *N. Z. J. Dairy Sci. Technol.*, **9**, 9 (1974).
11. Creamer, L. K., *J. Dairy Sci.*, **58**, 287 (1975).
12. Kaminogawa, S., Mizobuchi, H., and Yamauchi, K., *Agric. Biol. Chem.*, **36**, 2163 (1972).
13. Ohmiya, K., and Sato, Y., *Milchwissenschaft*, **27**, 417 (1972).
14. O'Keeffe, R. B., Fox, P. F., and Daly, C., *J. Dairy Res.*, **43**, 97 (1976).
15. Green, M. L., *J. Dairy Res.*, **44**, 159 (1977).
16. Sternberg, M., *Advan. Appl. Microbiol.*, **20**, 135 (1976).
17. Edwards, J. L., and Kosikowski, F. V., *J. Dairy Sci.*, **52**, 1675 (1969).
18. Czulak, J., *Aust. J. Dairy Technol.*, **14**, 177 (1959).
19. Richardson, B. C., and Creamer, L. K., *N. Z. J. Dairy Sci. Technol.*, **8**, 46 (1973).
20. Visser, S., Slangen, K. J., and Hup, G., *Neth. Milk Dairy J.*, **29**, 319 (1975).
21. IDF Annual Bulletin, 1977, Doc. 97, "Bitterness in Cheese", Int. Dairy Fed., Brussells.
22. Lowrie, R. J., and Lawrence, R. C., *N. Z. J. Dairy Sci. Technol.*, **7**, 51 (1972).
23. Ney, K. H., *Z. Lebensm. u.-Forsch.*, **147**, 64 (1971).
24. Wieser, H., and Belitz, H. D., *Z. Lebensm. u.-Forsch.*, **160**, 383 (1976).
25. Pelissier, J. P., Mercier, J. C., and Ribadeau-Dumas, B., *Annls. Biol. Anim. Biochim. Biophys.*, **14**, 343 (1974).

2.2 The Significance of Moisture to Food Quality

Marcus Karel*

The quality of foods as received by the consumer depends not only on initial composition but also on various quality changes occurring in processing, storage, and distribution. Many of these changes are affected by water content and the state of water in foods. The knowledge of the so-called "monolayer values" and of the amount of *nonsolvent water* is particularly significant. The monolayer value should not be construed as an amount of water uniformly covering the internal surfaces of foods but rather as the amount of water strongly absorbed on specific polar groups in the foods. Monolayer values for various food substances have been reported recently by Iglesias and Chirife (1976). With respect to nonsolvent water Duckworth and Kelley (1973) found that sucrose began to go into solution at an activity of ~ 0.88 in several water-polymer systems. At this activity the water contents of these systems were 0.34 g/g for agar, 0.27 for gelatin, 0.24 for starch, and 0.11 for cellulose. Glucose began to dissolve at an activity of ~ 0.85 and urea at an activity of ~ 0.45.

Many food components may be present in one of several states: crystalline solids, amorphous solids, aqueous solution, or bound to other components. Sorption in such systems is complex. It is known, for instance, that crystalline sugars sorb very little water; but amorphous sugars sorb substantially more water at the same conditions. However, the adsorption of water results in breaking of some H-bond and an increase in mobility of sugar molecules resulting eventually in the sugars transforming to the crystalline state. In this process the sugar loses water. History of samples is of paramount importance especially for materials such as sugars and polymers which can readily be prepared in a glassy state.

The effects of water on chemical reactions in foods are more complicated than are its effects on microbial growth. Water can act in one or more of the following roles: (a) as a solvent for reactants and products, (b) as a reactant (e.g. in hydrolysis reactions), (c) as a product of reactions (e.g. in condensa-

---
* *Department of Nutrition and Food Science, Massachusetts Institute of Technology, Cambridge, Massachusetts 02139, USA*

tion reactions such as occur in nonenzymic browning), and (d) as a modifier of the catalytic or inhibitory activities of other substances (e.g. water inactivates some metallic catalysts of lipid peroxidation). We shall consider here the following.

A. Action of water as plasticizer and solvent and consequences for physical and chemical changes.

B. Recent studies on enzymatic reactions at low water content.

C. Effect of water on reactions initiated by lipid peroxidation.

A. Action of water as plasticizer and solvent

Foods prepared by rapid dehydration or by dehydration from the frozen state (freeze-drying) often have a structure which is metastable. Addition of water and/or increase of temperature cause the phenomenon of "collapse" of this structure. Collapse may be defined as the appearance of adequate mobility to produce rearrangements of internal structure. Various important quality consequences follow:

1. Macroscopic flow resulting in caking, stickiness, and visual defects of the product.

2. Recrystallization.

3. Loss of entrapped volatile components.

Collapse of amorphous structure of dried food components results in disruption of internal "pockets" of molecular or larger size in which volatiles such as flavor compounds are entrapped until released by dissolving the entrapping matrix. Table 1, for instance, in recent studies by To and Flink at M.I.T. (To, 1978), the degree of collapse was quantitatively assessed by observing under the microscope the projected area of a flake of freeze-dried carbohydrate while it was heated to a specified temperature. As some collapse and flow occurred, at each temperature there was a decrease in the projected area up to the point where the complete liquification of the flake resulted in the final equilibrium shape. The fractional collapse was defined as an increase in the projected area at a given temperature over the maximum achievable increase in area. When this "fractional collapse" was plotted against the loss of entrapped flavors occurring because of exposure to the increased temperature (or increased moisture) causing the collapse, excellent correlations were obtained.

4. Collapse also allows penetration of gases and vapors into the food. Droplets of oxidizable lipids incorporated in an emulsion containing suitable solutes (such as carbohydrates as well as many polymers) may be freeze-dried and then washed with a nonpolar solvent such as hexane. All of the lipids are then entrapped and shielded from atmospheric oxygen. Subsequent exposure to water vapor which plasticizes the structure allows penetration of oxygen and consequent deterioration of lipids (Table 2).

B. Effects of water on enzyme-catalyzed reactions in foods

It has long been recognized that enzyme-catalyzed reactions can proceed in foods at relatively low water contents. Work in this field has been summarized recently by workers in Germany (Potthast *et al.*, 1975), in France (Drapron, 1972; Tome *et al.*, 1978), and in my group in the U.S.A. (Silver, 1976). Two features of the results of these studies are common to the experience of most investigators:

1. The rate of hydrolysis increases with increasing water activity with the reaction extremely slow at very low activities.
2. At each water activity there appears to be a maximum extent of hydrolysis which also increased with water content.

The apparent cessation of the reaction cannot be because of irreversible inactivation of the enzyme, because upon humidification to a higher water activity, hydrolysis is resumed at a rate characteristic of the newly obtained water activity. Silver (1976) investigated a model system consisting of Avicel, sucrose, and invertase and found that the reaction velocity increased with water activity. Complete conversion of the substrate was observed for water activities ≥ 0.75. Below water activities of 0.75 the reaction continued toward 100 percent hydrolysis.

Examination of the results in the light of the hypothesis of the existence of a mobilization point for the substrate showed that a sharp demarcation of the onset of reaction was not obtained. Chemical as well as microscopic studies showed that at least some of the amorphous sucrose in the system was in solution at relatively low water activities, thus allowing reaction to proceed in these solution pools. Effects of varying the enzyme to substrate ratios on reaction velocity and the effect of water activity on the activation energy for the reaction could not be explained by a simple diffusional model but required more complex postulates including the following:

1. The diffusional resistance is localized in a "shell" adjacent to the enzyme.
2. At low water activities, the reduced hydration produces conformational changes in the enzymes affecting its catalytic activity.

The very recent work of Toma *et al.* (1978) casts equally severe doubts on the simple diffusional hypothesis on the basis of experiments in liquid systems in which water activity was reduced by addition of glycerol, ethylene glycol, diethylene glycol, or sorbitol. In these solutions polyphenoloxidase activity on tyrosine showed features very similar to those obtained in solid systems. In particular, the rate increased rapidly with increasing water activity; and the reaction stopped at a certain level before all reactants were consumed; the higher the water content, the higher was this plateau. The authors were unable to find a correlation of enzyme activity with either viscosity or dielectric constant.

C. Effects of water on peroxidation of lipids and associated reactions

At low water contents and especially in porous substrates in complete absence of water, peroxidation of unsaturated lipids proceeds very rapidly. Addition of small quantities of water tends to produce a protective effect especially if the substrate is still free of oxidation products and reactive intermediates. However, reactions of oxidation products with proteins follow a more complex pattern.

In a model system consisting of methyl linoleate and lysozyme, the free radicals and other reactive species formed by the linoleate react with the protein resulting in increased fluorescence, decreased enzyme activity, and decreased protein solubility. Water activity has an inhibitory effect on the initial oxidation of the lipid, but the secondary reactions of the lipid degradation products with the protein are accelerated by increasing water activity (Kanner and Karel, 1967; Yong, 1978). Schaich (1974) studied free radical formation in proteins reacted with peroxidizing lipids and found that the amount and type of free radicals formed in the proteins were strongly affected by water activity. It appears that water facilitates recombination of free radicals, and as a consequence the steady state concentration of radicals decreases, whereas various radical-initiated processes such as protein cross-linking increase at high water contents.

REFERENCES

Drapron, R., *Ann. Technol. Agr.,* **24** (4), 487 (1972).

Duckworth, R. B. and Kelly, C. E., *J. Food. Technol.,* **8**, 105 (1973).

Iglesias, H. A. and Chirife, J., *Lebensm. -Wiss. u. -Technol.,* **9**, 123 (1976).

Kanner, J. and Karel, M., *J. Agr. Food Chem.,* **24**, 468 (1976).

Potthast, K., Hamm, R. and Acker, L., "Enzymic Relations in Low Moisture Foods" in R. B. Duckworth (ed.), Water Relations of Foods, p. 365 Academic Press, (1975).

Schaich, K. M., Free Radical Formation in Proteins Exposed to Peroxidizing Lipids, Sc. D. Thesis, M. I. T. Department of Nutrition and Food Science, Cambridge, Massachusetts, 1974.

Silver, M. E., The Behavior of Invertase in Model Systems at Low Moisture Contents, Ph. D. Thesis, M. I. T. Department of Nutrition and Food Science, Cambridge, Massachusetts, 1976.

To, E. C. H., Collapse, A Structural Transition in Freeze-dried Matrices, Sc. D. Thesis, M. I. T. Department of Nutrition and Food Science, Cambridge, Massachusetts, 1978.

Tome, D., Nicolas, J. and Drapron, R., *Lebensm.—Wiss. u. Technol.,* **11**, 38 (1978).

Yong, S. H., Reactions between Peroxidizing Methyl Linoleate and Histidine, or Histidyl Residue Analogues, Ph. D. Thesis, M. I. T. Department of Nutrition and Food Science, Cambridge, Massachusetts, 1978.

2.3 Formation of Aroma Compounds from Oxidized Lipids

Caj E. Eriksson*

Lipids comprise a group of compounds from which numerous aroma compounds are derived. For example, the volatile fraction of unblanched frozen peas contains, at least 42 compounds, 26 carbonyls and 16 alcohols, as a result of oxidation of the minor amounts of lipids contained in peas, as proposed by Murray et al.[1] Many factors are involved in the sequence of reactions leading to the formation of aroma from oxidized unsaturated fatty acids, such as lipid content and localization, lipid class and fatty acid composition, structure of the fatty acids, presence of various catalysts, treatment of the lipid, and the reactions of the aroma compounds themselves. The properties of individual aroma compounds are also important. The actual combination of these factors is important in deciding the final result.

The present paper, while not giving a survey of lipid oxidation which embraces the vast amount of published information, gathers together examples of recent advances in this field which have led to a greater understanding of aroma development from oxidized lipids. A survey covering aroma formation from oxidized edible oils has recently been given by Kochar and Meara.[2] Another survey on enzymic and non-enzymic catalysts involved in lipid oxidation and the further reactions of the primarily produced aroma compounds has been given by Eriksson.[3]

The amount of lipids as such does not appear to be an important factor. Large amounts of lipids in a tissue often mean a large amount of depot fat, while, when only small amounts of lipids are present, the lipids are almost exclusively contained in membranes. Most of the depot fat is built up from triglycerides where unsaturated fatty acids, when present, are predominantly found in the 2–position. In membranes, the polar lipids contain fatty acids only in the 1– and 2–positions. Unsaturated fatty acids are found first of all in the 2–position of such polar lipids. Sometimes, long chain unsaturated fatty acids, e.g. eruric acid, resemble saturated fatty acids in their position specificity. Since the different positions in both neutral and polar lipids are not equivalent, the membership of a lipid to one class or another may influence the hydrolysis of fatty acids which is sometimes an import-

* SIK-The Swedish Food Institute, Fack, S-400 23 Göteborg, Sweden

ant step prior to the key reactions in lipid oxidation as will be discussed later. Our knowledge of the classes, localization, chemical composition and structure of lipids has recently been surveyed for plant tissues by Galliard and Mercer.[4]

Lipid oxidation in various tissues where the fat is located, is not only influenced by lipid class and localization but also by the presence of lipid oxidation protection systems such as tocopherol. The tocopherol content of soy oil protects its lipids from oxidation while, for instance in animal fatty tissues, there are no such protecting systems. Hence, animal fat tends to be more susceptible to lipid oxidation and the development of rancidity even though it is less unsaturated than soy oil. This lack of protection is even more obvious in mutton and beef containing an increased proportion of polyunsaturated fatty acids as a result of feeding a lipid protected diet containing large amounts of polyunsaturated fatty acids to the animals. The flavor difference of these meats from normal ones has been partially attributed to increased levels of *trans*-2, *trans*-4–decadienal[5].

The low odor threshold values and high intensity factors of aroma compounds which are developed from non-volatile compounds can overrule many of the other factors involved in the formation of aroma, since so little of such low threshold and high flavor intensity compounds is required to produce a sensory response and flavor quality impression. Two examples of this phenomenon will be considered. They also illustrate the large differences in odor properties which may exist between closely related aroma compounds.

cis-4–Heptenal was found by McGill *et al.*[6] as an oxidation product derived from the small amounts of lipids present in cod muscle. The absolute flavor threshold of *cis*-4–heptenal was determined as 0.04 ppb in water and 0.5–1.6 ppb in oil. This makes *cis*-4–heptenal a far more potent aroma compound than its *trans* isomer (*trans*-4–heptenal), the flavor threshold of which was found to be 2 ppb in water and 100–320 ppb in oil. A shift from *cis* to *trans* configuration thus gives rise to a large difference in properties. The second example concerns the strong metallic odor produced by octa-1, *cis*-5–dien-3–one in butter fat. This compound is formed from oxidized trace amounts of (*n*-3) pentaenoic fatty acids, as shown by Swoboda and Peers.[7] Octa-1, *cis*-5–dien-3–one can be detected at a concentration of one part per 10^{12} parts of water and at one part per about 5×10^{10} parts of oil. This represents detection at a concentration which is about 100 times lower than that for octa-1–en-3–one formed from (*n*-6) pentaenoic fatty acid and containing one double bond less.

Besides autoxidation, several catalysts or environmental changes are involved in the breakdown of lipids, finally leading to aroma formation (see Fig. 1). As already pointed out, hydrolysis is an important step since

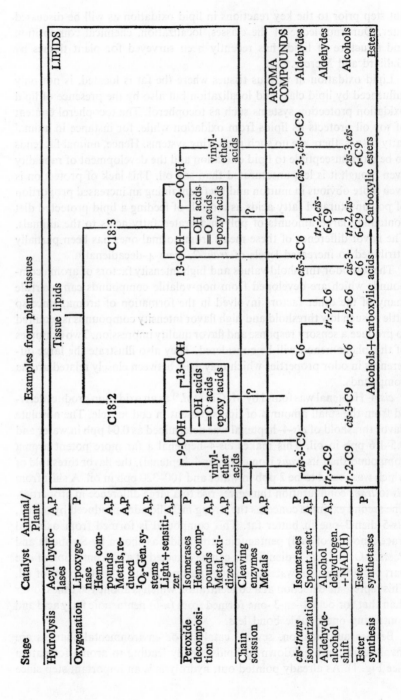

Fig. 1. Reaction sequence of lipid breakdown. Examples from plant tissues.

free fatty acids often react more efficiently than esterified ones. This is particularly true for the enzyme lipoxygenase present in many plant tissues. Lipoxygenase is active almost exclusively towards free polyunsaturated fatty acids. Hydrolysis occurs rapidly in plant itssues by the action of acyl hydrolases. The acyl hydrolases of potato, tomato and cucumber have been extensively investigated by Galliard who also summarized the nature of these enzymes[4]. The properties of the enzyme lipoxygenase from different plant sources have been studies in detail during the last 5 years. Most of our present knowledge of lipoxygenase has been reviewed by Veldink *et al.*[8] Plant lipoxygenase isoenzymes differ in their ability to introduce the hydroperoxy group at the 9–and 13–carbon atoms in linoleic and linolenic acids. This difference in specificity is reflected in the ability of different enzyme systems and plant tissues to produce flavor compounds from lipids. Fischer and Grosch[9] incubated linoleic acid with soybean lipoxygenase isoenzyme L-1 having an optimum pH of 9.0 and the isoenzyme L-2 with an optimum pH of 6.5, and compared the formation of volatile aldehydes. L-1 at pH 8.5 produced mainly hexanal and *trans*-2, *trans*-4–decadienal. At pH 7.0 it produced exclusively hexanal, whereas L-2 at this pH produced a wider range of volatile compounds involving hexanal, *trans*-2, *trans*-4–decadienal, *trans*-2,*cis*-4–decadienal, *trans*-2–heptenal, *trans*-2–octenal, *trans*-2,*trans*-4–nonadienal and heptanal in decreasing order.

Heme compounds occur in animal and plant tissues in the form of hemoglobin, myoglobin, peroxidases and cytochromes. All these heme compounds catalyze lipid oxidation in their native state and sometimes even more in their denatured state such as after heat treatment. For example, the milk enzyme lactoperoxidase was found to increase its non-enzymic lipid oxidation activity 16 times after heat treatment at 125°C for 5 min. The same set of volatile compounds were produced from linoleic acid both when the native and the heat denatured lactoperoxidase were used as the catalyst according to Eriksson[10]. It was shown later by Gregory *et al.* that a heme compound is associated with the milk fat globule membrane and that this compound may be involved in the peroxidation of milk lipids[11]. Allen and Humphries[12] found that a prooxidative fraction from milk fat globule membrane contained high activities of xanthine oxidase and that the activity of this fraction increased after heat treatment. These authors suggest that increased exposure of a prosthetic group, in this case ferredoxin, is responsible for the increased prooxidative effect as previously found in the case of lactoperoxidase.

One of the major differences between enzymic and non-enzymic catalysis of unsaturated fatty acid oxidation has so far been considered to lie in different specificities. Lipoxygenase catalysis can give rise to a varying ratio of 9- and 13-hydroperoxides produced on oxygenation of linoleic and linolenic acid depending on the presence of isoenzymes specific for either 9- or 13-attack, while the non-enzymatic type of catalysis always gives equal amounts of these hydroperoxy isomers. However, Chan et al.[13] have recently found that when hemoglobin, myoglobin, cupric and ferrous ions were used as catalysts in the oxygenation of linoleic acid under conditions similar to those employed for assaying lipoxygenase activity, the percentage ratio between the 9- and 13-peroxy isomers produced was about 30:70 instead of the expected 50:50. When methyl linoleate was used as the substrate, the ratio was found to be close to 50:50. It was suggested that this difference arose from different conformational preferences of the lipid molecules in aqueous media. This observation may be of fundamental importance for understanding aroma formation in material where heme compounds and metal ions are the major catalysts of lipid oxidation.

Considerable attention has recently been paid to the role of singlet oxygen in the oxygenation of unsaturated fatty acids. Singlet oxygen ($^1O_2$) is produced from the superoxide radical (O_2^-) which can be generated via a great number of enzymic and non-enzymic systems, many of them related to foods. Examples include many oxidoreductases, such as xanthine oxidase and the autoxidation of reduced glutathione. Most of our present knowledge of the nature of the superoxide radical and its production in biological systems has been reviewed by Bors et al.[14] The formation of singlet oxygen from the superoxide radical can be inhibited by the action of the enzyme superoxide anion dismutase (SOD) which converts the superoxide radical to hydrogen peroxide and ground state (triplet) oxygen. This is proposed to be the mechanism of lipid oxidation inhibition by SOD[15,16]. Thomas et al. in a very recent paper[17] have reported that the initial hydroperoxide concentration influenced xanthin oxidase-catalyzed linoleic acid oxidation. They propose that the hydroperoxides react with O_2^- to produce alkoxy radicals which initiate the oxidation.

Photosensitized lipid oxidation leads to aroma development which may differ for different systems, due largely to the nature of the sensitizer. Chan[18] has investigated the photosensitized oxidation of methyl oleate and methyl linoleate, and shown that riboflavin and erythrosine as sensitizers yielded mixtures of isomeric hydroperoxides with both substrates. The hydroperoxide mixture in the riboflavin-sensitized reaction was similar to that obtained in normal autoxidation while the erythrosine-sensitized reaction proceeded via singlet oxygen oxygenation and gave another hydroperoxide mixture. Erythrosine is widely used as a food color, and it has been shown by Chan[19] that this colored compound added to luncheon meat influenced the rapid development of detrimental aroma of the meat upon exposure to light.

Decomposition of hydroperoxides is known to be accelerated by certain enzymes, hydroperoxide isomerases, found in flax seed, corn, barley, wheat, soybean, mung bean, peanut and potato. This reaction gives rise to a number of isomeric acids. The reactions and their products have been reviewed by Veldink *et al.*[8]

Non-enzymatic catalysis of hydroperoxide decomposition occurs also with heme compounds and metals. Gardner *et al.*[20] using a ferric ion-cysteine complex as catalyst, found that 9 oxygenated fatty acids were formed from a mixture of linoleic acid hydroperoxides. Hamberg[21] showed that hemoglobin-catalyzed decomposition of 13-hydroperoxy linoleic acid yielded 5 new compounds involving keto acids, hydroxy acids and hydroxy-epoxy acids. However, little is known about the role of these hydroxy, keto and epoxy acids in the formation of aroma compounds. It has been proposed that 12-oxo-13-hydroxy-octadec-*trans*-10-enoic acid derived from 13-hydroperoxy acids in tomato is a precursor of hexanal· Galliard[22] investigated the formation of aroma compounds from potato, tomato and cucumber. The lipoxygenases of all three tissues predominantly yield the 9-hydroperoxy isomers of linoleic and linolenic acid. These tissues differ, however, as regards the subsequent reactions. Potato enzymes convert the 9-hydroperoxy isomers into vinylether acids which then are cleaved by enzyme systems present in the potato into *cis*-3-nonenal and *cis*-3, *cis*-6-nonadienal. Tomato enzymes, even though the 9-hydroperoxy isomer is present in larger amounts than the 13-hydroperoxy isomer, cleave only the 13-isomer. Cucumber enzymes cleave both the 9- and 13-hydroperoxy isomers. Matthew and Galliard[23] recently showed that cell-free extracts of bean leaves contain enzymes which cleave both 9- and 13-hydroperoxides of linoleic acid with the formation of C_9 and C_6 aldehydes. Hatanaka *et al.*[24] studied the distribution of an enzyme system producing *n*-hexanal and *cis*-3-hexenal in a large number of plants. They found that green leaves contained a higher activity of this enzyme system than edible green leaves and fruits. Seasonal variation of activity was also observed.

The above-mentioned reactions are incorporated into Fig. 1, which also shows that the primarily formed aroma compounds can undergo further reactions such as *cis-trans* isomerisation. It has been suggested that there are particular enzymes in tomato capable of such transfer. Even the presence of double bond-reducing enzyme systems has been proposed to exist in tomato. However, better known is the conversion of aldehydes into alcohols by the action of alcohol dehydrogenase and NADH. Recently, Yamashita *et al.*[25] showed that intact strawberry can synthesize a number of carboxylic esters from volatile aliphatic alcohols and acids added to the gas phase around the strawberry. Many of these alcohols can be regarded as products of lipid oxidation in plant material. This observation, together with the identification of cis-3-hexen-1-ylacetate in parsley leaves by Free-man et al.,[26] provides support for the hypothesis that a number of carboxylic esters have their origin in lipid oxidation. The different conversions shown in the figure have recently been reviewed by Eriksson[27].

REFERENCES

1. Murray, K. E., Shipton, J., Whitfield, F. B., and Lark, J. H., *J. Sci. Food Agr.*, **27**, 1093 (1976).
2. Kochar, S. P. and Meara, M. L., BFMIRA, Scientific and Technical Surveys No. 87 (1975).
3. Eriksson, C. E., *J. Agr. Food Chem.*, **23**, 126 (1975).
4. Galliard, T. and Mercer, E. I., (ed.), *Recent Advances in the Chemistry and Biochemistry of Plant Lipids*, Academic Press (1975).
5. Ford, A. L., Park, R. J., and Ratcliff, D., *J. Food Sci.*, **41**, 94 (1976).
6. McGill, A. S., Hardy, R., Burt, J. R., and Gunstone, F. D., *J. Sci. Food Agr.*, **25**, 1477 (1974).
7. Swoboda, P. A. T. and Peers, K. E., *J. Sci. Food Agr.*, **28**, 1010 (1977).
8. Veldink, G. A., Vliegenthart J. F. G., and Boldingh, J., *Progr. Chem. Fats Other Lipids*, **15**, 1649 (1970).
9. Fischer, K.-H. and Grosch, W., *Z. Lebensm. Unters.-Forsch.*, **165**, 137 (1977).
10. Eriksson, C. E., *J. Dairy Sci.*, **53**, 1649 (1970).
11. Gregory, J. F., Babish, J. G., and Shipe, W. F., *J. Dairy Sci.*, **59**, 364 (1977).
12. Allen, J. C. and Humphries, C., *J. Dairy Res.*, **44**, 495 (1977).
13. Chan, H. W.-S., Newby, V. K., and Levett, G., *J. C. S. Chem. Commun.*, **82**, 1978.
14. Bors, W., Saran, M., Lengfelder, E., Spöttl, R., and Michel, C., *Current Topics in Radiation Research Quarterly*, **9**, 247 (1974).
15. Kellogg, E. W. and Fridovich, I., *J. Biol. Chem.*, **250**, 8812 (1975).
16. Aurand, L. W., Boone, N. H., and Giddings, G. G., *J. Dairy Sci.*, **60**, 363 (1977).
17. Thomas, M. J., Mehl, K. S., and Pryor, W. A., *Biochem. Biophys. Res. Commun.*, **83**, 927 (1978).
18. Chan, H. W.-S., *J. Am. Oil Chem. Soc.*, **54**, 100 (1977).
19. Chan, H. W.-S., Levett, G., and Griffiths, N. M., *J. Sci. Food Agr.*, **28**, 339 (1977).
20. Gardner, H. W., Kleiman, R., and Weisleder, D., *Lipids*, **9**, 696 (1974).
21. Hamberg, M., *Lipids*, **10**, 87 (1975).
22. Galliard, T., Proc. Seminar on Metabolism and Functions of Lipids in Higher Plants, Cooperative USA-Japan Science Porgram, Tokyo, Sept. 1976.
23. Matthew, J. A. and Galliard, T., *Phytochemistry*, **17**, 1043 (1978).

24. Hatanaka, A., Sekiya, J., and Kajiwara, T., *Phytochemistry*, **17**, 869 (1978).
25. Yamashita, I., Nemoto, Y., and Yoshikawa, S., *Agr. Biol. Chem.*, **39**, 2303 (1975).
26. Freeman, G. G., Whenkam, R. J., Self, R., and Eagles, J., *J. Sci. Food Agr.*, **26**, 465 (1975).
27. Eriksson, C. E., Proc. 2nd Weurman Flavour Symp., Norwich, UK, April 2–6, 1978, Applied Science Publications, Ltd., U.K. (in press).

3. Taste and Chemical Structure

3.1 Structural Basis of Taste Substances

R. S. Shallenberger*

During the past decade there have been remarkable developments in our knowledge of the interrelation between structure and taste activity. Many of the taste-activity relationships that have evolved are centered about the unidimensional AH,B theory of sweet taste introduced by myself and T. E. Acree[1] in 1967 and expanded by Kier[2] in 1972 to include a third component.

The third component now seems to be necessary for intense sweetness or whenever AH,B needs to be "activated" through a hydrophobic interaction[3]. It is not, however, prerequisite for sweet taste whereas the AH,B unit is prerequisite.

Perhaps the most general approach to the relation between structure and taste quality is to consider the structural dimensions required of compounds needed to elicit the sensation. These are summarized in Table 1.

The sour taste is primarily a function of the hydrogen ion. Any substance capable of dissociation to yield a proton to the solution will, therefore, taste sour. As shown in the table, the sour taste phenomenon is dimensionless.

The salt taste can be defined as the sensory response to solutions of sodium chloride above the detection threshold. At the identification threshold it appears to be related to the simultaneous action of the sodium and the chlorine ions. It is therefore, unidimensional. It is interesting to find that, at about the detection threshold, solutions of sodium and potassium chloride are distinctly but weakly sweet. For this reason the dimensionality of the salt and the sweet tastes in the table have been grouped together. It

* New York State Agricultural Experiment Station, Cornell University, Geneva, NY 14456, USA

TABLE 1. The general chemical nature and dimensionality of taste substances

Chemical parameters	Unit taste sensation	Dimensionality	General chemical unit
One	Sour	0	H^+
Two	Salty	1	Na^+ Cl^-
	Sweet	1	AH,B
Three	Very sweet	2	AH,B,γ

is possible that the hydrated sodium cation and the hydrated chlorine anion constitute the structural requirement for sweetness as individual AH and B units respectively.

Since AH and B are prerequisite for sweetness, whether they occur alone or are contained within the structure of a single compound, it is clear that this basic quality attribute is unidimensional only. It is also clear that when AH and B are contained within the structure of a single compound, sweetness is enhanced above and beyond the action of individual moieties, probably because of a relatively rigid AH proton to B orbital distance of about 3 Angstrom units. This is the distance parameter of an AH,B unit that is presumably common to all compounds that taste sweet, and includes the sugars, amino acids, chloroform, saccharine and the cyclamates and so on.

Based on the finding that sugar sweetness is inversely proportionate to the ability of certain sugar hydroxyl groups to intramolecularly hydrogen bond, we[1] proposed that at the level of the initial set of events responsible for sweetness, the initial chemistry of sweetness must be a concerted intermolecular hydrogen bonding reaction between AH,B of the sweet compound and a sterically commensurate AH,B unit at the receptor site.

With this latter deduction we created, from the structural viewpoint, a chiral (handedness) recognition problem of the first magnitude. However, its resolution[3] seems to contribute greatly to our understanding of the relation between structure and taste, and suggests that perhaps we are on the right track at least some of the time. Its resolution also shows that several times during the course of our studies, we apparently came to the correct conclusions using premises that were only partly correct.

The chiral recognition problem is simply that the enantiomeric amino acids are capable of eliciting different tastes. The D-series are usually sweet whereas the L-series are usually tasteless or bitter. On the other hand, the enantiomeric sugars, the D-and the L-sugars, are equally sweet. How can such a chiral anomaly be resolved when the dimensionality of sweet taste is essentially unidimensional for the basic quality attribute, and at best as shown in the table, two dimensional for intense sweetness?

One complicating characteristic of chirality is that in the final analysis, there is no absolute handedness distinction possible unless the dimension-ality of the system is rigidly defined. Any handedness distinction that is made within the confines of a given dimension is nonexistent in the next highest dimensional realm. In one dimension, for example, the line seg-ment A---B is the nonsuperposable mirror image structure of the enantio-meric line segment B---A. In two dimensions, however, the chiral distinction is lost because the structures possess a 2-fold axis of symmetry, and are therefore superposable. By the same token, the simplest chiral structure in two dimensions is the scalene triangle. A triangle ABC possessing three unequal sides, being one-sided in two dimensions, is not superposable upon its mirror image structure ACB. Yet, such a chiral specification is nonexistent in Euclidean space because rotation in space leads to superposability and therefore equivalency.

I need to emphasize strongly that the Kier tripartite structure for intense sweetness is the scalene triangular structure and it is present in the sugars as shown below.

γ

5.25Å

3.14Å

AH   3Å   B

For the sugars we indicate Kier's third site as γ to indicate a hydrophobic function and a lipophilic[4] property. The diagram is possible for the sugars because it is now known, through the work of Birch[5] and others in En-gland, that OH-4 and the oxygen atoms of OH-3 is the primary AH,B unit

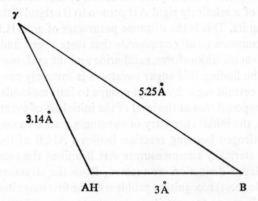

for sweet taste in the aldohexoses. Furthermore, the proton of OH-4 is "activated" by virtue of the "Lemieux effect" as shown below.

The Lemieux effect states[6] that, in a relatively nonpolar environment, the C-6 OH group will hydrogen bond intramolecularly and activate the proton donating capacity of OH-4, the very group identified as AH in the aldohexose structure. The tripartite structure for the sweet unit of these sugars is shown superposed on glucose in the next drawing.

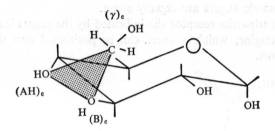

For β-D-fructopyranose, the tripartite saporous unit is

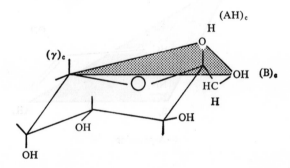

The primary AH and B moieties for fructopyranose were also made by the Birch School, and the tripartite saporous unit for fructose is identical to that of glucose, but only in its geometry.

It is clear, therefore, that for even a relatively weak sweet taste, as shown

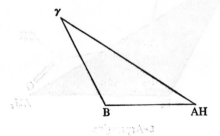

by the sugars, there is a potential tripartite saporous unit and it must describe the sterically commensurate tripartite receptor site.

That receptor site is shown below.

It is important to note that while the tripartite receptor site for sweetness is two-dimensionally chiral, it is diastereoisomeric with the sweet unit of the sugars, and not enantiomeric with that unit.

We can now return to, and explain the chiral anomaly posed by the fact that the D-and L-amino acids are sweet and not sweet respectively while the enantiomeric sugars are equally sweet.

Using the tripartite receptor site indicated by the sugars it can be seen that D-asparagine, which is sweet, can be positioned over the receptor site as follows.

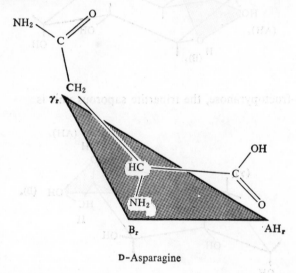

D-Asparagine

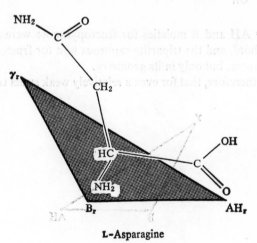

L-Asparagine

However, as shown next, L-asparagine, which is tasteless, cannot be positioned over the receptor site to make a tripartite fit. Apparently, the tripartite fit for these amino acids is needed to "activate" AH and B.

Turning to the D-and L-sugars, it was deduced that the saporous unit for either a D-or an L-sugar could be equally positioned over the same receptor site keeping in mind that the receptor is chiral in two dimensions while the D- and the L-sugars are chiral in three dimensions. This finding is shown below.

β-D-Glucose β-L-Glucose

The important point to be made, however, is that the enantiomeric sugars are equally sweet because the chirality of their two-dimensional tripartite saporous unit is lost in their three dimensional structure, but this happens because the sugars possess multiple chirality and not because their chirality is lost in an even higher dimension.

It would now seem that the very fact that the chiral anomaly posed by the enantiomeric amino acids and sugars can be resolved by the application of symmetry (chiral) principles, encourages us to believe that the identification of the structural nature of the sweet unit contained in sweet substances, and also the structural nature of the receptor site, is approximately correct.

REFERENCES

1. Shallenberger, R. S., and Acree, T. E., Molecular theory of sweet taste, *Nature* (London), **216**, 480–482 (1967).
2. Kier, L. B., A molecular theory of sweet taste, *J. Pharm. Sci.*, **61**, 1394–1397 (1972).

3. Shallenberger, R. S., Chemical clues to the perception of sweetness, *In Sensory Properties of Foods* (G. G. Birch *et al.*, eds.), p. 91, Applied Science Publishers, Ltd., London, (1977).
4. Shallenberger, R. S., and Lindley, M. G., A lipophilic-hydrophobic attribute and component in the stereochemistry of sweetness, *Food Chem.*, **2**, 145–153 (1977).
5. Birch, G. G., Structural relationships of sugars to taste, *Critical Rev. Food Sci.*, **8** (1), 57–95 (1976).
6. Shallenberger R. S., Intrinsic chemistry of fructose, *J. Pure and Appl. Chem.*, **50**, 1409–1420. (1978)

3.2 Chemical Structure and Sweetness of Sugars

G.G. Birch*

3.2.1 INTRODUCTION

Sugars appear to be the most convenient class of compounds available for the study of sweet taste in relation to chemical structure. The simplicity of their cyclic structures gives rise to a degree of certainty about their absolute stereochemistry and the precise location of their sweet-eliciting functions in space. Additionally they are optically active molecules and indeed exhibit multiple chirality. These properties make them eminently suitable as models and candidates for chemical modification in studying the sweet response (Birch, 1976, 1977).

Because of their marked hydrogen-bonding properties sugars are virtually devoid of vapour pressure. This means that they possess no odours or flavours in the strict sense and even after chemical modification their taste may be studied without olfactory complication. The sweetness of sugars differs in type from the sweetness of other molecules, such as amino acids and artificial sweetness, and the sugar type seems to be preferred. Relative sweetness is always determined in comparison to sucrose, by trained taste-panellists. However, the intensity of response may be distorted by the temporal qualities of the sweetener and sugars, with their short impact time and low persistence, differ markedly from newer types of sweetener in this respect.

Generally sugars have a good image with regard to toxicity which is an important asset in any extensive programme of tasting in relation to chemical structure. The only disadvantage of sugars in relation to other classes of compound is their rather low relative sweetness.

3.2.2 SELECTION OF MODEL SUGARS FOR STUDY

Much of the early structure/taste work was done with free reducing sugars such as glucose and fructose in the form in which they normally exist in foods. As such they are unsuitable for detailed study of structure/

* *National College of Food Technology, University of Reading, St. George's Avenue, Weybridge, Surrey KT13 ODE, England*

activity relationships because they isomerise rapidly into mixtures of components as soon as they dissolve in saliva. There is thus no certainty about the precise isomeric species responsible for eliciting sweetness if free sugars are used as models.

The ideal model for gustatory studies in relation to chemical structure would be the simplest possible non-reducing, conformationally stable, sweet and easily modifiable sugar. There is only one sugar which meets all these requirements and this is α,α-trehalose or mushroom sugar (Birch, 1963) shown in Fig.1. Some hundreds of simple derivatives of this unique

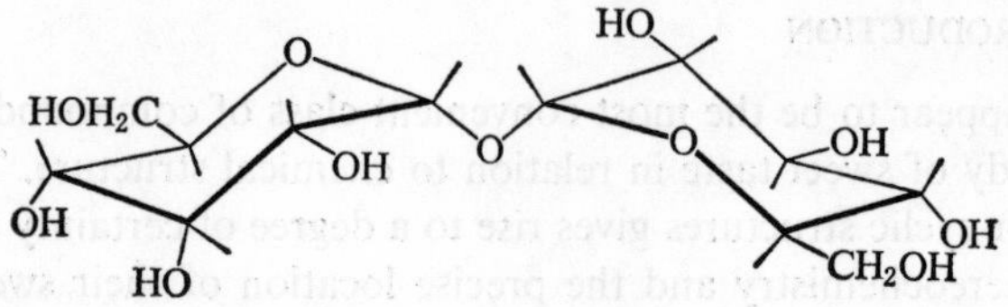

FIG. 1. α, α-Trehalose (mushroom sugar).

sugar have now been prepared and compared with those of its analogue, methyl α-D-glucopyranoside. Since every glucose residue in these derivatives is probably in the preferred $^4C_1$ conformation we can be reasonably certain about the precise location of each hydroxyl substituent in space.

3.2.3 Theory of Sweetness

The only comprehensive theory of seeetness which has so far been adopted for serious study is that of R.S. Shallenberger who suggested that hydrogen bonding might explain all aspects of the peripheral phenomenon. He imagined two electronegative atoms A and B in suitable geometric proximity, A containing an acidic proton and therefore acting as an acid function and B consequently acting as a base. The AH,B system of a sweetener can hydrogen bond to a similar AH,B system on the taste receptor as shown in Fig.2. to give a doubly hydrogen-bonded complex, the strength of which depends (Shallenberger & Acree, 1967) on the molecular archi-

FIG. 2. Shallenberger and Acree's (1967) AH,B theory.

tecture of the AH,B system which in turn governs the intensity of the sweet response. This elegant hypothesis could explain the sweetness of sugars, proteins, peptides and artificial sweeteners and has been invoked by taste chemists for about fifteen years to explain their gustatory structure/activity relationships.

When models such as α,α-trehalose and methyl α-D-glucopyranoside are used to search for AH,B systems in sugars one α-glycol group (i.e. the 3,4 α-glycol group) appears to be involved with sweetness and thus to fulfill the AH,B role. Such information becomes available only after some hundreds of taste studies in structurally related derivatives and in the course of these studies one is struck by the consistent taste properties which modified sugars exhibit. Some are sweet, some are bitter and some are bitter/sweet. It is rare and indeed almost impossible to find either tastelessness or other types of taste.

The most unequivocal results so far obtained are those of the deoxy sugars (Birch and Lee, 1974) which are prepared by selectively removing oxygen atoms one by one or two by two stepwise around the sugar ring. This process defines active hydroxyl groups and allows the identification of the AH,B system..

It is interesting that the α-glycol group at the 3,4–positions of glucopyranoside structures is at the least chemically reactive and most undisturbed area of the molecules and yet constitutes the AH,B system for sweetness. Some deoxy sugars are bitter or bitter/sweet and it appears that the very features of the molecules furthest removed from the sweet AH,B system (i.e. the area of the molecule surrounding the anomeric centre) are those which are involved in the bitter response. This finding has been extended to several other types of modified sugar and, in the case of the bitter/sweet glycoside methyl α-D-mannopyranoside (Fig.3) there is now good reason to believe that the molecule may align itself (Birch and Mylvaganam, 1976)

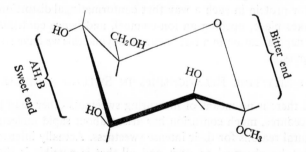

Fɪɢ. 3. Polarisation of methyl-α-D-mannopyranoside molecule on taste receptor.

in such a way that it spans both sweet and bitter receptors simultaneously. This of course conflicts with some accepted notions of discreet basic tastes, but attempts to refute the finding (McBurney and Gent, 1978) by alternative psychophysical methodology have been inappropriate (Birch, 1978).

Overall, a good deal of molecular evidence now exists to support Shallenberger's sweetness hypothesis and by proceeding in this methodical way with conformationally defined model structures we may hope to unfold the mysteries of the hypothetical receptor site itself.

3.2.4 THE NATURE OF THE SWEET RECEPTOR

Although some workers (Horowitz and Gentili 1971) have conjectured about the receptor in animated corporeal form, others (Khan, 1978) have preferred to consider it as an amorphous and ill-defined entity. However, it might well be a structural component of a protein surface embedded in the phospholipid environment of the taste cell membrane. Beets (1978) prefers the 'general concept' of a chemoreceptor as an entity only more or less fitted to interact with a stimulus molecule. A particular taste response then only arises as the integral of many different interactions eventually being decodified in the taste centre of the brain. Since the lipophilic environment of the receptor must influence the hydrogen bonding potential of sugar molecules, it should probably be taken into account when the alignment of the molecule occurs at the receptor. Somehow the sugar molecule transposes from an aqueous (hydrophilic) environment to a lipophilic environment before it is able to elicit a taste response.

It is a natural aspiration of taste chemists that their studies should lead to a better understanding of the nature of the receptor site. However, very little understanding of the nature of the taste receptor has yet emerged and it is possible that our concept of the chemoreceptive events involved when sweet molecules interact with receptors is inadequate for any progress to be made. It seems logical that the stimulus molecule should align itself on the receptor protein in such a way that conformational distortion of the protein takes place, opening an ion-channel, and hence contributing an elemental depolarisation in a taste neuron. Beyond this we have still made little progress.

3.2.5 INTENSITY/TIME RELATIONSHIPS IN SWEETNESS RESEARCH

Because there is no means of measuring sweetness other than by taste panel procedures, much confusion has arisen about sapid molecules and the structural reasons for their intense sweetness. Actually intense sweetness cannot be observed as such and all that is possible is that comparable sweetness (to normal sucrose concentrations) is experienced when a suitably intense sweetener such as thaumatin is diluted some hundreds of thousand times. In other words extreme dilutions of intense sweeteners are efficient in eliciting the sweet response and are therefore probably bound efficiently at or near to the receptor. There is thus no need to suppose that an intense protein sweetener opens ion channels any better than say a sugar. Each type of sweetener may contain similarly effective AH,B systems for this. They differ only in the tripartite nature of their sweet pharmacophores, the third site of the intense sweeteners facilitating the approach of the stimulus molecule (Birch, Latymer and Hollaway, 1978) to ionophor trigger mechanism. The approach of the sweet molecule might be in the form of a queue which accounts for the persistence of taste as well as onset time and these temporal qualities affect the overall profile of a sweetener. No new intense sweetener is yet close enough to sugars in its taste profile to be completely acceptable in food science and technology as a replacement. There is thus currently much interest in taste modification using tasteless adjuncts to alter time/intensity relationships of sweeteners. Such work is more likely to succeed if the separate mechanisms accounting for intensity and persistence are fully understood.

3.2.6 CONCLUSIONS

The past fifteen years has seen a methodical chemical structural approach to the understanding of sweetness and sweeteners and a step by step unfolding of the structural features which are necessary for sweet-eliciting molecules. Sugars have proved invaluable models for this study despite their low relative sweetness and modern research has led to the conclusion that stimulus molecules approach the receptor in an ordered, aligned manner. The key to understand this more fully seems to lie in the peculiar time/intensity properties exhibited by each sweet structure and thus lead to a sound basis for the design of safe, nutritionally useful sweet molecules for the future.

REFERENCES

1. Beets, M. G. J., Structure Activity Relationships in Human Chemoreception, Applied Science. London, (1978).
2. Birch, G. G., Interaction of bitter/sweet sugars with receptor sites, *Chemical Senses and Flavour*, **3**, 247–248 (1978).
3. Birch, G. G., Structural relationships to taste in the sugar, *Crit. Rev. Food Sci. Nutr.*, **8**, 57–95 (1976).
4. Birch, G. G., Taste properties of sugar molecule. In: "Olfaction and Taste. VI", (eds. J. Le Magnen and P. MacLeod). IRL. London, (1977).

5. Birch, G. G., Trehaloses, *Advan. Carbohydrate Chem.*, **18**, 201–225 (1963).

6. Birch, G. G., Latymer, Z. and Hollaway, M. J., An orderly queue hypothesis in sugar taste chemoreception, *IRCS Med. Sci.*, **6**, 214 (1978).

7. Birch, G. G. and Lee, C. K., Sensory properties of deoxy sugars, *J. Food Sci.*, **39**, 947–949 (1974).

8. Birch, G. G. and Mylvaganam, A. R., Evidence for the proximity of sweet and bitter receptor sites, *Nature*, **260**, 362–364 (1976).

9. Horowitz, R. M. and Gentili, B., Dihydrochalcone sweeteners. In: "Sweetness and Sweeteners". (eds. G. G. Birch, L. F. Green and C. B. Coulson). Applied Science. London, (1971).

10. Khan, R., Advances in sucrochemistry. In: "Sugar Science and Technology". (eds. G. G. Birch and K. J. Parker). Applied Science, London, (1978).

11. McBurney, D. H. and Gent, J. F., Taste of methyl- -D-mannopyranoside: Effects of cross adaptation and Gymnema sylvestre, *Chemical Senses and Flavour*, 3 45–50 (1978).

12. Shallenberger, R. S. and Acree, T. E., Molecular theory of sweet taste, *Nature*, **216**, 480–482 (1967).

3.3 Physiological Functions of Sweeteners

Morley R. Kare*

A robin will avidly consume ripe strawberries. What qualities attract the bird to these berries? Is it the sweetness, the texture, the acidity, or the color?

We know that birds have color vision, are uniquely tolerant of acid pH, and are extremely sensitive to texture. However, the robin, as with many avian species, does not respond to solutions of the common simple sugars. Nevertheless, the common belief persists that birds are attracted to fruit by the sweetness. Perhaps this is because it is generally assumed that all life exists in a common sensory world—ours.

In human nutrition there are also misconceptions on the role of sensory qualities of food. It is surprising that the physiological functions of the most widely used flavoring agent, sugar, has experienced so little investigation.

Many species of fish, birds, and even some mammals, e.g. tigers, domestic cats, hedgehogs, and sea lions, avoid or at least do not avidly consume tha common sugars. This failure to respond to the taste of carbohydrates, the commonest sources of energy in the environment, is startling.

Man displays a sweet tooth even before birth. The seven month fetus will respond to sweet stimulation introduced into the amniotic fluid. Histological studies indicate that taste buds appear between the second and third fetal month.

In a series of extensive studies[1,2], human infants, one to three days of age, have been observed to respond to sugar solutions. The range of concentrations that was effective was similar to that of adult humans. Further, the newborn differentiated between sugars (sucrose, fructose, glucose, and lactose) as well as between concentrations of the sugar solution offered. It is clear that the drive for sweet in man is an innate sense.

Studies have indicated that the adolescent prefers a higher concentration of sucrose solution than does an adult[3]. Almost 50 % of the adolescents tested preferred a 0.6 M sucrose, the adults preference was divided almost equally between the four concentrations ranging from 0.075 M to

---

* *Monell Chemical Senses Center and University of Pennsylvania, Philadelphia, PA, USA*

373

0.6 M. There are substantial individual differences in response to sugar, which permits one to conclude that the human response to sweets is not homogeneous.

In our laboratory we conducted a study to compare the taste sensitivities and preferences of control (40–45 years), mature (65–70) and aged (80–85) individuals. Subjects in reasonably good health were selected, and an experiment suited to the aged was designed. For example, a generous amount of time was allowed for the subjects to respond and the differences in concentration of taste ingredients among tested choices was large (e.g. plus or minus 20 % sucrose in chocolate). In the precise testing for detection threshold, there were small declines in sensitivity; however, preference behavior for sweet was not significantly different in the aged as compared to the controls.

Studies with cadavers[4] suggest that there is approximately an eighty percent reduction in the numbers of functioning taste buds by the age of eighty years. It should be noted that taste cells are constantly being replaced and have a life expectancy of about ten days.

Man's response to sweet is sufficiently important to be present at birth and to be maintained relatively unimpaired into old age. The question arises as to what physiological functions, if any, does our perception of sweet serve?

Taste does serve in discriminating between food choices. It is conceivable that the sweet taste encouraged early man to obtain vitamins, e.g. from ripe fruit, or the bitter taste helped him to avoid poisons, e.g. alkaloids. However, these senses are not totally reliable guides for man or animals, particularly when nutrients are out of their natural context. The toxic substance lead acetate is sweet to humans, and many preferred foods, e.g. chocolate and nuts, are bitter.

The role of taste and other sensory qualities of food in the nutritional maintenance of the body has received almost no systematic investigation, and is usually dismissed as trivial. The digestive system normally accepts nutrients to maintain body homeostasis: input of nutrients must equal output of nutrients plus expended energy. The maintenance of this balance is largely attributed to post-absorptive phenomena.

The facts indicate something quite different. From the outset the oral cavity determines what will enter the digestive system. It meters and monitors the intake, and apparently is involved in many aspects of digestion.

Attempts have been made to increase the intake of cereal based diets to fill the nutritional needs of children[5]. A variety of preferred flavors failed to increase intake significantly. Only sucrose, added to a bland porridge of corn, soy flour, and milk, increased intake (by 25 %). On the other hand the sensitivity of the obese to sucrose is no different than that of persons of normal weight, and in fact their preference is for lower concentrations of this sugar.

Taste can influence the length of time food is chewed, as well as the pattern of swallowing. Strong taste stimuli can slow gastric contractions and enhance intestinal motility.

At the first step in feeding, at the peripheral level, taste initiates early and anticipatory metabolic modifications[6]. The respiratory quotient (RQ) is 0.7 during fasting and approaches 1.0 after feeding. This is attributed to the metabolic needs after the absorption of nutrients. However, precise observation indicates that the time of the rise in the RQ coincides with oral stimulation. Apparently the preparation of the digestive tract for the reception of food may be initiated in part by taste. The nervous system pathways responsible for these reflexes are not well characterized, but probably involve gustatory-vagal interactions.

Orally administered glucose can trigger an immediate rise in circulating levels of immunoreactive insulin (IRI). This initial response may be characterized by a second peak after a few moments. A second phase of the rise in circulating IRI occurs after about 20 minutes, paralleling the hyperglycemia[7]. With gastric feeding or intravenous administration there is no early rise in circulating insulin; only the subsequent rise in response to the elevated circulating blood glucose[8].

The nature of a taste stimulus substantially influenced the volume and protein content of exocrine pancreatic secretion obtained from dogs with gastric and intestinal fistulas[9]. An appealing sucrose solution increased the output as compared to an offensive quinine mixture. Contrary to the effects of oral stimulation recent work[10] has demonstrated that gastrically administered taste mixtures, regardless of sensory quality, did not alter pancreatic flow.

Summarizing, oral stimulation (i.e. taste) can modify chewing, swallowing, activity along the gut, preparing the tract for metabolism (RQ), metabolic hormone release, and exocrine pancreatic function. Clinical observations suggest that these effects serve a relevant role in nutritional maintenance. The question as to whether these taste functions specifically affect food utilization is being pursued.

In the healthy young animal digestive enzymes are present in excess, so that a taste related increase in output is redundant. Under normal conditions the body's mechanisms which control food digestion can more than cope with taste problems or enzyme needs that they might encounter.

A series of randomly selected aversive stimuli, changed daily, was added to the food of young rats[11]. This resulted in a substantial drop in the efficiency of food utilization. Rats fed diets containing a combination of aversive taste stimuli and soybean trypsin inhibitors suffered an additional inhibition of growth efficiency.

It is apparent that the sensory stimulation produced by orally consumed sugar can affect volume of food intake where it is depressed, and under some circumstances of sub-optimal functioning influence the effective use of nutrients.

It was not very long ago that most people's main concern about food was for an adequate supply. Nutrition and more recently toxicity have captured general attention.

For a variety of reasons highly appealing food, including sugar, is commonly linked to poor nutrition. No doubt on occasion the two can be associated. In the instances where flavor has been purposely removed from a food product, e.g. sugar from baby food, no effort was made to asses the impact of reduced sensory stimulation on digestion.

The results reported indicate that oral stimulation could, under some circumstances, contribute significantly to digestion and metabolism. This would be particularly true in the young, old, or infirm where activity of the gut, metabolic hormones, or exocrine products of the pancreas are limited.

While nutrient content and toxicity are obviously important, preliminary physiological evidence suggests that it could be a grave error to focus on these parameters and ignore the palatability of food.

Taste can be a vehicle for good nutrition as easily as it can be for bad. At a modest expense to an optimum diet, and with a minimum hazard, the scientific evidence warrants devoting some of our energy to adding to the quality of life.

REFERENCES

1. Desor, J., Maller, O., and Turner, R., Taste in Acceptance of Sugars by Human Infants, *J. Comp. Physiol. Psychol.*, **84**, 496–501 (1973).
2. Maller, O., and Desor, J., Effect of Taste on Ingestion by Human Newborns, in Bosma, H. (ed): *Fourth Symposium on Oral Sensation and Perception*, Washington, U. S. Govt. Printing Office, 1974.
3. Desor, J., Greene, L. S., and Maller, O., Preferences for Sweet and Salty in 9-to 15-Year-Old and Adult Humans, *Science*, **190**, 686–687, (1975).
4. Arey, L. B., Tremaine, M. J., and Monzingo, F. L., The Numerical and Topographical Relations of Taste Buds to Human Circumvallate Papillae Throughout the Lifespan, *Anat. Record*, **64**, 9, (1935).

5. Grewal, T., Gopaldas, T., Hartenberger, P., Ramakushnan, I., and Rama-chndran, G., Influence of Sugar and Flavor on the acceptability of Instant CSM: Trials on Young Children from an Urban Orphanage, *J. Food Sci. Technol.*, **10**, 149–152, (1973).

6. Nicolaidis, S., Early Systematic Responses to Orogastric Stimulation in the Regulation of Food and Water Balance: Functional and Electrophysiological Data, in *Neural Regulation of Food and Water Intake, Ann. N. Y. Acad. Sci.*, **157**, 1176–1203, (1969).

7. Fischer, U., Hommel, H., Ziegler, M., and Lutzi, E., The Mechanism of Insulin Secretion after Oral Glucose Administration, *Diabetologia*, **8**, 385–390, (1972).

8. Steffens, A. B., Influence of the Oral Cavity on Insulin Release in the Rat, *Am. J. Physiol.*, **230**, 1411–1415, (1976).

9. Behrman, H. R., and Kare, M. R., Canine Pancreatic Secretion in Response to Acceptable and Aversive Taste Stimuli, *Proc. Soc. Exp. Biol. Med.*, **129**, 343–346, (1968).

10. Naim, M., Kare, M. R., and Merrit, A. Med., Effects of Oral Stimulation on the Cephalic Phase of Pancreatic Exocrine Secretion in Dogs, *Physiol. Behav.*, **20**, 563–570 (1978).

11. Naim, M., and Kare, M. R., Taste Stimula and Pancreatic Function, in *The Chemical Senses and Nutrition*, pp. 145–162. Eds. M. R. Kare and O. Maller, Academic Press, New York, (1977).

3.4 Taste-Giving Peptides

Yasuo Ariyoshi*

It is known that the chemical structures of sweet-tasting compounds vary widely. In order to establish a structure-taste relationship, a large number of compounds have been tested, and several molecular theories of sweet taste have been proposed by different groups. At present, the phenomenon of sweet taste seems best explained by the tripartite functioning of the postulated AH, B (proton donor-acceptor) system and hydrophobic site X.[1-4] Space-filling properties are also important as well as the charge properties. The hydrophile-hydrophobe balance in a molecule seems to be another important factor.

After the finding of a sweet taste in L-Asp-L-Phe-OMe (aspartame) by Mazur et al.[5], a number of aspartyl dipeptide esters were synthesized by several groups in order to deduce structure-taste relationships. In the case of peptides, the configuration and the conformation of the molecule are important in connection with the space-filling properties. The preferred conformations of amino acids can be shown by application of the extended Hückel theory calculation. However, projection of reasonable conformations for di- and tripeptide molecules is not easily accomplished.

In an attempt to find a convenient method for predicting the sweet-tasting property of new peptides and, in particular, to elucidate more definite structure-taste relationships for aspartyl dipeptide esters, we previously applied the Fischer projection technique in drawing sweet molecules[4,6].

The sweet-tasting property of aspartyl dipeptide esters has been successfully explained on the basis of the general structures shown in Fig. 1.[4,6] A peptide will taste sweet when it takes the formula (1a), but not when it takes the formula (1b), where R_2 is larger than R_1. R_1 is a small hydrophobic side chain with a chain length of 1–4 atoms, and R_2 is a larger hydrophobic side chain with a chain length of 3–6 atoms. R_1 in formula (1a) serves as the hydrophobic binding site, X. In the formula (1a), when R_1 and R_2 are sufficiently dissimilar in size, the sweetness potency will be intense, whereas when R_1 and R_2 are of similar size, the potency will be

* Central Research Laboratories, Ajinomoto Co., Inc., Suzuki-cho, Kawasaki-ku, Kawasaki 210, Japan

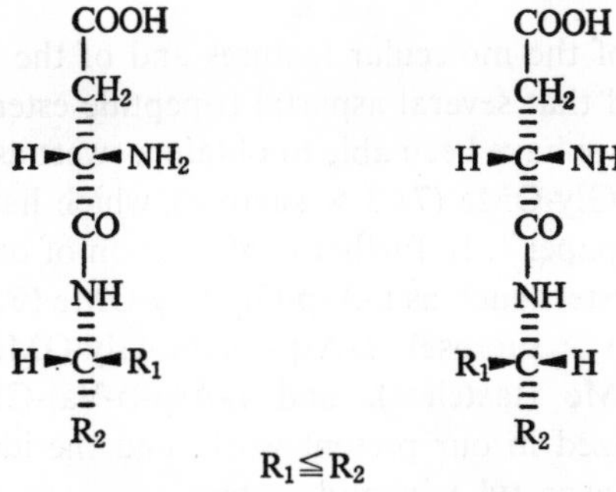

COOH
|
CH₂
‖
H►C◄NH₂
‖
CO
|
NH
‖
H►C◄R₁
‖
R₂

(1a)
Sweet

COOH
|
CH₂
‖
H►C◄NH₂
‖
CO
|
NH
‖
R₁►C◄H
‖
R₂

R₁≦R₂

(1b)
Not sweet

R₁ = Small hydrophobic side chain (chain length of 1–4 atoms)
R₂ = Larger hydrophobic side chain (chain length of 3–6 atoms)

FIG. 1. General structure for sweet peptides.[4]

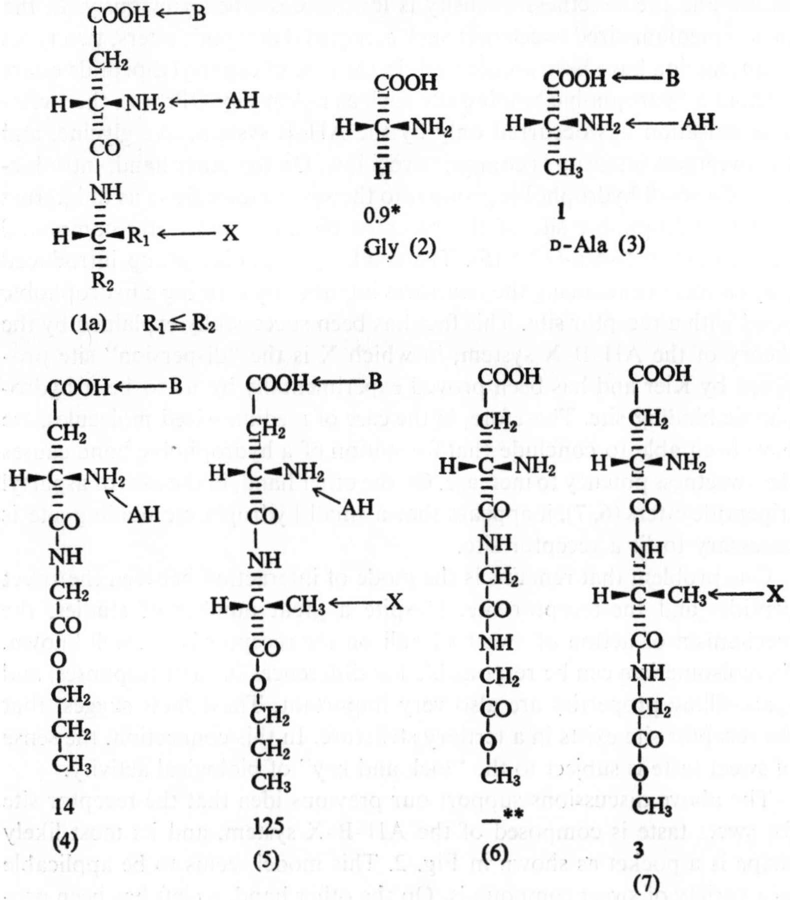

COOH ◄—B
|
CH₂
‖
H►C◄NH₂ ◄——AH
‖
CO
|
NH
‖
H►C◄R₁ ◄——X
‖
R₂

(1a)   R₁ ≦ R₂

COOH
|
CH₂
‖
H►C◄NH₂
‖
H

0.9*

Gly (2)

COOH ◄——B
|
CH₂
‖
H►C◄NH₂ ◄——AH
‖
CH₃

1

D-Ala (3)

COOH◄—B
|
CH₂
‖
H►C◄NH₂ ◄AH
‖
CO
|
NH
|
CH₂
|
CO
|
O
|
CH₂
|
CH₂
|
CH₃

14
(4)

COOH◄—B
|
CH₂
‖
H►C◄NH₂ ◄AH
‖
CO
|
NH
‖
H►C◄CH₃ ◄—X
‖
CO
|
O
|
CH₂
|
CH₂
|
CH₃

125
(5)

COOH
|
CH₂
‖
H►C◄NH₂
‖
CO
|
NH
|
CH₂
|
CO
|
NH
|
CH₂
|
CO
|
O
|
CH₃

—**
(6)

COOH
|
CH₂
‖
H►C◄NH₂
‖
CO
|
NH
‖
H►C◄CH₃ ◄—X
‖
CO
|
NH
|
CH₂
|
CO
|
O
|
CH₃

3
(7)

* Numbers indicate the sweetness potency of the compound as a multiple of sucrose.
** Tasteless.

weak. Further examinations of the molecular features and of the model of the receptor have suggested that several aspartyl tripeptide esters may also taste sweet. As expected, we have been able to obtain a sweet aspartyl tripeptide ester, L-Asp-D-Ala-Gly-OMe (7; 3 × sucrose), which has been briefly reported in a previous paper[7]. In further confirmation of our previous idea, several tripeptide esters such as L-Asp-Gly-Gly-OMe (6; tasteless), L-Asp-D-Ala-Gly-OEt (1 × sucrose), L-Asp-D-Abu-Gly-OMe (1 × sucrose), L-Asp-D-Val-Gly-OMe (tasteless), and L-Asp-D-Val-Gly-OEt (tasteless), have been synthesized in our present work, and the idea has been successfully applied to aspartyl tripeptide esters.

In the case of small-sized sweeteners such as glycine (2) and alanine (3), the sweetness sensation occurs only by the AH–B system with an ionic nature and the sweetness intensity is low, as described previously. In the case of medium-sized sweeteners such as aspartyl dipeptide esters, two types of interaction have been considered. In the case of aspartyl dipeptide esters without a hydrophobic binding site such as L-Asp-Gly-OPr^n (4), the sweetness sensation has occurred only by the AH–B system, like glycine, and the sweetness intensity is comparatively low. On the other hand, introduction of a small hydrophobic group into the sweet molecule so as to interact with a hydrophobic site of the receptor results in a sweeter compound such as L-Asp-D-Ala-OPr^n (5). The small hydrophobic group introduced plays a role in enhancing the sweetness intensity by forming a hydrophobic bond with a receptor site. This fact has been successfully explained by the theory of the AH–B–X system, in which X is the "dispersion" site proposed by Kier and has been proved experimentally by us to be a hydrophobic binding site. Therefore, in the case of medium-sized molecules, we have been able to conclude that formation of a hydrophobic bond causes the sweetness potency to increase. On the other hand, in the case of aspartyl tripeptide esters (6, 7), it appears that a small hydrophobic binding site is necessary to fit a receptor site.

One problem that remains is the mode of interaction between the sweet peptides and the receptor site. Despite a great number of studies, the mechanism of action of sweet stimuli on the receptor is not well known. Stereoisomerism can be responsible for differences in taste responses, and space-filling properties are also very important. These facts suggest that the receptor site exists in a tertiary structure. In this connection, the sense of sweet taste is subject to the "lock and key" of biological activity.

The above discussions support our previous idea that the receptor site for sweet taste is composed of the AH–B–X system, and its most likely shape is a pocket as shown in Fig. 2. This model seems to be applicable to a variety of sweet compounds. On the other hand, a cleft has been proposed as a receptor model from NMR spectroscopic studies of aspartame

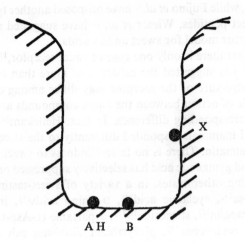

AH = Proton donor
B = Proton acceptor
X = Hydrophobic binding site
FIG. 2. Schematic representation of the receptor site for sweet peptides.[6]

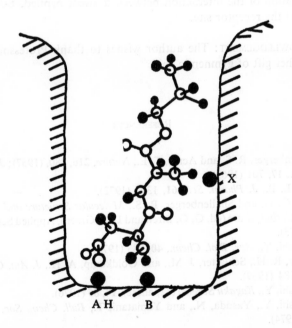

FIG. 3. Schematic representation of the interaction between L-Asp-D-Ala-Opr*
and the receptor.

by Lelj et al.[8], while Fujino et al.[9] have proposed another type of receptor model for sweet peptides. Wieser et al.[10] have suggested a hydrophobic tube as a receptor model for sweet amino acids.

It appears that there is only one type of sweet receptor,[11] although another group[12] has suggested the existence of more than one type. Since the chemical structure of the receptor may differ among different mammals, the mode of action between the sweet compounds and the receptor will show a corresponding difference. In fact, Hellekant[13] has reported that individual mammals responded differently to the sweet taste of monellin and thaumatin. There is no taste-blindness to sweet taste in so far as we know, and gymnemic acid has selectively suppressed only sweet taste, without affecting other tastes, in a variety of sweet-tasting compounds such as sucrose[14], cyclamic acid[14], D-amino acids[14], inorganic compounds[14], miraculin[15], stevioside[16,17], aspartame (L-Asp-L-Phe-OMe)[17], naringin dihydrochalcone[17], glycyrrhizin disodium salt (90%)[17], and saccharin sodium salt[17]. These findings, in conjunction with previous results, suggest that the receptor site of sweet taste may exist as a single type, and sweet sensation may occur in the same mode or in a very similar manner among a variety of sweet compounds. Fig. 3 gives a schematic representation of the interaction between a sweet peptied, L-Asp-D-Ala-OPr", and the receptor site.

ACKNOWLEDGEMENT: The author wishes to thank Professor Y. Kurihara for her gift of gymnemic acid.

REFERENCES

1. Shallenberger, R. S. and Acree, T. E., Nature, 216, 480, (1967); J. Agr. Food Chem., 17, 701 (1969).
2. Kier, L. B., J. Pharm. Sci., 61, 1394 (1972).
3. Birch G. G. and Shallenberger, R. S., Molecular Structure and Function of Food Carbohydrate (ed. G. G. Birch and L. F. Green), Applied Science Publ., 9 (1973).
4. Ariyoshi, Y., Agr. Biol. Chem., 40, 983 (1976).
5. Mazur, R. H., Schlatter, J. M., and Goldkamp, A. H., J. Am. Chem. Soc., 91, 2684 (1969).
6. Ariyoshi, Y., Kagaku Sosetsu (Japanese), 14, 85 (1976).
7. Ariyoshi, Y., Yasuda, N., and Yamatani, T., Bull. Chem. Soc. Japan, 47, 326 (1974).

8. Lelj, F., Tancredi, T., Temussi, P. A., and Toniolo, C., *J. Am. Chem. Soc.*, **98**, 6669 (1976).
9. Fujino, M., Wakimasu, M., Mano, M., Tanaka, K., Nakajima, N., and Aoki, H., *Chem. Pharm. Bull.*, **24**, 2112 (1976).
10. Wieser, H., Jugel, H., and Belitz, H.-D. *Z. Lebensm. Unters.-Forsch.*, **164**, 277 (1977).
11. Schoonhoven, L. M., *Transduction Mechanism in Chemoreception*, 189 (1973).
12. Beidler, L. M., *Symposium: Sweeteners* (ed. G. E. Inglett), The Avi Publ. Co. Inc., Westport, 10 (1974).
13. Hellekant, G., *Olfaction and Taste*, **5**, 15 (1975).
14. Kurihara, Y., *Life Sci.*, **8**, 537 (1969).
15. Diamant, H., Hellekant, G., and Zotterman,, Y., *Olfaction and Taste*, **4**, 241 (1972).
16. Kasahara, Y. and Kawamura, Y., Abstr. 9th Symp. Taste and Smell, Tokyo, 40 (1975).
17. Ariyoshi, Y., Unpublished results. (The sweet taste of these compounds was suppressed by gymnemic acid and only a bitter taste was felt.)

3.5 Taste and Structure Relations of Flavonoid Compounds

Robert. M. Horowitz* and Bruno Gentili*

Within the past twenty years it was found that flavonoids, particularly citrus flavonoids, give rise to taste phenomena which can be correlated with chemical structure.[1] Moreover, some of the compounds yield derivatives that are valuable as sweeteners or taste modifiers. The two most abundant flavonoids in *Citrus* are hesperidin and naringin. Both compounds are flavanone 7-β-glycosides and both contain a disaccharide made up of L-rhamnose and D-glucose. Here the similarity ends: hesperidin is tasteless and naringin is bitter. In the late fifties we showed that the disaccharide in naringin is different than that in hesperidin, which was known to contain rutinose (6-O-α-L-rhamnosyl-β-D-glucose). We found that naringin contains the disaccharide neohesperidose and that neohesperidose is 2-O-α-L-rhamnosyl-β-D-glucose. Hesperidin, naringin and a third citrus flavanone, neohesperidin, are shown in Fig. 1. Neohesperidin, like naringin, contains neohesperidose and is intensely bitter. Examination of a number of other flavanone 7-β-rutinosides and 7-β-neohesperidosides confirmed that all the rutinosides were tasteless and all the neohesperidosides bitter. Thus, there can be no doubt that the point of attachment of rhamnose to glucose is a critical factor in determining bitterness or tastelessness in these compounds.

There is a wide range of sensitivity to naringin bitterness. In part, this may be due to the fact that commercial naringin contains varying proportions of the 2S-and 2R-isomers and that some tasters find the 2R-isomer more bitter than the 2S-isomer.[2] The differences between samples of naringin are attributed to the fact that its chirality changes as a function of grapefruit maturity.

In order to delineate in more detail the structural factors for taste we converted naringin to its chalcone and then to the dihydrochalcone (DHC). The chalcone, and especially the dihydrochalcone, were found to be intensely sweet. Other flavanones also yielded sweet DHC's, as shown in Table 1. In general, in both the flavanone and DHC series, neohesperidose

* U.S. Department of Agriculture, Fruit and Vegetable Chemistry Laboratory, Pasadena, California 91106, USA

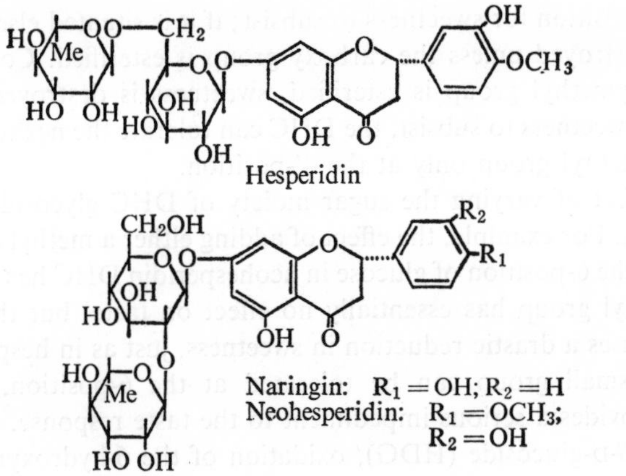

FIG. 1. Structures of some citrus flavanones

TABLE 1. Taste and relative sweetness of dihydrochalcones (DHC's)

Compound	Taste	Relative sweetness
Naringin DHC	Sweet	1
Neohesperidin DHC	Sweet	6.5
Poncirin DHC	Slightly bitter	
Neoeriocitrin DHC	Slightly sweet	
Hesperidin DHC	Tasteless	
Hesperetin DHC 4'-glucoside	Sweet	1
Hesperetin DHC	Sweet	
Naringenin DHC	Slightly sweet	

promotes or allows the expression of taste; rutinose suppresses it entirely. Neohesperidose itself, however, is neither necessary nor sufficient to confer taste on flavonoids in this series: many examples of tasteless neohesperidosides or sapid non-glycosides can be cited.

A large number of DHC B-ring variants have been synthesized. The most favorable arrangement for sweetness is a single hydroxy group at the 3- or 4-position, a 3-hydroxy-4-alkoxy group or a 2-hydroxy-3-alkoxy group. The 3-alkoxy-4-hydroxy arrangement abolishes sweetness, as does any trisubstitution. The absence of a hydroxy group results in compounds that are either tasteless or bittersweet.

In order to overcome limited solubility many DHC derivatives containing ionized groups have been made. These include carboxymethyl[1c,3] and sulfoalkyl[3] substituents. The carboxymethyl group must be located at the 4'-position for sweetness to subsist; if it is situated elsewhere sweetness is destroyed unless the carboxy group is esterified. Conversely, if a 4'-carboxymethyl group is esterified, sweetness is destroyed. It appears that, for sweetness to subsist, the DHC can tolerate the negatively charged carboxymethyl group only at the 4'-position.

The effect of varying the sugar moiety of DHC glycosides is an area of interest. For example, the effect of adding either a methyl or rhamnosyl group to the 6-position of glucose in neohesperidin DHC has been studied. The methyl group has essentially no effect on taste, but the rhamnosyl group causes a drastic reduction in sweetness, just as in hesperidin DHC. Thus, a small group can be tolerated at the 6-position, but a large group provides a serious impediment to the taste response. In hesperetin DHC 4'-β-D-glucoside (HDG), oxidation of the 6-hydroxymethyl group to carboxyl (to give the glucuronide) results in complete loss of sweetness, but if the carboxyl group is allowed to form the methyl ester sweetness returns, giving a compound 2.5 × sweeter than HDG. Again, this illustrates the extreme sensitivity of the taste receptor to location of charge on the molecule. In two other examples—the xyloside and galactoside derivatives—there is also an increase in sweetness over that of HDG (1.5 — 2X) and both compounds have excellent taste quality. A large number of hesperetin DHC 4'-disaccharides have been reported recently;[4] the best compound was the 2-α-L-rhamnosyl-β-D-galactosyl derivative, which was about equal to neohesperidin DHC in sweetness.

With regard to taste, availability, utility and safety, three DHC's that claim attention are neohesperidin DHC, naringin DHC, and HDG (Fig.2). These were early compounds in the series and a large body of information about their taste and toxicology is available. Many glycosidic and non-glycosidic variants of these compounds have been synthesized, but none of them exhibits any clear overall superiority to Neohesperidin DHC. Moreover, because the non-glycosidic derivatives contain alkyl substituents of a type not found in naturally occurring flavonoids, their introduction does away with one of the chief attractions of a compound such as neohesperidin DHC, i.e., that it is only a short step removed from an innocuous natural product.

Naringin is readily available as a byproduct from grapefruit. Neohesperidin is obtained from the bitter orange and is not available commercially. Instead, it must be obtained from naringin, which is converted through phloracetophenone neohesperidoside to neohesperidin and thence to the DHC in overall yield of about 30%. Hesperidin, the starting material for HDG, is available in almost unlimited quantity from sweet oranges and lemons.

Can the DHC's be used as sweeteners? They appear to meet many of

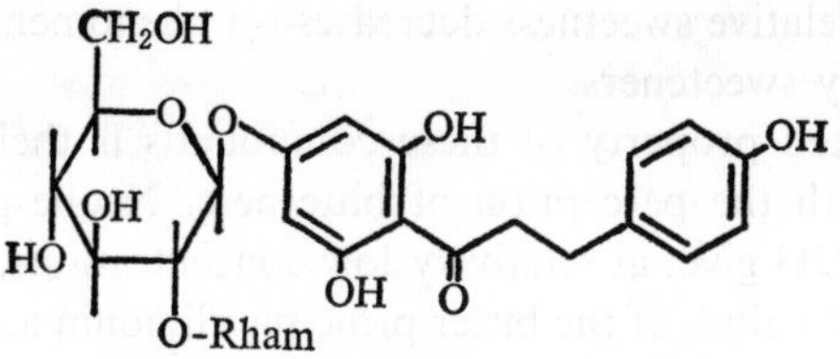

CH₂OH

O-Rham

Naringin Dihydrochalcone (1x)

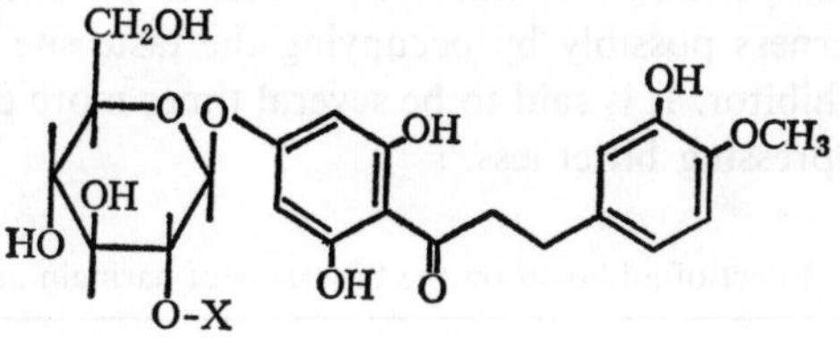

CH₂OH

OCH₃

O-X

Neohesperidin Dihydrochalcone (6.5x)
(X=Rhamnosyl)
Hesperetin Dihydrochalcone Glucoside (1x)
(X=H)

FIG. 2. Structures of some sweet dihydrochalcones

the criteria for sweeteners. Their taste is pleasant, unmarred by bitterness and usually of great intensity. The onset of sweetness, however, is somewhat slow and generally of rather long duration. At threshold neohesperidin DHC is almost 1900 times sweeter than sucrose, while naringin DHC and HDG are almost 300 times sweeter (Table 2). As concentration

TABLE 2. Relative sweetness of dihydrochalcones and sucrose compared at various concentrations of sucrose[1]

Sucrose (mg/kg)	(Sucrose)/(Sweetener)		Naringin DHC
	Neohesperidin DHC	HDG	
1300[2]	1857	289	289
5000	927	193	156
10000	667	135	102
20000	400	111	69
25000	368	100	63
50000	250	78	50

[1] Data of D. G. Guadagni, *et al.*, *J. Sci. Food Agr.*, **25**, 1199 (1974).
[2] Calculated from threshold values; all other figures obtained on basis of sweetness equivalent to that of sucrose.

increases, the relative sweetness decreases—a phenomenon often observed in high-potency sweeteners.

An unexpected property of these compounds is their ability to mask or interfere with the perception of bitterness. Neohesperidin DHC and particularly HDG give, at relatively low concentrations, striking increases in the threshold values of the bitter principles limonin and naringin (Table 3). A compound that seems able to interfere with the perception of bitterness even more effectively than the DHC's is neodiosmin, the flavone analog of neohesperidin. Neodiosmin is tasteless but it appears to interfere with bitterness possibly by occupying the taste site and acting as a competitive inhibitor. It is said to be several times more effective than the DHC's in suppressing bitterness.[5]

TABLE 3. Effect of additives on the bitterness of naringin and limonin[1]

Compound added	Concentration (ppm)	Threshold concentration (ppm) of	
		Naringin	Limonin
None	—	20	1.0
Sucrose	10,000 (1%)	25	1.0
Sucrose	30,000 (3%)	30	1.0
Neo DHC	16[2]	34	1.4
HDG	80[2]	34	3.2
HDG	300[3]	45	3.5
Neodiosmin	10	65	4.0

[1] Data of D. G. Guadagni et al., J. Sci. Food Agr., 25, 1199 (1974); J. Food Sci., 41, 681 (1976)
[2] Equivalent to 1% sucrose in sweetness.
[3] Equivalent to 3% sucrose in sweetness.

Dihydrochalcone sweeteners work best where long-lasting sweetness is advantageous—in chewing gums, confections, toothpastes, mouthwashes and similar products. They could probably be used to provide some of the sweetness in soft drinks. Other applications of DHC's or neodiosmin would be in products where it is desirable to reduce bitterness; these include many pharmaceuticals, some fruit juices and other beverages.

Neohesperidin DHC has been fed to rats and dogs for 2 years at various dose levels[6]; it has been examined in the Ames mutagenicity test[7]; and the excretion and metabolism of the C-14 labed compound have been studied. In rats over 90% of the label is excreted within 24 hours and no evidence of mutagenicity was found in the Ames test. DHC's are flavonoids and, as a group, flavonoids are usually regarded as innocuous. They contain neither nitrogen nor sulfur—elements often associated with toxicity—

and are believed to be metabolized to CO_2 and various aromatic acids. Perhaps of most importance is the fact that since flavonoids occur in all higher plants, they are, and always have been, a common constituent of the diet.

REFERENCES

1. **a**. Horowitz, R. M., in *Biochemistry of Phenolic Compounds*, ed. J. B. Harborne, Academic Press, New York, pp. 545–571 (1964); **b**. Horowitz R. M., and Gentili, B., *J. Agr. Food Chem.*, **17**, 696 (1969); **c**. Horowitz R. M. and Gentili, B., in *Symposium: Sweeteners*, ed. G. E. Inglett, Avi Publishing Co., Westport, Connecticut, pp. 182–193 (1974).
2. Gaffield, W., Lundin, R. E., Gentili, B., and Horowitz, R. M., *Bioorganic Chem.*, **4**, 259 (1975).
3. Dubois, G. E., Crosby, G. A., Stephenson, R. A., and Wingard, R. E., *J. Agr. Food Chem.*, **25**, 763 (1977).
4. Kamiya, S., and Esaki, S., *Nippon Shokuhin Kogyo Gakkaishi*, **23**, 432 (1976).
5. Guadagni, D. G., Maier, V. P., Turnbaugh, J. G., *J. Food Sci.*, **41**, 681 (1976).
6. Gumbmann, M. R., Gould, D. H., Robbins, D. J., and Booth, A. N., in *Sweeteners and Dental Caries*, ed. J. H. Shaw and G. G. Roussos, Information Retrieval, Inc., Washington, D. C., pp. 301–310 (1978).
7. Batzinger, R. P., Ou, S. L., Bueding, E., *Science*, **198**, 944 (1977).

Appendix

Contributed Paper Sessions

Section 1   Exploitation of Food Resources

Protein resources

AUTOLYSIS OF ANTARCTIC KRILL (*EUPHAUSIA SUPERBA*)
Doi, E., Kawamura, Y., Igarashi, S., and Yonezawa, D.(Japan)

NUTRITIVE VALUE OF PROTEIN IN ANTARCTIC KRILL
Kobatake, Y., Innami, S., Iwaya, M., and Tamura, E. (Japan)

UTILIZATION OF SALTED ANTARCTIC KRILL
Kawabata, M., Taguchi, K., and Ohtsuki, K. (Japan)

PROTEINS OF FROZEN STORED ANTARCTIC EUFAUSIA MUSCLE
Suzuki, T., and *Matsumoto, J.J.* (Japan)

DEVELOPING A NEW PROTEIN CONCENTRATE FROM ANTARCTIC KRILL
Suzuki, T., Kanna, K., Suzuki, M., Okazaki, E., and Morita, N. (Japan)

"MARINE LAGOON", A PLAN FOR THE ENHANCEMENT IN MARINE PRODUCTION BY TROPHIC WASTES
Nakayama, O., Kohno, T., and Amemiya, Y. (Japan)

THE CARBAMIDE PROCESS FOR WASTE PROTEIN RECOVERY AND SINGLE CELL PROTEIN PRODUCTION
Eriksson, C.E. (Sweden)

PROTEIN RECOVERY AND LYSINOALANINE FORMATION IN SCANDINAVIAN TRADITIONAL, ALKALINE FISH PRODUCTION
Eriksson, C.E. (Sweden)

PROTEIN PRODUCTION FROM ANIMAL WASTE
Tochikura, T., Yano, T., Hatanaka, M., Lee, L., Tachiki, T., and Kumagai, H. (Japan)

PREPARATION AND RHEOLOGICAL CHARACTERISTICS OF
PROTEIN CONCENTRATES FROM SLAUGHTERHOUSE BLOOD
Quaglia, G.B., Alessandroni, A., Lombardi, M., and Massacci, A. (Italy)

POTENTIAL VALUE OF RICE BRAN FRACTIONS AS PROTEIN
FOOD INGREDIENTS
Barber, S., Benedito de Barder, C., and Martinez, J. (Spain)

STUDIES ON LEAF PROTEIN FROM LADINO CLOVER I.
PHYSICOCHEMICAL PROPERTIES OF FRACTION-1 PROTEIN
Noguchi, H., Satake, I., and Fujimoto, S. (Japan)

STUDIES ON LEAF PROTEIN FROM LADINO CLOVER II.
NUTRITIONAL EVALUATION OF LEAF PROTEIN
CONCENTRATE
Yoshida, A., Satanachote, C., Kimura, T., Noguchi, H., and Ino, K.
(Japan)

LEAF PROTEIN CONCENTRATE. PROCESSING, INCLUDING
ULTRAFILTRATION AND ISOPROPANOL EXTRACTION, AND
ITS INFLUENCE ON PRODUCT PROPERTIES
Trägardh, Ch. (Sweden)

QUICK-COOKING WINGED BEANS (*PSOPHOCARPUS
TETRAGONOLOBUS*)
Rockland, L. B.*, Zaragosa, E.M.*, and Orraca-Tetteh, R. † (*USA,
† Ghana)

NUTRITIONAL PROPERTIES OF RAPESEED PROTEIN
CONCENTRATE
Anjou, K. (Sweden)

PRODUCTION OF INTERMEDIATE AMYLOSE STARCHES AND
PROTEIN ISOLATES FROM LEGUME SEEDS (FIELD PEAS AND
HORSEBEANS).
Vose, J.R. (Canada)

"FRACTIONING" BARLEY PROTEINS BY FACTOR ANALYSIS
Martens, H.*, and Bach Knudsen, K.E. (*Norway, Denmark)

SOME FUNCTIONAL PROPERTIES OF PEA AND SOYBEAN
PREPARATIONS
Gwiazda, S., *Rutkowski, A.,* and Kocoń, J. (Poland)

A NUTRITIVE SYRUP FROM GRAINS
Dahiqvist, A., Conrad, E., Rockström, E., and Theander, O. (Sweden)

PRODUCTION OF SCP BY METHANOL FED-BATCH CULTURE
Yano, T., Mori, H., Kobayashi, T., and Shimizu, S. (Japan)

PROTEIN EVALUATION OF PHOTOSYNTHETIC BACTERIA AS
FEED RESOURCES
Ibuki, F., Kaneko, S., Doi, H., and Kanamori, M. (Japan)

ODD–NUMBERED FATTY ACIDS APPEARED IN ADIPOSE
TISSUE FAT OF RATS FED ON SINGLE-CELL PROTEIN AND
CONVENTIONAL DIETS
Tajima, M., Hayakawa, S., and Yoshikawa, S. (Japan)

SOME TRIALS ON THE UTILIZATION ON WHEY, BLACK
WATER OF OLIVE AND VINASSE FOR PRODUCTION OF SCP
IN TURKEY
Yaziciğlu, T., Çelikkol, E., Öcal, Ş., Aran, N., and Ömeroğlu, S. (Turkey)

PRODUCTION OF PROTEIN, β-CAROTENE AND GLYCEROL
FROM ALGAE
Dolev, A., Nativ, A., Evron, M., and Ben-Amotz, A. (Israel)

THE EFFECT OF TECHNOLOGICAL TREATMENT ON THE
ULTRASTRUCTURE AND MECHANICAL PROPERTIES OF
SINGLE CELL PROTEIN CURD
Tsintsadze, T.*, Lee, C.†, and Rha, C.† (*USSR, †USA)

THE CHIHUAHUA, MEXICO HIGH NUTRITION LOW COST
FOOD PROGRAM
Del Valle, F.R., Camacho, A., Acosta, H., and Luján, F.J. (Mexico)

AN INVESTIGATION INTO INSECT PROTEIN
Del Valle, F.R., and Mena, M.H. (Mexico)

Carbohydrate resources

NEW GELIFYING MALTODEXTRINS FOR APPLICATION IN
LOW ENERGY FOOD
Schierbaum, F.R., Richter, M., and Augustat, S. (GDR)

PRODUCTION AND PROPERTIES OF ELSINAN, A NEW
α–D–GLUCAN ELABORATED BY *ELSINOE LEUCOSPILA*
Tsumuraya, Y., and *Misaki, A.* (Japan)

BATCH FERMENTATION WITH BACTERIA OF PRETREATED
PITH FROM BAGASSE WITH A MIXTURE OF SULFURIC AND
NITRIC ACIDS TO OBTAIN PROTEIN FOR ANIMAL
CONSUMPTION
López Planes, R., Iglesias, G., and Hernández, L. (Cuba)

KINETIC STUDY OF THE PREHYDROLYSIS OF PITH FROM
BAGASSE WITH A MIXTURE OF SULFURIC AND NITRIC ACID
TO OBTAIN FERNENTABLE SUGARS AND POLYSACCHARIDES
López Planes, R., Iglesias, G., and Hernández, J. (Cuba)

Fat and oil resources

SOME IMPRESSIONS OF FOOD SCIENCE AND TECHNOLOGY
IN EAST AFRICA
Henderson, H.M.*, Saint-Hilaire, P.†, and Schulthess, W.† (*Canada,
† Kenya)

TECHNOLOGICAL, NUTRITIONAL AND TOXICOLOGICAL
EVALUATION OF A TRANSESTERIFIED FRACTIONATED
LIQUID FRACTION OF PALM OIL
Mokady, S., Yannai, S., Cogan, U., and *Dolev, A.* (Israel)

Section 2   Food Safety

Food safety assessment

RADIATION-INDUCED CHANGES IN FOOD MODELS: PROTEIN
AGGREGATION
Diehl, J.F.*, Delincee, H.*, and Paul, P. † (*FRG, † India)

DNA BREAKING ACTIVITY OF POLYPHENOLS IN
FOODSTUFFS
Yamada, K., Murakami, H., Shinohara, K., Shirahata, S., Hori, C., and
Omura, H. (Japan)

UTILIZATION OF INDUCIBILITY OF RAT LIVER DRUG
HYDROXYLATION SYSTEM AS AN INDEX FOR FOOD SAFETY
ASSESSMENT
Sugimoto, E., and Kitagawa, Y. (Japan)

CAECAL ENLARGEMENT IN THE TOXICOLOGICAL
EVALUATION OF FOOD ADDITIVES
Walker, R. (UK)

MIGRATION OF INDIRECT FOOD ADDITIVES
Gilbert, S.G. (USA)

EXPOSURE OF HIGH FISH CONSUMERS TO METHYL
MERCURY IN CONTAMINATED COASTAL AREAS OF THE
UNITED KINGDOM
Hubbard, A.W., and Lindsay, D.G. (UK)

EFFECT OF POLYCHLORINATED BIPHENYLS (PCB) AND
NITRITE ON VITAMIN A STORAGE IN PATS
Ikegami, S., Nakamura, A., Ono, S., Nagayama, S., Nishide, E., and
Innami, S. (Japan)

Toxic substances

A COMPARATIVE STUDY ON AFLATOXIN AND CHEMICAL

COMPOSITION OF PISTACHIO NUTS (PISTACIA vera L.)
Karbassi, A.*, and Luh, B.S. †(*Iran, †USA)

MYCOTOXIN PRODUCING FUNGI
Ayres, J.C. (USA)

NITRITE AS A FOOD ADDITIVE: THE PIGMENTATION OF CURED MEAT
Bonnett, R., Charalambides, A.A., Mahmoud, S.A., Sales K.D., and Scourides, P.A. (UK)

REACTION OF SODIUM NITRITE WITH MEAT PROTEINS
Cassens, R.G., Ito, T., Nakai, H., and Greaser, M.L. (USA)

NITROSATION REACTION IN SOLVENT-AQUEOUS SYSTEMS: EFFECTS OF VARIOUS SOLVENTS AND SODIUM ASCORBATE ON THE NITROSOPYRROLIDINE FORMATION
Ohshima, H., and *Kawabata, T.* (Japan)

TOXICITY OF THERMALLY POLYMERIZED OIL
Saito, M., and Kaneda, T. (Japan)

EFFECT OF 1–AMINOPROLINE, A LINSEED TOXIN, ON METHIONINE METABOLISM IN RATS
Sasaoka, K., Ogawa, T., and Kimoto, M. (Japan)

INHIBITION OF INTESTINAL HISTAMINE-METABOLIZING ENZYMES BY AMINES KNOWN TO OCCUR IN SCOMBROID FISH
Lieber, E., and Taylor, S. (USA)

TOXIC CONSTITUENTS IN BRACKEN INDUCING ABNORMAL DEVELOPMENT IN SEA URCHIN EMBRYOGENESIS
Kobayashi, A., Koshimizu, K., and Kobayashi, N. (Japan)

EFFECTS OF CYANOGENIC GLYCOSIDE ON REPRODUCTION AND NEONATAL DEVELOPMENT IN RATS.
Olusi, S.O., *Oke, O.L.*, and Odusote, A. (Nigeria)

SOME PROBLEMS IN THE USE OF CASSAVA AS FOOD
Oke, O.L. (Nigeria)

Section 3   Food Engineering and Technology

Food engineering

"CLOSED-LOOP" FOOD/WATER ENGINEERING SYSTEMS
Gallop, R.A., Hydamaka, A.W., and Stephen, P. (Canada)

DIRECT ENERGY CONSUMPTION IN LEMON AND ORANGE

PACKING PLANTS
Singh, R.P., Mayou, L.P., and O'Brien, M. (USA)

CAUSES OF TOMATO DAMAGE AND LOSSES BEFORE PROCESSING
O'Brien, M., and Singh, R.P. (USA)

DAMAGE TO FOODS OF PLANT ORIGIN: AN ENGINEERING APPROACH
LeMaguer, M.(Canada)

MECHANICAL PROPERTIES OF SELECTED INDICA RICE AS COMPARED WITH JAPONICA
Hoki, M., and Kobayashi, H. (Japan)

ACTUAL EXAMPLES OF DESIGNS OF AUTOMATED FOOD PROCESSING MACHINES WHICH ARE APPLIED RHEOLOGICAL PROPERTY OF FOOD MATERIALS
Hayashi, T. (Japan)

EFFECT OF CONCENTRATION ON APPARENT VISCOSITY OF A GLOBULAR PROTEIN SOLUTION
Pradipasena, P.*, and Rha, C.K. †(*Thailand, †USA)

VISCOELASTIC BEHAVIOR OF WHEAT FLOUR DOUGH: EFFECT OF EITHER AIR CLASSIFICATION OR GLUTEN FORTIFICATION
Kohda, Y. (Japan)

RHEOLOGICAL PROPERTIES OF *SARDINELLA BRASILIENSIS* SOLUBLE EXTRACT
Forster, R.J., Martucci, E.T., and *Gasparetto, C.A.* (Brazil)

A PURIFIED AND FUNCTIONAL PROTEIN-FAT CONCENTRATE FROM SOYBEANS BY ULTRAFILTRATION
Cheryan, M. (USA)

THE FOULING ON THE MEMBRANE DURING REVERSE OSMOSIS CONCENTRATION OF MANDARIN ORANGE JUICE
Watanabe, A., Kimura, S., and Kimura, S. (Japan)

ANALYSIS OF DISPERSION MECHANISM IN GEL CHROMATOGRAPHY AND ITS APPLICATION
Nakanishi K., Yamamoto, S., Matsuno, R., and Kamikubo, T. (Japan)

OPTIMIZATION OF RINSING PROCESSES
Thor, W., and *Loncin, M.* (FRG)

PREDICTION OF DIFFUSION IN SOLID FOODSTUFFS
Stahl, R., and *Loncin, M.* (FRG)

PRELIMINARY RESULTS ON THE KINETICS OF MEAT
DEHYDRATION BY SODIUM CHLORIDE-GLYCEROL
SOLUTIONS
Favetto, G., *Chirife, J.*, and Bartholomai, G.B. (Argentina)

THE DRYING OF FOOD IN SUPERLOW DEHUMIDIFIED AIR
WITH LOW TEMPERATURE
Hosaka, H., Suzuki, K., Kubota, K., and Kuri, S. (Japan)

NEW TECHNOLOGY IN THE PRODUCTION OF FREEZE DRIED
COMPRESSED FOODS
Rahman, A.R., Kelley, N.J., Ayoub, J.A., Westcott, D.E., and *Hollender,
H.A.* (USA)

AROMA RETENTION DURING DRYING OF FOODSTUFFS
Voilley, A.*, and Loncin, M. †(*France, †FRG)

DETERMINATION AND PREDICTION OF DRYING RATES OF
POTATOES AND CARROTS IN LAYERS IN TUNNEL DRIER
Nääs, I.A. (Brazil)

FUNDAMENTAL STUDY OF SPRAY DRYING - DRYING OF A
NON-SUPPORTED DROPLET
Toei, R., Okazaki, M., and Furuta, T. (Japan)

AN ELECTRONIC INDICATOR OF TIME-TEMPERATURE
HISTORY FOR THE DISTRIBUTION OF FROZEN FOODS
Kobayashi, T., Toyoshima, T., Togawa, T., Hayakawa, A., and Kamiya,
A. (Japan)

PREDICTION OF THERMAL CONDUCTIVITY OF "TOFU" AND
MEATS
Yano, T., Kong, J.Y., Miyawaki, O., and Nakamura, K. (Japan)

ELECTRO-CONDUCTIVE HEATING BY LIQUID CONTACT:
USAGE IN BLANCHING AND THAWING
Kopelman, I.J., and Mizrahi, S. (Israel)

DRY COOKING OF GRAINS
Akao, T., Aonuma, T., Nishizawa, Y., Tsukada, N., and Yamanaka, Y.
(Japan)

HEAT TRANSFER CONSIDERATIONS FOR EFFECTIVE
CONTAINER AND PACKAGING EQUIPMENT STERILIZATION
IN ASEPTIC PACKAGING
Toledo, R.T. (USA)

DESTRUCTION OF BACTERIAL SPORES ON PACKAGING
MATERIALS

Han, B.H.*, and *Loncin, M.* †(*Korea, †FRG)

HEAT TRANSFER DURING FORCED AIR COOLING OF HOT FILLED CANNED FOODS
Husain, A. (USA)

RELATIONSHIP BETWEEN HEAT TRANSFER PARAMETERS AND THE CHARACTERISTIC DAMAGE VARIABLES FOR THE FREEZING OF BEEF
Mascheroni, R.H., and *Calvelo, A.* (Argentina)

NEW DESIGN CRITERIA OF AIR-CHILLING EQUIPMENT FOR POULTRY
Veerkamp, C.H. (Netherlands)

FOULING OF HEAT EXCHANGE SURFACES BY SOLUBLE PROTEINS
Ling, A., and *Lund, D. B.* (USA)

EVALUATION OF THERMAL INACTIVATION OF ENZYMES
Park, K.H.*, and *Loncin, M.* (*Korea, †FRG)

FRACTIONATION OF PALM OIL BY MEANS OF CRYSTALLIZATION ON A COOLED SURFACE
Hahn, G., Weisser, H., and *Loncin, M.* (FRG)

Food processing

LOW-ACID CANNED FOOD REGULATIONS
Schaffner, R., Mulvaney, T., and Pretanik, S. (USA)

EFFECT OF SOME OPERATING CONDITIONS ON THE SOLUBILIZATION PROCESS DURING COFFEE BREWING
Voilley, A., and Simatos, D. (France)

INFLUENCE OF SOME PROCESSING CONDITIONS ON THE QUALITY OF COFFEE BREW
Voilley, A., Sauvageot, F., Simatos, D., and Wojcik, G. (France)

INCREASE OF BITTERNESS BY SUFFERING FROM THE COLD IN CITRUS FRUITS AND ITS MECHANISM
Takakuwa, M., and Miyamoto, H. (Japan)

ELECTICAL STIMULATION OF PIG CARCASSES
Højmark Jensen, J., *Jul, M.*, and Zinck, O. (Denmark)

ELECTRICAL STIMULATION OF CHICKENS
Højmark Jensen, J., *Jul, M.*, and Zinck, O. (Demark)

DEVELOPMENT OF ACTIVE FISH PROTEIN POWDER
Niki, H., Deya, E., Kato, T., Doi, T., Igarashi, S., and Hayashi, H. (Japan)

A NUTRITIOUS DRIED FISH PRODUCT SUITABLE FOR USE IN VENEZUELA
Bello, R. A., and Pigott, G.M. (USA)

A COMPARATIVE STUDY OF IMPORTANT WHEAT VARIETIES IN PAKISTAN, FOR THEIR PROTEIN CHARACTERISTICS AND BAKING BEHAVIOUR
Musarrat, B., and *Kausar, P.* (Pakistan)

SOME PROCESSING PARAMETERS FOR PRODUCTION OF WHEY-SOY DRINK MIX
Holsinger, V. H., DellaMonica, E.S., and Sinnamon, H.I. (USA)

DEVELOPMENT OF MAYONNAISE-LIKE FOOD WITH SOYBEAN PROTEIN
Eida, T., Harakawa, K., Saitoh, T., Suematsu, A., and Yomoto, C. (Japan)

ENZYMATIC HYDROLYSIS OF SOY PROTEIN. PROCESSING DEVELOPMENTS AND APPLICATIONS IN LOW pH FOODS
Sejr Olsen, H., Adler-Nissen, J., Jensen, H.J., and Møller, O. (Demmark)

EXPANSION MECHANISM OF SOYBEAN PROTEIN GEL
Saio, K., and Hashizume, K. (Japan)

FUNDAMENTAL STUDIES OF SPUN FIBER FROM SOYA PROTEIN
Hayakawa, I., and Nomura, D. (Japan)

IMPROVEMENT OF EMULSIFYING PROPERTIES OF SOY PROTEINS
Aoki, H., Orimo, N., Kitagawa, I., Shimazu, R., and Wakabayashi, K. (Japan)

HOMOGENIZATION OF OIL IN WATER EMULSIONS
Treiber, A., Kiefer, P., and *Loncin, M.* (FRG)

SOME ASPECTS FOR UTILIZING THE W/O/W-TYPE MULTIPLE-PHASE EMULSIONS IN THE FIELD OF FOOD TECHNOLOGY
Matsumoto, S. (Japan)

PREPARTION OF THE WATER SOLUBLE POWDER STABILIZED SPARINGLY SOLUBLE ORGANICS
Sugisawa, H., Iwai, Y., and Watanabe, I. (Japan)

BOUND WATER, QUANTITATIVE DETERMINATION AND APPLICATION TO THE STABILITY OF INTERMEDIATE MOISTURE FOODS
Soekarto, S.T.*, and Steinberg, M.P. †(*Indonesia, †USA)

AIR DRYING OF VEGETABLES WITH SODIUM CHLORIDE

PRETREATMENT
Solms, J., Speck, P., and Escher, F. (Switzerland)

Food preservation

ULTRASTRUCTURAL CHANGES ASSOCIATED WITH CHILLING INJURY DURING STORAGE AT LOW TEMPERATURE AND FACTORS AFFECTING ON DEGENERATION OF MEMBRANE SYSTEM IN EGGPLANT FRUITS
Abe, K., Chachin, K., and Ogata, K. (Japan)

STUDIES ON PHYSIOLOGICAL AND BIOCHEMICAL PROPERTIES AND KEEPING QUALITY OF SHIITAKE (*LENTINUS EDODES SING.*)
Minamide, T., and Ogata, K. (Japan)

SHELF-LIFE OF ASEPTICALLY FILLED ORANGE JUICE IN BOTTLES
Mannheim, C.H., and Havkin, M. (Israel)

AROMA RECOVERY AND SULPHUR DIOXIDE PRESERVATION OF ORAGNE JUICE
Pérez, R., Gasque, F., Izquierdo, L. J., and *Lafuente, B.* (Spain)

A STUDY OF VOLATILE RETENTION DURING FREEZE DRYING OF TOMATO JUICE
Gerschenson, L.M., *Bartholomai, G.B.*, and Chrife, J. (Argentina)

EFFECT OF SOLIDS LOSS IN CENTRIFUGING FROZEN CHINESE CABBAGE ON RESIDUAL MOISTURE CONTENT
Okamura, T., and Ishibashi, K. (Japan)

RESPIRATORY CHANGES AND CYANIDE-RESISTANT RESPIRATION IN POTATOES INDUCED BY GAMMA RADIATION
Chachin, K., and Ogata, K. (Japan)

EFFECT OF IRRADIATION ON MICROBIAL, ORGANOLEPTIC QUALITY AND CHEMICAL COMPOSITION OF ONION POWDER
Silberstein, O., Henzi, W., Penniman, J., Bednarczyk, A., Eiss, M., Galetto, W., and Welbourn, J. (USA)

STORAGE AND PROCESSING OF TROPICAL FRUITS AND VEGETABLES
Olorunda, A.O., and Fafunso, M. (Nigeria)

APPLICATION OF GAMMA RADIATION FOR DISINFESTATION OF SUNDRIED STRIPED MACKEREL (*RASTRELLIGER CHRYSOZONUS*)
Pablo, I.S. (Philippines)

Packaging

TEMPERATURE AND MOISTURE TRANSPORT REGULATION
BY LETTUCE CONTAINER MATERIALS
Erickson, L.R., *Singh, R. P.*, Garrett, R.E., and Morris, L.L. (USA)

Enviornmental engineering

RECOVERY OF PROTEIN BY BUBBLE SEPARATION
Iibuchi, S., *Chiang, W.C.*, and Yano, T. (Japan)

THE ENVIRONMENTAL PROBLEMS OF MEAT BY PRODUCTS
PROCESSING.
Wix, P. (UK)

Section 4   Organoleptic Properties

Flavor

VOLATILE COMPONENTS OF RICE AND RICE BRAN
Kato, H., Tsugita, T., Kurata, T., and Fujimaki, M. (Japan)

VOLATILE FLAVOR COMPONENTS OF COOKED ODOROUS
RICE (KAORIMAI)
Nakamura, M., Sakakibara, H., Yanai, T., Yajima, I., and Hayashi, K.
(Japan)

FORMATION OF ALDEHYDES- ALCOHOLS AND ESTERS FROM
α-KETO ACIDS IN STRAWBERRY
Yamashita, I., Iino, K., and Yoshikawa, S. (Japan)

STUDIES ON BIOSYNTHESIS OF VOLATILE ESTER IN BANANA
FRUIT
Ueda, Y., and Ogata, K. (Japan)

FLAVOR STABILITY OF LEMON JUICE
Friedrich, H., and *Gubler, B.A.* (Switzerland)

THE CHARACTERISTIC FLAVOR COMPONENTS OF JAPANESE
FERMENTED SHOYU (SOY SAUCE)
Nunomura, N., Sasaki, M., Asao, Y., and Yokotsuka, T. (Japan)

STATISTICAL ANALYSIS OF GAS CHROMATOGRAPHIC
PROFILES OF SOY SAUCE AROMA
Aishima, T., Nagasawa, M., and Fukushima, D. (Japan)

ENZYMES IN FLAVOR DEVELOPMENT IN SHIITAKE
MUSHROOM (*LENTINUS EDODES*)
Iwami, K., Yasumoto, K., and Mitsuda, H. (Japan)

SOME ASPECTS OF GLUCOSINOLATE DECOMPOSITION

MacLeod, A.J., and Gil, V. (UK)

EXPLORING THE RELATIONSHIP BETWEEN SENSORY AND
CHEMICAL PROPERTIES OF VINEGARS
Mori, A., and Nakamura, N. (Japan)

OXIDATIVE DEGRADATION OF ISOHUMULONES IN
RELATION TO BEER FLAVOR
Hashimoto, N., Shimazu, T., and Eshima, T. (Japan)

ORIGIN OF ALKYL SUBSTITUTED PYRIDINES IN FOOD
FLAVORS: FORMATION OF THE PYRIDINES FROM FATTY
ALDEHYDES AND AMINO ACIDS
Suyama, K., and Adachi, S. (Japan)

1, 3-DIOXOLANES IN SOME SIMULATED MEAT FLAVOURS
MacLeod, G., Seyyedain-Ardebili, M., and MacLeod, A.J. (UK)

PRODUCTION OF DAIRY FLAVOURS BY MICROBIAL LIPASE
Kanisawa, T., and Hattori, S. (Japan)

SENSORY EVALUATION OF A SPLIT-RICE AND FISH SOUP
FORMULATION.
Moraes, M.A.C., and Fujimura, C.Q. (Brazil)

SENSORY EVALUATION OF "CHARQUE"
Moraes, M.A.C., and Costa, A.R.S. (Brazil)

Taste

BITTERING CONTRIBUTION OF THE TRANSFORMATION
PRODUCTS OF HUMULONES AND LUPULONES TO BEER
Kowaka, M. (Japan)

RELATIONSHIP BETWEEN BITTERNESS AND CHEMICAL
STRUCTURE OF BITTER PEPTIDE BPIa FROM CASEIN
HYDROLYZATE
Okai, H., Fukui, H., Shigenaga, T., Kanehisa, H., and Oka, S. (Japan)

FORMATION AND ACCUMULATION OF CAPSAICINOID, THE
PUNGENT PRINCIPLE OF HOT PEPPERS, IN *CAPSICUM FRUITS*
Iwai, K., Suzuki, T., *Fujiwake, H.,* Kohashi, M., and Watanabe, S. (Japan)

ASTRINGENCY AND CONDENSED TANNIN OF SEVERAL
FRUITS
Matsuo, T., and Itoo, S. (Japan)

STUDIES ON THE IRRITANT SUBSTANCE
Okuyama, K. (Japan)

SENSORY EVALUATION OF STEVIOSIDE AND NEWLY

ISOLATED DITERPENE GLYCOSIDES AS SWEETNERS
Ishima, T., Katayama, O., and Yokoyama, Y. (Japan)

PSYCHOMETRICAL STUDIES ON THE TASTE OF MONOSODIUM
GLUTAMATE
Yamaguchi, S., and Kimizuka, A. (Japan)

CONTRIBUTION OF EXTRACTIVE COMPONENTS TO THE
TASTE OF BOILED CRABS
Hayashi, T., Yamaguchi, K., and Konosu, S. (Japan)

Texture

MECHANICAL PROPERTIES OF WAXY RICE CAKE
Horiuchi, H. (Japan)

CHANGING CARRAGEENAN GEL TEXTURE BY ADDITION
OF OTHER HYDROCOLLOIDS
Christensen, O., and Trudsoe, J. (Denmark)

RHEOLOGICAL STUDIES OF GELATIN GELS
Nishinari, K., and Watase, M. (Japan)

TEXTURE AND COLOUR CHANGES IN MEAT DURING
COOKING RELATED TO THERMAL DENATURATION OF
DIFFERENT PROTEINS
Martens, M. Stabursvik, E., and *Martens, H.* (Norway)

METHOD OF RATING ON THE TEXTURE OF BAKED
PRODUCTS BY MULTI-POINT MENSURATION METHOD.
Tsuji, S. (Japan)

FLOW PROPERTIES OF MILK IN A CAPILLARY AT LOW
SHEAR STRESSES
Mineshita, T., Yamamoto, A., Nagano, K., and Fujii, S. (Japan)

EATING QUALITY OF NON-GLUTINOUS COOKED RICE, RICE
CAKE AND GELATINATION, RETROGRADATION OF RICE
STARCH GRAIN
Kurasawa, H., Shoji, I., and Kondo, E. (Japan)

Section 5 Basic Problems on Food Constituents

Proteins

FREEZE-THAW GELATION OF YOLK LIPOPROTEIN
Kurisaki, J., Yamauchi, K., and Kaminogawa, S. (Japan)

CHANGES OF CHALAZAE AND VITELLINE MEMBRANE
DURING STORAGE OF CHICKEN EGG

Sato, Y., and Kato, T. (Japan)

VISCOMETRIC BEHAVIOUR OF THE SOLUBLE OVOMUCIN
Hayakawa, S., and Sato, Y. (Japan)

EFFECT OF MAILLARD REACTION ON THE CHEMICAL-
PHYSICOCHEMICAL PROPERTIES OF OVALBUMIN
Watanabe, K., Kato, Y., and Sato, Y. (Japan)

WATER BINDING PATTERNS OF NATIVE AND DENATURED
LYSOZYME AS DETERMINED BY INFRARED SPECTROSCOPY
Frasco, C.B., *Karmas, E.,* and Gilbert, S.G. (USA)

INTERACTION OF IMMOBILIZED CHICKEN FLAVOPROTEIN
WITH FLAVINS
Ohtsuki, K., Kawabata, M., and Taguchi, K. (Japan)

EFFECT OF HEATING ON THE FUNCTIONAL PROPERTIES OF
OVOTRANSFERRIN
Nakamura, R., Takemoto, H., and Umemura, O. (Japan)

INTRACELLULAR TRANSPORT AND POSTSYNTHETIC
MODIFICATION OF CASEINS
Sasaki, M., Eigel, W.N., and Keenan, T.W. (USA)

PROPERTIES OF SOLUBLE CASEIN REMOVED FROM CASEIN
MICELLE AT LOW TEMPERATURE
Niki, R., and Arima S. (Japan)

A SIMPLE METHOD FOR FRACTIONATION OF α_{S_1}-CASEIN
Chiba, H., Ueda, M., Yoshikawa, M., and Sasaki, R. (Japan)

CALCIUM INSENSITIVITY OF α_{S_1}-CASEIN
Kaminogawa, S., Yamauch, K., and Yoon, C.H. (Japan)

FRACTIONATION AND PROPERTIES OF A PEPTIDASE OF
STREPTOCOCCUS CREMORIS WHICH DECOMPOSES
CHYMOSINTREATED α_{S_1}-CASEIN
Yamauchi, K. Kaminogawa, S., and Hwang, I.K. (Japan)

STUDIES ON THE STRUCTURE OF CASEIN MICELLE. I.
LOCALIZATION OF κ-CASEIN ON THE SURFACE
Sasaki, R., Takahata, K., Yoshikawa, M., and Chiba, H. (Japan)

STUDIES ON THE STRUCTURE OF CASEIN MICELLE. II. ROLE
OF PHOSPHATE GROUPS OF CASEIN COMPONENTS
Yoshikawa, M., Sasaki, R., and Chiba, H. (Japan)

DESTRUCTION AND RECONSTRUCTION OF CASEIN MICELLE
Ono, T., and Odagiri, S. (Japan)

PROTEOLYTIC COAGULATION OF CASEIN IN MODEL
SYSTEMS WITH DIFFERENT IONS CONCENTRATIONS
Carić, M. (Yugoslavia)

HETEROGENEITY AND CARBOHYDRATES OF BOVINE
κ-CASEIN
Kanamori, M., *Doi, H.*, and Ibuki, F. (Japan)

CHARACTERIZATION OF MILK MEAT PREPARED FROM
BOVINE CASEIN.
Miyanaka, A., Yagi, N., and Kanamori, M. (Japan)

LIPOLYSIS OF COW'S MILK AND SOME PROPERTIES OF MILK
LIPASES
Saito, Z. (Japan)

COMPARISON OF PROTEIN COMPOSITION BETWEEN MILK
FAT GLOBULE MEMBRANE AND PLASMA MEMBRANE OF THE
LACTATING MAMMARY GLAND
Kanno, C., Hattori, R., and Yamauchi, K. (Japan)

CONFORMATIONAL CONTRIBUTION ON THE GELATION OF
SOYBEAN 11S GLOBULIN
Okubo, K., and Shibasaki, K. (Japan)

EFFECT OF LOW TEMPERATURE TREATMENT ON GEL
FORMATION OF SOYBEAN PROTEIN
Soeda, T., and Baba, K. (Japan)

ISOLATION AND SUBUNIT STRUCTURE OF γ-CONGLYCININ
IN SOYBEAN GLOBULIN
Yamauchi, F., Sato, W., Kamata, Y., and Shibasaki, K. (Japan)

STUDIES ON SESAME PROTEINS: SUBUNIT STRUCTURE,
PROTEIN ISOLATE, AND GELATION CHARACTERISTICS
Hasegawa, K., Maeda, K., Fujino, Y., Wakinaga, T., and Fujino, S. (Japan)

SUBUNIT STRUCTURE OF ARACHIN
Yamada, T., Aibara, S. and Morita, Y. (Japan)

ANALYSIS OF SUBUNIT COMPOSITION OF LEGUMINS FROM
VARIOUS CULTIVARS OF BROAD BEAN SEEDS
Mori, T., and Utsumi, S. (Japan)

EXTRACTION OF WHEAT GLUTENIN WITH SODIUM DODECYL
SULFATE AND ITS MOLECULAR WEIGHT DISTRIBUTION
Danno, G., Kanazawa, K. and Natake, M. (Japan)

SELECTIVE CLEAVAGE OF INTER-SUBUNIT DISULFIDE
BONDS OF WHEAT GLUTENINS

Yonezawa, D., Yoshida, M., Hamauzu, Z., and Kawamura, Y. (Japan)

CHANGE IN PROTEINS DURING FROZEN STORAGE OF COD
AS DETECTED BY SDS-ELECTROPHORESIS
Connell, J.J., Laird, W., Mackie, I.M., and Ritchie, A. (UK)

STUDIES ON THE CATIONIC PROTEIN IN *SURIMI*
Yamamoto, A., and Nagao, K. (Japan)

EFFECT OF TEMPERATURES ON FISH ALKALINE PROTEASE,
MUSCLE ACTOMYSIN AND TEXTURE QUALITY
Deng, J.C. (USA)

ENZYMATIC RELEASE OF LYSINOALANINE FROM
PROTEINS AND ITS UTILIZATION BY LYSINE DEPENDENT
MICROORGANISMS
Sternberg, M., and *Kim*, C.Y. (USA)

RECONSTITUTION OF THE Z-DISK
Suzuki, A., Saito, M., and Nonami, Y. (Japan)

EFFECTS OF ATP CONCENTRATION, pH AND SARCOMERE
LENGTH ON RIGOR TENSION DEVELOPMENT AND
DISSOCIATION OF RIGOR COMPLEXES IN GLYCERINATED
RABBIT SKELETAL MUSCLE FIBER
Izumi, K., and Fukazawa, T. (Japan)

STUDIES ON THE HEAT-GELLING PROPERTIES OF MYOSIN
FROM SKELETAL MUSCLE
Samejima, K., and Yasui, T. (Japan)

SEPARATION AND SOME PROPERTIES OF CATHEPSIN B AND
CATHEPSIN B-LIKE PROTEASE FROM RABBIT SKELETAL
MUSCLE
Okitani, A., Matsukura, U., Watanabe, M., Otsuka, Y., Kato, H., and
Fujimaki, M. (Japan)

A PEPTIDE WITH DELICIOUS TASTE
Yamasaki, Y., and *Maekawa*, K. (Japan)

INHIBITION MECHANISM OF AMYLASE INHIBITOR FROM
KIDNEY BEAN (PHASEOLAMIN) FOR PORCINE PANCREATIC
α-AMYLASE
Nakatani, H., Shibata, K., Araiye, K., *Kondo*, H., and Hiromi, K. (Japan)

Carbohydrates

PROPERTIES OF STARCHES OF *OPAQUE*-2, *SUGARY*-2
OPAQUE-2 AND *WAXY OPAQUE*-2 MUTANTS OF MAIZE
VARIETIES ADAPTED TO TEMPERATE AREAS

Fuwa, H.*, Glover, D.V.†, Sugimoto, Y.*, Ikawa, Y.*, and Takaya, T.*
(*Japan, †USA)

STRUCTURE AND PROPERTIES OF AMYLO-WAXY AND ITS
RELATED MAIZE STARCHES
Yamada, T., Akaki, M., and Taki, M. (Japan)

PROPERTIES AND USES OF HORNY AND FLOURY
ENDOSPERMS OF CORN
Kikuchi, K., Takatsuji, I., Miyake, K., and Tokuda, M. (Japan)

STRUCTURAL CHANGES OF STARCH MOLECULES DURING
THE MALTING OF BARLEY
Kano, Y., Kunitake, N., and Karakawa, T. (Japan)

THE GELATINIZATION OF STARCH IN BAKED PRODUCTS
Lineback, D.R., and Wongsrikasem, E. (USA)

STUDY ON PROPERTIES AND STRUCTURE OF
RETROGRADATED STARCH
Takeshita, S., Suzuki, E., and Konishi, H. (Japan)

MEANS TO PREVENT STARCH TO SUGAR CONVERSION IN
POTATO TUBERS DURING COLD STORAGE
Amir, J., and Kahn, V. (Israel)

FREE RADICAL GENERATION IN CRYSTALLINE
SACCHARIDES UNDER GRINDING PROCESSES
Hasegawa, H., Tsuchita, H., Yamamoto, Y., and Tsuchiya, F. (Japan)

STRUCTURE OF XYLOGLUCAN, β-GLUCAN AND
ARABINOXYLAN IN A HEMICELLULOSE COMPONENT
ISOLATED FROM RICE ENDOSPERM CELL WALLS
Shibuya, N., Iwasaki, T., and Misaki, A. (Japan)

THE COMPOSITION AND PROPERTIES OF GUM EXTRACTED
FROM OKRO CAPSULES
Woolfe, M.L.*, and Johnston, K.A.† (*Brazil, †UK)

CHANGES IN PECTIC SUBSTANCES, HEMICELLULOSE AND
CELLULOSE IN RADISH (DAIKON) DURING GROWTH
Manabe, M., *Otsuka, N.*, Kurata, H., and Tarutani, T. (Japan)

CONSTITUTION OF JUNSAI, EDIBLE HETEROPOLYSACCHARIDE
OF WATER PLANT, *BRASENIA SCHREBERI J.F. GMEL*
Kakuta, M., and Misaki, A. (Japan)

ANTITUMOR ACTIVITY OF LIGNIN
Murakami, H., and Yamaguchi, N. (Japan)

EFFECT OF *CHLORELLA* EXTRACT ON THE PHAGOCYTIC ACTIVITY OF THE RETICULOENDOTHELIAL SYSTEM
Nakamura, H., Tamura, A., and Yamazaki, K. (Japan)

Fats and oils

STUDIES ON THE LIPID IN PUMPKIN SEEDS
Tsuyuki, H., Itoh, S., and Yamagata, K. (Japan)

LIPID CONTENT AND FATTY ACID COMPOSITION IN BAMBOO SHOOTS
Kozukue, E. (Japan)

APPLICATION OF HIGH-PERFORMANCE LIQUID CHROMATOGRAPHY TO THE STUDY OF FATTY ACID COMBINATION OF TRIGLYCERIDE IN BEEF LIPID
Wada, S., Koizumi, C., Takiguchi, A., and Nonaka, J. (Japan)

FATTY ACID DISTRIBUTION IN LIPIDS EXTRACTED FROM SHEEP BONE MARROWS
Ohtake, Y., and Watanabe, M. (Japan)

"INTERNAL LIPID" IN RICE STARCH
Ito, S., Sato, S., and Fujino, Y. (Japan)

ANTIOXIDANT ACTIVITY OF SOYBEANS AND SOYBEAN PRODUCTS
Pratt, D.E., and Birac, P.M. (USA)

ANTIOXIDANT PROPERTIES OF BRANCHED-CHAIN AMINO ACID DERIVATIVES
Kawashima, K., Itoh, H., Miyoshi, M., and Chibata, I. (Japan)

ANTIOXIDATIVE EFFECT OF MAILLARD REACTION PRODUCTS
Lingnert, H., and *Eriksson, C.E.* (Sweden)

EFFECTS OF METAL SALTS AND ANTIOXIDANTS ON THE OXIDATION OF FISH LIPID DURING STORAGE UNDER THE CONDITIONS OF LOW AND INTERMEDIATE MOISTURES
Zama, K., Takama, K., and Mizushima, Y. (Japan)

STUDIES ON THE ISOMERIC MONOHYDROPEROXIDES FROM CHLOROPHYLL SENSITIZED PHOTOOXIDATION OF UNSATURATED FATTY ACID ESTERS
Terao, J., and Matsushita, S. (Japan)

STUDIES ON DETERIORATION OF PALM OIL AT ELEVATED TEMPERATURE

Wada, T., Chiokki, S., Maekawa, A., Suzuki, T., and Hirayama, H. (Japan)

INCORPORATION OF SECONDARY DEGRADATION
PRODUCTS FROM AUTOXIDIZED LINOLEIC ACID INTO RAT
Kanazawa, K., Danno, G., and Natake, M. (Japan)

LIPOLYTIC ENZYMES IN VICIA FABA MINOR-AN OVERVIEW
Henderson, H. M., Eskin, N.A.M., and Atwal, A.S. (Canada)

Interactions of food constituents

CHARACTERIZATION OF SOME REACTION PRODUCTS
FORMED BY THE REACTION OF L-SCORBAMIC ACID WITH
DEHYDRO-L-ASCORBIC ACID
Kurata, T., Tsuge, N., Kato, H., and Fujimaki, M. (Japan)

FREE RADICAL AND ITS PRECURSOR PRODUCED BY THE
REACTION OF DEHYDRO-L-ASCORBIC ACID WITH AMINO
ACID
Hayashi, T., and Namiki, M. (Japan)

BROWNING REACTION OF TRIOSE REDUCTONE WITH SOME
AMINO ACIDS OR NUCLEIC ACID-RELATED COMPOUNDS
AND PREPARATION OF THE INTERMEDIATES
Shinohara, K., Lee, J-H., Tseng, Y-K., Murakami, H., and Omura, H.
(Japan)

STUDY OF NON-VOLATILE CONSTITUENTS PRODUCED FROM
THE REACTION OF D-GLUCOSE AND CYSTEAMINE
Kitamura, K., Sakaguchi, M., Okamoto, Y., and Shibamoto, T. (Japan)

EPR SPECTRAL STUDY ON THE KINETIC BEHAVIOUR OF THE
NONENZYMATIC BROWNING REACTION
Milić, B.Lj., Piletić, M. B., Grujić-Injac, B., and Premović, P.I.
(Yugoslavia)

ASSOCIATION OF PHOSPHATIDYLCHOLINE WITH SOYBEAN
PROTEIN
Ohtsuru, M., Kanamoto, R., and Kito, M. (Japan)

MICELLE FORMATION OF PROTEIN-CARBOHYDRATE
SOLUTION AND ITS APPLICATION TO OIL-SOLUBILIZATION
Ono, F., and Aoyama, Y. (Japan)

LOWERING OF WATER ACTIVITY ACCOMPANYING
EMULSION FORMATION
Koiwa, Y., and Ohta, S. (Japan)

PROTECTIVE EFFECT OF MILK PROTEINS ON PRECIPITATION OF HEAT-DENATURED OVALBUMIN AND CONALBUMIN
Sato, Y., and *Hayakawa, M.* (Japan)

IMPROVER INTERACTIONS WITH WEAKER BREAD FLOURS
Frazier, P.J., Brimblecombe, F.A., Daniels, N.W.R., and *Russell Eggitt, P.W.* (UK)

AN ASPECT ON THE INTERACTION BETWEEN GLUTEN AND LIPID IN WHEAT FLOUR DOUGH
Nishiyama, J., Kuninori, T., and Matsumoto, H. (Japan)

FOAMING ACTIVITY OF WHEAT FLOOR SUSPENSION AND ITS RELATION TO BREADMAKING
Ohta, S., Inoue, S., and Totigoe, T. (Japan)

FACTORS AFFECTING ANTHOCYANIN COLOR IN BEVERAGES
Timberlake, C.F., and Bridle, P. (UK)

PROPERTIES OF LIPOXYGENASE IN RICE GERM
Yamamoto, A., Fujii, Y., Yasumoto, K., and Mitsuda, H. (Japan)

CHLOROHYDRINS IN PROTEIN HYDROLYSATES
Davídek, J., Velíšek, J., and Janíček, G. (Czechoslovakia)

STUDY OF VOLATILES PRODUCED IN 2-HYDROXY-3-METHYL-CYCLOPENT-EN-1-ON WITH AMMONIA AND HYDROGEN SULFIDE
Nishimura, O., Sakaguchi, M., Aitoku, A., and Shibamoto, T. (Japan)

Food ingredients

PECTIC ENZYMES IN SOME SPANISH PRODUCTS USED FOR PICKLING
Minguez Mosquera, M.I., Castillo Gomez J., and *Fernandez Diez, M.J.* (Spain)

BOUND FORM OF VITAMIN B_6 IN CEREALS AND SEEDS
Yasumoto, K., Iwami, K., Okada, J., Tsuji, H., and Mitsuda, H. (Japan)

ANTHOCYANINS OF BOLIVIAN PURPLE CORN (*ZEA MAYS* L., MAIZE MORADO)
Nakatani, N., Fukuda, H., and Fuwa, H. (Japan)

D-AMINO ACIDS AS THE UBIQUITOUS CONSTITUENT OF HIGHER PLANTS
Ogawa, T., and Sasaoka, K. (Japan)

Section 6 Biochemical Techniques in Food Science

Application of enzymes

OPTIMIZATION OF THE CONTINUOUS GLUCOSE ISOMERASE
REACTOR SYSTEM FOR HIGH-FRUCTOSE CORN SYRUP
PRODUCTION
Ryu, D. Y.*, Chung, S.H.*, and *Katoh, K.*† (*Korea †Japan)

PROCESS DESIGN CONSIDERATIONS OF A COMMERCIAL
GLUCOSE ISOMERASE REACTOR SYSTEM
Harrow, L.S., and Venkatsubramanian, K. (USA)

PROPERTIES OF GLUCOSE ISOMERASE COVALENTLY BOUND
TO POLYACRYLAMIDE BEAD SURFACE
Nakamura, K., Hibino, K., and Yano, T. (Japan)

STUDIES ON THE GLUCOAMYLASE FROM *MONASCUS
RUBIGINOSUS* SATO
Zhang S.-A. *et al.* (People's Republic of China)

STUDIES ON THE MALTOSE SYRUP WITH A
STREPTOMYCES AMYLASE
Adachi, T., and Hidaka, H. (Japan)

SOLUBLE AND IMMOBILIZED ENZYME TECHNOLOGY IN
BIOCONVERSION OF BARLEY STARCH
Linko, Y.Y., Lindroos, A., and Linko, P. (Finland)

IMMOBILIZATION OF INVERTASE ON KONJAC MANNAN GEL
Maekaji, K., and Okimasu, S. (Japan)

PULSE RESPONSE IN IMMOBILIZED ENZYME COLUMN
Adachi, S., Nakanishi, K., *Matsuno, R.*, Hashimoto, K., and Kamikubo, T.
(Japan)

THE PROPERTIES OF β-GALACTOSIDASE-IMMOBILIZED IN
VARIOUS FORMS
Reimerdes, E.H., and Herlitz, E. (FRG)

PRODUCTION AND APPLICATION OF β-GALACTOSIDASE IN
FOOD PROCESSING
Park, Y.K., DeSanti, M.S.S., and Pastore, G.M. (Brazil)

AN ENZYMATIC CONVERSION OF CELLULOSE TO STARCH
Sasaki, T., Machida, K., and Kainuma, K. (Japan)

HYDROLYSIS OF CELLULOSE WITH *PELLICULARIA
FILAMENTOSA* CELLULASE. —EFFECT OF CRYSTALLINITY
OF CELLULOSE ON THE MECHANISM OF HYDROLYSIS.
Tanaka, M., Matsuno, R., and Kamikubo, T. (Japan)

CHROMATOGRAPHIC SEPARATION OF ORANGE
PECTINESTERASE ISOENZYMES ON SODIUM PECTATE,
CROSS-LINKED WITH EPICHLOROHYDRIN
Rombouts, F.M., Wissenburg, A.K., and Pilnik, W. (Netherlands)

LOW-METHOXYL PECTIN PREPARED BY PECTINESTERASE
FROM *ASPERGILLUS JAPONICUS*
Ishii, S., Kiho, K., Sugiyama, S., and Sugimoto, H. (Japan)

PECTOLYTIC ENZYMES IN PROCESSING OF BLACK
CURRANTS
Koivistoinen, P., Kosonen, O.-P., and Kiuru, K. (Finland)

ENZYMIC PRODUCTION OF PECTIN FROM CITRUS FRUIT
PEELINGS
Sakai, T., Okushima, M., and Tonomura, K. (Japan)

IMMOBILIZATION OF THE MICROBIAL CELL CONTAINING
AND KINASE ACTIVITY
Hayashi, T., *Kawashima*, K., and Tanaka, Y. (Japan)

A NEW ENZYMATIC PROCESS FOR IMPROVING THE AMINO
ACID COMPOSITION OF FOOD PROTEINS
Yamashita, M., Arai, S., and Fujimaki, M. (Japan)

ENZYMATIC REMOVAL OF BEANY FLAVOR FROM SOYBEAN
PRODUCTS. I. ALDEHYDE DEHYDROGENASE
Chiba, H., Takahashi, N., Yoshikawa, M., and Sasaki, R. (Japan)

ENZYMATIC REMOVAL OF BEANY FLAVOR FROM SOYBEAN
PRODUCTS. II. ALDEHYDE OXIDASE
Sasaki, R., Takahashi, N., Yoshikawa, M., and Chiba, H. (Japan)

USE OF FIBRE-ENTRAPPED ENZYMES IN FOOD TECHNOLOGY
Morisi, F. (Italy)

RAPID AND LARGE SCALE ISOLATION OF MILK CLOTTING
ENZYMES BY AFFINITY CHROMATOGRAPHY
Murakami, K., and Kobayashi, H. (Japan)

RIPENING AND DEBITTERING OF CHEESES AND PROTEIN
HYDROLYSATES
Mälkki, Y. (Finland)

APPLICATION OF IMMOBILIZED PROTEASES FOR
PRODUCTION OF CHEESE
Kobayashi, T., Tanimura, S., Murasaki, S., Ohmiya, K., and Shimizu, S.
(Japan)

THE ENZYMATIC DEGRADATION OF β-CASEIN AND ITS
TECHNOLOGICAL SIGNIFICANCE
Reimerdes, E.H. (FRG)

QUANTITATIVE COMPARISON OF PROTEASES FOUND IN
SKELETAL MUSCLE OF VARIOUS MUSCLE FOOD ANIMALS
Kang, C.K., Busch, W. A., Jodlowski, R.F., and Warner, W.D. (USA)

PRODUCTION OF ACID SOLUBLE SOY PROTEIN BY
ENZYMATIC HYDROLYSIS
Moretti, R.H. (Brazil)

APPLICATION OF EXTERNAL ENZYMES TO THE IMPROVING
OF BEER FILTRATION
Pajunen, E., and Enari, T.-M. (Finland)

ACID PROTEASES OF THE ANTARCTIC KRILL, *EUPHAUSIA
SUPERBA*: PURIFICATION AND SOME PROPERTIES.
Murakami, K., and *Kimoto, K.* (Japan)

ENZYMATIC PROTEIN HYDROLYSIS IN A MEMBRANE
REACTOR
Roozen, J.P., and Pilnik, W. (Netherlands)

OXIDATIVE IMPROVEMENT OF DOUGH WITH LIPOXYGENASE
AND GLUCOSE OXIDASE
Matsumoto, H., Nishiyama, J., Mita, T., and Kuninori, T. (Japan)

APPROACHES TO THE LIMONIN BITTERNESS PROBLEM IN
CITRUS JUICE
Hasegawa, S., and Maier, V.P. (USA)

THE FUNDAMENTALS OF FRUIT TREATMENT BY
PECTOLYTIC ENZYMES IN JUICE AND WINE PRODUCTION
Mikeladze, G.G. (USSR)

Utilization of microorganisms

PRODUCTION AND PROPERTIES OF MONASCUS PIGMENT
FOR COLORING FOODSTUFF
Yamanaka, S., Shimizu, E., and Takinami, K. (Japan)

DIRECT FERMENTATION OF L-ISOLEUCINE FROM SUGAR
MATERIAL
Tang, R.-T., Guo, Y.-F., and Chen, Q. (People's Republic of China)

LYSINE PRODUCTION BY LYSINE SULFUR ANALOG
RESISTANT-MUTANTS OF YEAST
Tanaka, H., Takenouchi, E., Nikolova, D.K., Yamamoto, T., and Soda,
K. (Japan)

UTILIZATION OF MICROORGANISMS IN THE PRODUCTION OF SUGAR FROM IRAQI DATES
Marouf, B. (Iraq)

HIGH β-AMYLASE PRODUCTION BY AN ASPOROGENOUS MUTANT OF *BACILLUS CEREUS* BQ10-S1 AND ISOLATION OF PEPTIDYL FACTORS EFFECTIVE β-AMYLASE PRODUCTION
Shinke, R., Aoki, K., Nishira, H., Kiyohara, T., and Yuki, S. (Japan)

SINGLE CELL PROTEIN FROM SYNTHETIC ETHANOL. UTILIZATION OF PURE O_2 IN A NEW DESIGN FERMENTER
Garrido, J., Del Amo, E., Fernández, M.J., Tabera, J., and Garrido, F.(Spain)

KINETIC STUDIES ON GROWTH AND SPORULATION OF *BACILLUS THURINGIENSIS*
Moraes, I.O., Hokka, C.O., and *Nakamura, I.M.* (Brazil)

BIOCHEMICAL DIFFERENCES OF PIGMENTED *STAPHYLOCOCCUS AUREUS* STRAINS AND THEIR NON PIGMENTED DERIVATIVES
Yokoya, F., and *Salzberg, S.P.* (Brazil)

Section 7 Food Analysis and Standard

Development of food analysis

INSTRUMENTAL METHODS OF FOOD MOISTURE MEASUREMENT
Groeninger, K. (Switzerland)

NITROGEN-TO-PROTEIN CONVERSION FACTORS WITH SPECIAL REGARD TO FOOD PROTEINS
Yamaguchi, M., Matsuno, N., Ohno, I., and Miyazaki, M. (Japan)

THE GAS CHROMATOGRAPHIC DETERMINATION OF FLUORIDE IN MILK AND WATER
Smith, G.D., Beswick, G., and Rosie, D.A. (UK)

DESIGN AND APPLICATION OF A NATIONWIDE SAMPLING PLAN TO ESTIMATE CONCENTRATIONS OF ZINC AND COPPER IN PROCESSED BABY FOODS
Butrum, R.R., and Wolf, W.A. (USA)

A NEW FLUORESCENT REAGENT N-(9-ACRIDINYL) MALEIMIDE (NAM) AND ITS APPLICATION TO THE SIMPLE MICRO DETERMINATION OF THIOLS IN SOME FOODSTUFF AND MAMMALLIAN TISSUES
Takahashi, H., Nara, Y., Tuzimura, K., and Megro, H. (Japan)

MEASUREMENT OF ULTRAWEAK CHEMILUMINESCENCE
FOR THE EVALUATION OF FOOD DETERIORATION
Part I. PHOTON COUNTING SYSTEMS FOR ULTRAWEAK LIGHT
DETECTION AND SPECTRAL ANALYSIS
Yamagishi, A., Takyu, C., Inaba, H., Usuki, R., and Kaneda, T. (Japan)

MEASUREMENT OF ULTRAWEAK CHEMILUMINESCENCE
FOR THE EVALUATION OF FOOD DETERIORATION
Part II. SOME APPLICATIONS TO THE DETECTION OF
OXIDATIVE DETERIORATION OF OILS AND FOODS.
Usuki, R., Kaneda, T., Yamagishi, A., Takyu, C., and Inaba, H. (Japan)

THE THIOCYANATE CONTENT OF EGG FROM HENS FED ON A
DIET CONTAINING RAPESEED MEAL
Shuaib, A.C.A., *Beswick, G.*, and Tomlins, R.I. (UK)

ANALYTICAL TECHNIQUES FOR THE IDENTIFICATION OF
TAINTS IN FOODS
Holmes, A. W. (UK)

ISOLATION AND IDENTIFICATION OF N-NITROSAMINES IN
BROWNING MODEL SYSTEMS
Sakaguchi, M., Aitoku, A., and Shibamoto, T. (Japan)

SIMPLIFIED POV DETERMINATION METHOD
Asakawa, T., and Matsushita, S. (Japan)

THE SEASONAL TRANSITION OF CONSTITUENTS DURING
GROWTH OF CITRUS UNSHU
Sawada, M., *Muraki, S.*, Yoshida, T., and Hattori, S. (Japan)

SPECTROPHOTOMETRIC DETERMINATION OF AMYLOSE IN
MILLED RICE
Karbassi, A.*, Ejlali, M.*, and Luh, B.S.† (*Iran, †USA)

SIMULTANEOUS DETERMINATION OF CAPSAICIN AND ITS
ANALOGUES BY HIGH PERFORMANCE LIQUID CHROMATOG-
RAPHY AND GAS CHROMATOGRAPH-MASS SPECTROMETER
Iwai, K., *Suzuki, T.*, Fujiwake, H., and Oka, S. (Japan)

NMR IN FOOD SCIENCE AND TECHNOLOGY
Lechert, H. (FRG)

DETERMINATION OF ARSENIC AND TIN IN CANNED FOOD
BY FLAMELESS ATOMIC ABSORPTION SPECTROPHOTOMETRY
Hu, C.T. (People's Republic of China)

DETECTION OF FRAUDS IN CITRUS JUICES.-XXI. CONTENT OF
TOTAL NITROGEN AND AMINO ACID NITROGEN IN THE

WHEYS OF JUICES FROM SPANISH LEMONS
Royo Iranzo, J., Peris Torán, Ma. J., and Grima, R.(Spain)

Food standard

MICROBIOLOGICAL IDENTIFICATION OF SCP YEAST BY PMR
SPECTRUM OF CELL-WALL MANNAN
Hirata, T., and Ishitani, T. (Japan)

APPROACHES TO STANDARDIZE MONITORING METHODS
OF MICROBIOLOGICAL IDENTITY OF SINGLE CELL PROTEINS
IN PRODUCTION
Katoh, K., Suzuki, A. and Ebine, H. (Japan)

DIASTASE AND HYDROXYMETHYLFURFURALDEHYDE IN
HONEY
Wix, P., and Mohamedally, S.M.(UK)

Section 8   Microorganism

Food sanitation

STUDIES ON THE REGULATION OF STAPHYLOCOCCAL
ENTEROTOXINS A AND B PRODUCED BY STRAIN S-6
Pereira, J.L., and *Salzberg, S.P.* (Brazil)

THE GERMICIDAL RESISTANCE OF *CLOSTRIDIUM
BOTULINUM* SPORES
Ito, K.A., and Seeger, M.L. (USA)

IMMUNOLOGICAL ASPECT OF *CLOSTRIDIUM PERFRINGENS*
FOOD POSIONING
Skjelkvåle, R.*, and Uemura, T.† (*Norway, †Japan)

DIRECT PLATING MEDIUM PROCEDURE FOR ISOLATING
AND ENUMERATING *VIBRIO PARAHAEMOLYTICUS* IN FISH
AND SHELLFISH.
Horie, S., and Yamada, M. (Japan)

EFFECTS OF OZONE TREATMENT ON SHELF LIFE AND
MICROFLORA OF POULTRY MEAT
Yang, P.P.W., and *Chen, T.C.* (USA)

MICROFLORA IN THE INDUSTRIALLY PRODUCED DOUGH
Žakula, R., and *Todorović, M.* (Yugoslavia)

QUALITY OF STORED PECAN NUTS AS AFFECTED BY LEVEL
OF MATURITY AT HARVEST AND TEMPERATURE AND TIME
OF STORAGE
Beuchat, L.R., and Heaton, E.K. (USA)

Pasteurization and sterilization

ALTERATION OF HEAT RESISTANCE OF MICROBES IN NON-ISOTHERMAL PROCESS OF HEAT STERILIZATION
Tsuchido, T., Hayashi, M., Takano, N., and Shibasaki, I. (Japan)

GROWTH INHIBITORY ACTIONS OF N^α-COCOYL-L-ARGININE ETHYLESTER TO FOOD MICROORGANISMS
Hasegawa, T., Takano, S., Aoki, S., and Suzuki, T. (Japan)

Fermentation food products

BIOLOGICAL AGING IN SHERRY WINES PRODUCTION
Garrido, J., Fernández, M.J. and Garrido, D. (Spain)

ENZYMATIC FORMATION OF ETHYL α-D-GLUCOSIDE IN SAKE
Oka, S., Masumoto, K., and Shigeta, S. (Japan)

EFFECT OF MIXED CULTURE METHOD ON PHILIPPINE FERMENTED UNDISTILIED RICE BEVERAGE
Quiason, S. (Philippines)

LIPID-DEGRADING ENZYMES IN GERMINATING BARLEY GRAINS AND THE POSSIBLE PARTICIPATION OF THEIR REACTION PRODUCTS IN THE FLAVOR OF BEER
Yabuuchi, S. (Japan)

SUGAR NUCLEOTIDE FERMENTATION AND ITS MECHANISM
Kawai, H. Yamamoto, K., Yano, T., and Tochikura, T. (Japan)

THE BIOSYNTHESIS OF CELLULOSE BY ACETOBACTER ACETI, A PRODUCER OF FERMENTATION FOOD
Yamanaka, S., Takinami, K., and Osumi, M. (Japan)

CITRUS UNSHIU PEEL AS A MEDIUM FOR THE EDIBLE MUSHROOM CULTURE
Yoshikawa, K., and Tsuetaki, H. (Japan)

GALACTOSE METABOLISM IN *BIFIDOBACTERIUM BIFIDUM*
Lee, L., Terao, S., and Tochikura, T. (Japan)

THE EFFECT OF AFLATOXIN B_1 ON THE MORPHOLOGICAL AND BIOCHEMICAL PROPERTIES OF LACTIC ACID BACTERIA FOR YOGHURT MANUFACTURING
Šutič, M., and Banina, A. (Yugoslavia)

INVESTIGATIONS INTO AN INDIGENOUS FERMENTED MILK FOOD
Ahmad, I.H. (Malaysia)

Section 9   Food and Nutrition

Food fortification

IMPROVEMENT OF "ASEAN" NUTRITIONAL STATUS BY
INCREASING FOOD INTAKE
Bhumiratana, A. (Thailand)

DIETARY DAIRY DRINKS FORTIFIED WITH PROTEINS,
VITAMINES AND MINERALS
Carić, M., Marić, S., and Gavarić, D. (Yugoslavia)

TECHNOLOGICAL APPROACHES IN THE HUMANIZATION OF
BUFFALO MILK
Ganguli, N. C., and Kuchroo, C.N. (India)

Loss of nutrients during storage and processing

PREDICTION OF NUTRIENT LOSSES
Labuza, T.P., Shapero, M., and Kamman, J. (USA)

EFFECT OF TIME AND TEMPERATURE OF UHT-MILK DURING
PROCESSING
Reuter, H., and Hoppe, A. (FRG)

THE EFFECT OF FAT AND TEMPERATURE ON THE
CONCENTRATION OF THIAMIN IN UHT-MILK DURING
STORAGE
Feldheim, W. (FRG)

NUTRITIVE DETERIORATION OF FOOD PROTEINS DUE TO
INTERACTION WITH OXIDIZED FATS
Sugano, M., and Yanagita, T. (Japan)

APPLICATION OF THERMODYNAMIC ACTIVATION
PARAMETERS TO AN UNDERSTANDING OF ASCORBIC ACID
STABILITY IN DEHYDRATED FOODS
Dennison, D. B., and *Kirk, J.R.* (USA)

THERMAL STABILITY OF VITAMIN B_6 IN FOOD PROCESSING
*Navankasattusas, S.**, and Lund, D.B.† (*Thailand, †USA)

RACEMIZATION OF AMINO ACID RESIDUES IN FOODS
DURING ROASTING
Hayase, F., Yamada, M., Kato, H., and Fujimaki, M. (Japan)

LYSINOALANINE IN THE ALKALI-TREATED FOOD
PROTEINS
Hasegawa, K., and Okamoto, N. (Japan)

THE EFFECT OF SPROUT INHIBITION ON THE QUALITY OF
POTATOES
Mondy, N. (USA)

Assessment of nutritional value

AN EVALUATION OF THE NUTRITIVE VALUE OF MILLET
PROTEIN
Maki, Z., and *Tashiro, M.* (Japan)

NUTRITIONAL EVALUATION OF FOOD PROTEINS BY
ENZYMATIC HYDROLYSIS AND AMINO ACID ANALYSIS
Nair, B.M., and Öste, R. (Sweden)

THE NUTRITIONAL IMPORTANCE OF HYDROXYPROLINE
BALANCE IN METABOLIC DISORDERS AFFECTING
CONNECTIVE TISSUE
Mohamedally, S.M., and Wix, P. (UK)

DIGESTIBILITY OF ACYLATED PROTEINS BY PEPSIN AND
PANCREATIC PROTEASES
Matoba, T., and Doi,E. (Japan)

NUTRITIONAL EVALUATION OF CEREAL-LEGUME
MIXTURES USING NORMAL AND GENETICALLY IMPROVED
CEREALS AND CHICKPEA.
Del Angel, A.R., and Sotelo, A. (Mexico)

Section 10   Food Additives and Adventitious Constituents

THE VALUE OF ADDED COLOURINGS IN FOOD AND
DRINKS
Hicks, D. (UK)

EFFECTS OF PHTHALIC ACID ESTERS ON THE LIVER
LIPID METABOLISM IN RATS
Yanagita, T., Kuzuhara, S., Enomoto, N., and Shimada, T. (Japan)

FISHY TAINTS IN EGGS
Curtis, R.F., Fenwick, G. R., Hobson-Frohock, A., Heaney, R., and
Land, D.G. (UK)

VOLATILE COMPOUNDS FROM STORAGE MITES IN
FOOD
Curtis, R.F., Hobson-Frohock, A., Fenwick, G.R., and Berreen,
J.M. (UK)

EFFECTS OF ADDITIVES ON THE STABILITY OF FROZEN MINCED FISH. I. MINCES OF BLUE WHITING (*MICROMESISTIUS POTASSOU*, RISSO) OBTAINED BY THE EXTRUSION METHOD WITH ADDITION OF PROTEIN PROTECTORS AND ANTIOXYDANTS
Moral, A., Borderías, A. J., and *García Matamoros, E.* (Spain)

EFFECTS OF ADDITIVES ON THE STABILITY OF FROZEN MINCED FISH. II. MINCES OF BLUE WHITING (*MICROMESISTIUS POTASSOU*, RISSO) OBTAINED BY THE "MINCING" METHOD WITH THE ADDITION OF PROTEIN PROTECTORS AND ANTIOXYDANTS
Borderías, A. J., Moral, A., Tejada, M. and *García Matamoros, E.* (Spain)

LIME AS A BREADMAKING IMPROVER USING A WHOLE MAIZE (ZEA MAYS) WHEAT FLOUR MIXTURE
Molina, M. R., de la Fuente, G., Quintana, S., and Bressani, R. (Guatemala)

ANTIOXIDANT ACTIVITY AND PUNGENCY OF CAPSAICIN HOMOLOGUES
Fujimoto, K., Kanno, Y., and Kaneda, T. (Japan)

Section 11   Traditional Local Foods

COMPARATIVE STUDIES ON JAPANESE AND SRILANKAN POLISHED RICES
Kailasapathy, K., Ito, S., and Fujino, Y. (Japan)

MAKOMO, AN EDIBLE SCLEROTIUM PRODUCED ON *ZIZANIA LATIFOLIA*
Kobayashi, A., Tadera, K., Yagi, F., and Hara, A. (Japan)

DEVELOPMENT OF A HEAT PROCESSED PRODUCT BASED ON YELLOW MAIZE (BASED ON TRADITIONAL NIGERIAN DISH-AGIDI)
Brennan, J. G.*, and *Ogazi, P O.*† (*UK, Nigeria)

INCREASING THE OIL STABILIZATION OF HALVA
Uluöz, M., *Yiğit, V.*, and Gözlü, S. (Turkey)

FISH SAUCE INSOUTHEAST ASIA
*Togano, T.**, Nakamura, H.*, and Sanchez, P.C. †(*Japan, †Philippines)

Round Table Meetings

DOCUMENTATION AND INFORMATION IN FOOD SCIENCE AND TECHNOLOGY
organized by Dardenne, G. (France)

PROBLEMS ASSOCIATED WITH QUALITIES OF MEAT AND MEAT PRODUCTS
organized by Ando, N. (Japan)

TRAINING FOR RESEARCH AND RESEARCH MANAGEMENT FOR DEVELOPING COUNTRIES
organized by Kefford, J. F. (Australia)

CONTRIBUTION OF MILK PROTEIN STUDY TO HUMAN NUTRITION AND DAIRY TECHNOLOGY
organized by Yamauchi, K. (Japan)

SERVICES FOR THE FOOD INDUSTRY IN DEVELOPING COUNTRIES
organized by Spensley, P. C. (UK)

FOOD PHYSICS TO BE FURTHERED
organized by Mohsenin, N. N. (USA), Sone, T., Yamashita, R., and Hoki, M. (Japan)

POTENTIAL OF POST HARVEST TECHNOLOGY FOR ALLEVIATING WORLD HUNGER
organized by The United Nations University (chairman: Jul, M.)

Author Index

Subject Index

A

acetyl CoA, 191
Achromobacter obae, 282
acid whey, 88
acrylonitrile, 135
Actinoplanes, 249
acyl-CoA-cholesterol-*O*-acyl trans-
    ferase, 187
acyl-glycerol-3-phosphoryl-choline
    transferase, 187
acylhydrolase, 354
adhesion, 319
Aerobactor cloacae, 247
aflatoxin, 136
after-processing infection, 236
D-alabinose isomerase, 245
alcohol dehydrogenase, 100
aleurone grain, 115
aleurone particle, 96
alkali treatment, straw, 52
allergy, 142
alnarp thermal treatment of cream,
    335
Amaranthus spp., 36
amino acid, 278
———— composition, 54
————, production, 279
DL-amino-ε-caprolactam, 281
amylase, food processing, 238
————, subsite structure, 242
amylograph, 106
animal feed, safety, 140
animal protein extender, 32
anti-nutrient, 140
anti-nutritional factor, 43
————, oil seed, 41
antioxidant, 186
L-arginine, 281
aroma compound, 352
aroma development, oxidized lipid,
    352
aromatic amino acid biosynthesis,
    281
ascorbic acid, 176
————, cooking loss, 200
————, retention, 228
Aspergillus flavus, 43
Aspergillus niger, 271

Aspergillus oryzae, 69, 71, 239, 298
atherosclerotic cerebro-cardiovascular
    disease, 136

B

Bacillus brevis, 285
Bacillus megaterium, 245
Bacillus natto, 72
Bacillus subtilis, 239
bean, nutritional value, 26
beany flavor, 74
beer, fermentation, 292
beer production, recent progress, 290
bioconvension of residue, 51
biotin, 279
bitter component, cheese, 343
bran protein, 115
Brevibacterium ammoniagenes, 283
Brevibacterium flavum, 280
brewing, 290
butter, physical structure, 334

C

cadmium level, food, 164
calcium, 200
———— caseinate, 332
cancer bioassays, 130
Candida lipolytica, 12
n-caproaldehyde, 103
carbon dioxide, 222
carbonyl compound, 99, 104, 176
carboxypeptidase, 291
carcinogen, 131
carcinogenic potential, 148
cardiovasculardisease, 130
carotene, *cis*-isomerization, 171
carotene content, carrot, 176
casein, 340
    κ-————, 264, 333
    para-————, 333
    para-κ-————, 264
casein micelle, 264
———— system, 332
cassaba, 9
————, cyano-phoric glycoside, 142
cellobiohydrolase, 257
cellobiose, 258
cellulase, 258, 260

429